Steins;Gate

Steins;Gate

The universe has no end, though it does have a beginning. --- Infinite.
Stars too have a beginning, though they are destroyed by their own power. --- Finite.
Those who believe they have wisdom, are often shown by history to be the most foolish.
The fish in the sea don't know what the world is like on the land. Wisdom would destroy them as well.
Man to exceeding the speed of light would be more ridiculous than fish to living on land.
This is God's final warning to any who rebel.

Chapter 7 ◎ Fantasy Homeostasis III

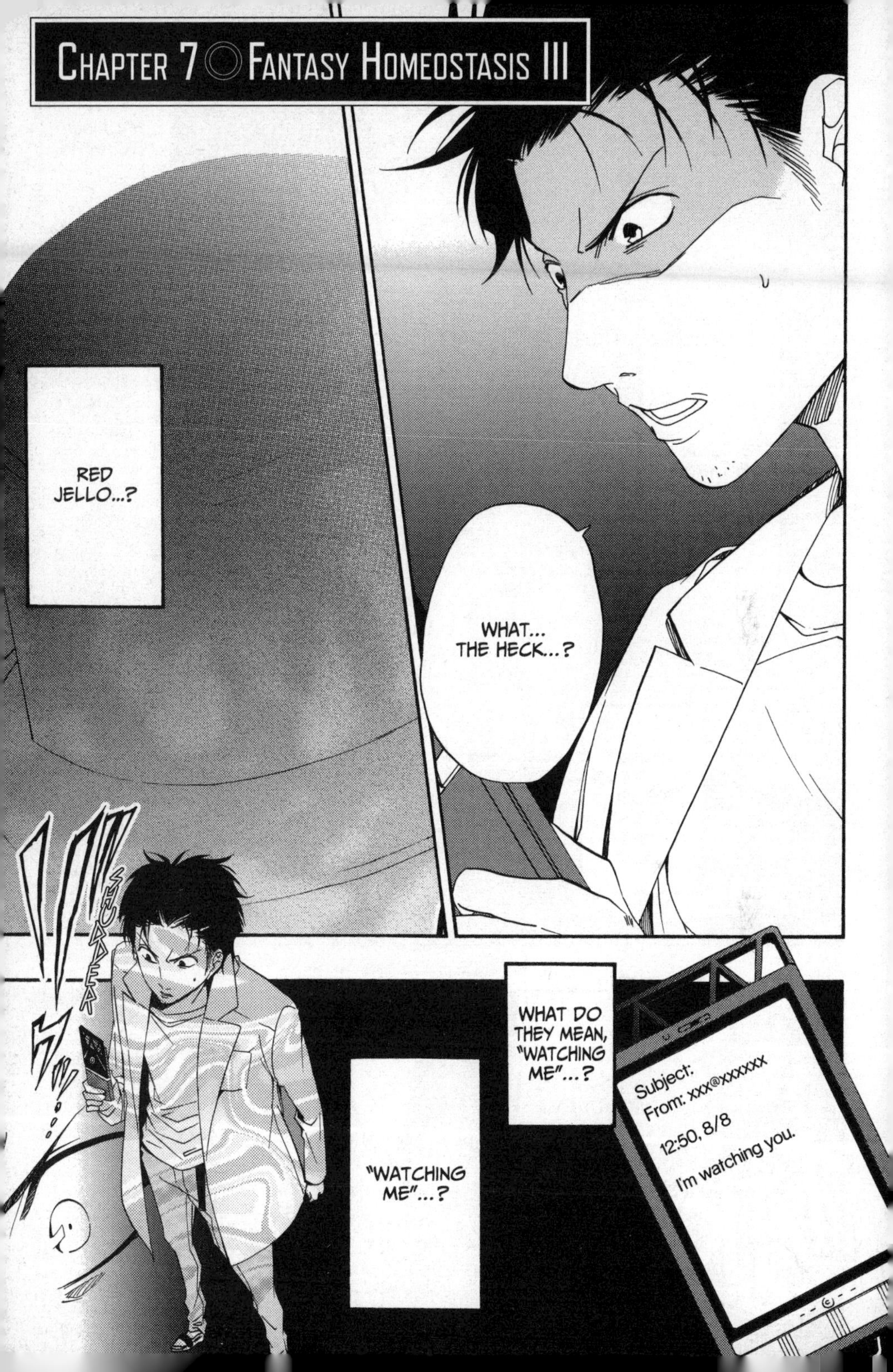
WHAT... THE HECK...?
RED JELLO...?
Subject:
From: xxx@xxxxxx
12:50, 8/8
I'm watching you.
WHAT DO THEY MEAN, "WATCHING ME"...?
"WATCHING ME"...?
SHUDDER

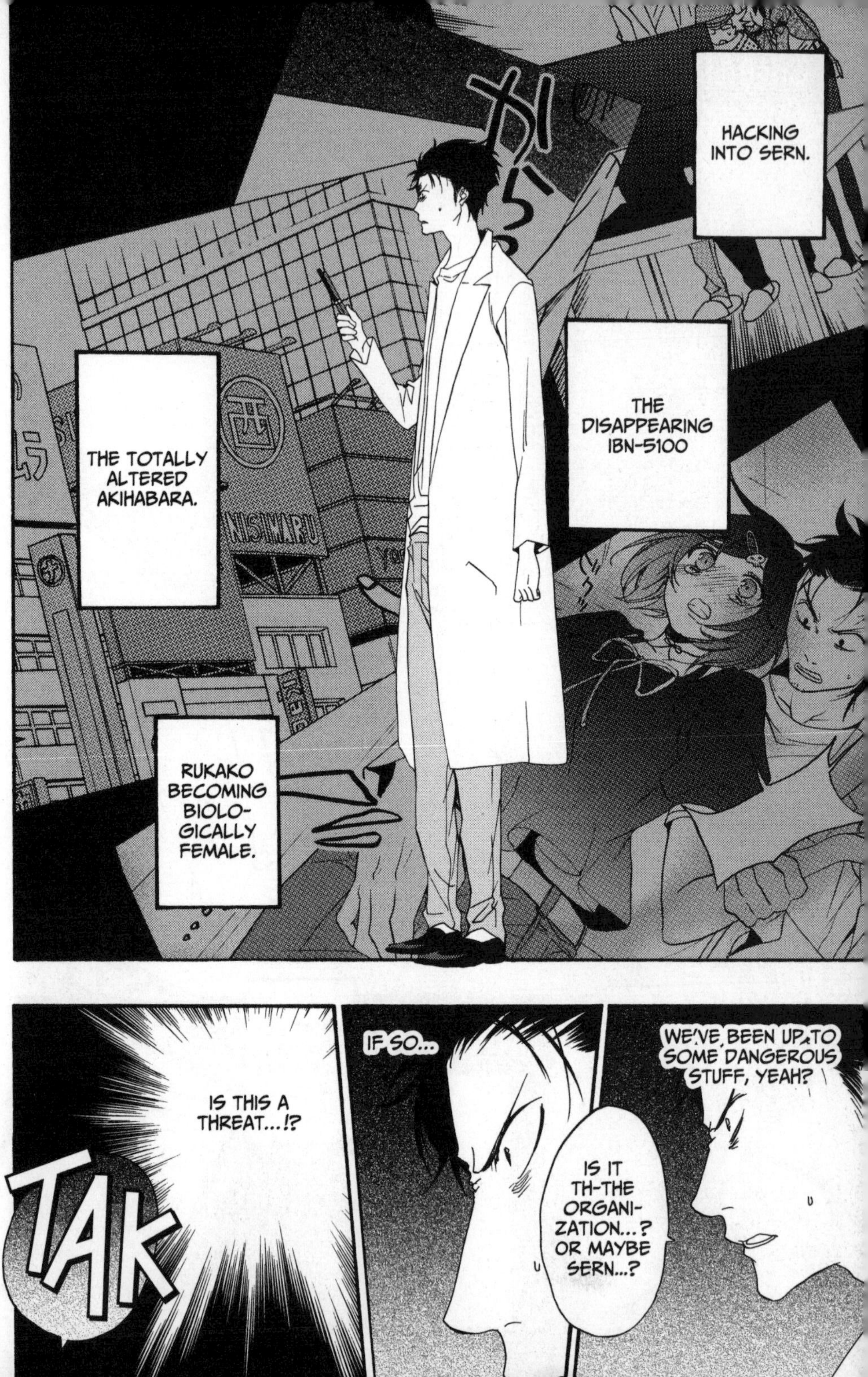
HACKING INTO SERN.
THE DISAPPEARING IBN-5100
THE TOTALLY ALTERED AKIHABARA.
RUKAKO BECOMING BIOLO-GICALLY FEMALE.
WE'VE BEEN UP TO SOME DANGEROUS STUFF, YEAH?
IF SO...
IS IT TH-THE ORGANI-ZATION...? OR MAYBE SERN...?
IS THIS A THREAT...!?
TAK

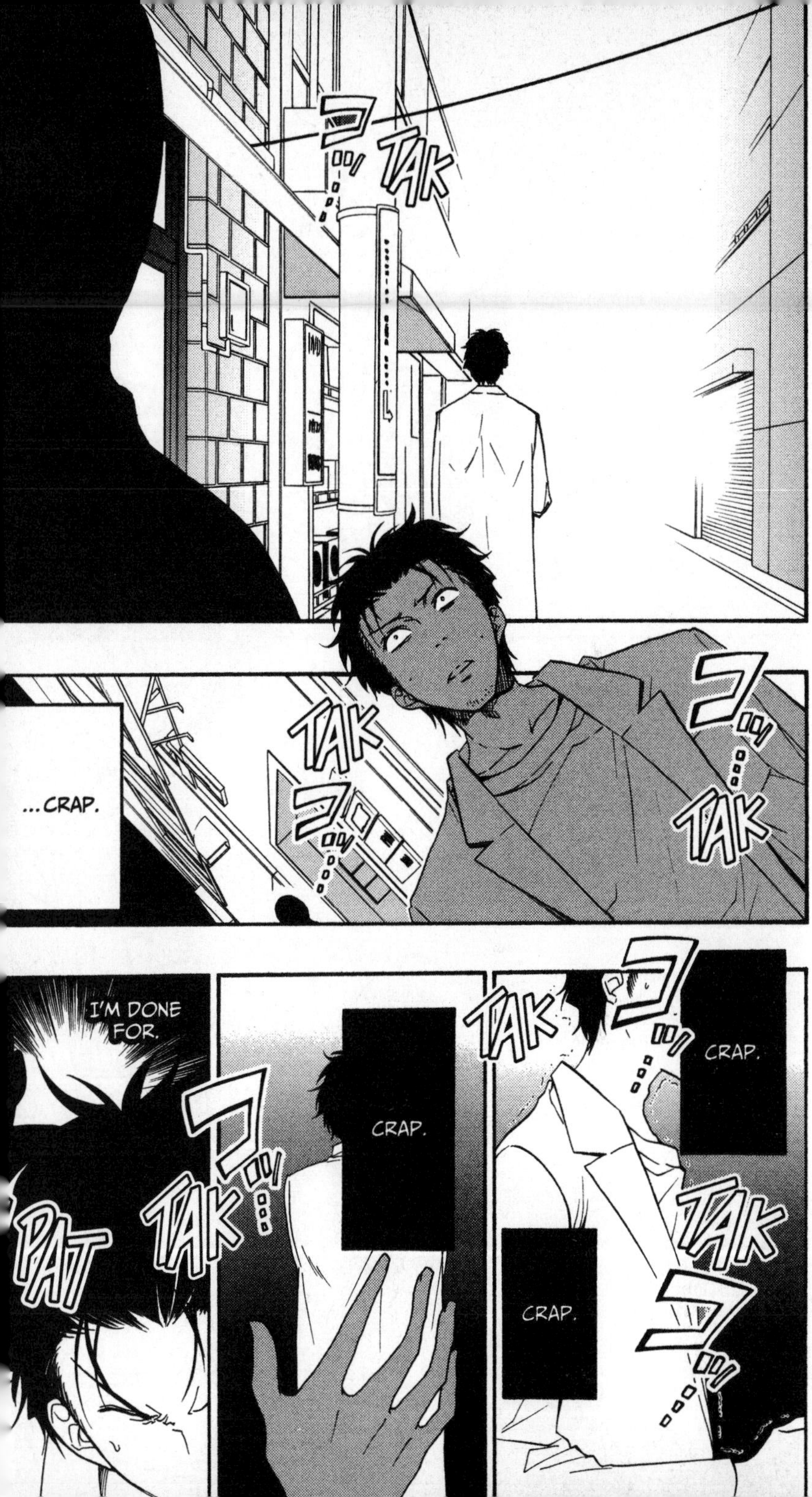
コッ
TAK
コッ
TAK
TAK
コッ
...CRAP.
コッ
TAK
CRAP.
TAK
CRAP.
コッ
CRAP.
コッ
TAK
I'M DONE FOR.
PAT

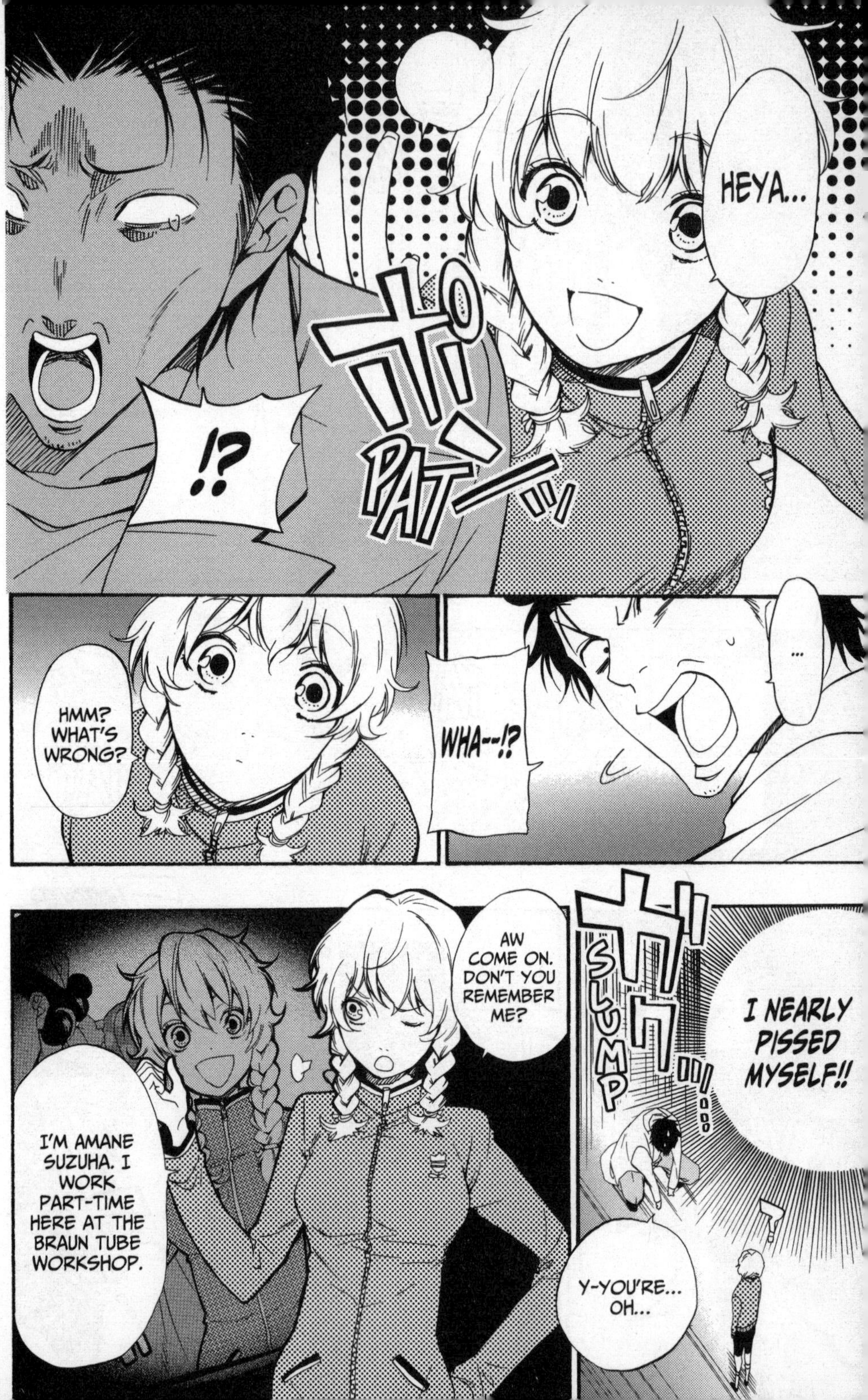
HEYA...
PAT
!?
...
WHA--!?
HMM? WHAT'S WRONG?
I NEARLY PISSED MYSELF!!
SLUMP
Y-YOU'RE... OH...
AW COME ON. DON'T YOU REMEMBER ME?
I'M AMANE SUZUHA. I WORK PART-TIME HERE AT THE BRAUN TUBE WORKSHOP.

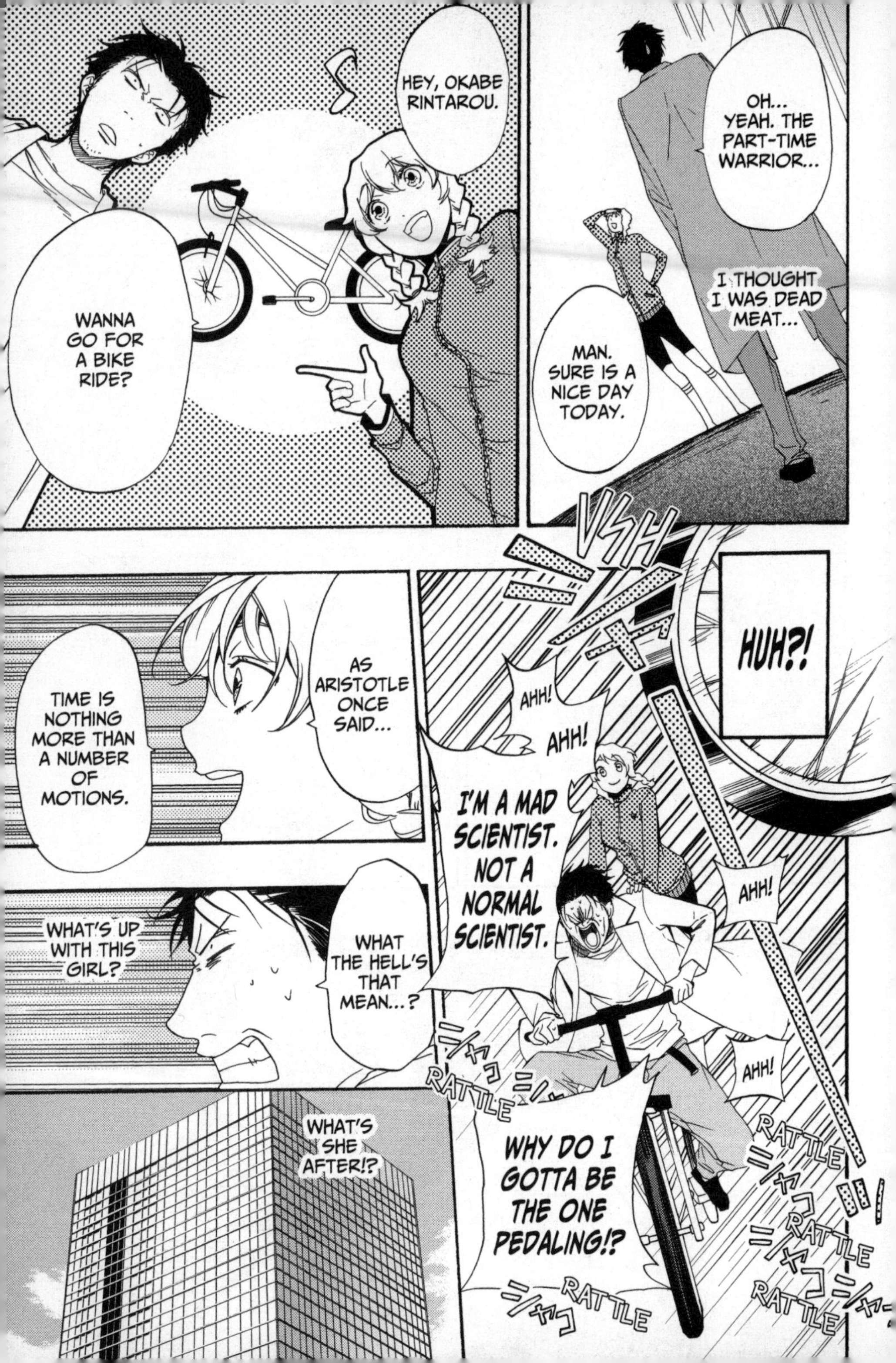
OH... YEAH. THE PART-TIME WARRIOR...
I THOUGHT I WAS DEAD MEAT...
MAN. SURE IS A NICE DAY TODAY.
HEY, OKABE RINTAROU.
WANNA GO FOR A BIKE RIDE?
VSH
HUH?!
AHH!
AHH!
I'M A MAD SCIENTIST. NOT A NORMAL SCIENTIST.
AHH!
AHH!
RATTLE
WHY DO I GOTTA BE THE ONE PEDALING!?
RATTLE
RATTLE
RATTLE
RATTLE
AS ARISTOTLE ONCE SAID...
TIME IS NOTHING MORE THAN A NUMBER OF MOTIONS.
WHAT THE HELL'S THAT MEAN...?
WHAT'S UP WITH THIS GIRL?
WHAT'S SHE AFTER!?

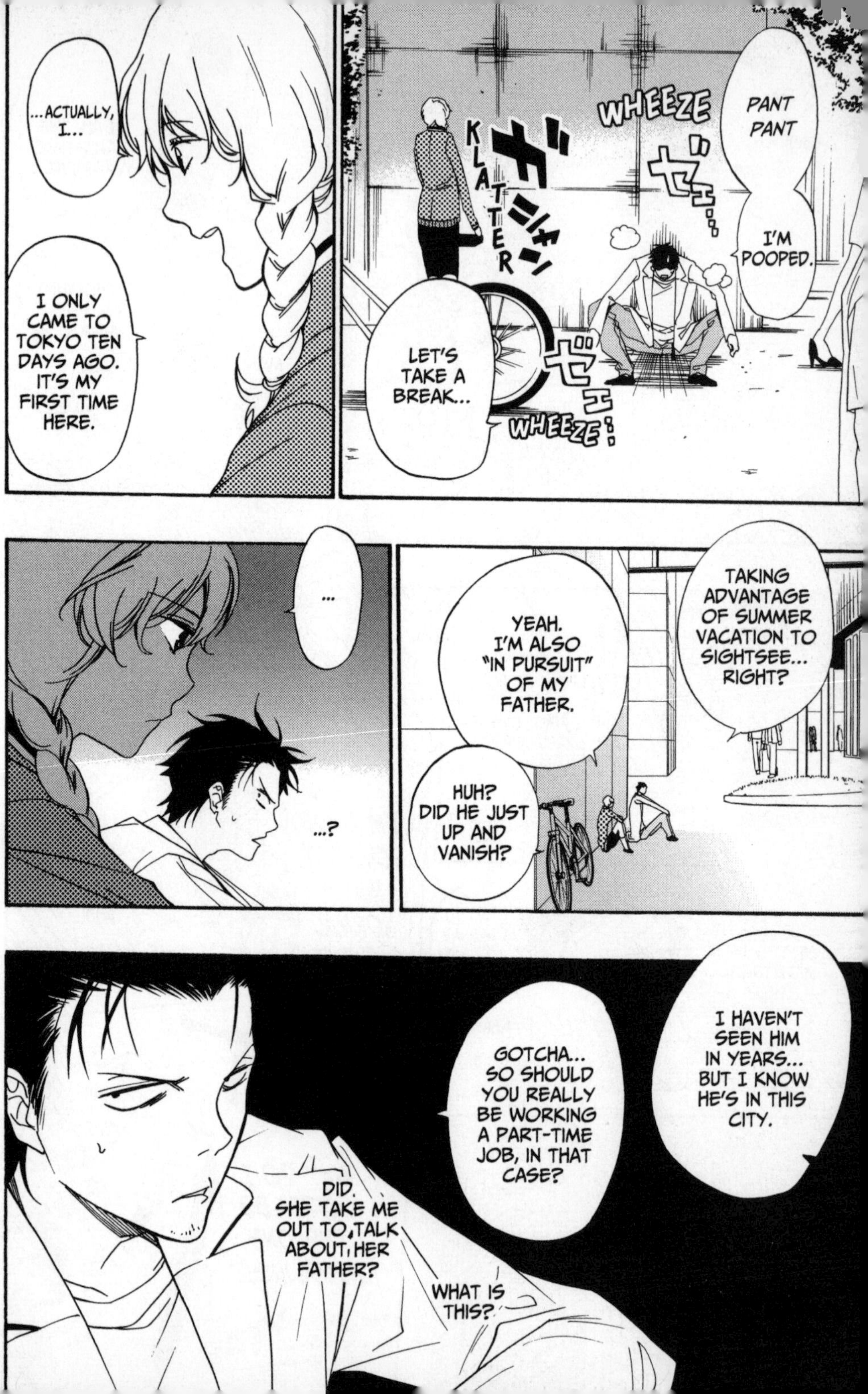
PANT PANT
I'M POOPED.
WHEEZE
KLATTER
LET'S TAKE A BREAK...
WHEEZE
...ACTUALLY, I...
I ONLY CAME TO TOKYO TEN DAYS AGO. IT'S MY FIRST TIME HERE.
TAKING ADVANTAGE OF SUMMER VACATION TO SIGHTSEE... RIGHT?
YEAH. I'M ALSO "IN PURSUIT" OF MY FATHER.
HUH? DID HE JUST UP AND VANISH?
...
...?
I HAVEN'T SEEN HIM IN YEARS... BUT I KNOW HE'S IN THIS CITY.
GOTCHA... SO SHOULD YOU REALLY BE WORKING A PART-TIME JOB, IN THAT CASE?
WHAT IS THIS?
DID SHE TAKE ME OUT TO TALK ABOUT HER FATHER?

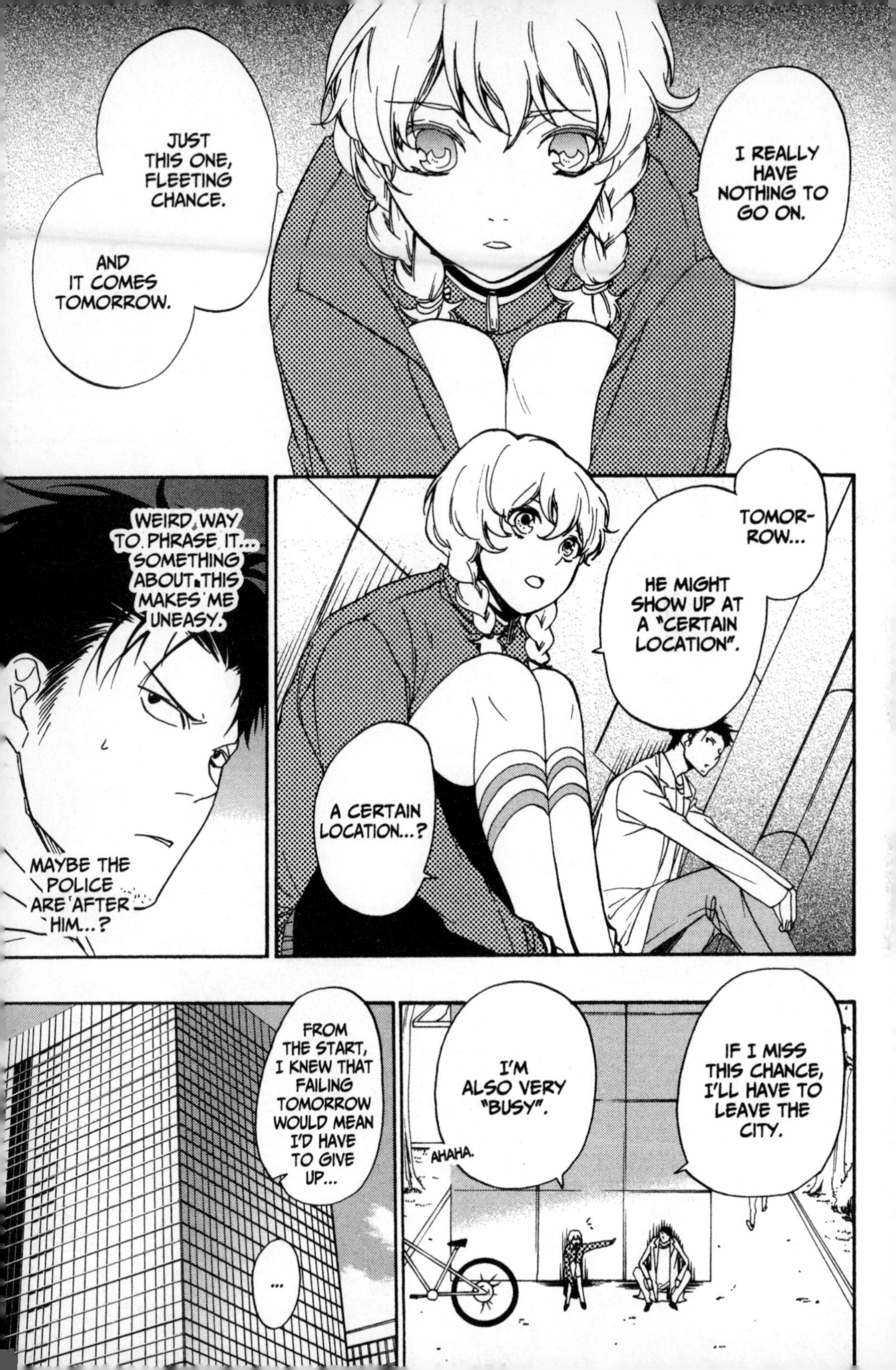
I REALLY HAVE NOTHING TO GO ON.
JUST THIS ONE, FLEETING CHANCE.
AND IT COMES TOMORROW.
TOMORROW...
HE MIGHT SHOW UP AT A "CERTAIN LOCATION".
A CERTAIN LOCATION...?
WEIRD WAY TO PHRASE IT... SOMETHING ABOUT THIS MAKES ME UNEASY.
MAYBE THE POLICE ARE AFTER HIM...?
IF I MISS THIS CHANCE, I'LL HAVE TO LEAVE THE CITY.
I'M ALSO VERY "BUSY".
AHAHA.
FROM THE START, I KNEW THAT FAILING TOMORROW WOULD MEAN I'D HAVE TO GIVE UP...
...

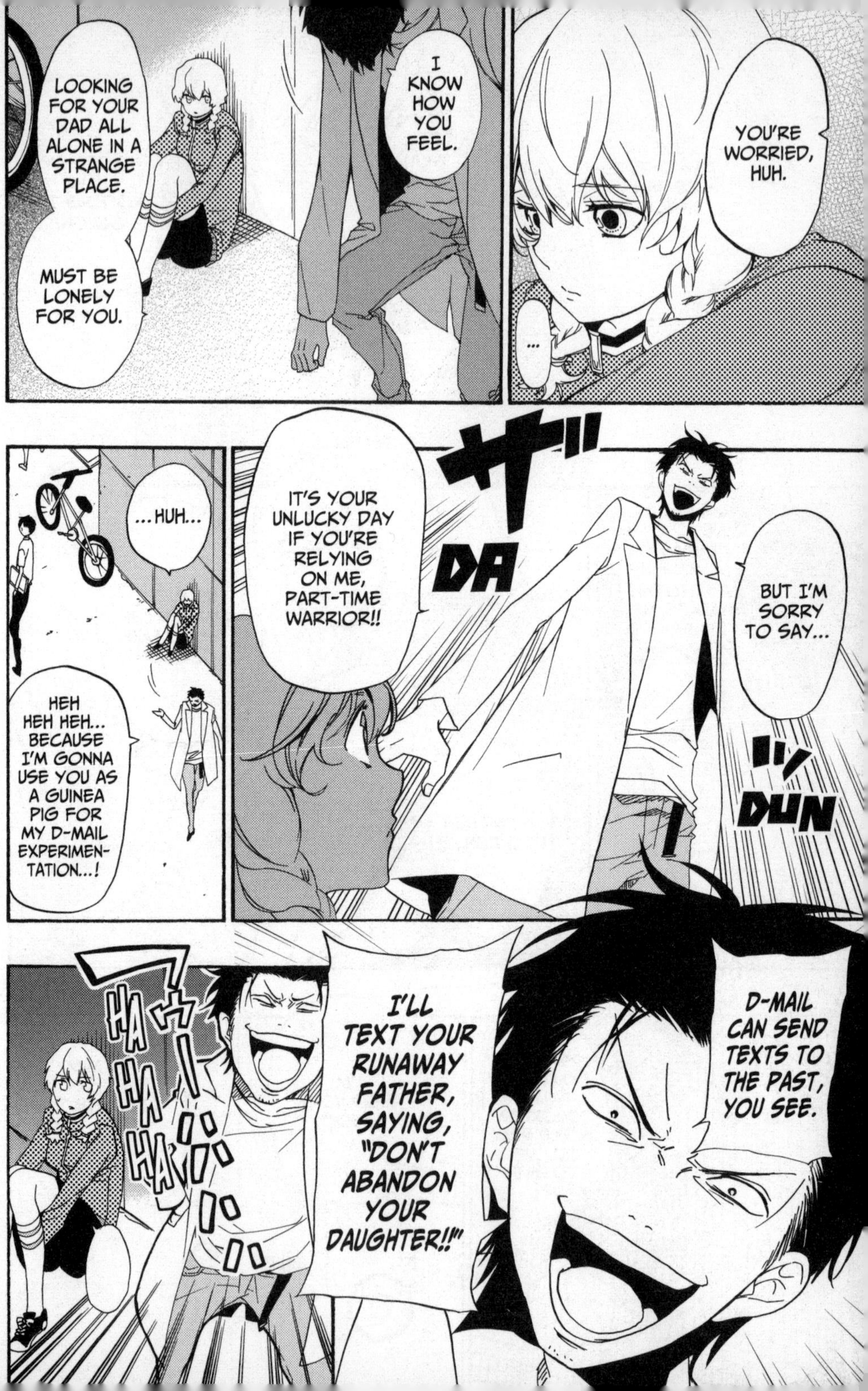
YOU'RE WORRIED, HUH.
...
I KNOW HOW YOU FEEL.
LOOKING FOR YOUR DAD ALL ALONE IN A STRANGE PLACE.
MUST BE LONELY FOR YOU.
BUT I'M SORRY TO SAY...
DA
DUN
IT'S YOUR UNLUCKY DAY IF YOU'RE RELYING ON ME, PART-TIME WARRIOR!!
...HUH...
HEH HEH HEH... BECAUSE I'M GONNA USE YOU AS A GUINEA PIG FOR MY D-MAIL EXPERIMENTATION...!
D-MAIL CAN SEND TEXTS TO THE PAST, YOU SEE.
I'LL TEXT YOUR RUNAWAY FATHER, SAYING, "DON'T ABANDON YOUR DAUGHTER!!"
HA HA HA

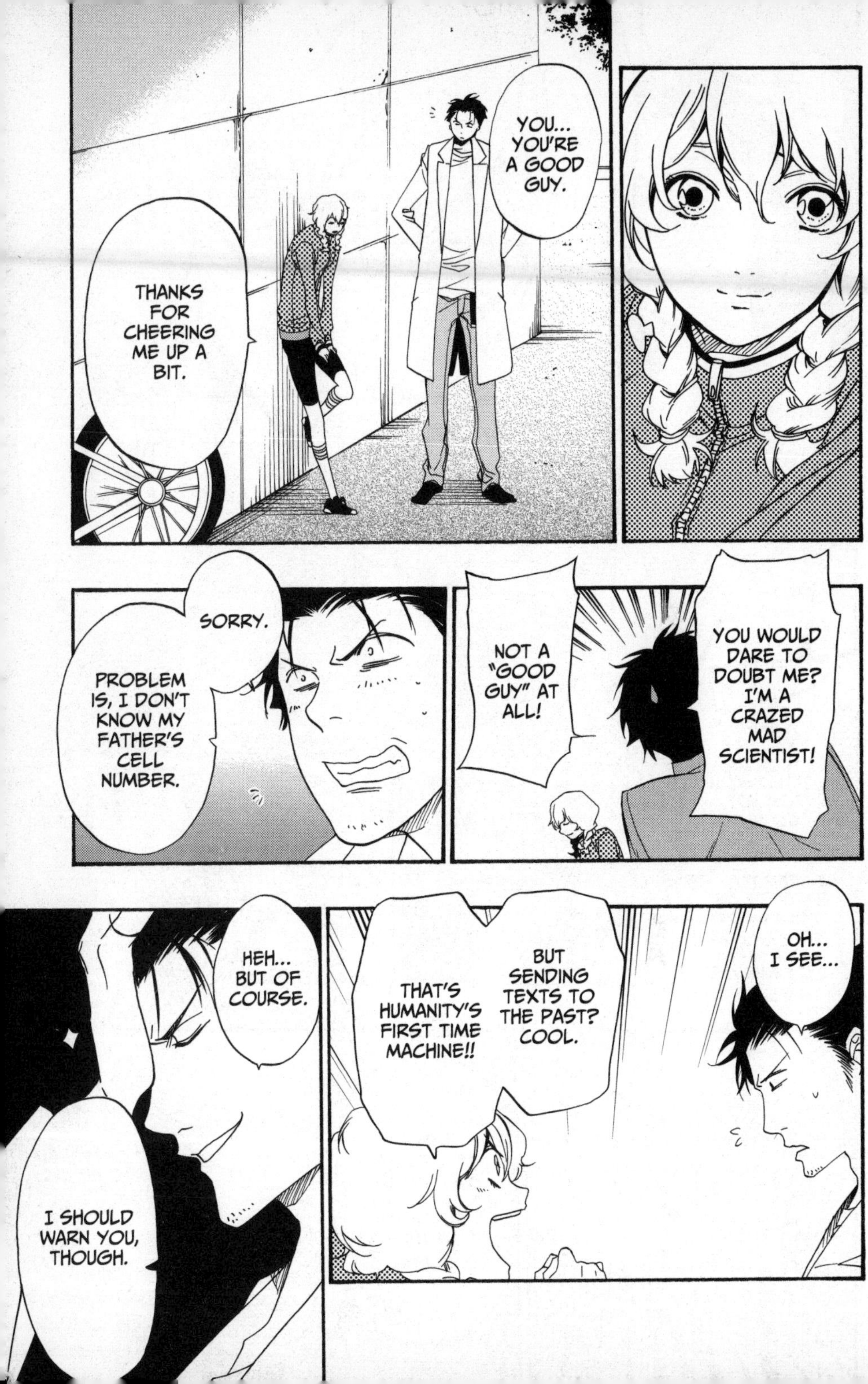
YOU... YOU'RE A GOOD GUY.
THANKS FOR CHEERING ME UP A BIT.
YOU WOULD DARE TO DOUBT ME? I'M A CRAZED MAD SCIENTIST!
NOT A "GOOD GUY" AT ALL!
SORRY.
PROBLEM IS, I DON'T KNOW MY FATHER'S CELL NUMBER.
OH... I SEE...
BUT SENDING TEXTS TO THE PAST? COOL.
THAT'S HUMANITY'S FIRST TIME MACHINE!!
HEH... BUT OF COURSE.
I SHOULD WARN YOU, THOUGH.

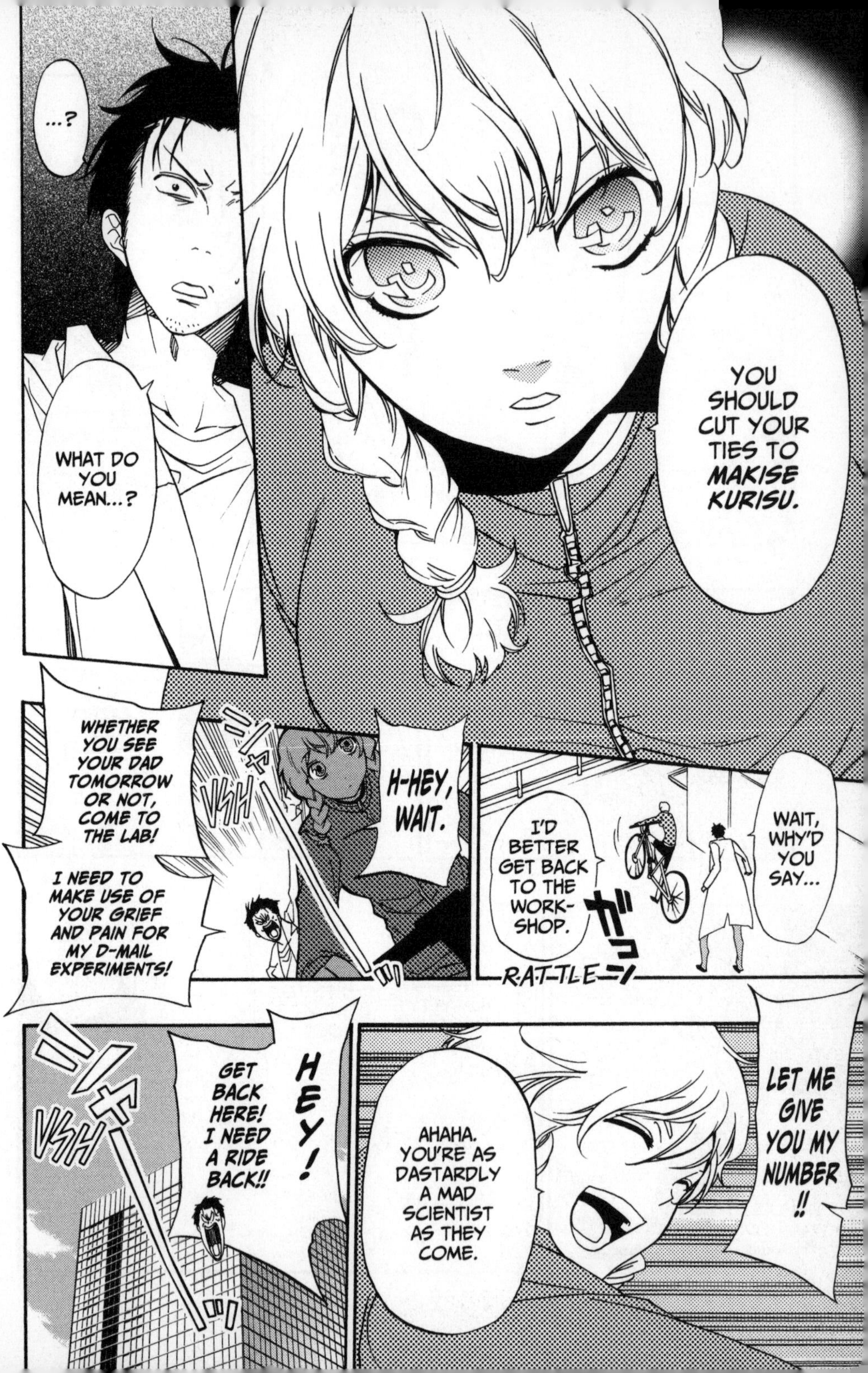
YOU SHOULD CUT YOUR TIES TO *MAKISE KURISU.*
...?
WHAT DO YOU MEAN...?
WAIT, WHY'D YOU SAY...
I'D BETTER GET BACK TO THE WORK-SHOP.
RATTLE
H-HEY, WAIT.
VSH
WHETHER YOU SEE YOUR DAD TOMORROW OR NOT, COME TO THE LAB!
I NEED TO MAKE USE OF YOUR GRIEF AND PAIN FOR MY D-MAIL EXPERIMENTS!
LET ME GIVE YOU MY NUMBER!!
AHAHA. YOU'RE AS DASTARDLY A MAD SCIENTIST AS THEY COME.
HEY!
GET BACK HERE! I NEED A RIDE BACK!!
VSH

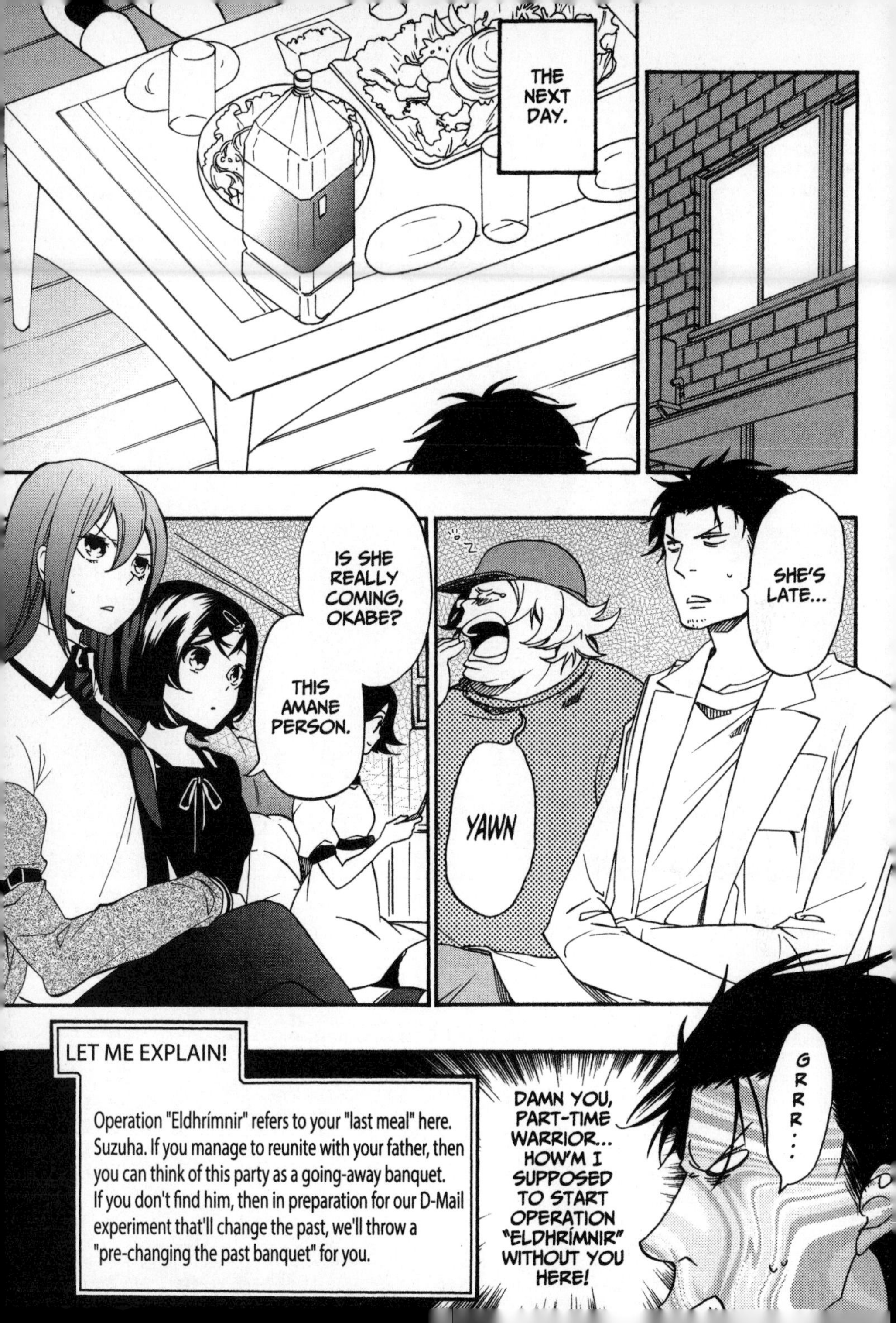
THE NEXT DAY.
SHE'S LATE...
YAWN
IS SHE REALLY COMING, OKABE?
THIS AMANE PERSON.
GRRR...
DAMN YOU, PART-TIME WARRIOR... HOW'M I SUPPOSED TO START OPERATION "ELDHRÍMNIR" WITHOUT YOU HERE!
LET ME EXPLAIN!
Operation "Eldhrímnir" refers to your "last meal" here. Suzuha. If you manage to reunite with your father, then you can think of this party as a going-away banquet. If you don't find him, then in preparation for our D-Mail experiment that'll change the past, we'll throw a "pre-changing the past banquet" for you.

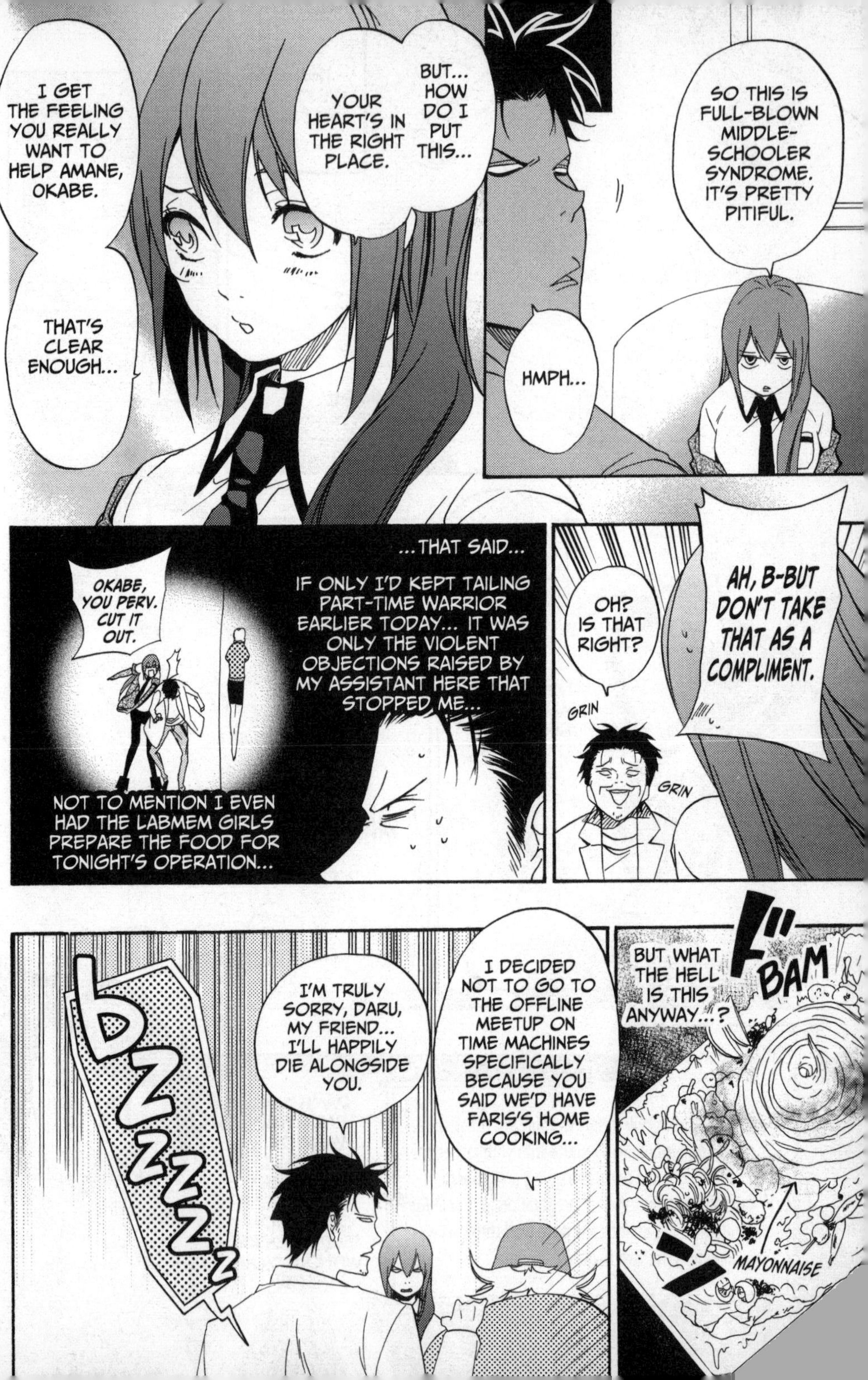
SO THIS IS FULL-BLOWN MIDDLE-SCHOOLER SYNDROME. IT'S PRETTY PITIFUL.
HMPH...
BUT... HOW DO I PUT THIS...
YOUR HEART'S IN THE RIGHT PLACE.
I GET THE FEELING YOU REALLY WANT TO HELP AMANE, OKABE.
THAT'S CLEAR ENOUGH...
AH, B-BUT DON'T TAKE THAT AS A COMPLIMENT.
OH? IS THAT RIGHT?
GRIN
GRIN
...THAT SAID...
IF ONLY I'D KEPT TAILING PART-TIME WARRIOR EARLIER TODAY... IT WAS ONLY THE VIOLENT OBJECTIONS RAISED BY MY ASSISTANT HERE THAT STOPPED ME...
OKABE, YOU PERV. CUT IT OUT.
NOT TO MENTION I EVEN HAD THE LABMEM GIRLS PREPARE THE FOOD FOR TONIGHT'S OPERATION...
BUT WHAT THE HELL IS THIS ANYWAY...?
BAM
MAYONNAISE
I DECIDED NOT TO GO TO THE OFFLINE MEETUP ON TIME MACHINES SPECIFICALLY BECAUSE YOU SAID WE'D HAVE FARIS'S HOME COOKING...
I'M TRULY SORRY, DARU, MY FRIEND... I'LL HAPPILY DIE ALONGSIDE YOU.
bZZZZz

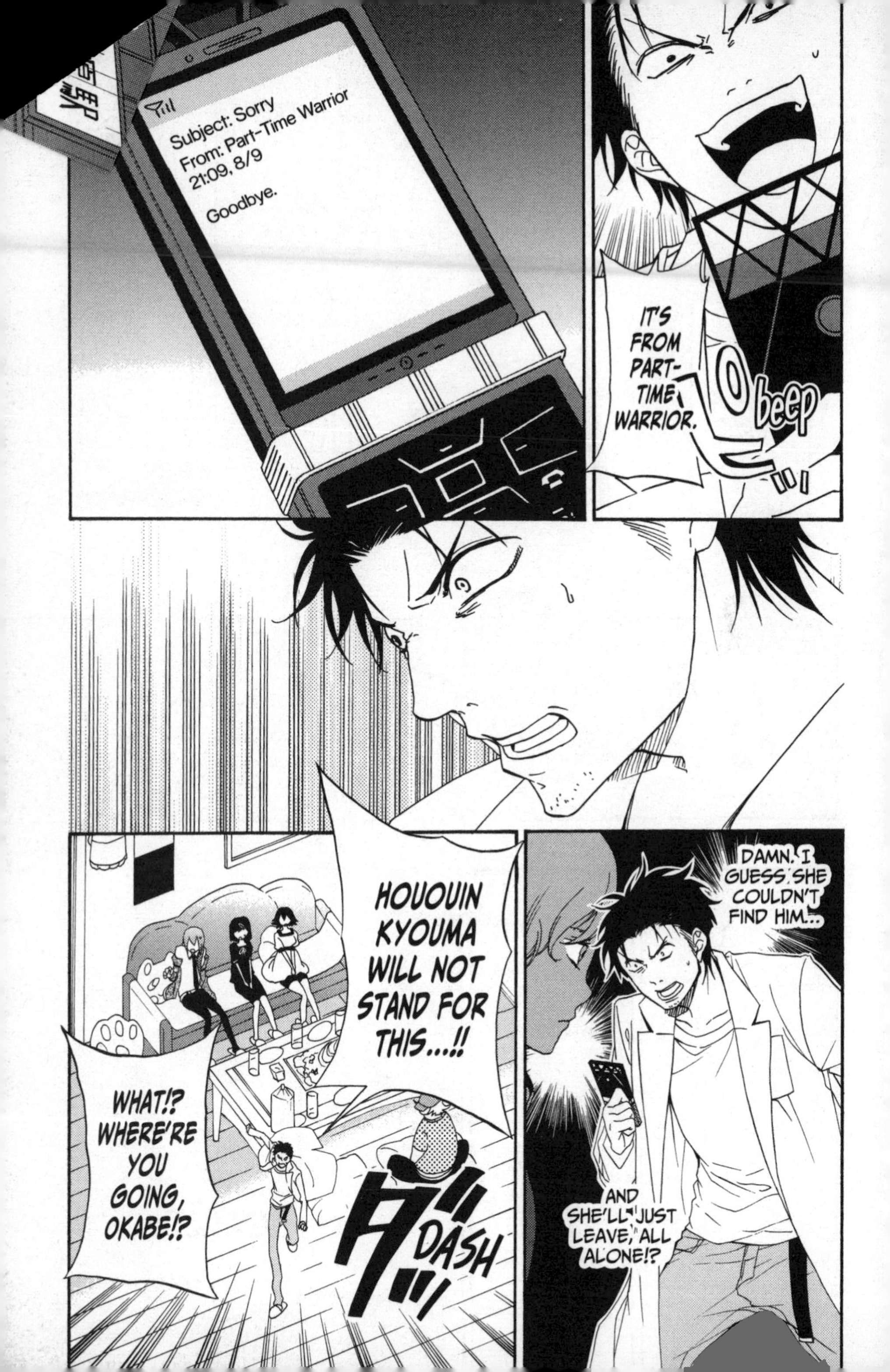
IT'S FROM PART-TIME WARRIOR.
beep
Subject: Sorry
From: Part-Time Warrior
21:09, 8/9
Goodbye.
DAMN. I GUESS SHE COULDN'T FIND HIM...
AND SHE'LL JUST LEAVE, ALL ALONE!?
HOUOUIN KYOUMA WILL NOT STAND FOR THIS...!!
WHAT!? WHERE'RE YOU GOING, OKABE!?
DASH

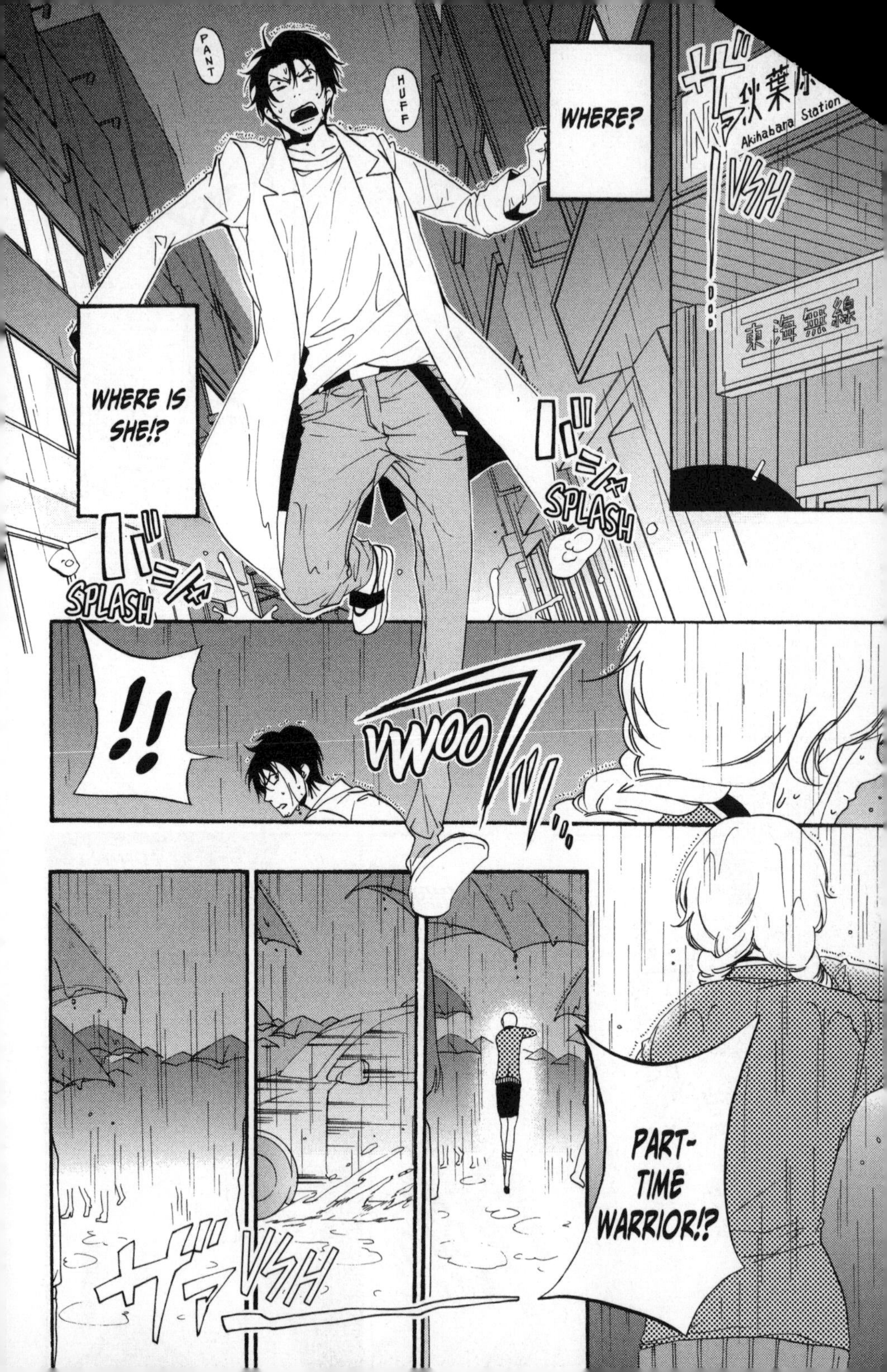

Akihabara Station
ザァ
VSH
WHERE?
PANT
HUFF
東海無線
バシャ
SPLASH
WHERE IS SHE!?
バシャ
SPLASH
VWOO
!!
PART-TIME WARRIOR!?
ザァ
VSH

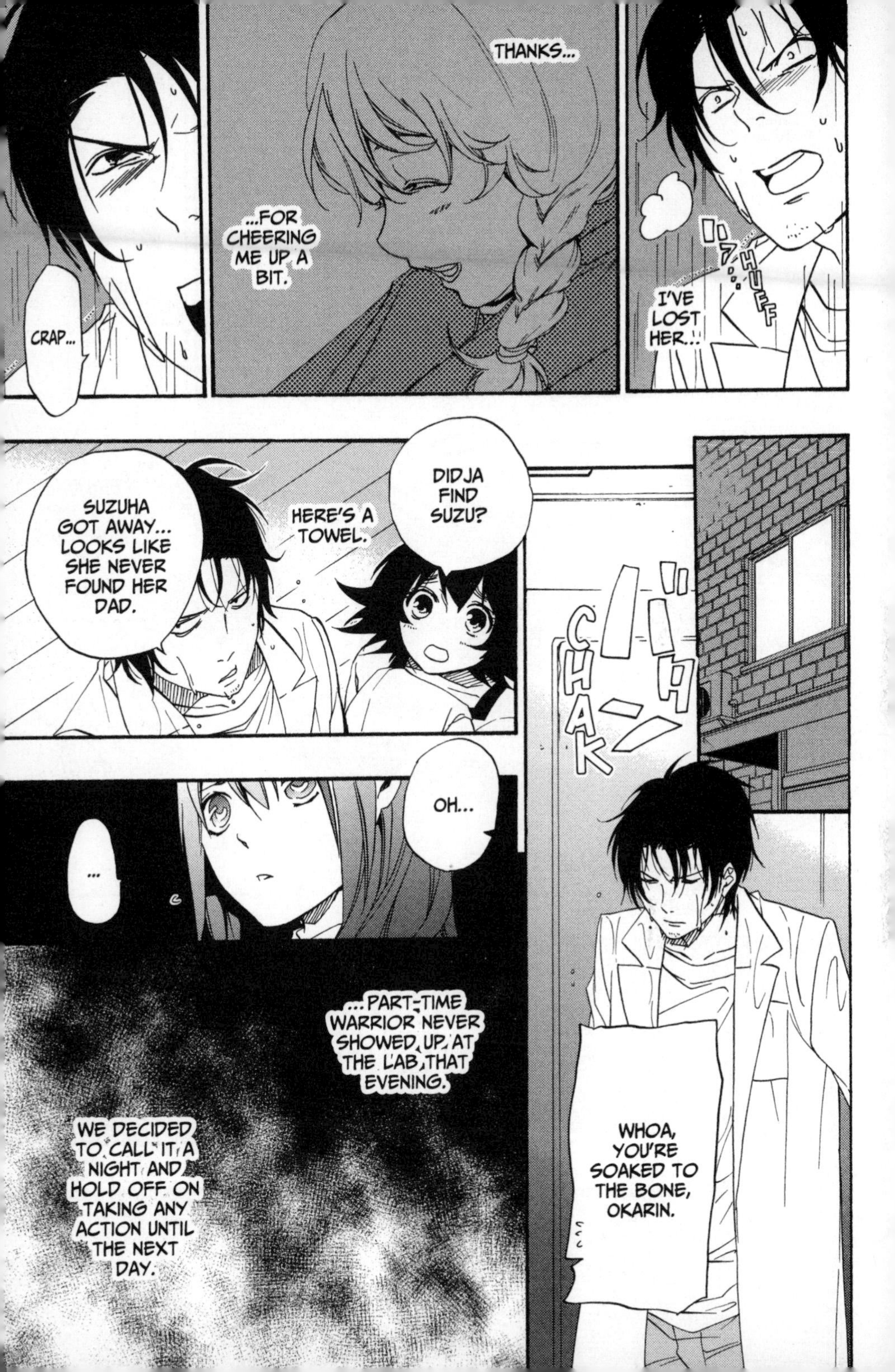
HUFF
I'VE LOST HER...
THANKS...
...FOR CHEERING ME UP A BIT.
CRAP...
CHAK
WHOA, YOU'RE SOAKED TO THE BONE, OKARIN.
DIDJA FIND SUZU?
HERE'S A TOWEL.
SUZUHA GOT AWAY... LOOKS LIKE SHE NEVER FOUND HER DAD.
OH...
...
...PART-TIME WARRIOR NEVER SHOWED UP AT THE LAB THAT EVENING.
WE DECIDED TO CALL IT A NIGHT AND HOLD OFF ON TAKING ANY ACTION UNTIL THE NEXT DAY.

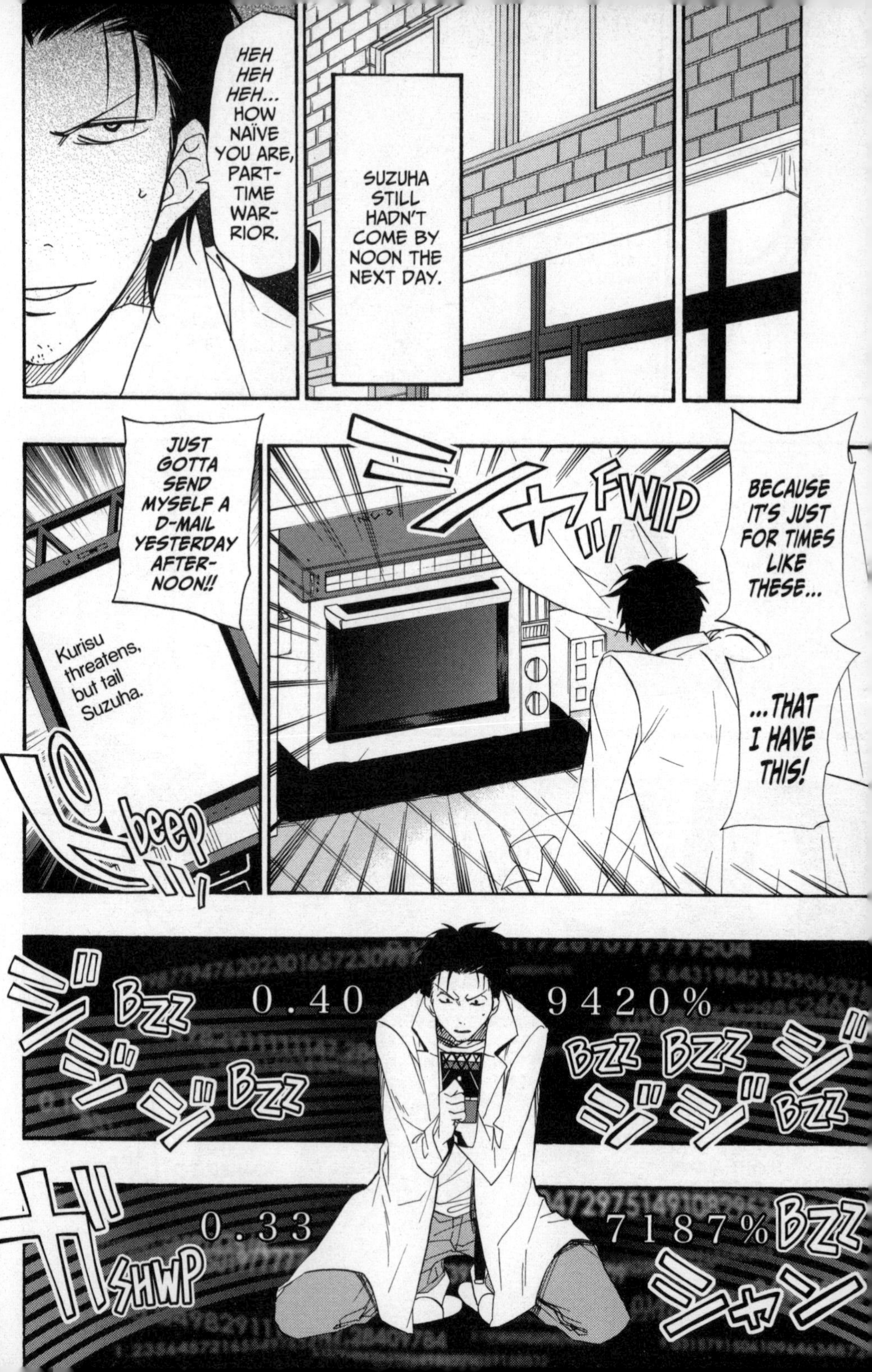
SUZUHA STILL HADN'T COME BY NOON THE NEXT DAY.
HEH HEH HEH... HOW NAÏVE YOU ARE, PART-TIME WARRIOR.
BECAUSE IT'S JUST FOR TIMES LIKE THESE...
FWIP
...THAT I HAVE THIS!
JUST GOTTA SEND MYSELF A D-MAIL YESTERDAY AFTERNOON!!
Kurisu threatens, but tail Suzuha.
beep
0.409420%
BZZ BZZ BZZ
BZZ BZZ
0.337187%
BZZ
SHWP

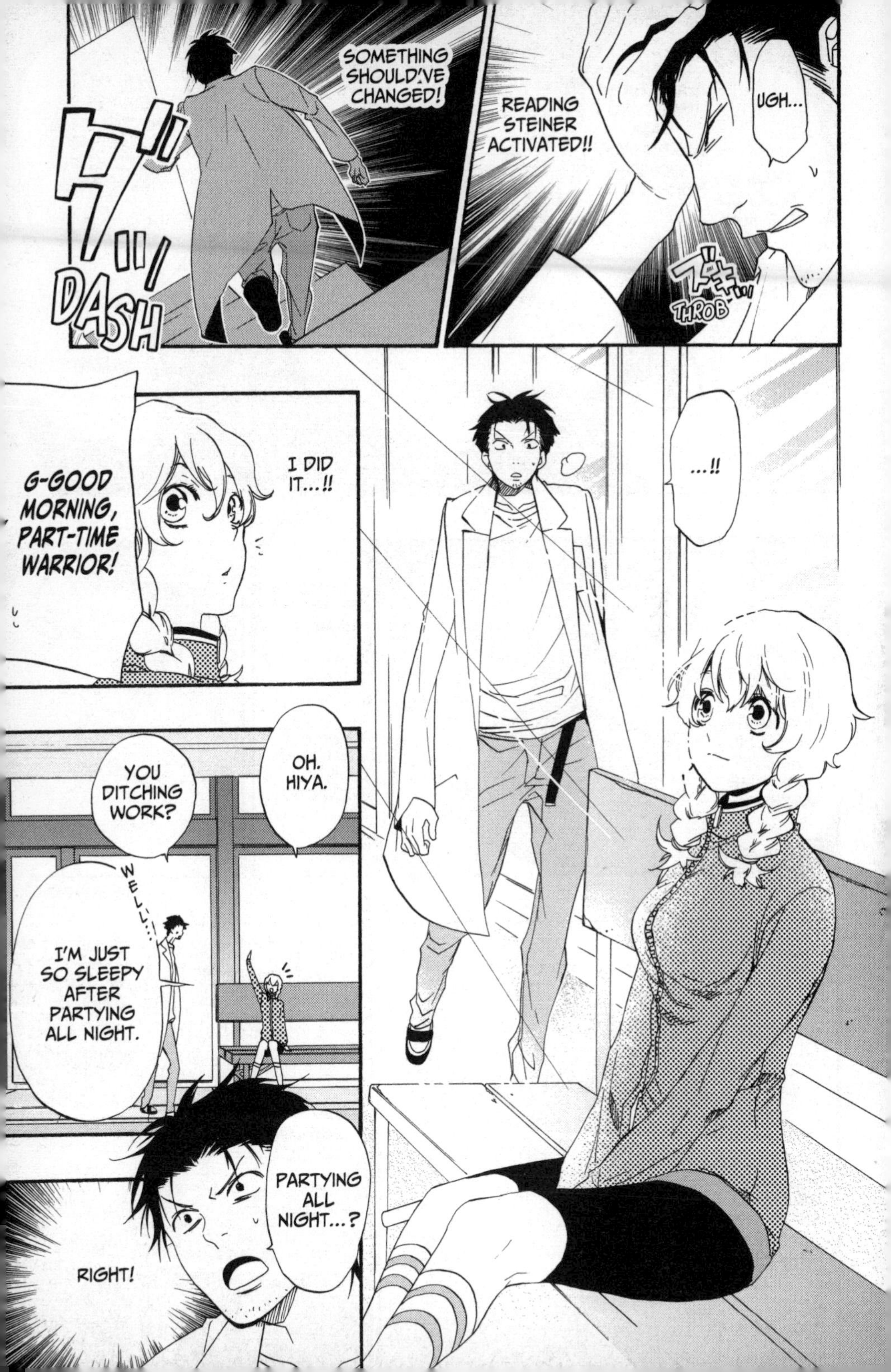
UGH...
READING STEINER ACTIVATED!!
THROB
SOMETHING SHOULD'VE CHANGED!
DASH
...!!
I DID IT...!!
G-GOOD MORNING, PART-TIME WARRIOR!
OH. HIYA.
YOU DITCHING WORK?
WELL...
I'M JUST SO SLEEPY AFTER PARTYING ALL NIGHT.
PARTYING ALL NIGHT...?
RIGHT!

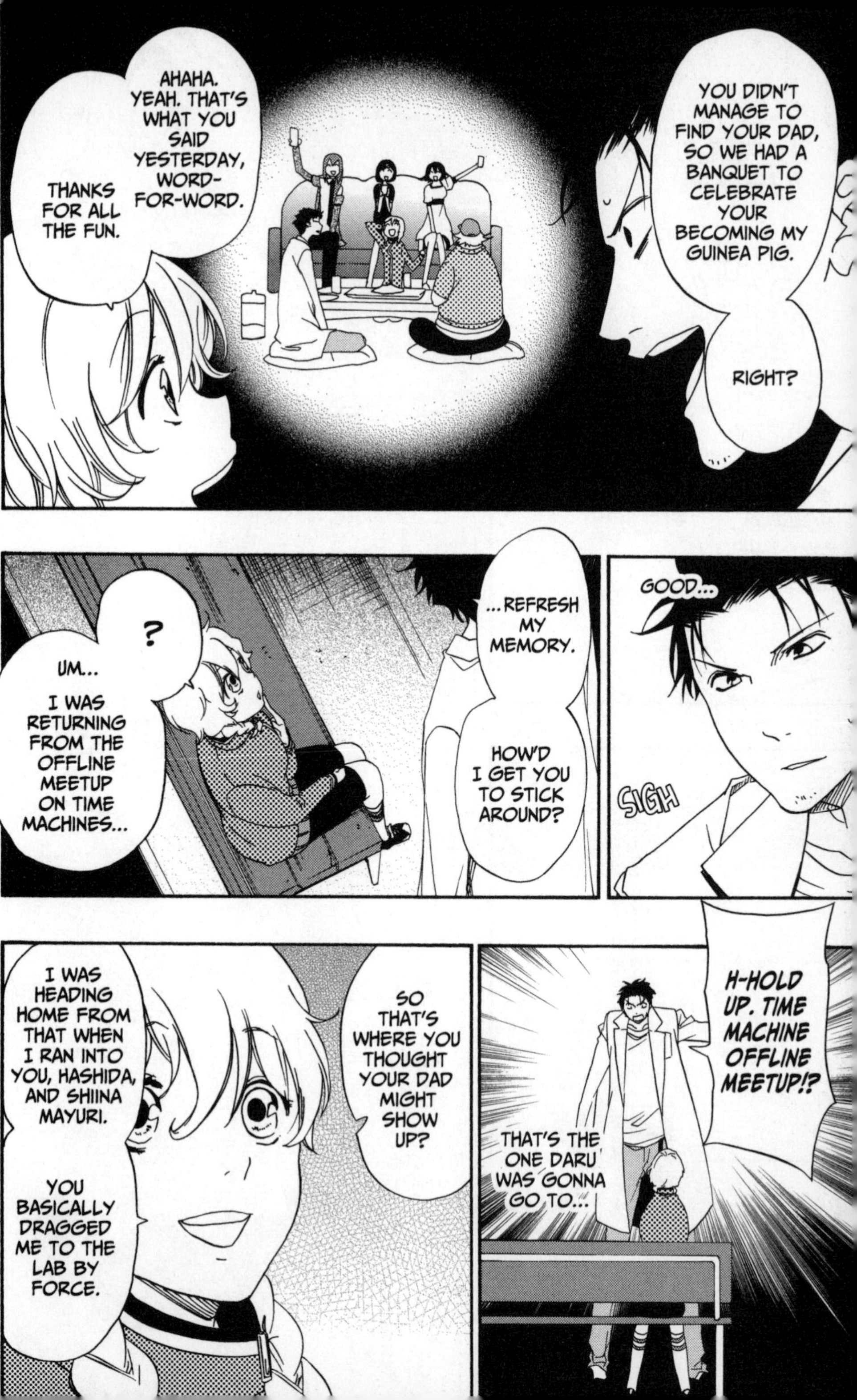
YOU DIDN'T MANAGE TO FIND YOUR DAD, SO WE HAD A BANQUET TO CELEBRATE YOUR BECOMING MY GUINEA PIG.
RIGHT?
AHAHA. YEAH. THAT'S WHAT YOU SAID YESTERDAY, WORD-FOR-WORD.
THANKS FOR ALL THE FUN.
GOOD...
SIGH
...REFRESH MY MEMORY.
HOW'D I GET YOU TO STICK AROUND?
?
UM...
I WAS RETURNING FROM THE OFFLINE MEETUP ON TIME MACHINES...
H-HOLD UP. TIME MACHINE OFFLINE MEETUP!?
THAT'S THE ONE DARU WAS GONNA GO TO...
SO THAT'S WHERE YOU THOUGHT YOUR DAD MIGHT SHOW UP?
I WAS HEADING HOME FROM THAT WHEN I RAN INTO YOU, HASHIDA, AND SHIINA MAYURI.
YOU BASICALLY DRAGGED ME TO THE LAB BY FORCE.

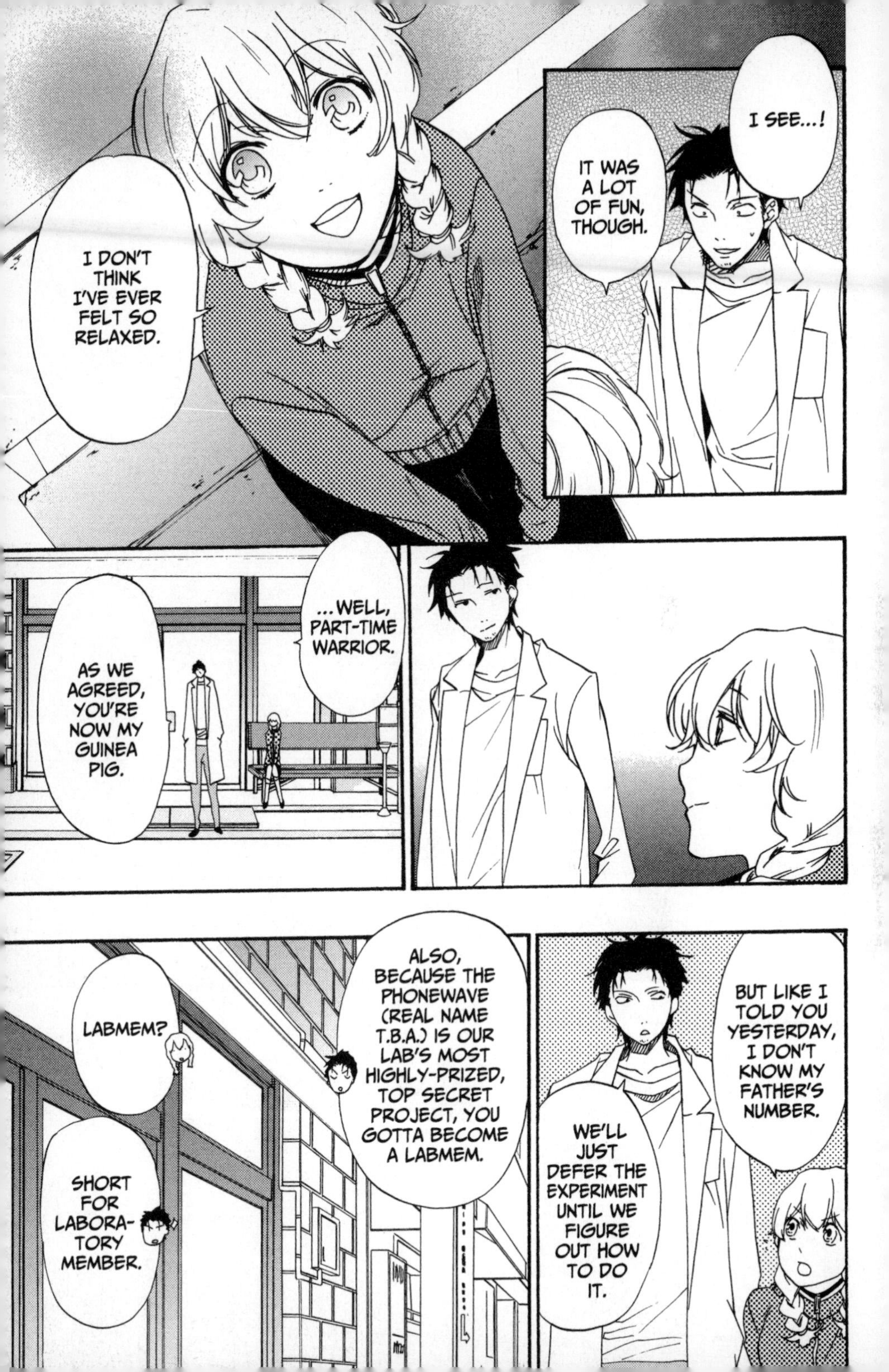
I SEE...!
IT WAS A LOT OF FUN, THOUGH.
I DON'T THINK I'VE EVER FELT SO RELAXED.
...WELL, PART-TIME WARRIOR.
AS WE AGREED, YOU'RE NOW MY GUINEA PIG.
BUT LIKE I TOLD YOU YESTERDAY, I DON'T KNOW MY FATHER'S NUMBER.
WE'LL JUST DEFER THE EXPERIMENT UNTIL WE FIGURE OUT HOW TO DO IT.
ALSO, BECAUSE THE PHONEWAVE (REAL NAME T.B.A.) IS OUR LAB'S MOST HIGHLY-PRIZED, TOP SECRET PROJECT, YOU GOTTA BECOME A LABMEM.
LABMEM?
SHORT FOR LABORA-TORY MEMBER.

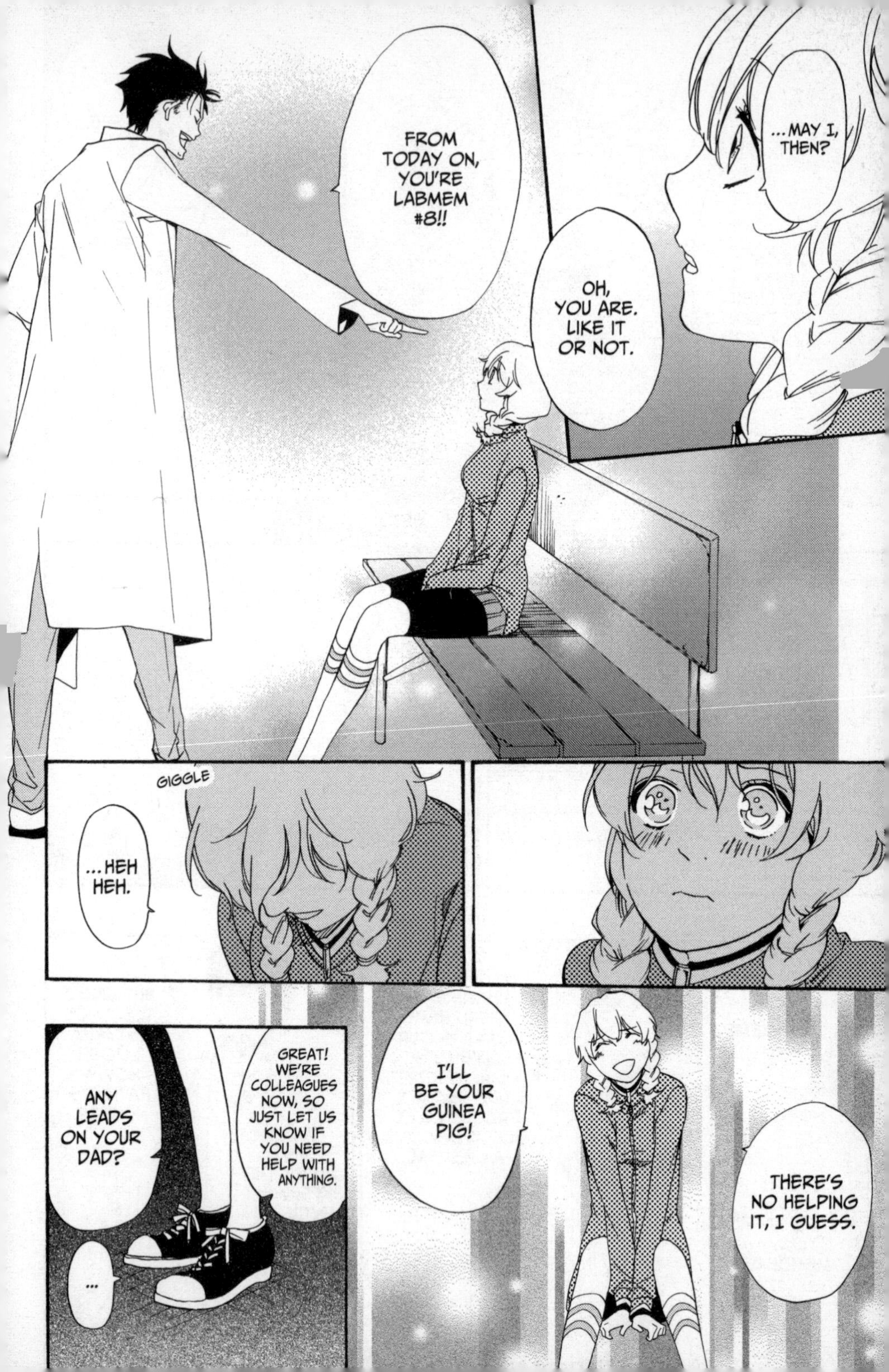
...MAY I, THEN?
OH, YOU ARE. LIKE IT OR NOT.
FROM TODAY ON, YOU'RE LABMEM #8!!
GIGGLE
...HEH HEH.
THERE'S NO HELPING IT, I GUESS.
I'LL BE YOUR GUINEA PIG!
GREAT! WE'RE COLLEAGUES NOW, SO JUST LET US KNOW IF YOU NEED HELP WITH ANYTHING.
ANY LEADS ON YOUR DAD?
...

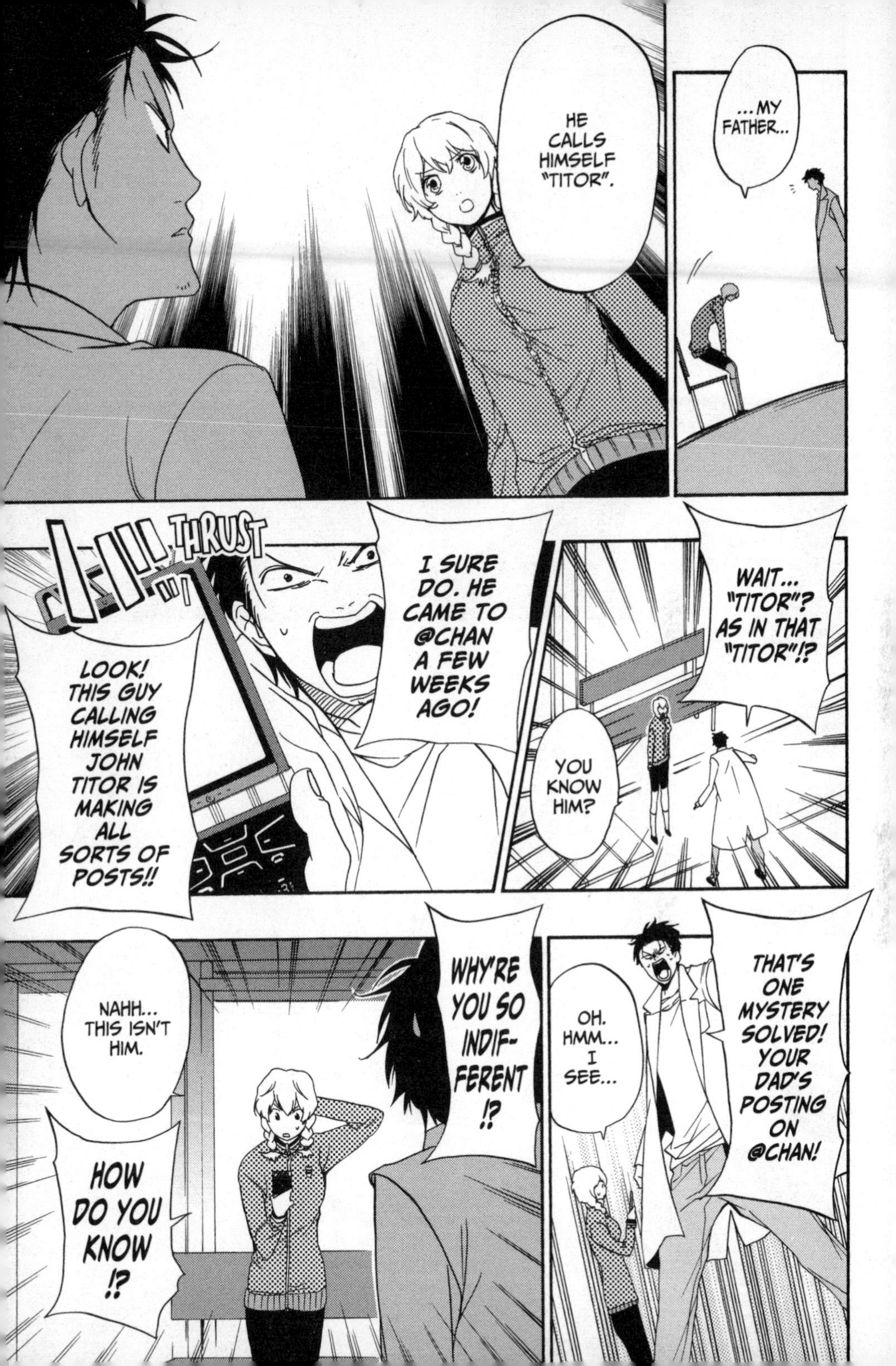
...MY FATHER...
HE CALLS HIMSELF "TITOR".
WAIT... "TITOR"? AS IN THAT "TITOR"!?
YOU KNOW HIM?
I SURE DO. HE CAME TO @CHAN A FEW WEEKS AGO!
THRUST
LOOK! THIS GUY CALLING HIMSELF JOHN TITOR IS MAKING ALL SORTS OF POSTS!!
THAT'S ONE MYSTERY SOLVED! YOUR DAD'S POSTING ON @CHAN!
OH. HMM... I SEE...
WHY'RE YOU SO INDIF-FERENT!?
NAHH... THIS ISN'T HIM.
HOW DO YOU KNOW!?

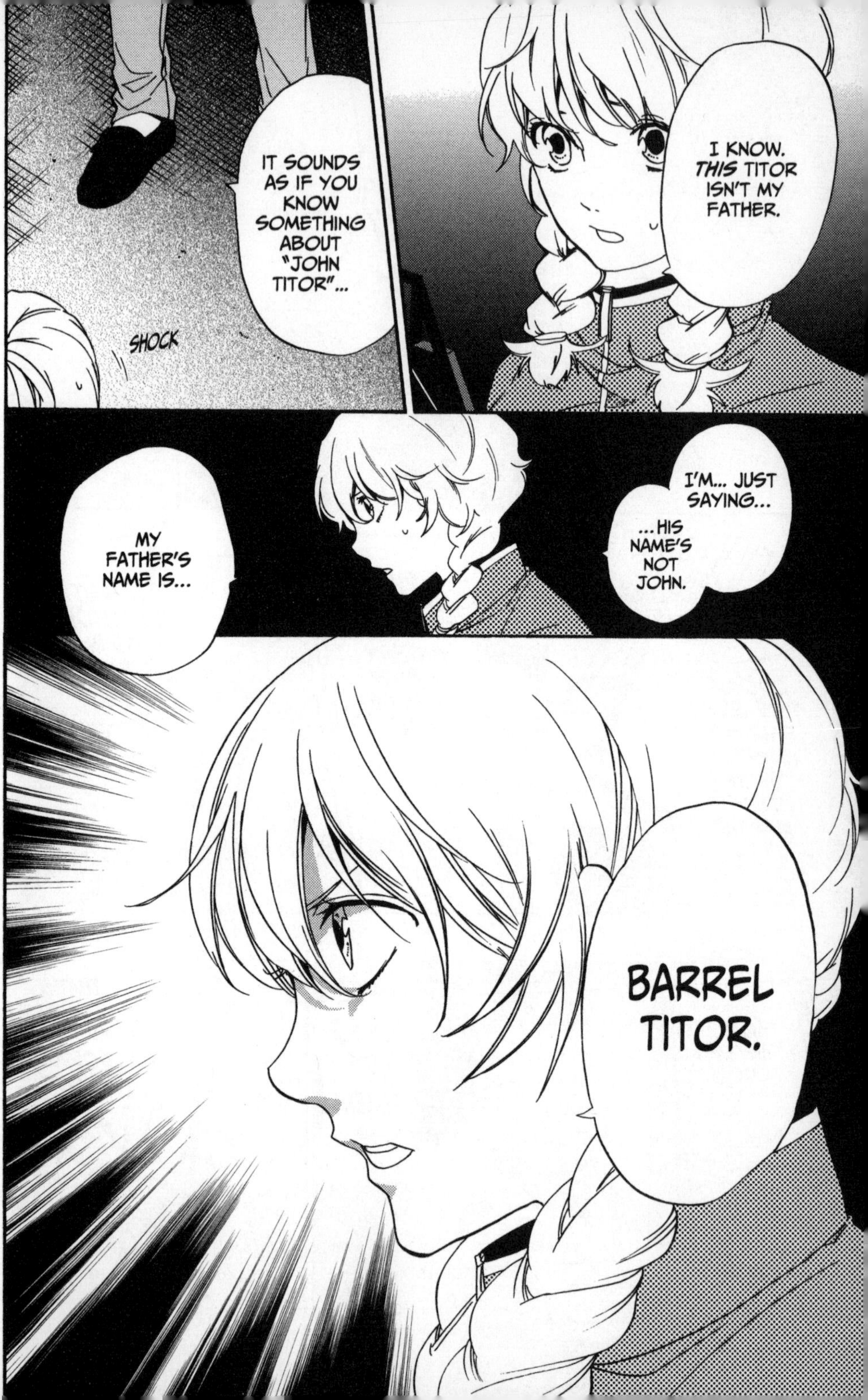
I KNOW. *THIS* TITOR ISN'T MY FATHER.
IT SOUNDS AS IF YOU KNOW SOMETHING ABOUT "JOHN TITOR"...
SHOCK
I'M... JUST SAYING...
...HIS NAME'S NOT JOHN.
MY FATHER'S NAME IS...
BARREL TITOR.

T I P S ◆ L I S T

[JOHN TITOR]

On November 2nd, 2000, someone appeared on an American internet message board claiming to be from the year 2036. The internet went crazy, flooding the board with doubts and questions for the supposed time traveler. The individual called himself John Titor and spoke of the accomplishments of the near future and of the physics behind time travel. The most notable of his comments was the following: "SERN will achieve an understanding of the mechanics behind time travel and complete the first time machine in 2034." Four months after appearing, he claimed, "My mission here is done, so I'm returning to my own world", and then vanished.

The universe has no end, though it does have a beginning. --- Infinite.
Stars too have a beginning, though they are destroyed by their own power. --- Finite.
Those who believe they have wisdom, are often shown by history to be the most foolish.
The fish in the sea don't know what the world is like on the land. Wisdom would destroy them as well.
Man to exceeding the speed of light would be more ridiculous than fish to living on land.
This is God's final warning to any who rebel.

Chapter 8 ◎ Space-Time Boundary Dogma I

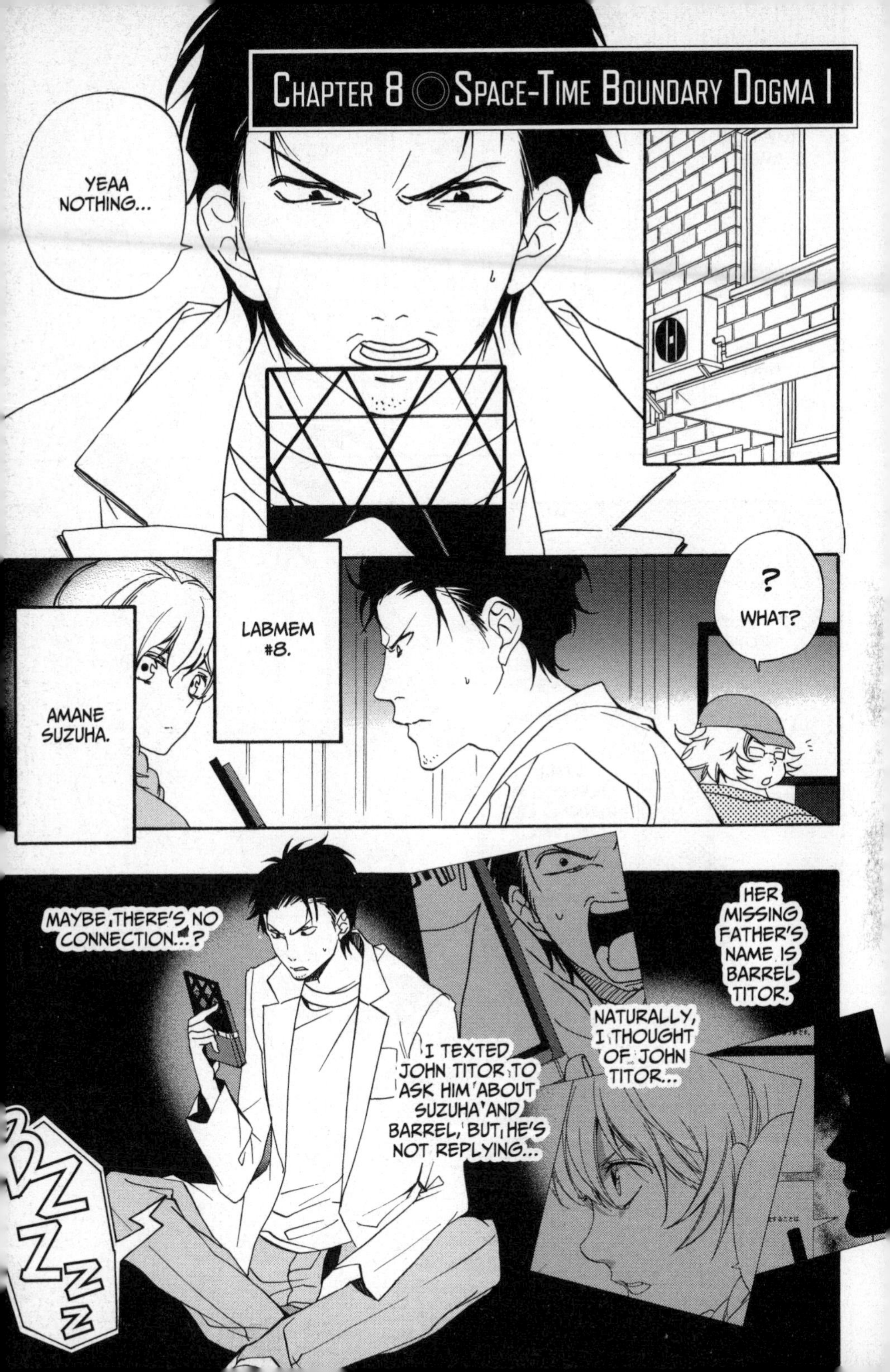
YEAA NOTHING...
?
WHAT?
LABMEM #8.
AMANE SUZUHA.
HER MISSING FATHER'S NAME IS BARREL TITOR.
NATURALLY, I THOUGHT OF JOHN TITOR...
MAYBE THERE'S NO CONNECTION...?
I TEXTED JOHN TITOR TO ASK HIM ABOUT SUZUHA AND BARREL, BUT HE'S NOT REPLYING...
BZZZZZ

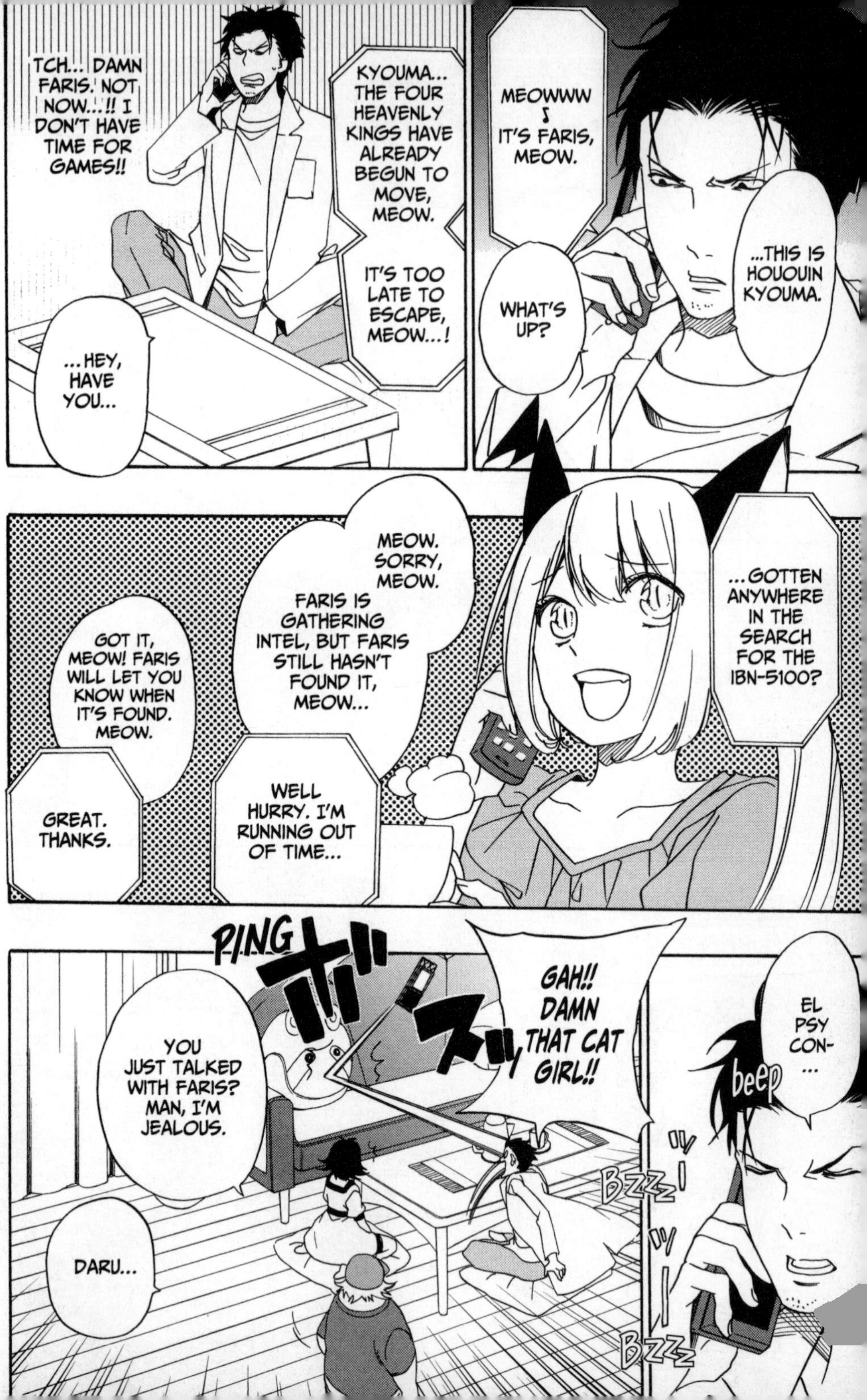
...THIS IS HOUOUIN KYOUMA.
MEOWWW ♪ IT'S FARIS, MEOW.
WHAT'S UP?
KYOUMA... THE FOUR HEAVENLY KINGS HAVE ALREADY BEGUN TO MOVE, MEOW.
IT'S TOO LATE TO ESCAPE, MEOW...!
TCH... DAMN FARIS. NOT NOW...!! I DON'T HAVE TIME FOR GAMES!!
...HEY, HAVE YOU...
...GOTTEN ANYWHERE IN THE SEARCH FOR THE IBN-5100?
MEOW. SORRY, MEOW. FARIS IS GATHERING INTEL, BUT FARIS STILL HASN'T FOUND IT, MEOW...
WELL HURRY. I'M RUNNING OUT OF TIME...
GOT IT, MEOW! FARIS WILL LET YOU KNOW WHEN IT'S FOUND. MEOW.
GREAT. THANKS.
EL PSY CON-...
beep
BZZZ
BZZZ
PING
GAH!! DAMN THAT CAT GIRL!!
YOU JUST TALKED WITH FARIS? MAN, I'M JEALOUS.
DARU...

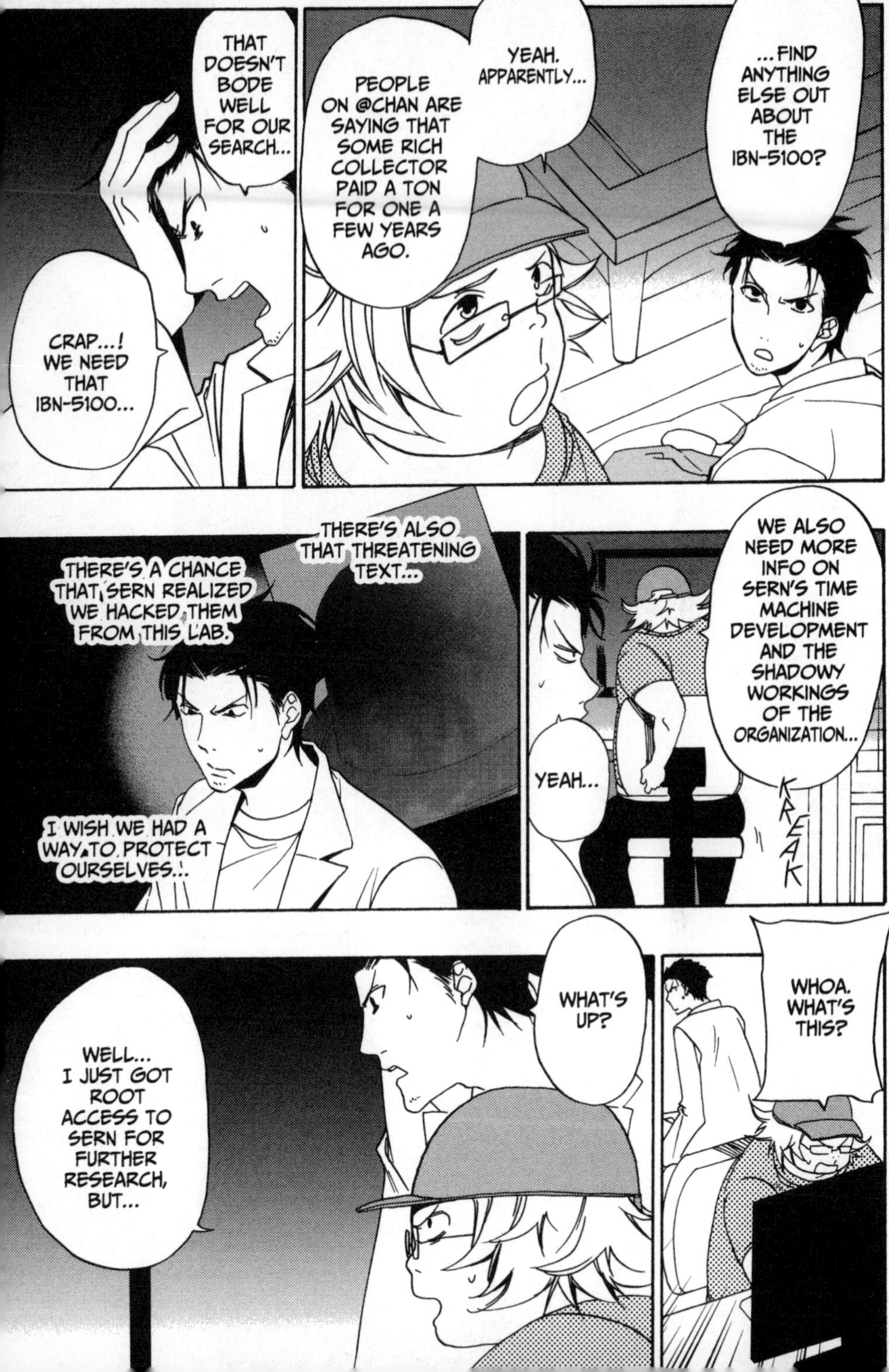
...FIND ANYTHING ELSE OUT ABOUT THE IBN-5100?
YEAH. APPARENTLY...
PEOPLE ON @CHAN ARE SAYING THAT SOME RICH COLLECTOR PAID A TON FOR ONE A FEW YEARS AGO.
THAT DOESN'T BODE WELL FOR OUR SEARCH...
CRAP...! WE NEED THAT IBN-5100...
WE ALSO NEED MORE INFO ON SERN'S TIME MACHINE DEVELOPMENT AND THE SHADOWY WORKINGS OF THE ORGANIZATION...
KREAK
YEAH...
THERE'S ALSO THAT THREATENING TEXT...
THERE'S A CHANCE THAT SERN REALIZED WE HACKED THEM FROM THIS LAB.
I WISH WE HAD A WAY TO PROTECT OURSELVES...
WHOA. WHAT'S THIS?
WHAT'S UP?
WELL... I JUST GOT ROOT ACCESS TO SERN FOR FURTHER RESEARCH, BUT...

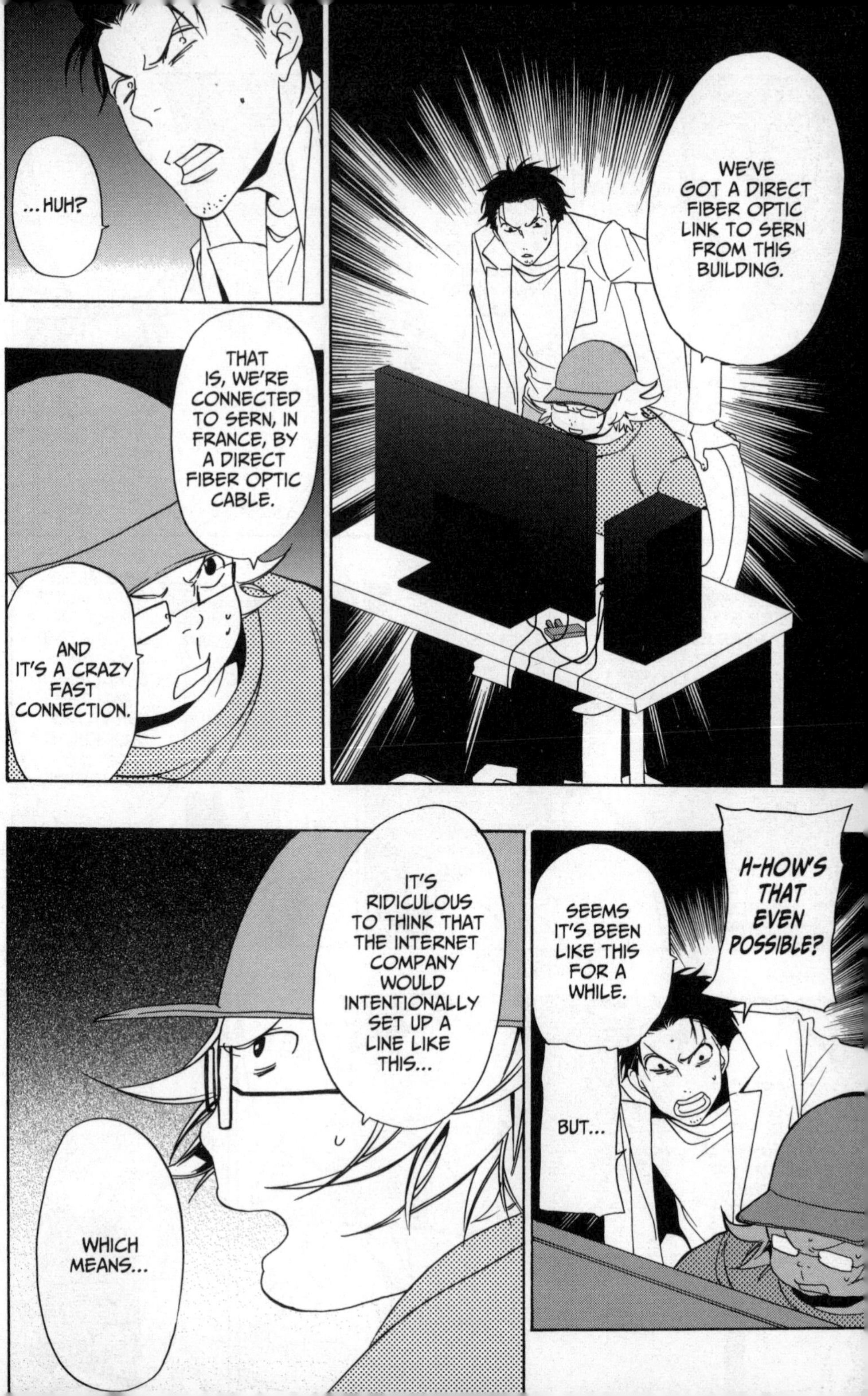
WE'VE GOT A DIRECT FIBER OPTIC LINK TO SERN FROM THIS BUILDING.
...HUH?
THAT IS, WE'RE CONNECTED TO SERN, IN FRANCE, BY A DIRECT FIBER OPTIC CABLE.
AND IT'S A CRAZY FAST CONNECTION.
H-HOW'S THAT EVEN POSSIBLE?
SEEMS IT'S BEEN LIKE THIS FOR A WHILE.
BUT...
IT'S RIDICULOUS TO THINK THAT THE INTERNET COMPANY WOULD INTENTIONALLY SET UP A LINE LIKE THIS...
WHICH MEANS...

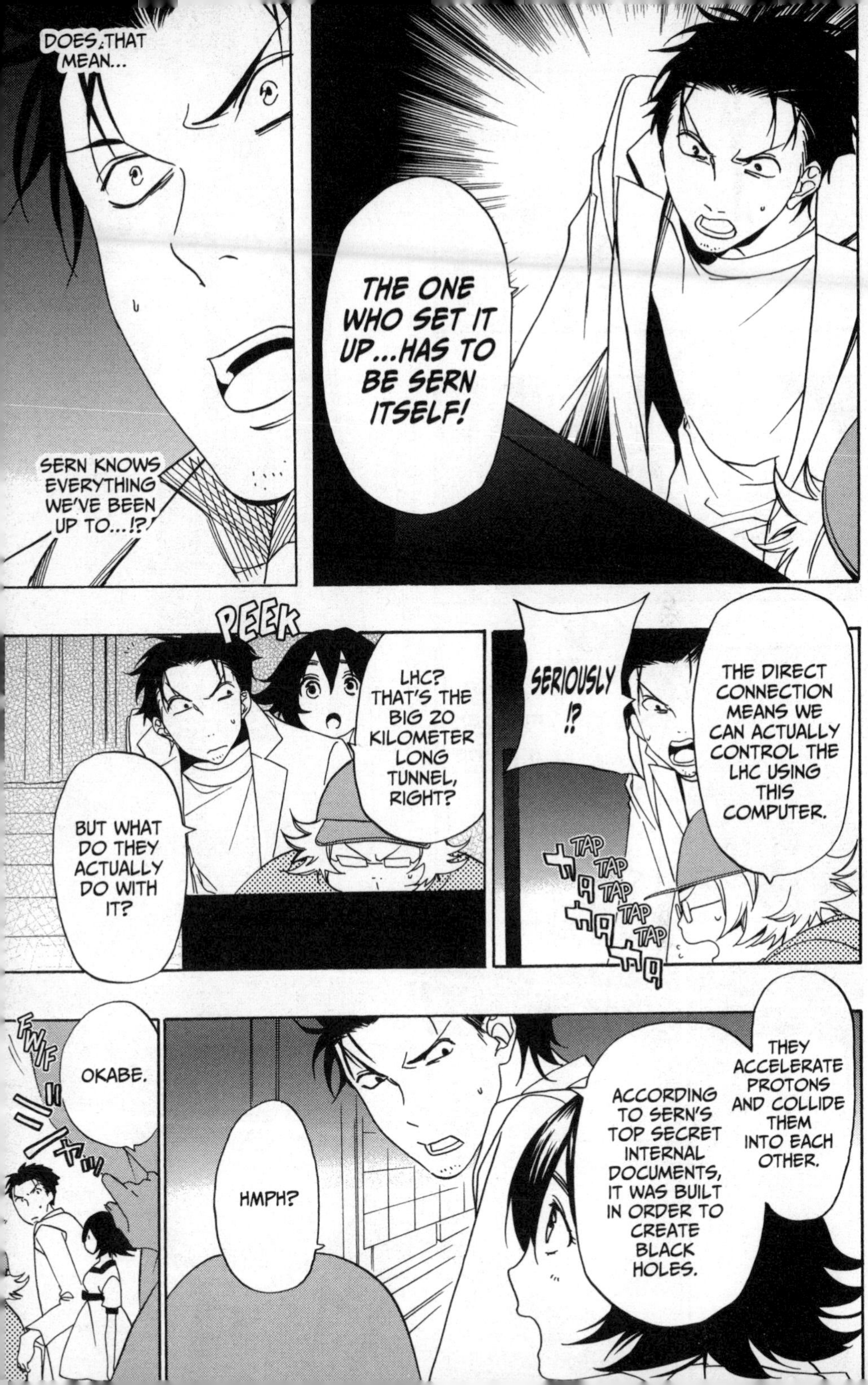
THE ONE WHO SET IT UP...HAS TO BE SERN ITSELF!
DOES THAT MEAN...
SERN KNOWS EVERYTHING WE'VE BEEN UP TO...!?!
THE DIRECT CONNECTION MEANS WE CAN ACTUALLY CONTROL THE LHC USING THIS COMPUTER.
SERIOUSLY !?
TAP TAP TAP TAP TAP
PEEK
LHC? THAT'S THE BIG 20 KILOMETER LONG TUNNEL, RIGHT?
BUT WHAT DO THEY ACTUALLY DO WITH IT?
THEY ACCELERATE PROTONS AND COLLIDE THEM INTO EACH OTHER.
ACCORDING TO SERN'S TOP SECRET INTERNAL DOCUMENTS, IT WAS BUILT IN ORDER TO CREATE BLACK HOLES.
HMPH?
OKABE.
FWIF

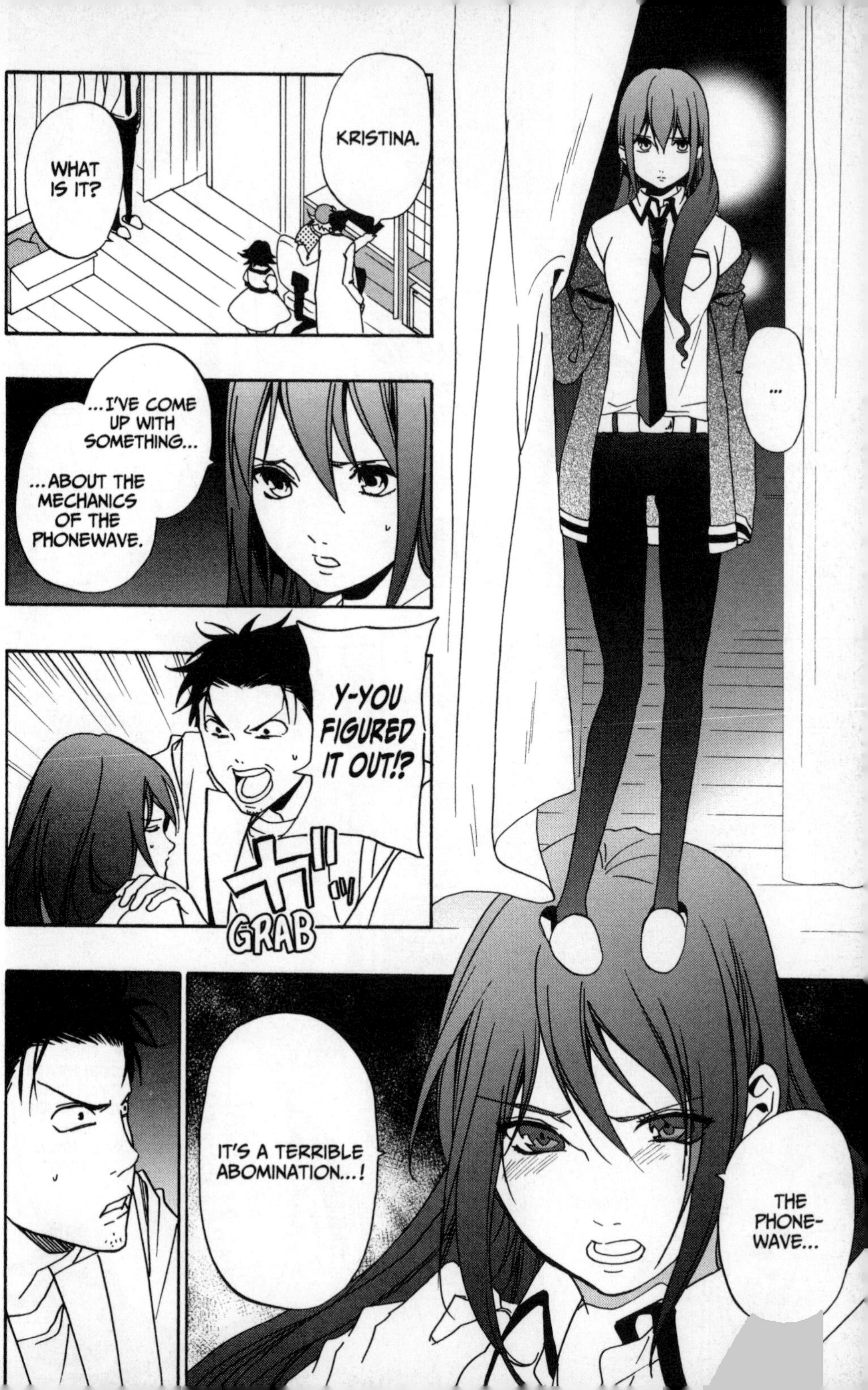
...
KRISTINA.
WHAT IS IT?
...I'VE COME UP WITH SOMETHING...
...ABOUT THE MECHANICS OF THE PHONEWAVE.
Y-YOU FIGURED IT OUT!?
GRAB
THE PHONE-WAVE...
IT'S A TERRIBLE ABOMINATION...!

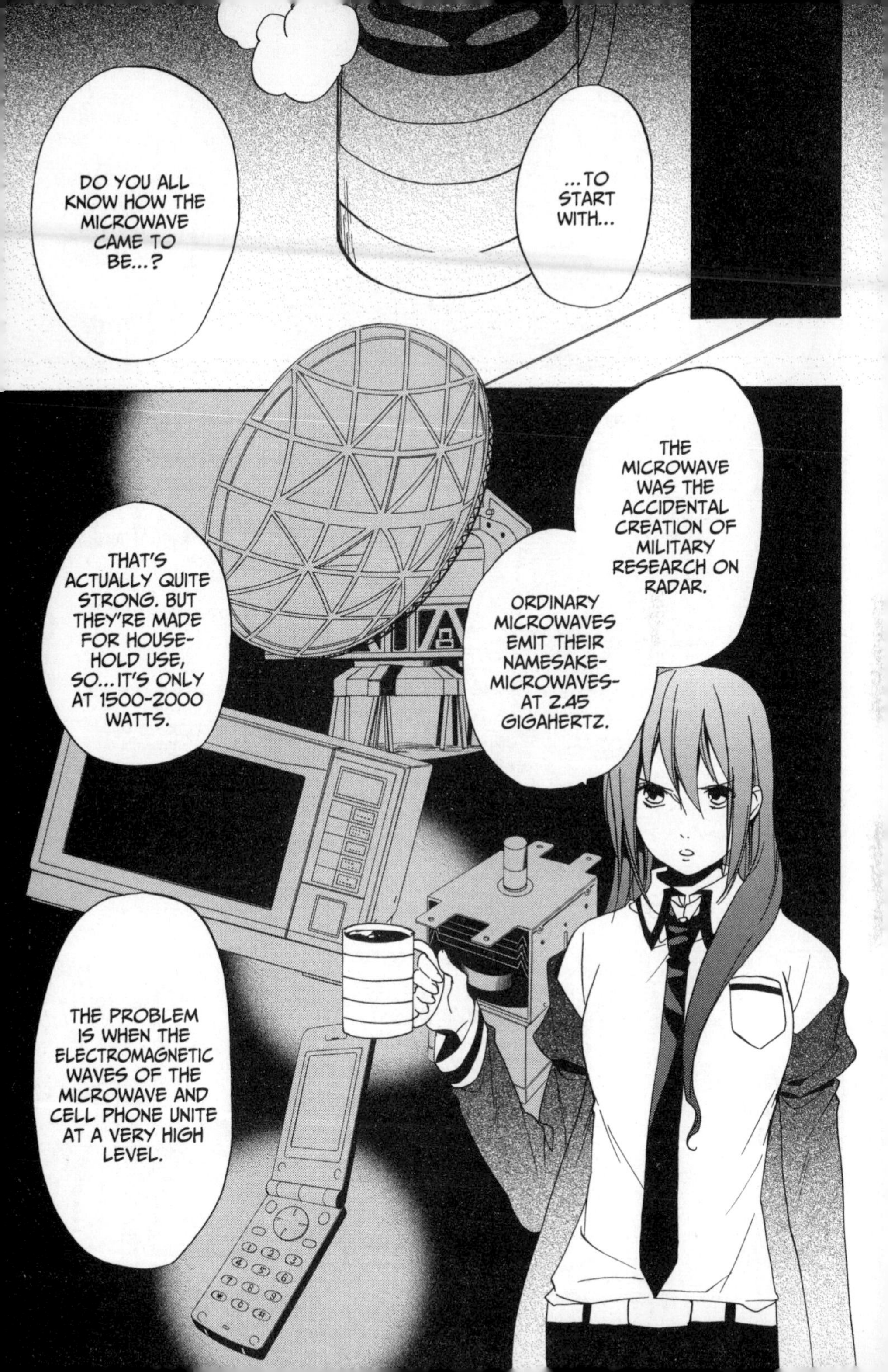
...TO START WITH...
DO YOU ALL KNOW HOW THE MICROWAVE CAME TO BE...?
THE MICROWAVE WAS THE ACCIDENTAL CREATION OF MILITARY RESEARCH ON RADAR.
ORDINARY MICROWAVES EMIT THEIR NAMESAKE-MICROWAVES-AT 2.45 GIGAHERTZ.
THAT'S ACTUALLY QUITE STRONG. BUT THEY'RE MADE FOR HOUSE-HOLD USE, SO...IT'S ONLY AT 1500-2000 WATTS.
THE PROBLEM IS WHEN THE ELECTROMAGNETIC WAVES OF THE MICROWAVE AND CELL PHONE UNITE AT A VERY HIGH LEVEL.

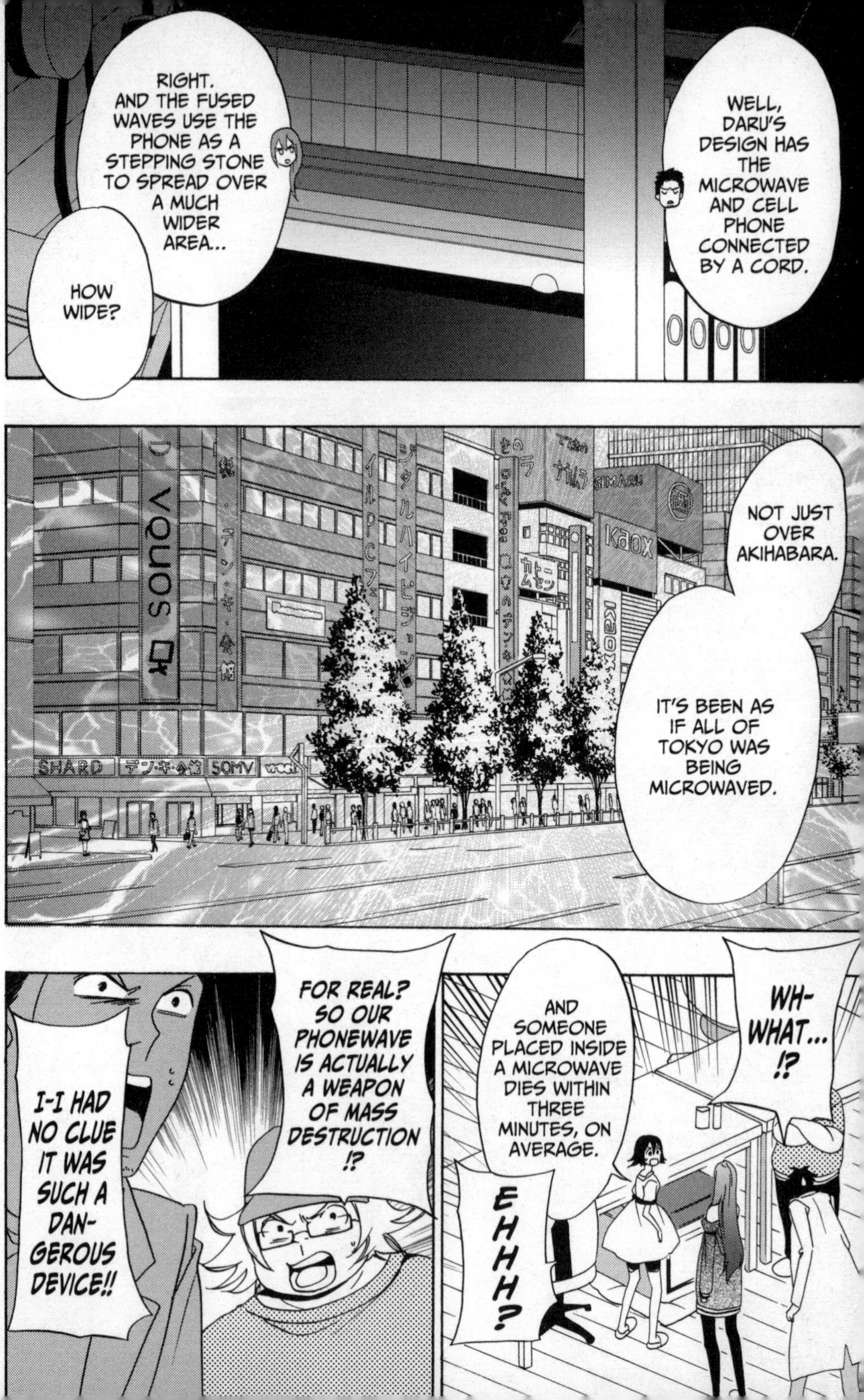
WELL, DARU'S DESIGN HAS THE MICROWAVE AND CELL PHONE CONNECTED BY A CORD.
RIGHT. AND THE FUSED WAVES USE THE PHONE AS A STEPPING STONE TO SPREAD OVER A MUCH WIDER AREA...
HOW WIDE?
NOT JUST OVER AKIHABARA.
IT'S BEEN AS IF ALL OF TOKYO WAS BEING MICROWAVED.
VQUOS
SHARD
SOMV
Kaox
WH-WHAT...!?
AND SOMEONE PLACED INSIDE A MICROWAVE DIES WITHIN THREE MINUTES, ON AVERAGE.
EHHH?
FOR REAL? SO OUR PHONEWAVE IS ACTUALLY A WEAPON OF MASS DESTRUCTION!?
I-I HAD NO CLUE IT WAS SUCH A DANGEROUS DEVICE!!

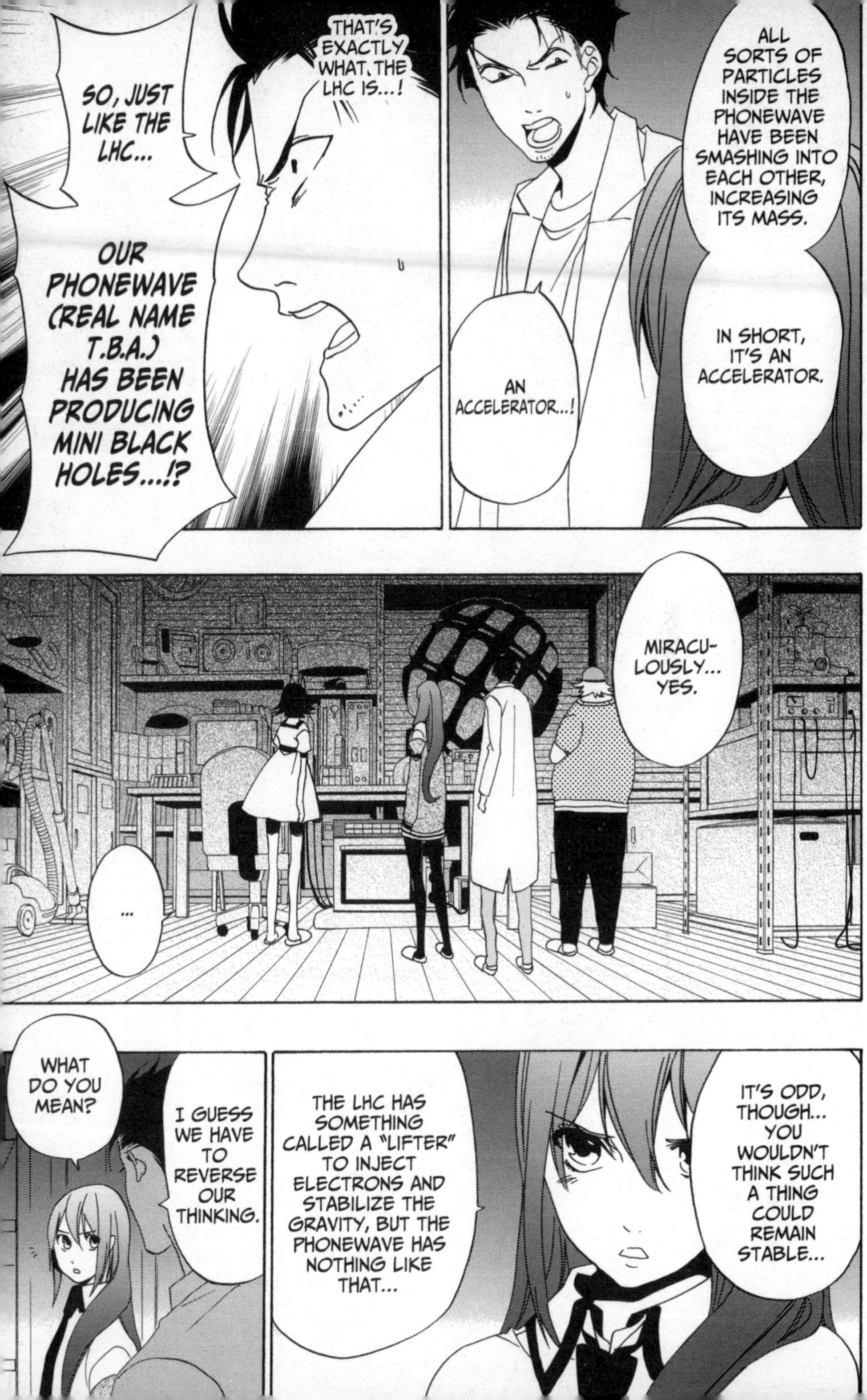
ALL SORTS OF PARTICLES INSIDE THE PHONEWAVE HAVE BEEN SMASHING INTO EACH OTHER, INCREASING ITS MASS.
IN SHORT, IT'S AN ACCELERATOR.
AN ACCELERATOR...!
THAT'S EXACTLY WHAT THE LHC IS...!
SO, JUST LIKE THE LHC...
OUR PHONEWAVE (REAL NAME T.B.A.) HAS BEEN PRODUCING MINI BLACK HOLES...!?
MIRACU-LOUSLY... YES.
...
IT'S ODD, THOUGH... YOU WOULDN'T THINK SUCH A THING COULD REMAIN STABLE...
THE LHC HAS SOMETHING CALLED A "LIFTER" TO INJECT ELECTRONS AND STABILIZE THE GRAVITY, BUT THE PHONEWAVE HAS NOTHING LIKE THAT...
I GUESS WE HAVE TO REVERSE OUR THINKING.
WHAT DO YOU MEAN?

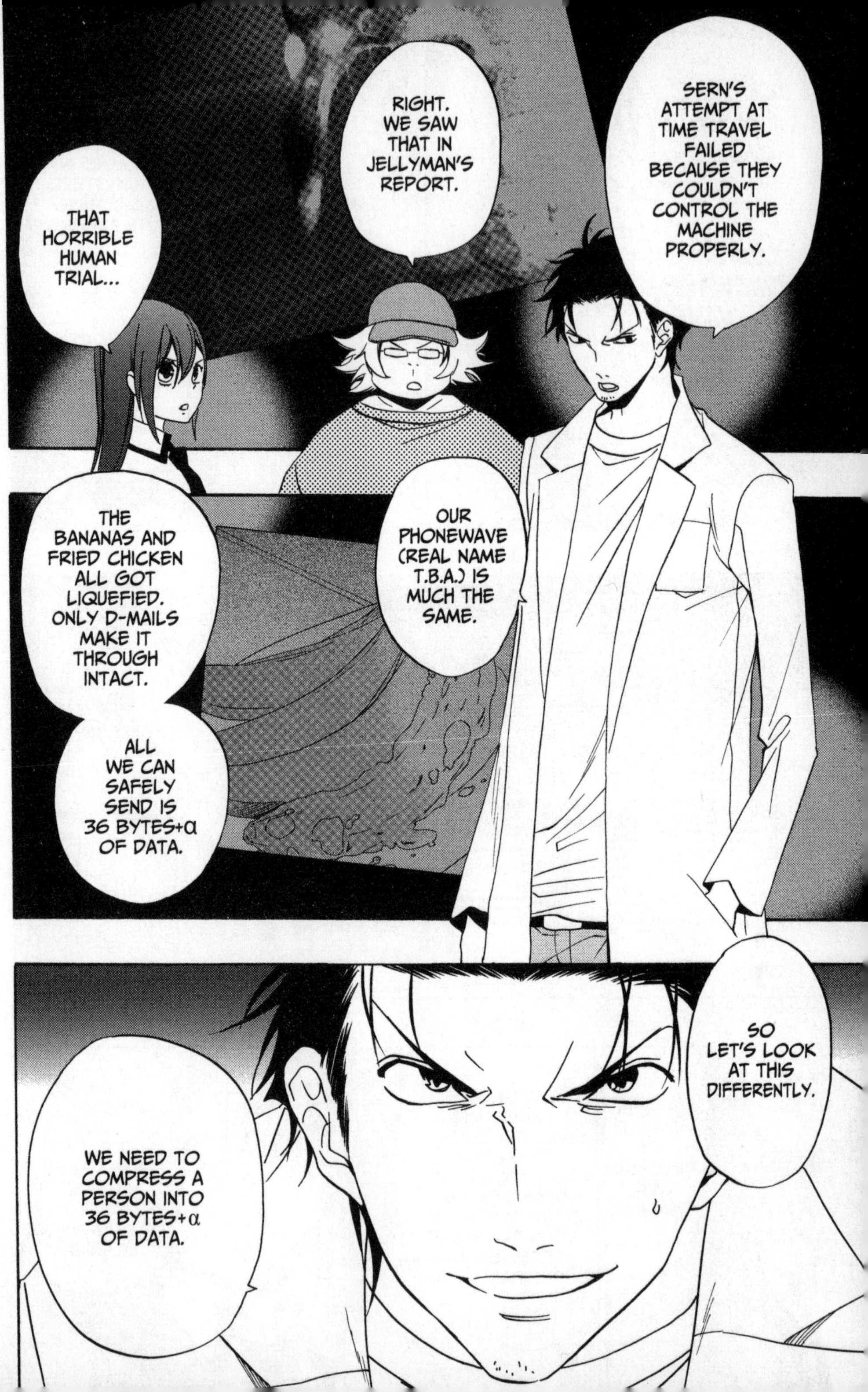
SERN'S ATTEMPT AT TIME TRAVEL FAILED BECAUSE THEY COULDN'T CONTROL THE MACHINE PROPERLY.
RIGHT. WE SAW THAT IN JELLYMAN'S REPORT.
THAT HORRIBLE HUMAN TRIAL...
OUR PHONEWAVE (REAL NAME T.B.A.) IS MUCH THE SAME.
THE BANANAS AND FRIED CHICKEN ALL GOT LIQUEFIED. ONLY D-MAILS MAKE IT THROUGH INTACT.
ALL WE CAN SAFELY SEND IS 36 BYTES+α OF DATA.
SO LET'S LOOK AT THIS DIFFERENTLY.
WE NEED TO COMPRESS A PERSON INTO 36 BYTES+α OF DATA.

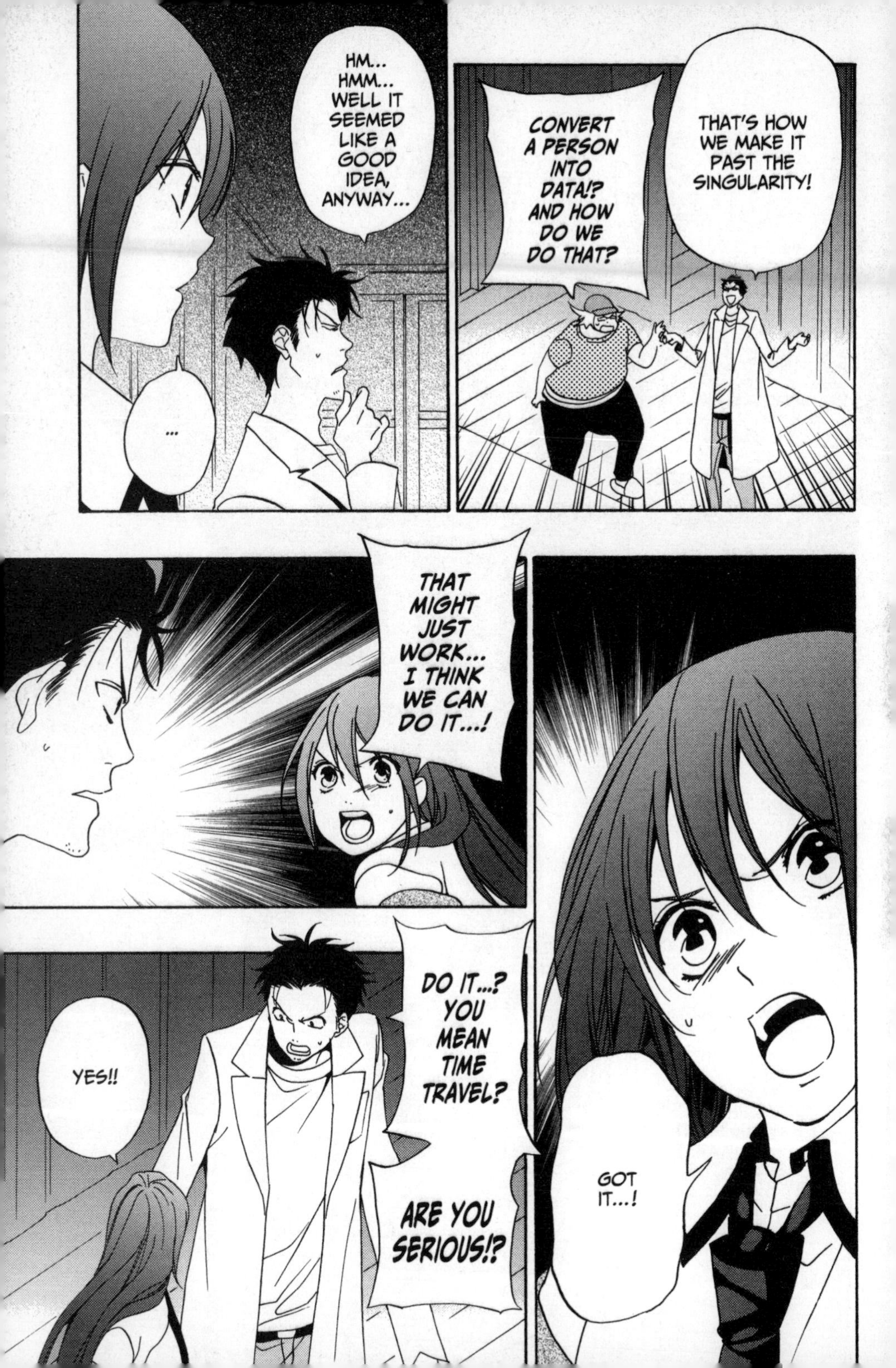
THAT'S HOW WE MAKE IT PAST THE SINGULARITY!
CONVERT A PERSON INTO DATA!? AND HOW DO WE DO THAT?
HM... HMM... WELL IT SEEMED LIKE A GOOD IDEA, ANYWAY...
...
GOT IT...!
THAT MIGHT JUST WORK... I THINK WE CAN DO IT...!
DO IT...? YOU MEAN TIME TRAVEL?
ARE YOU SERIOUS!?
YES!!

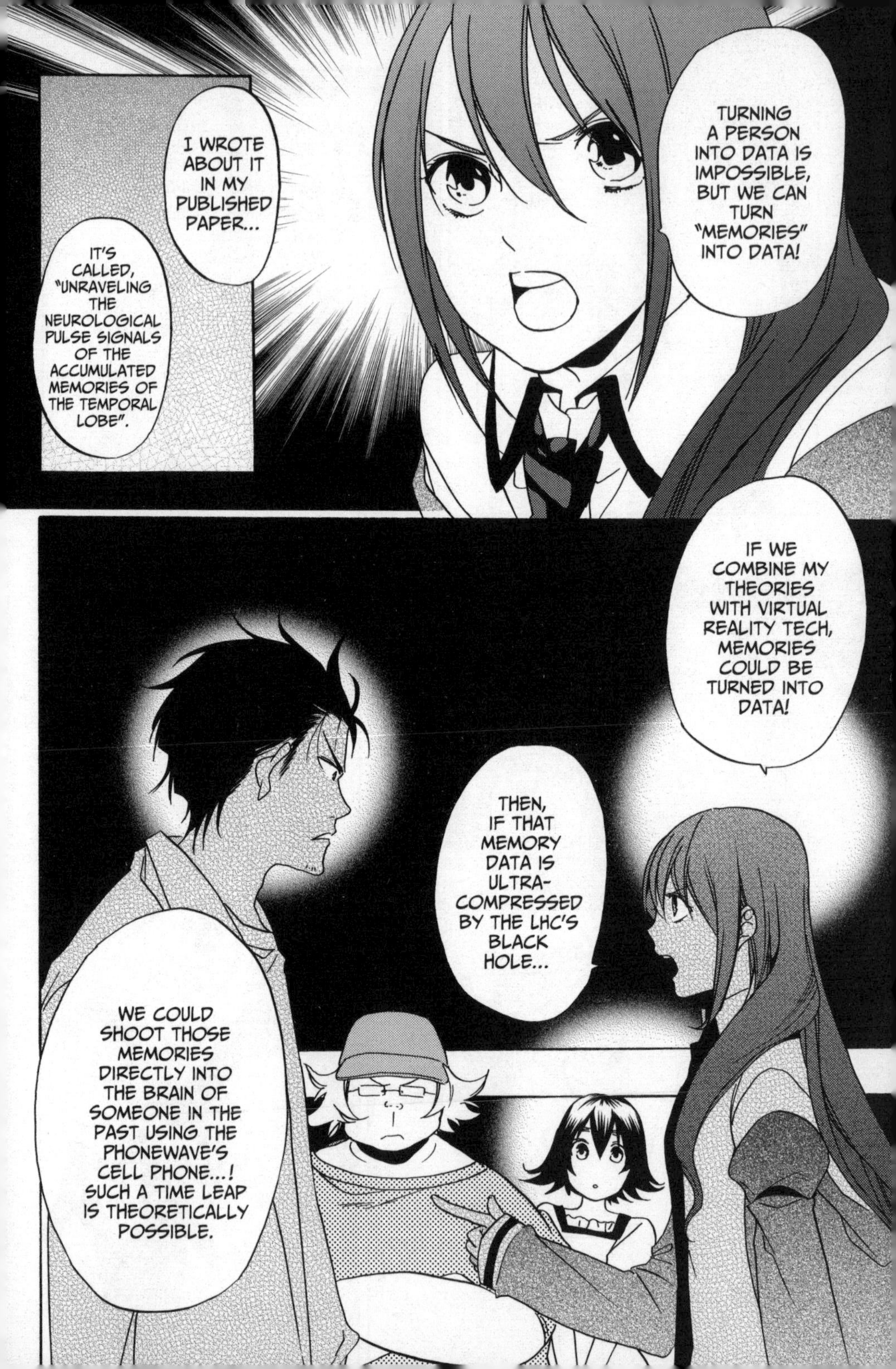
TURNING A PERSON INTO DATA IS IMPOSSIBLE, BUT WE CAN TURN "MEMORIES" INTO DATA!
I WROTE ABOUT IT IN MY PUBLISHED PAPER...
IT'S CALLED, "UNRAVELING THE NEUROLOGICAL PULSE SIGNALS OF THE ACCUMULATED MEMORIES OF THE TEMPORAL LOBE".
IF WE COMBINE MY THEORIES WITH VIRTUAL REALITY TECH, MEMORIES COULD BE TURNED INTO DATA!
THEN, IF THAT MEMORY DATA IS ULTRA-COMPRESSED BY THE LHC'S BLACK HOLE...
WE COULD SHOOT THOSE MEMORIES DIRECTLY INTO THE BRAIN OF SOMEONE IN THE PAST USING THE PHONEWAVE'S CELL PHONE...! SUCH A TIME LEAP IS THEORETICALLY POSSIBLE.

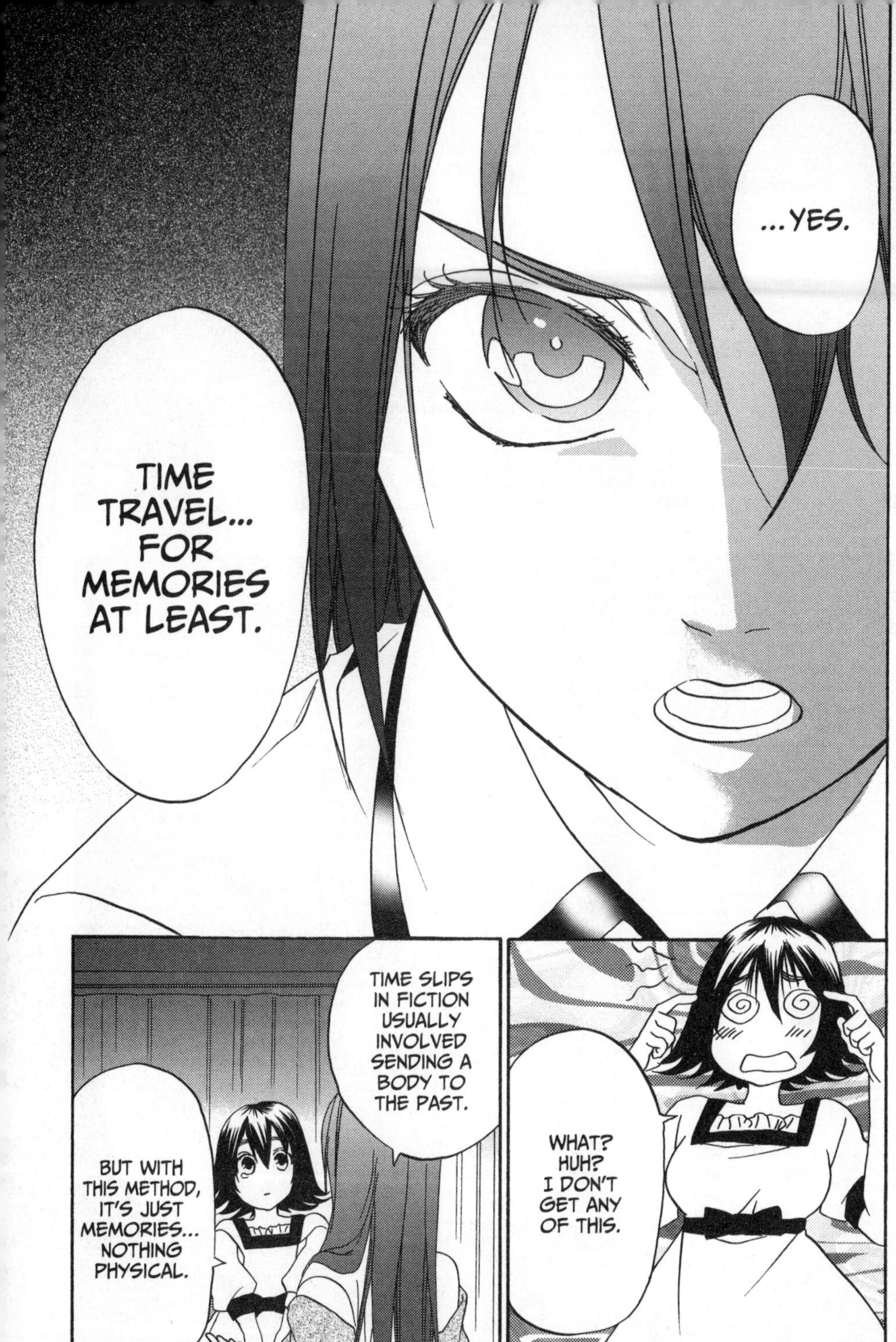
...YES.
TIME TRAVEL... FOR MEMORIES AT LEAST.
WHAT? HUH? I DON'T GET ANY OF THIS.
TIME SLIPS IN FICTION USUALLY INVOLVED SENDING A BODY TO THE PAST.
BUT WITH THIS METHOD, IT'S JUST MEMORIES... NOTHING PHYSICAL.

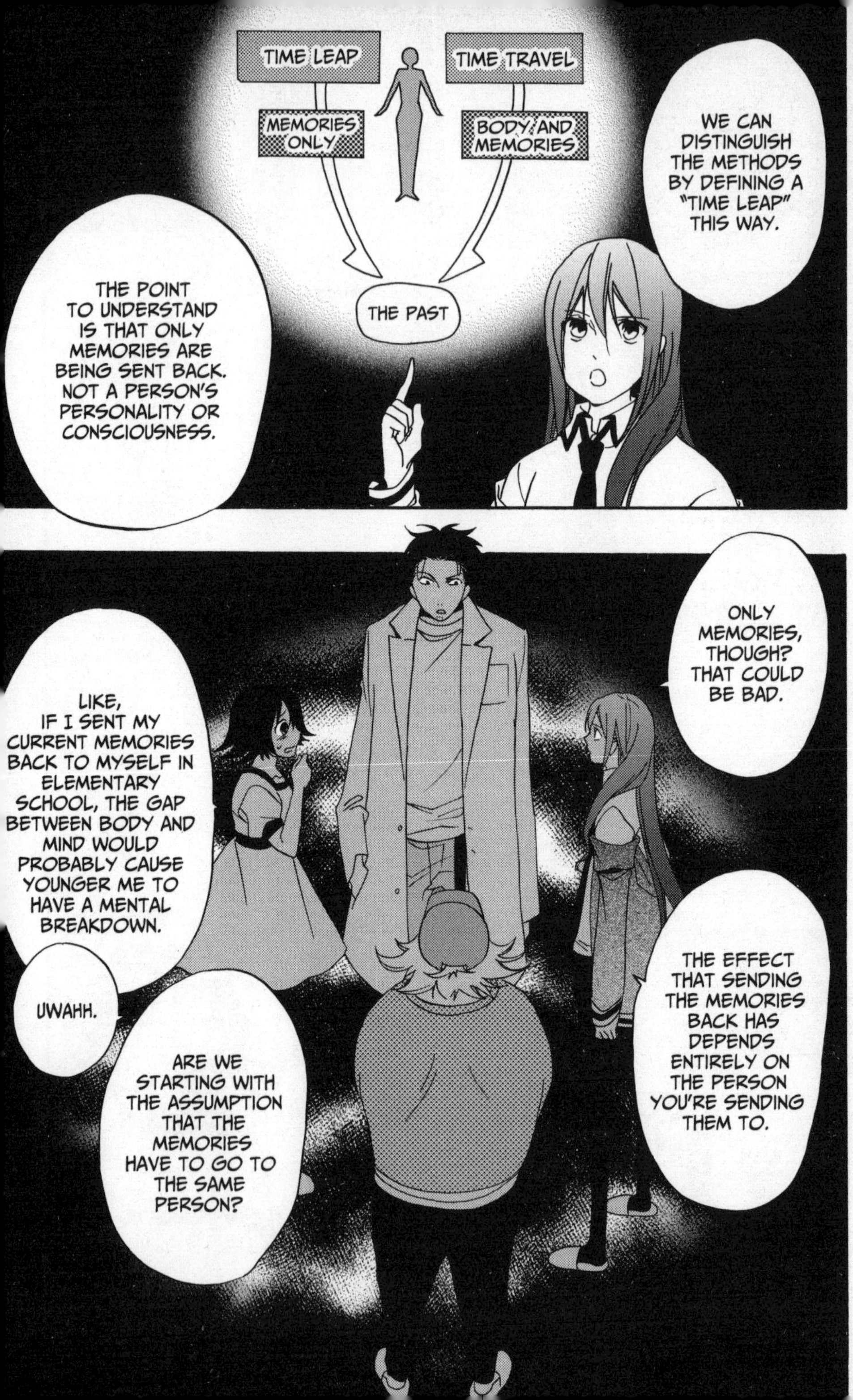
WE CAN DISTINGUISH THE METHODS BY DEFINING A "TIME LEAP" THIS WAY.
TIME TRAVEL
BODY AND MEMORIES
TIME LEAP
MEMORIES ONLY
THE PAST
THE POINT TO UNDERSTAND IS THAT ONLY MEMORIES ARE BEING SENT BACK. NOT A PERSON'S PERSONALITY OR CONSCIOUSNESS.
ONLY MEMORIES, THOUGH? THAT COULD BE BAD.
LIKE, IF I SENT MY CURRENT MEMORIES BACK TO MYSELF IN ELEMENTARY SCHOOL, THE GAP BETWEEN BODY AND MIND WOULD PROBABLY CAUSE YOUNGER ME TO HAVE A MENTAL BREAKDOWN.
THE EFFECT THAT SENDING THE MEMORIES BACK HAS DEPENDS ENTIRELY ON THE PERSON YOU'RE SENDING THEM TO.
UWAHH.
ARE WE STARTING WITH THE ASSUMPTION THAT THE MEMORIES HAVE TO GO TO THE SAME PERSON?

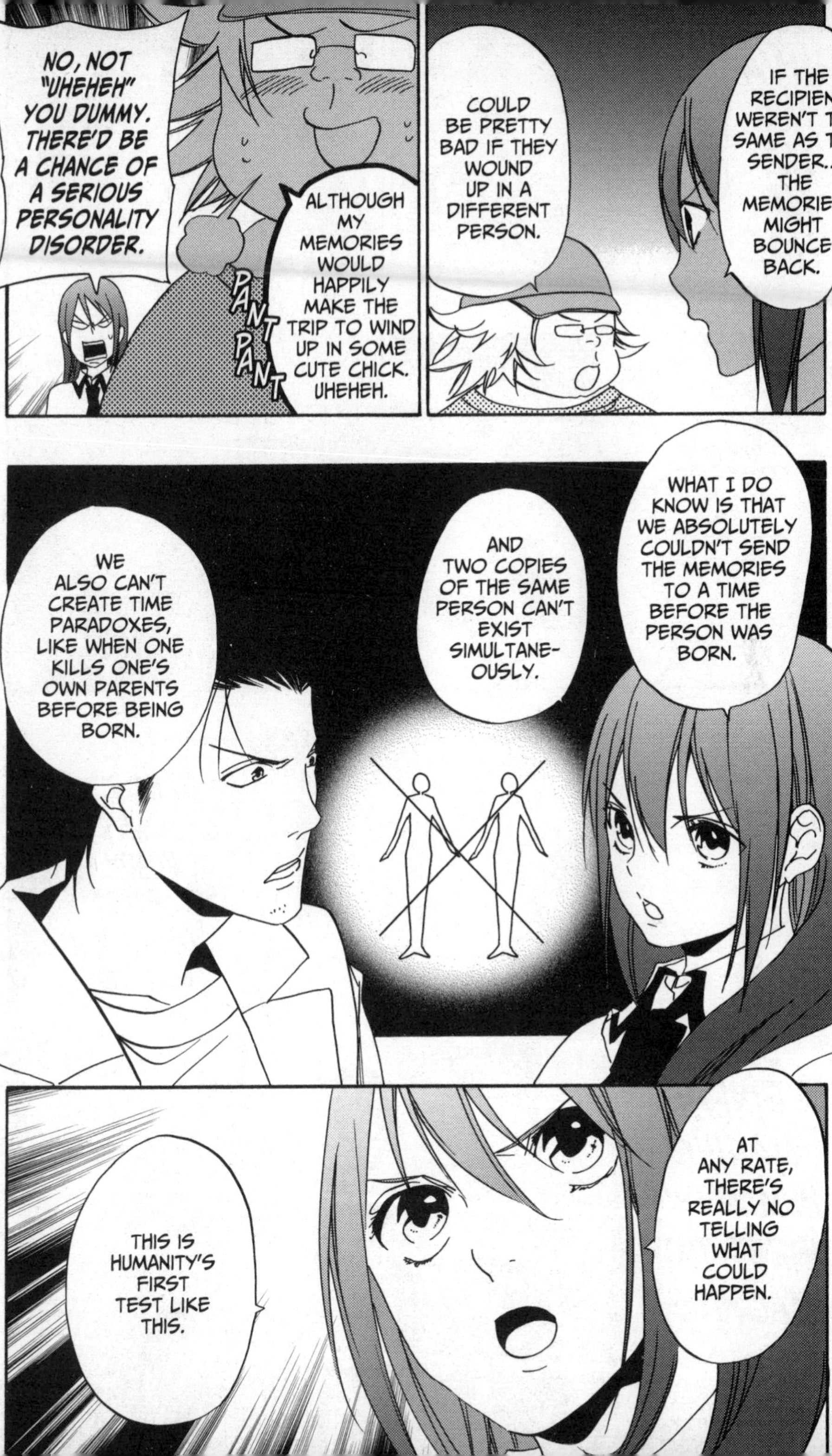
IF THE RECIPIENT WEREN'T THE SAME AS THE SENDER... THE MEMORIES MIGHT BOUNCE BACK.
COULD BE PRETTY BAD IF THEY WOUND UP IN A DIFFERENT PERSON.
ALTHOUGH MY MEMORIES WOULD HAPPILY MAKE THE TRIP TO WIND UP IN SOME CUTE CHICK. UHEHEH.
PANT PANT
NO, NOT "UHEHEH" YOU DUMMY. THERE'D BE A CHANCE OF A SERIOUS PERSONALITY DISORDER.
WHAT I DO KNOW IS THAT WE ABSOLUTELY COULDN'T SEND THE MEMORIES TO A TIME BEFORE THE PERSON WAS BORN.
AND TWO COPIES OF THE SAME PERSON CAN'T EXIST SIMULTANE-OUSLY.
WE ALSO CAN'T CREATE TIME PARADOXES, LIKE WHEN ONE KILLS ONE'S OWN PARENTS BEFORE BEING BORN.
AT ANY RATE, THERE'S REALLY NO TELLING WHAT COULD HAPPEN.
THIS IS HUMANITY'S FIRST TEST LIKE THIS.

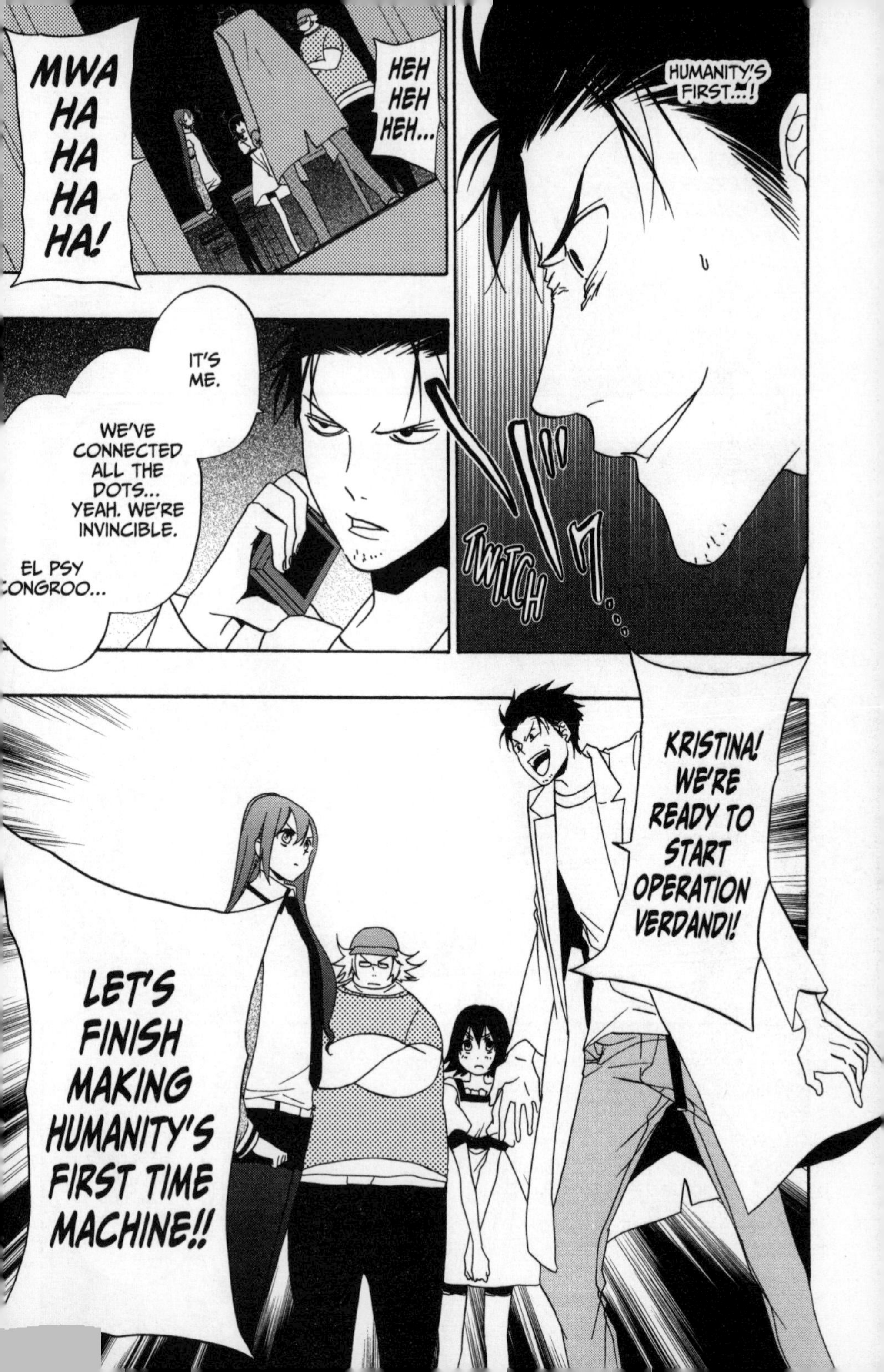
HUMANITY'S FIRST...!
TWITCH
HEH HEH HEH...
MWA HA HA HA HA HA!
IT'S ME.
WE'VE CONNECTED ALL THE DOTS... YEAH. WE'RE INVINCIBLE.
EL PSY CONGROO...
KRISTINA! WE'RE READY TO START OPERATION VERDANDI!
LET'S FINISH MAKING HUMANITY'S FIRST TIME MACHINE!!

[LHC- LARGE HADRON COLLIDER]

SERN's famed, massive (27 km long) particle accelerator. The device is said to be capable of producing mini black holes based on how it's used. According to John Titor, the mini black hole that SERN produces with this device in 2034 is used to make time travel a reality.

[ACCELERATOR]

A device used in particle physics experiments. Accelerating electrons, protons, and ions to high speeds transforms them into large amounts of energy. The current limits of science have allowed us to accelerate particles up to 99.7% of the speed of light. At that point, a particle's mass increases by a factor of 13 (as compared to when it's motionless). In other words, the closer an object is to the speed of light, the more massive (or heavier) it becomes. Within the constraints of our current laws of physics, there exists a phenomenon we can't comprehend called distortion. We can think of this as a law implemented into reality by a desperate creator, stating that "humans cannot exceed the speed of light".

The universe has no end, though it does have a beginning. --- Infinite.
Stars too have a beginning, though they are destroyed by their own power. --- Finite.
Those who believe they have wisdom, are often shown by history to be the most foolish.
The fish in the sea don't know what the world is like on the land. Wisdom would destroy them as well.
Man to exceeding the speed of light would be more ridiculous than fish to living on land.
This is God's final warning to any who rebel.

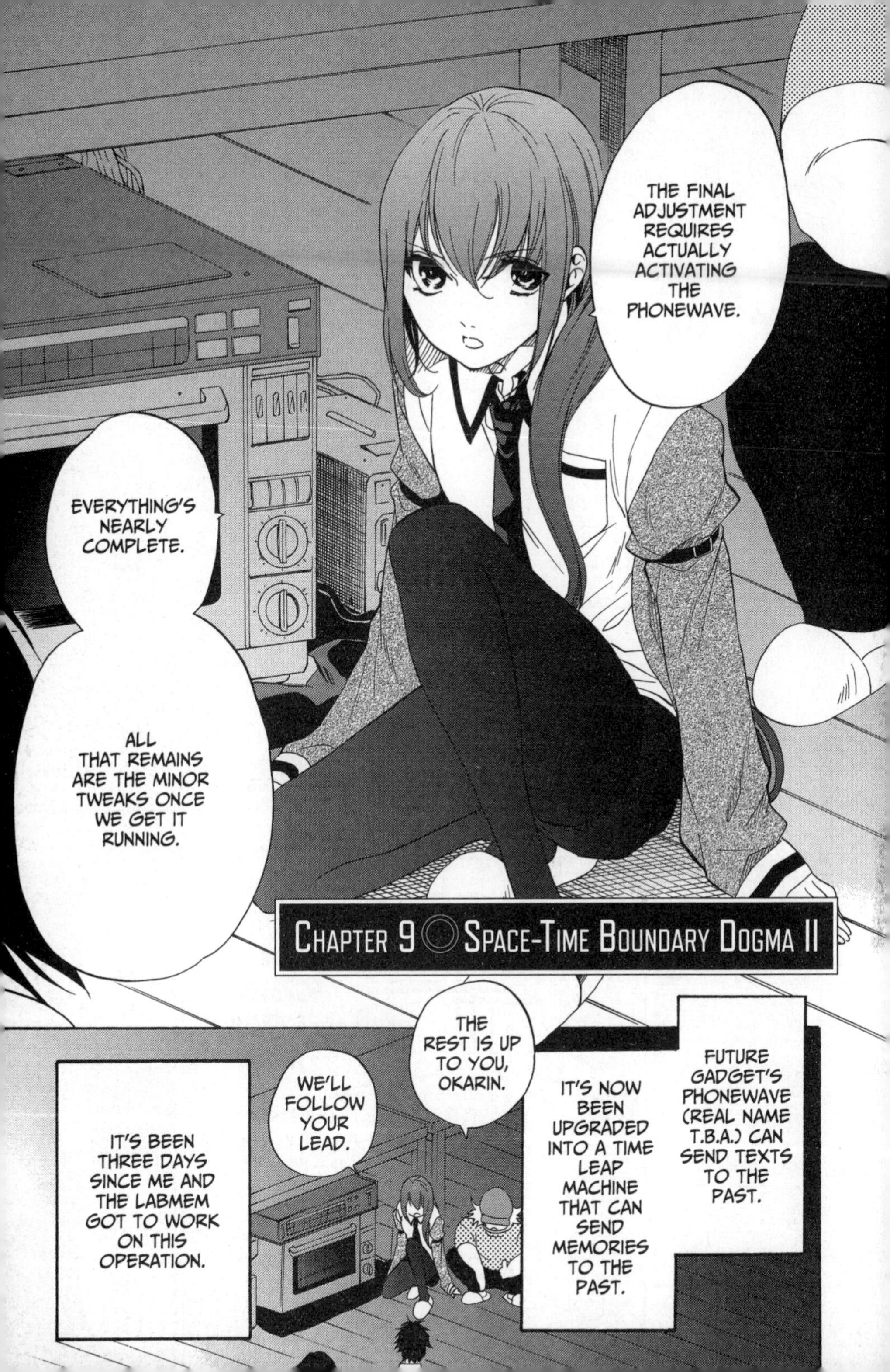
THE FINAL ADJUSTMENT REQUIRES ACTUALLY ACTIVATING THE PHONEWAVE.
EVERYTHING'S NEARLY COMPLETE.
ALL THAT REMAINS ARE THE MINOR TWEAKS ONCE WE GET IT RUNNING.
CHAPTER 9 ◎ SPACE-TIME BOUNDARY DOGMA II
FUTURE GADGET'S PHONEWAVE (REAL NAME T.B.A.) CAN SEND TEXTS TO THE PAST.
IT'S NOW BEEN UPGRADED INTO A TIME LEAP MACHINE THAT CAN SEND MEMORIES TO THE PAST.
THE REST IS UP TO YOU, OKARIN.
WE'LL FOLLOW YOUR LEAD.
IT'S BEEN THREE DAYS SINCE ME AND THE LABMEM GOT TO WORK ON THIS OPERATION.

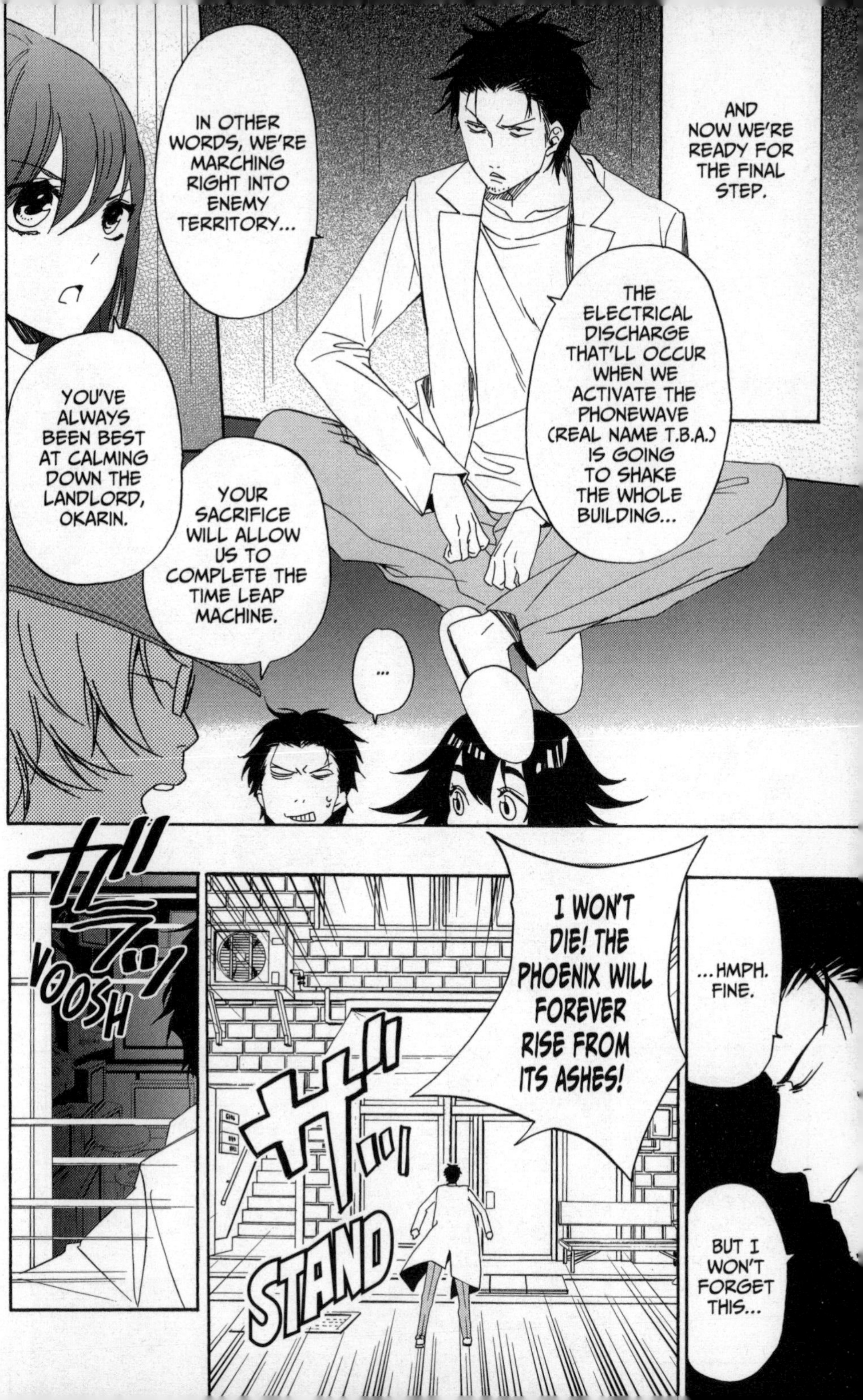
AND NOW WE'RE READY FOR THE FINAL STEP.
THE ELECTRICAL DISCHARGE THAT'LL OCCUR WHEN WE ACTIVATE THE PHONEWAVE (REAL NAME T.B.A.) IS GOING TO SHAKE THE WHOLE BUILDING...
IN OTHER WORDS, WE'RE MARCHING RIGHT INTO ENEMY TERRITORY...
YOU'VE ALWAYS BEEN BEST AT CALMING DOWN THE LANDLORD, OKARIN.
YOUR SACRIFICE WILL ALLOW US TO COMPLETE THE TIME LEAP MACHINE.
...
...HMPH. FINE.
BUT I WON'T FORGET THIS...
I WON'T DIE! THE PHOENIX WILL FOREVER RISE FROM ITS ASHES!
STAND
VOOSH

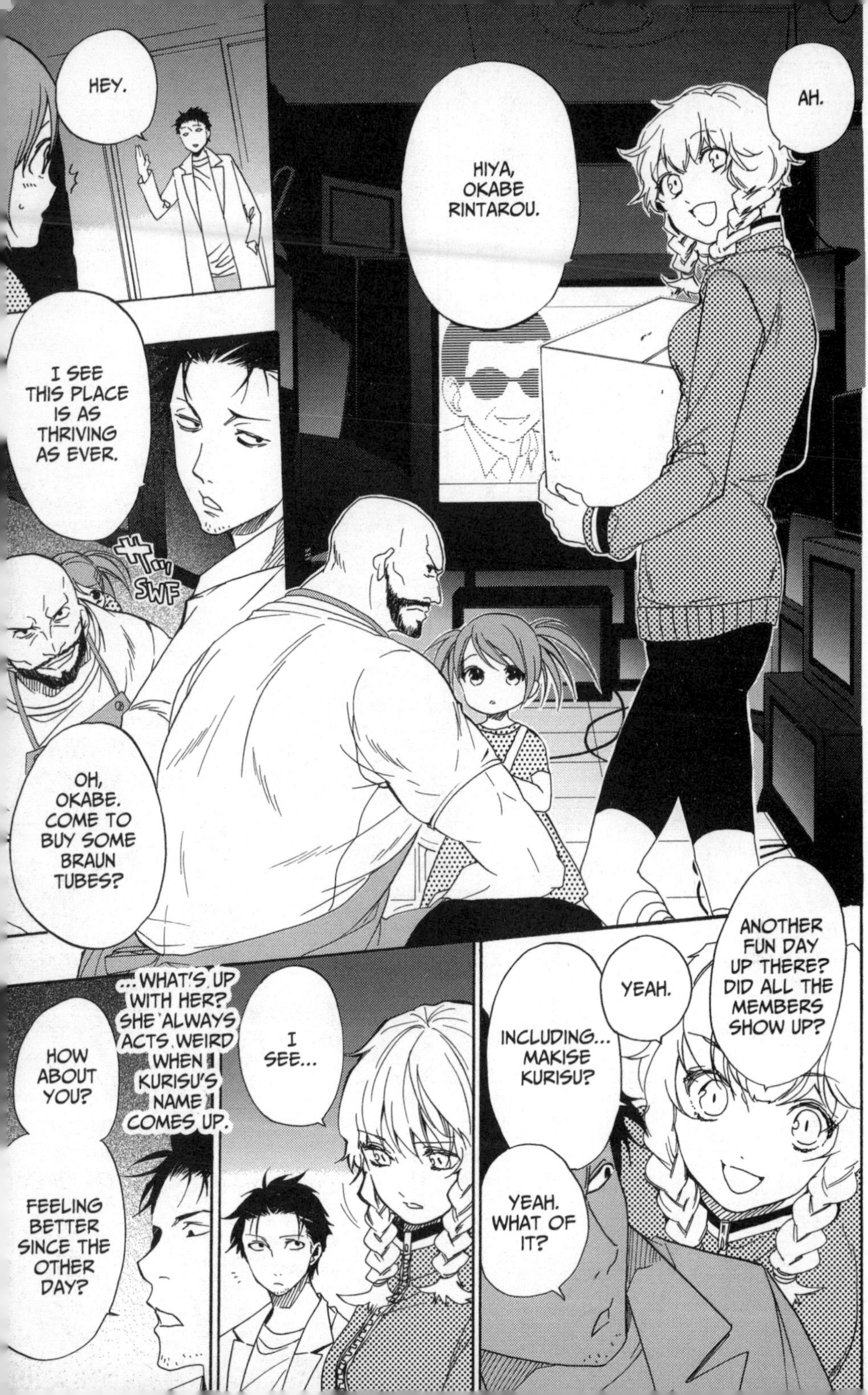
AH.
HIYA, OKABE RINTAROU.
HEY.
I SEE THIS PLACE IS AS THRIVING AS EVER.
SWF
OH, OKABE. COME TO BUY SOME BRAUN TUBES?
ANOTHER FUN DAY UP THERE? DID ALL THE MEMBERS SHOW UP?
YEAH.
INCLUDING... MAKISE KURISU?
YEAH. WHAT OF IT?
I SEE...
...WHAT'S UP WITH HER? SHE ALWAYS ACTS WEIRD WHEN KURISU'S NAME COMES UP.
HOW ABOUT YOU?
FEELING BETTER SINCE THE OTHER DAY?

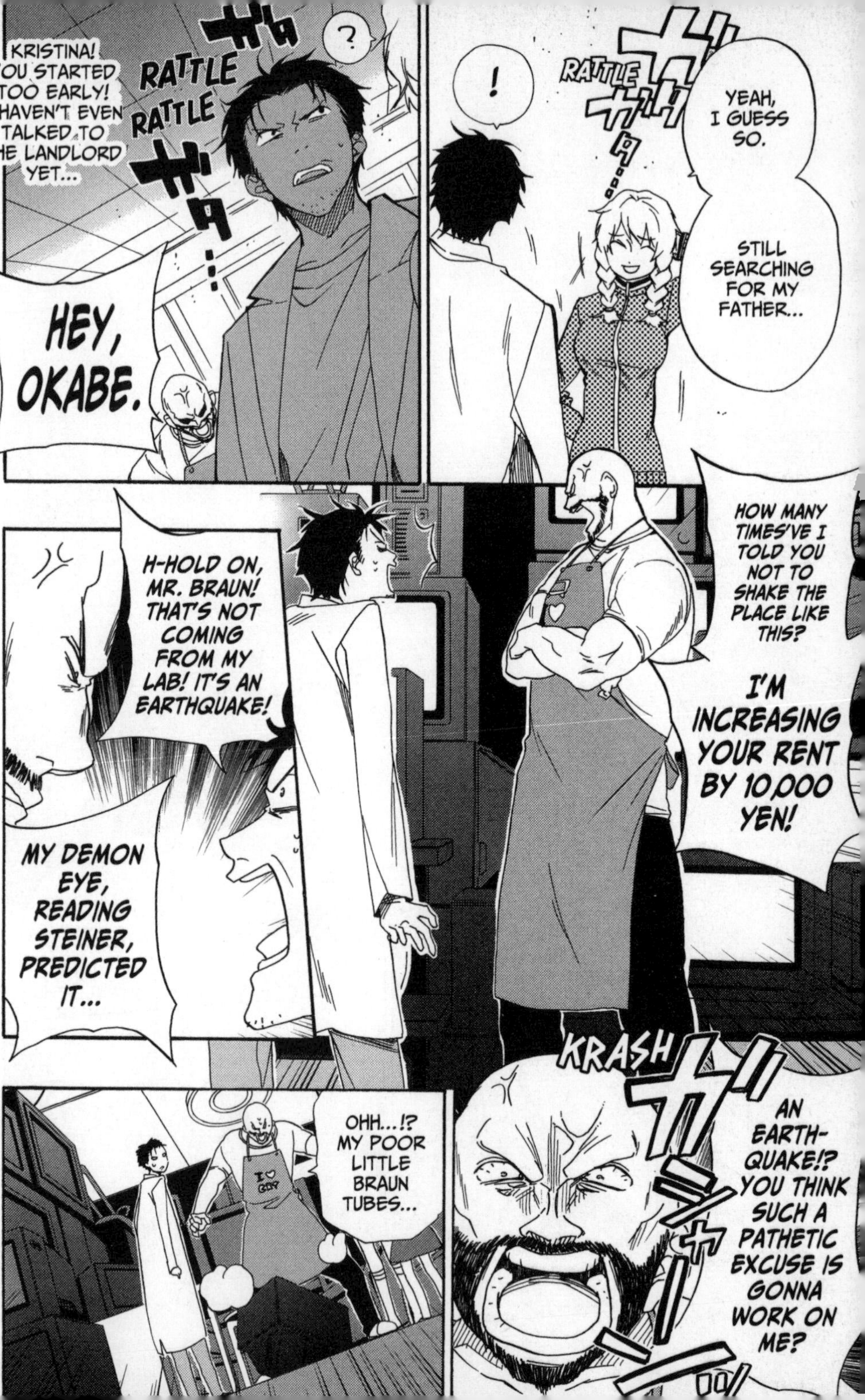
!
RATTLE
YEAH, I GUESS SO.
STILL SEARCHING FOR MY FATHER...
?
RATTLE RATTLE
KRISTINA! YOU STARTED TOO EARLY! I HAVEN'T EVEN TALKED TO THE LANDLORD YET...
HEY, OKABE.
HOW MANY TIMES'VE I TOLD YOU NOT TO SHAKE THE PLACE LIKE THIS?
I'M INCREASING YOUR RENT BY 10,000 YEN!
H-HOLD ON, MR. BRAUN! THAT'S NOT COMING FROM MY LAB! IT'S AN EARTHQUAKE!
MY DEMON EYE, READING STEINER, PREDICTED IT...
KRASH
AN EARTHQUAKE!? YOU THINK SUCH A PATHETIC EXCUSE IS GONNA WORK ON ME?
OHH...!? MY POOR LITTLE BRAUN TUBES...

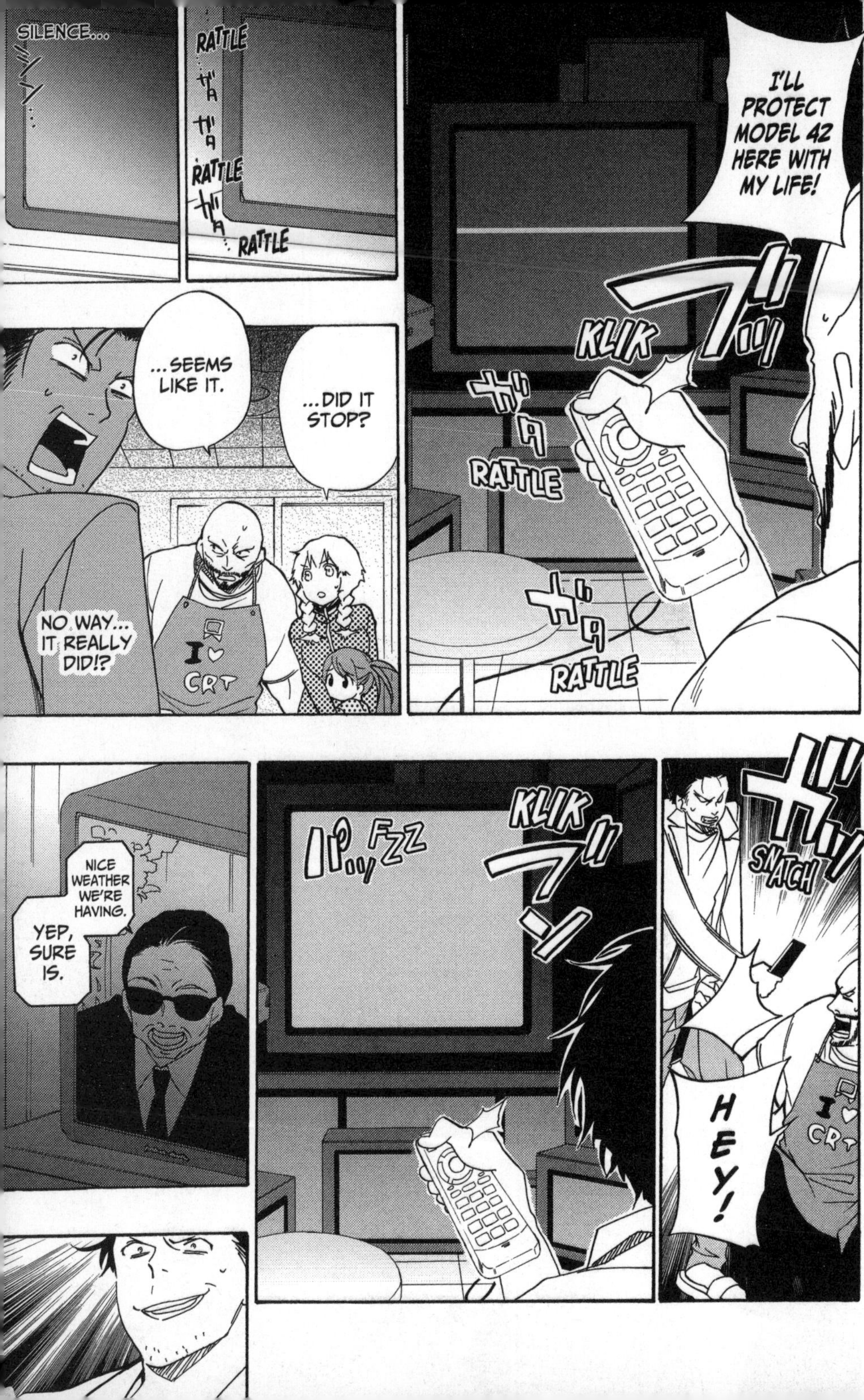
I'LL PROTECT MODEL 42 HERE WITH MY LIFE!
KLIK
RATTLE
RATTLE
RATTLE
RATTLE
RATTLE
SILENCE...
...DID IT STOP?
...SEEMS LIKE IT.
NO WAY... IT REALLY DID!?
SNATCH
HEY!
KLIK
FZZ
NICE WEATHER WE'RE HAVING.
YEP, SURE IS.

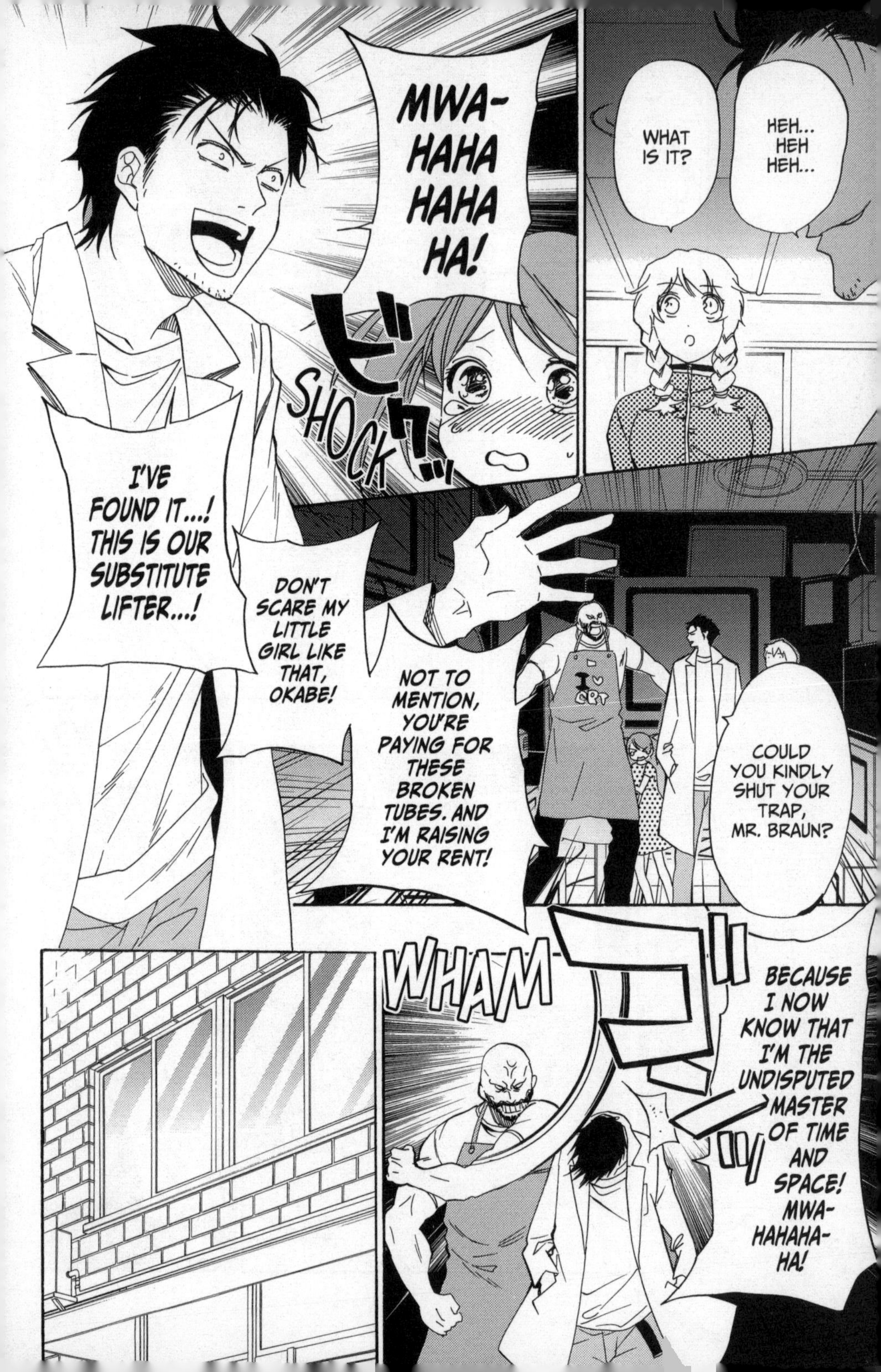
HEH... HEH HEH...
WHAT IS IT?
MWA-HAHA HAHAHA HA!
SHOCK
I'VE FOUND IT...! THIS IS OUR SUBSTITUTE LIFTER...!
DON'T SCARE MY LITTLE GIRL LIKE THAT, OKABE!
NOT TO MENTION, YOU'RE PAYING FOR THESE BROKEN TUBES. AND I'M RAISING YOUR RENT!
COULD YOU KINDLY SHUT YOUR TRAP, MR. BRAUN?
WHAM
BECAUSE I NOW KNOW THAT I'M THE UNDISPUTED MASTER OF TIME AND SPACE! MWA-HAHAHA-HA!

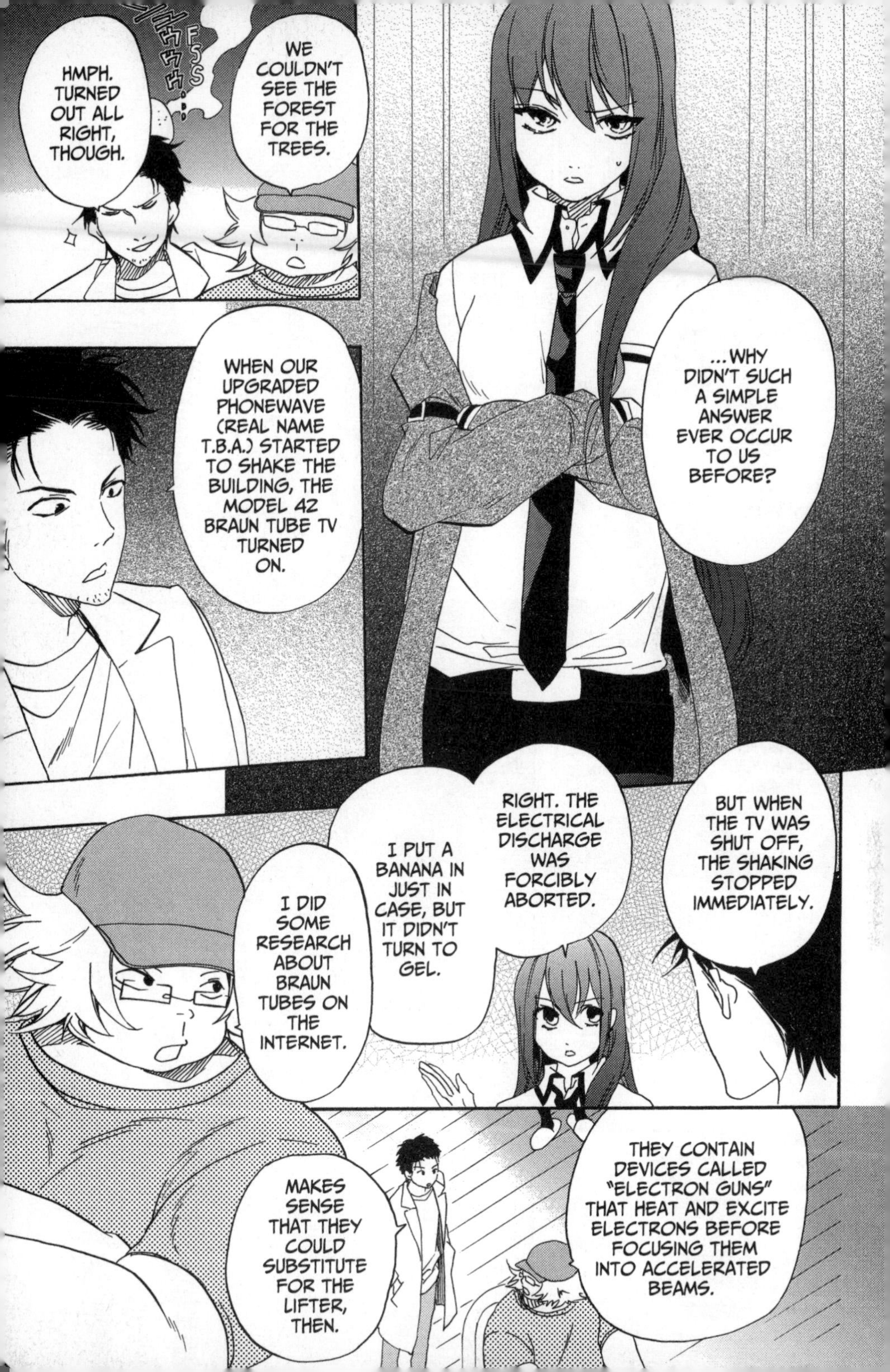
...WHY DIDN'T SUCH A SIMPLE ANSWER EVER OCCUR TO US BEFORE?
FSS
WE COULDN'T SEE THE FOREST FOR THE TREES.
HMPH. TURNED OUT ALL RIGHT, THOUGH.
WHEN OUR UPGRADED PHONEWAVE (REAL NAME T.B.A.) STARTED TO SHAKE THE BUILDING, THE MODEL 42 BRAUN TUBE TV TURNED ON.
BUT WHEN THE TV WAS SHUT OFF, THE SHAKING STOPPED IMMEDIATELY.
RIGHT. THE ELECTRICAL DISCHARGE WAS FORCIBLY ABORTED.
I PUT A BANANA IN JUST IN CASE, BUT IT DIDN'T TURN TO GEL.
I DID SOME RESEARCH ABOUT BRAUN TUBES ON THE INTERNET.
THEY CONTAIN DEVICES CALLED "ELECTRON GUNS" THAT HEAT AND EXCITE ELECTRONS BEFORE FOCUSING THEM INTO ACCELERATED BEAMS.
MAKES SENSE THAT THEY COULD SUBSTITUTE FOR THE LIFTER, THEN.

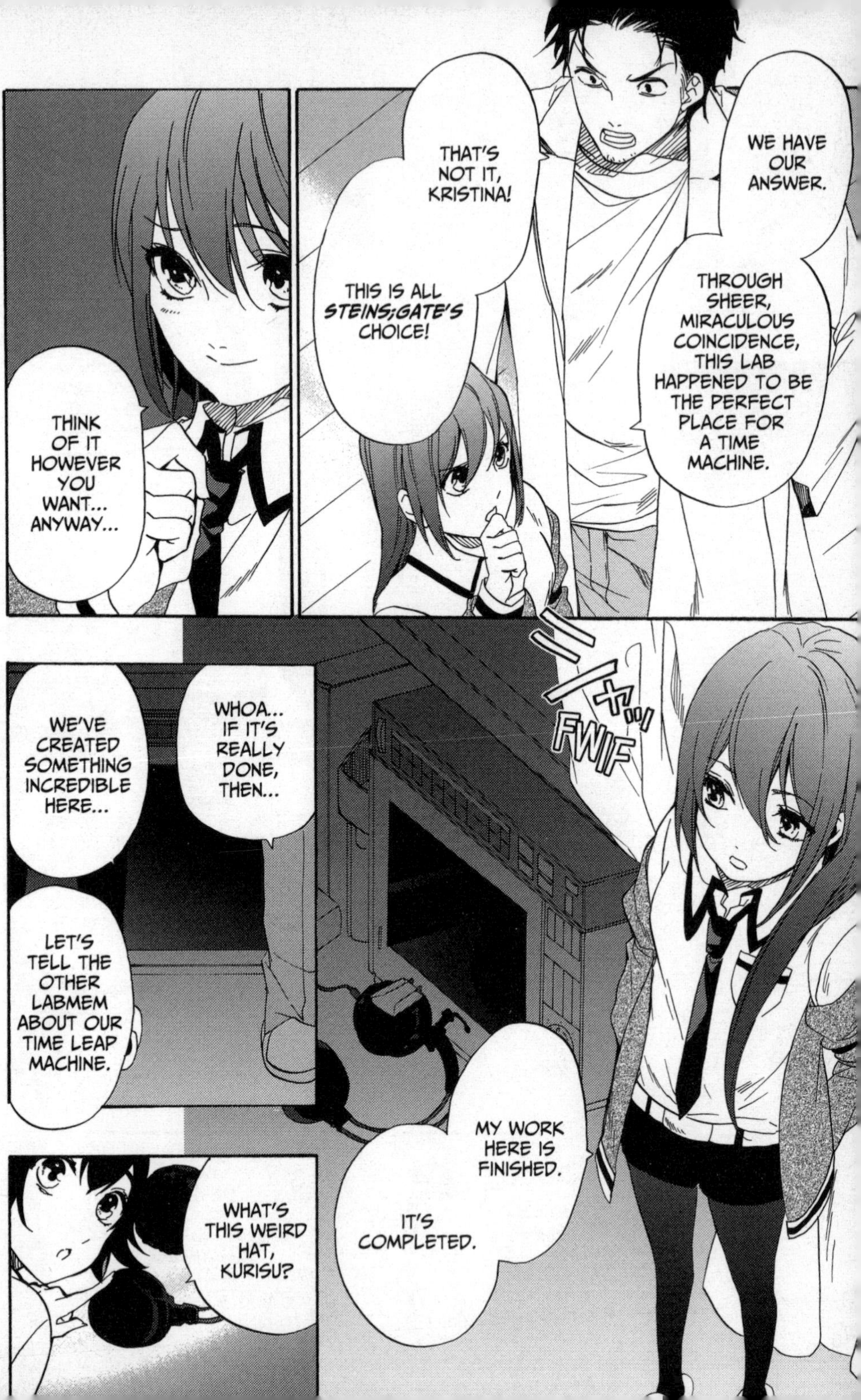
WE HAVE OUR ANSWER.
THROUGH SHEER, MIRACULOUS COINCIDENCE, THIS LAB HAPPENED TO BE THE PERFECT PLACE FOR A TIME MACHINE.
THAT'S NOT IT, KRISTINA!
THIS IS ALL *STEINS;GATE'S* CHOICE!
THINK OF IT HOWEVER YOU WANT... ANYWAY...
FWIF
MY WORK HERE IS FINISHED.
IT'S COMPLETED.
WHOA... IF IT'S REALLY DONE, THEN...
WE'VE CREATED SOMETHING INCREDIBLE HERE...
LET'S TELL THE OTHER LABMEM ABOUT OUR TIME LEAP MACHINE.
WHAT'S THIS WEIRD HAT, KURISU?

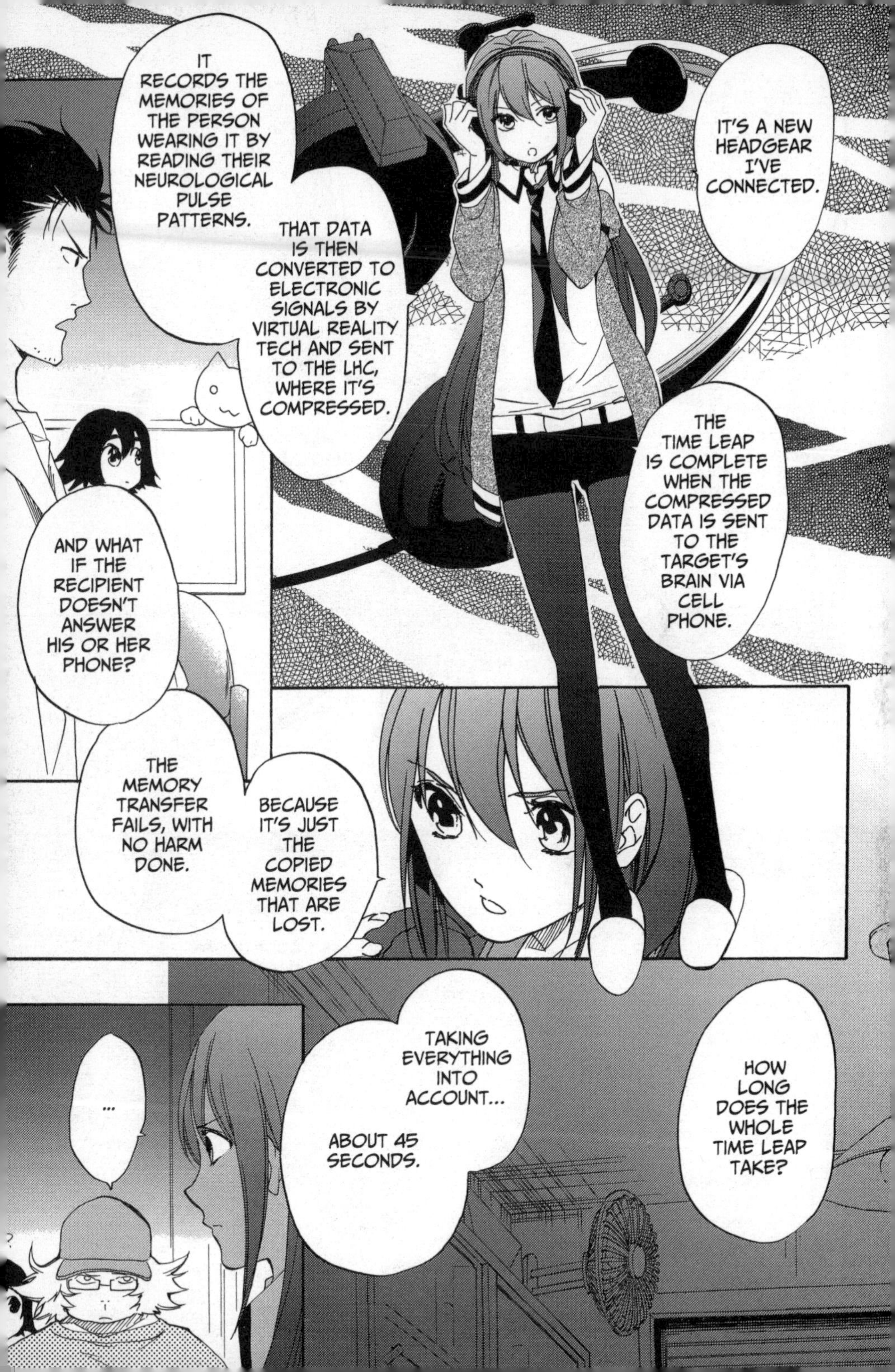
IT'S A NEW HEADGEAR I'VE CONNECTED.
IT RECORDS THE MEMORIES OF THE PERSON WEARING IT BY READING THEIR NEUROLOGICAL PULSE PATTERNS.
THAT DATA IS THEN CONVERTED TO ELECTRONIC SIGNALS BY VIRTUAL REALITY TECH AND SENT TO THE LHC, WHERE IT'S COMPRESSED.
THE TIME LEAP IS COMPLETE WHEN THE COMPRESSED DATA IS SENT TO THE TARGET'S BRAIN VIA CELL PHONE.
AND WHAT IF THE RECIPIENT DOESN'T ANSWER HIS OR HER PHONE?
THE MEMORY TRANSFER FAILS, WITH NO HARM DONE.
BECAUSE IT'S JUST THE COPIED MEMORIES THAT ARE LOST.
HOW LONG DOES THE WHOLE TIME LEAP TAKE?
TAKING EVERYTHING INTO ACCOUNT...
ABOUT 45 SECONDS.
...

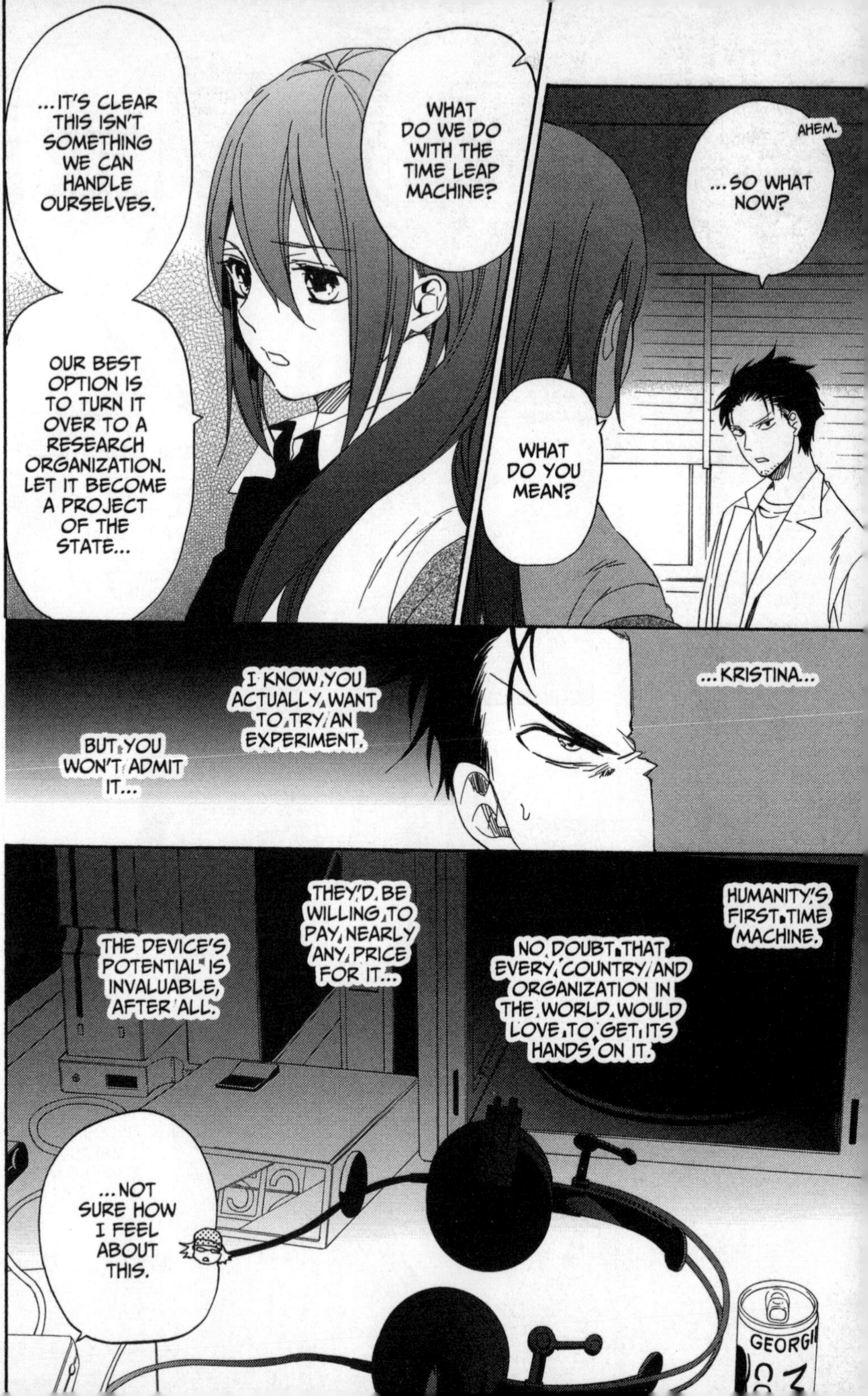
AHEM.
...SO WHAT NOW?
WHAT DO YOU MEAN?
WHAT DO WE DO WITH THE TIME LEAP MACHINE?
...IT'S CLEAR THIS ISN'T SOMETHING WE CAN HANDLE OURSELVES.
OUR BEST OPTION IS TO TURN IT OVER TO A RESEARCH ORGANIZATION. LET IT BECOME A PROJECT OF THE STATE...
...KRISTINA...
I KNOW YOU ACTUALLY WANT TO TRY AN EXPERIMENT.
BUT YOU WON'T ADMIT IT...
HUMANITY'S FIRST TIME MACHINE.
NO DOUBT THAT EVERY COUNTRY AND ORGANIZATION IN THE WORLD WOULD LOVE TO GET ITS HANDS ON IT.
THEY'D BE WILLING TO PAY NEARLY ANY PRICE FOR IT...
THE DEVICE'S POTENTIAL IS INVALUABLE, AFTER ALL.
...NOT SURE HOW I FEEL ABOUT THIS.

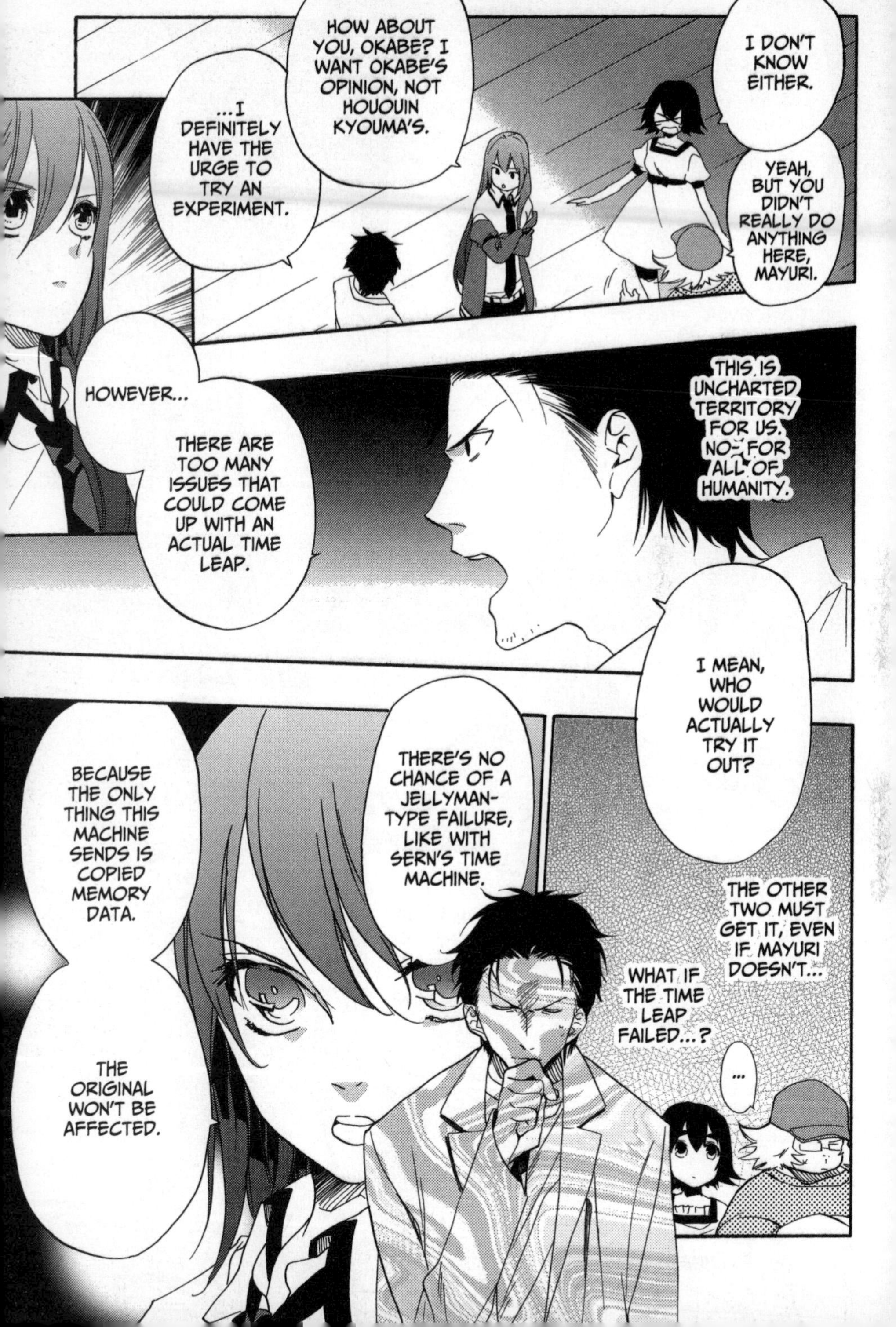
I DON'T KNOW EITHER.
YEAH, BUT YOU DIDN'T REALLY DO ANYTHING HERE, MAYURI.
HOW ABOUT YOU, OKABE? I WANT OKABE'S OPINION, NOT HOUOUIN KYOUMA'S.
...I DEFINITELY HAVE THE URGE TO TRY AN EXPERIMENT.
THIS IS UNCHARTED TERRITORY FOR US. NO— FOR ALL OF HUMANITY.
HOWEVER...
THERE ARE TOO MANY ISSUES THAT COULD COME UP WITH AN ACTUAL TIME LEAP.
I MEAN, WHO WOULD ACTUALLY TRY IT OUT?
THE OTHER TWO MUST GET IT, EVEN IF MAYURI DOESN'T...
WHAT IF THE TIME LEAP FAILED...?
...
THERE'S NO CHANCE OF A JELLYMAN-TYPE FAILURE, LIKE WITH SERN'S TIME MACHINE.
BECAUSE THE ONLY THING THIS MACHINE SENDS IS COPIED MEMORY DATA.
THE ORIGINAL WON'T BE AFFECTED.

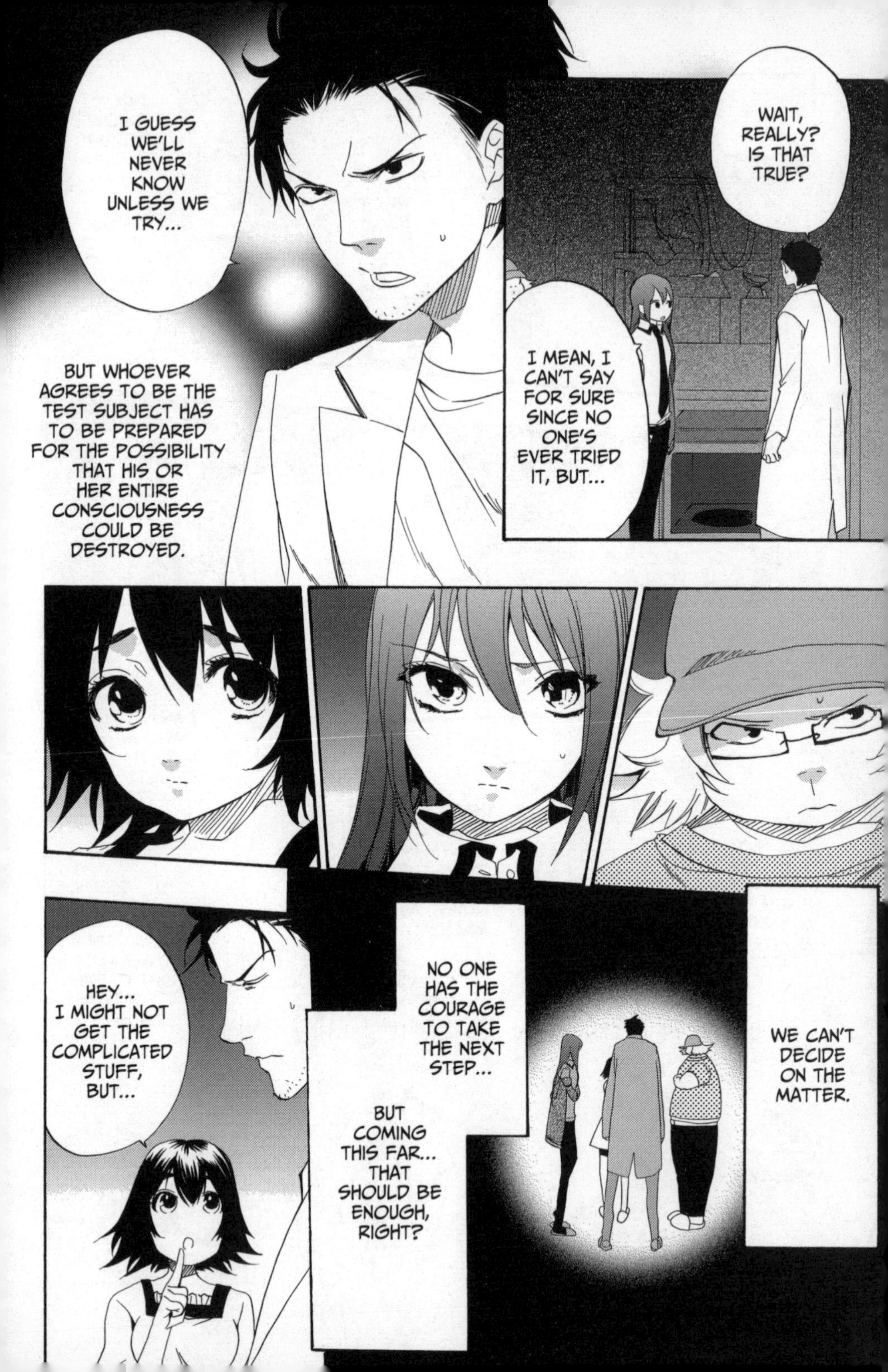
WAIT, REALLY? IS THAT TRUE?
I MEAN, I CAN'T SAY FOR SURE SINCE NO ONE'S EVER TRIED IT, BUT...
I GUESS WE'LL NEVER KNOW UNLESS WE TRY...
BUT WHOEVER AGREES TO BE THE TEST SUBJECT HAS TO BE PREPARED FOR THE POSSIBILITY THAT HIS OR HER ENTIRE CONSCIOUSNESS COULD BE DESTROYED.
WE CAN'T DECIDE ON THE MATTER.
NO ONE HAS THE COURAGE TO TAKE THE NEXT STEP...
BUT COMING THIS FAR... THAT SHOULD BE ENOUGH, RIGHT?
HEY... I MIGHT NOT GET THE COMPLICATED STUFF, BUT...

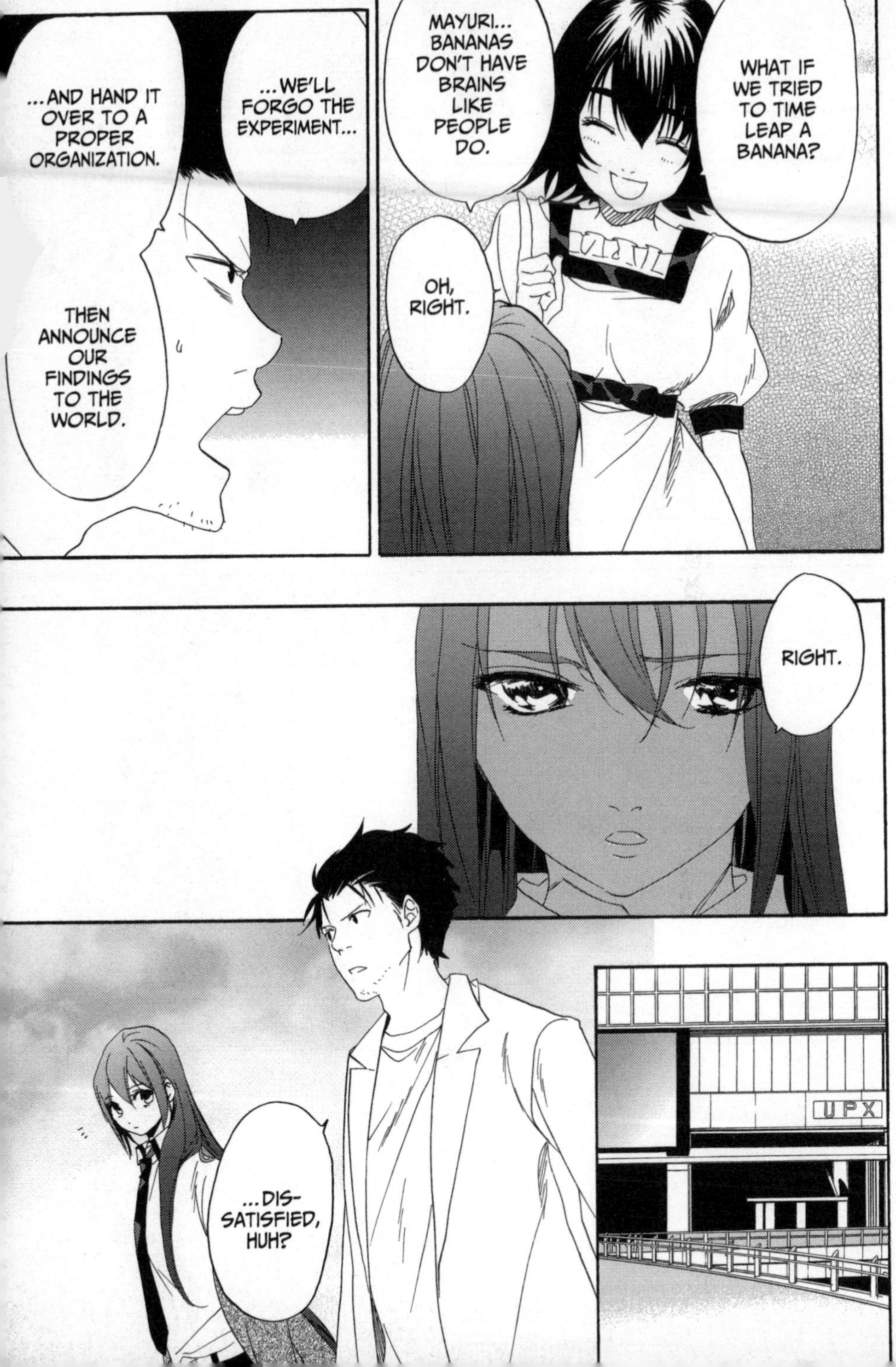
WHAT IF WE TRIED TO TIME LEAP A BANANA?
MAYURI... BANANAS DON'T HAVE BRAINS LIKE PEOPLE DO.
OH, RIGHT.
...WE'LL FORGO THE EXPERIMENT...
...AND HAND IT OVER TO A PROPER ORGANIZATION.
THEN ANNOUNCE OUR FINDINGS TO THE WORLD.
RIGHT.
UPX
...DIS-SATISFIED, HUH?

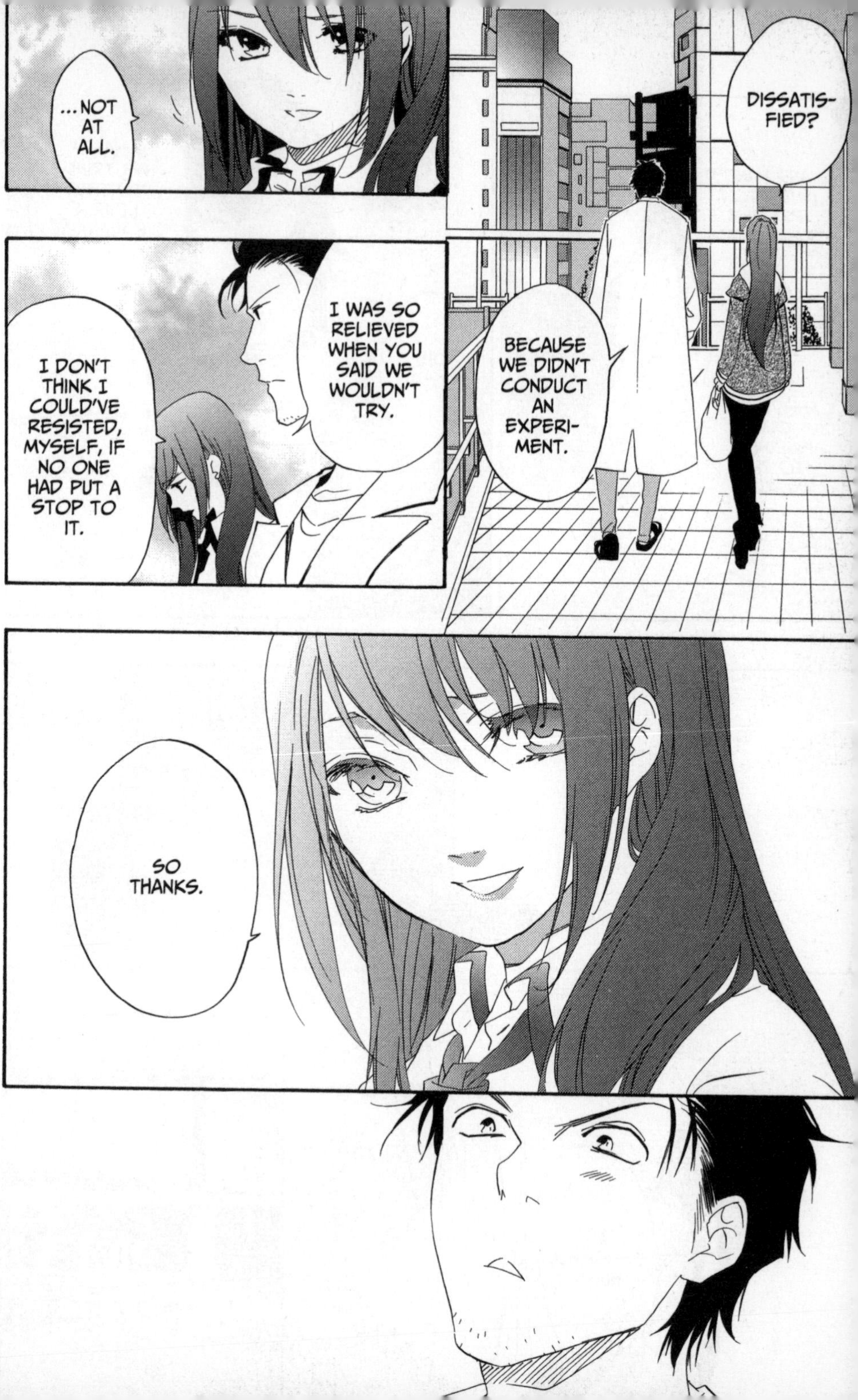
DISSATIS-
FIED?
BECAUSE WE DIDN'T CONDUCT AN EXPERIMENT.
...NOT AT ALL.
I WAS SO RELIEVED WHEN YOU SAID WE WOULDN'T TRY.
I DON'T THINK I COULD'VE RESISTED, MYSELF, IF NO ONE HAD PUT A STOP TO IT.
SO THANKS.

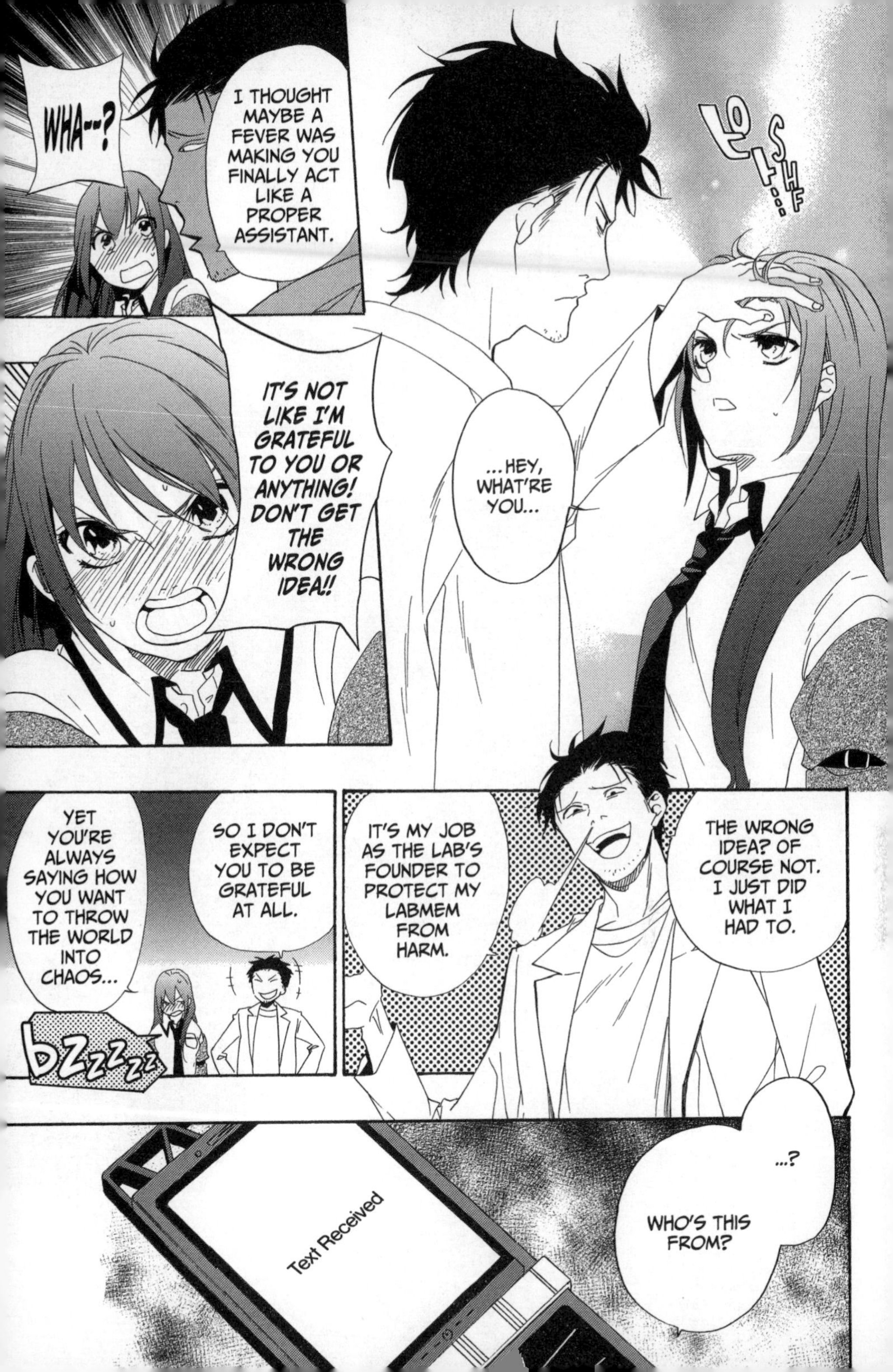
ピト…
SHF
...HEY, WHAT'RE YOU...
I THOUGHT MAYBE A FEVER WAS MAKING YOU FINALLY ACT LIKE A PROPER ASSISTANT.
WHA--?
IT'S NOT LIKE I'M GRATEFUL TO YOU OR ANYTHING! DON'T GET THE WRONG IDEA!!
THE WRONG IDEA? OF COURSE NOT. I JUST DID WHAT I HAD TO.
IT'S MY JOB AS THE LAB'S FOUNDER TO PROTECT MY LABMEM FROM HARM.
SO I DON'T EXPECT YOU TO BE GRATEFUL AT ALL.
YET YOU'RE ALWAYS SAYING HOW YOU WANT TO THROW THE WORLD INTO CHAOS...
bZzzzz
...?
WHO'S THIS FROM?
Text Received

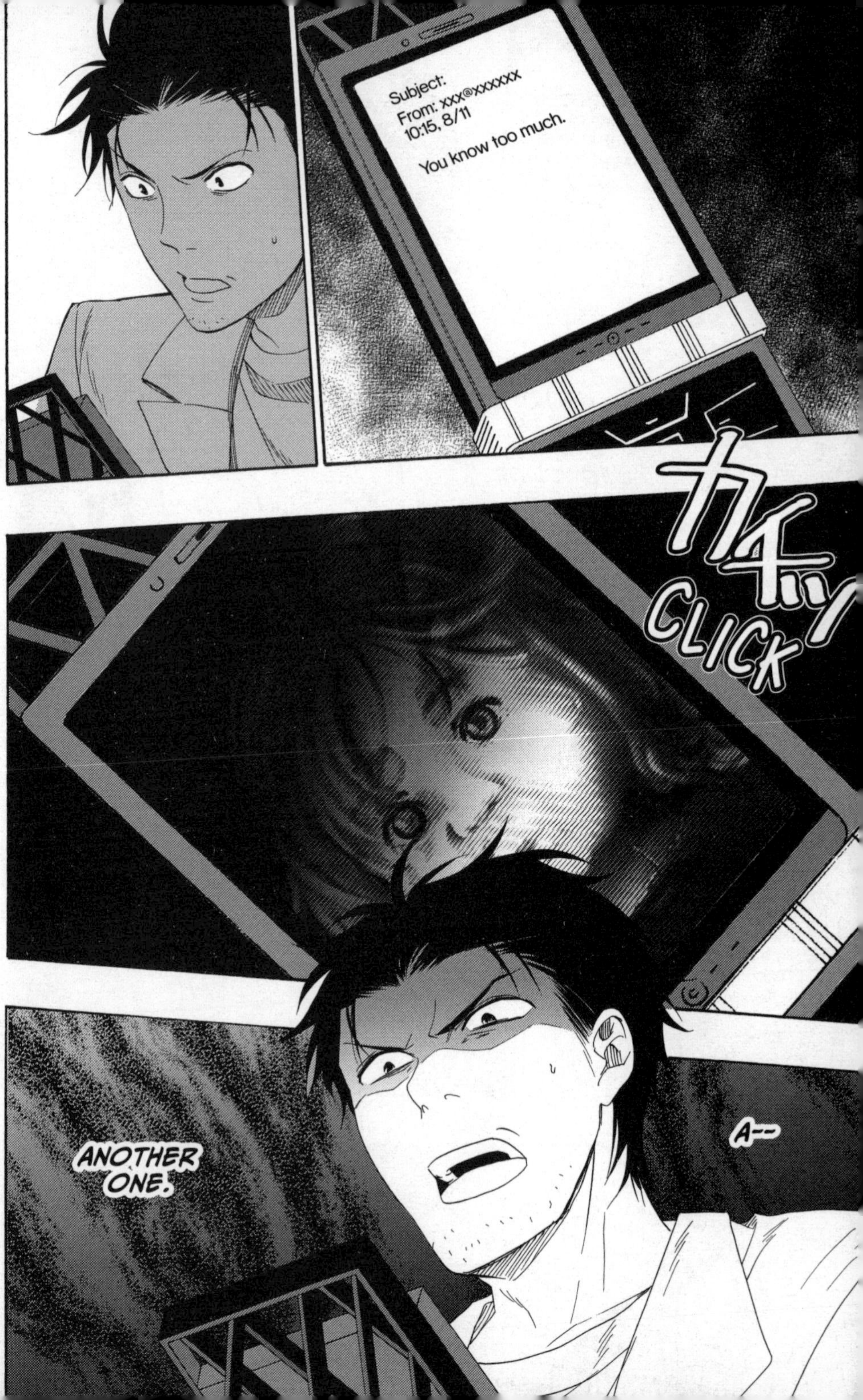
Subject:
From: xxx@xxxxxx
10:15, 8/11
You know too much.
カチッ
CLICK
A--
ANOTHER ONE.

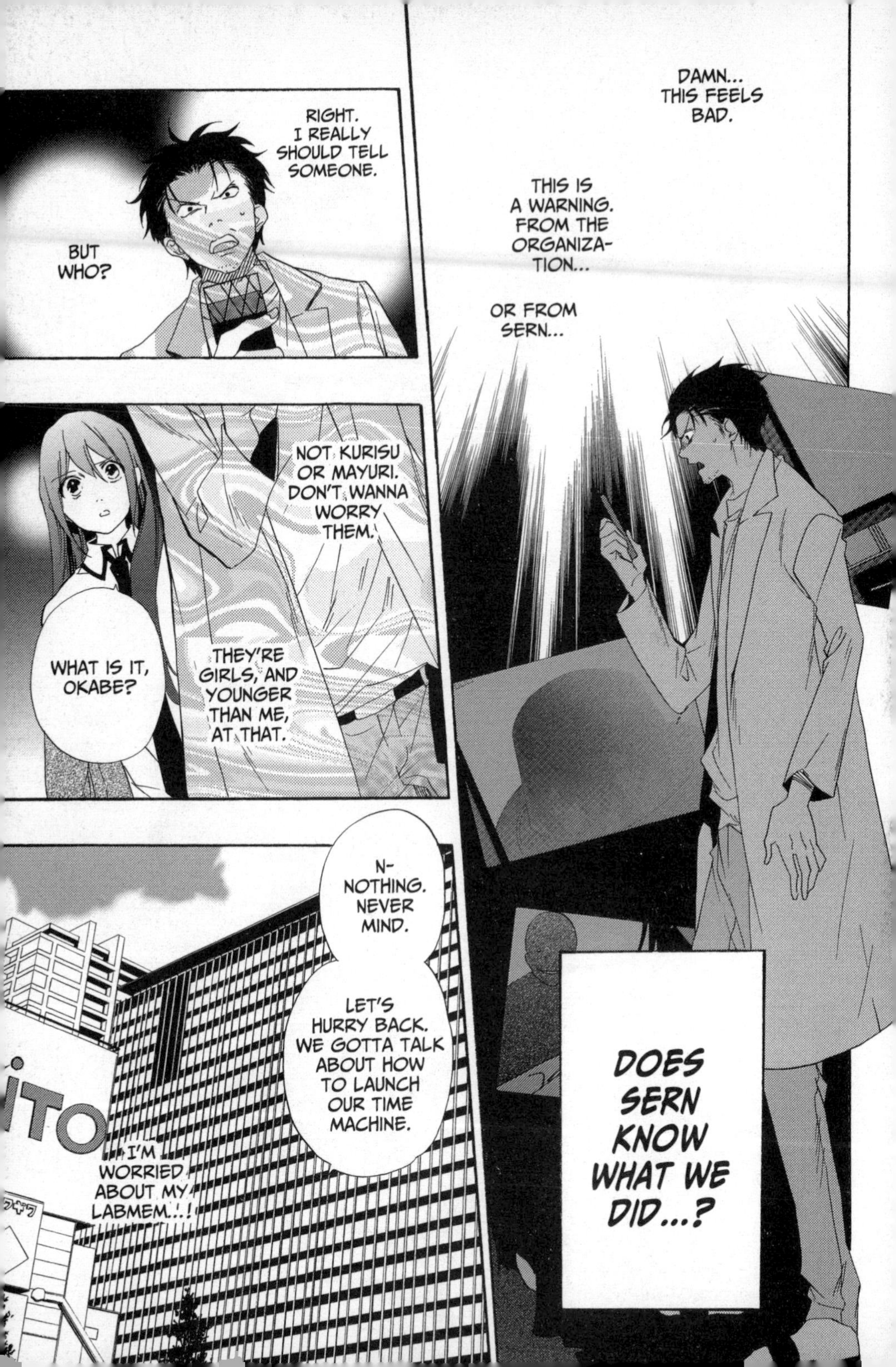
DAMN... THIS FEELS BAD.
THIS IS A WARNING. FROM THE ORGANIZATION...
OR FROM SERN...
DOES SERN KNOW WHAT WE DID...?
RIGHT. I REALLY SHOULD TELL SOMEONE.
BUT WHO?
NOT KURISU OR MAYURI. DON'T WANNA WORRY THEM.
THEY'RE GIRLS, AND YOUNGER THAN ME, AT THAT.
WHAT IS IT, OKABE?
N-NOTHING. NEVER MIND.
LET'S HURRY BACK. WE GOTTA TALK ABOUT HOW TO LAUNCH OUR TIME MACHINE.
I'M WORRIED ABOUT MY LABMEM...!

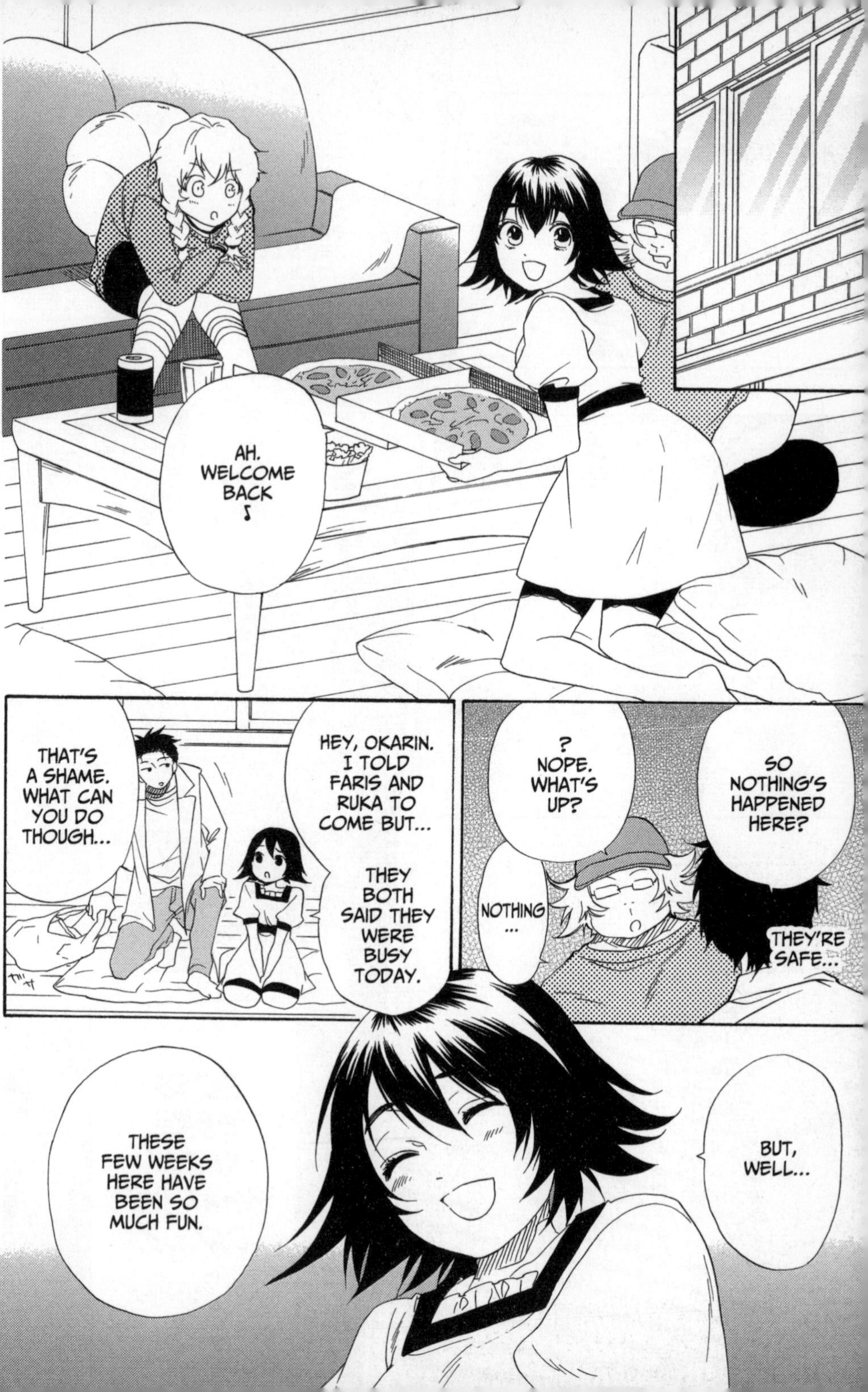
AH. WELCOME BACK ♪
SO NOTHING'S HAPPENED HERE?
? NOPE. WHAT'S UP?
NOTHING ...
THEY'RE SAFE...
HEY, OKARIN. I TOLD FARIS AND RUKA TO COME BUT...
THEY BOTH SAID THEY WERE BUSY TODAY.
THAT'S A SHAME. WHAT CAN YOU DO THOUGH...
BUT, WELL...
THESE FEW WEEKS HERE HAVE BEEN SO MUCH FUN.

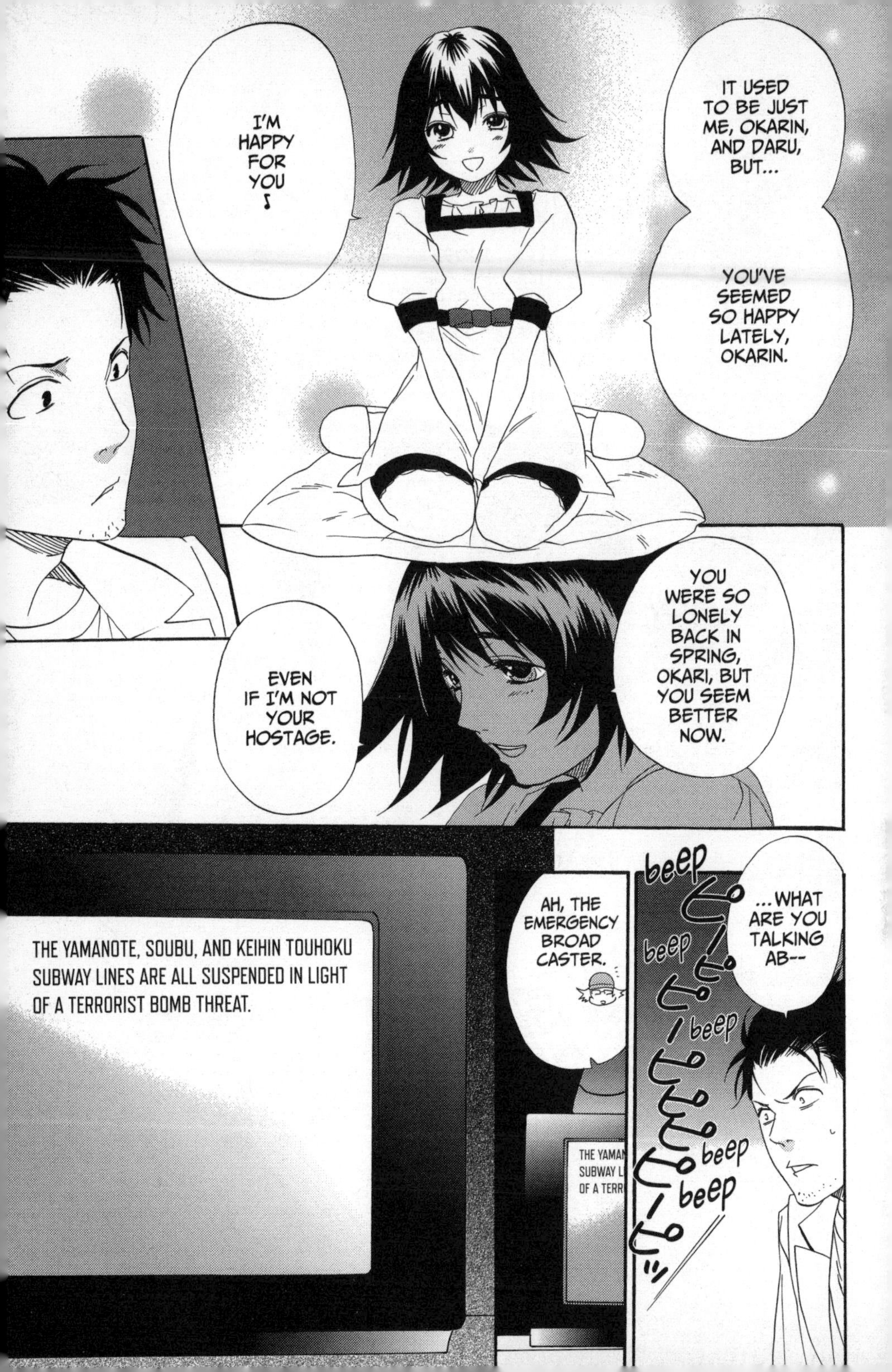

IT USED TO BE JUST ME, OKARIN, AND DARU, BUT...
YOU'VE SEEMED SO HAPPY LATELY, OKARIN.
I'M HAPPY FOR YOU ♪
YOU WERE SO LONELY BACK IN SPRING, OKARI, BUT YOU SEEM BETTER NOW.
EVEN IF I'M NOT YOUR HOSTAGE.
...WHAT ARE YOU TALKING AB--
beep
beep
beep
beep
beep
AH, THE EMERGENCY BROAD CASTER.
THE YAMANOTE, SOUBU, AND KEIHIN TOUHOKU SUBWAY LINES ARE ALL SUSPENDED IN LIGHT OF A TERRORIST BOMB THREAT.

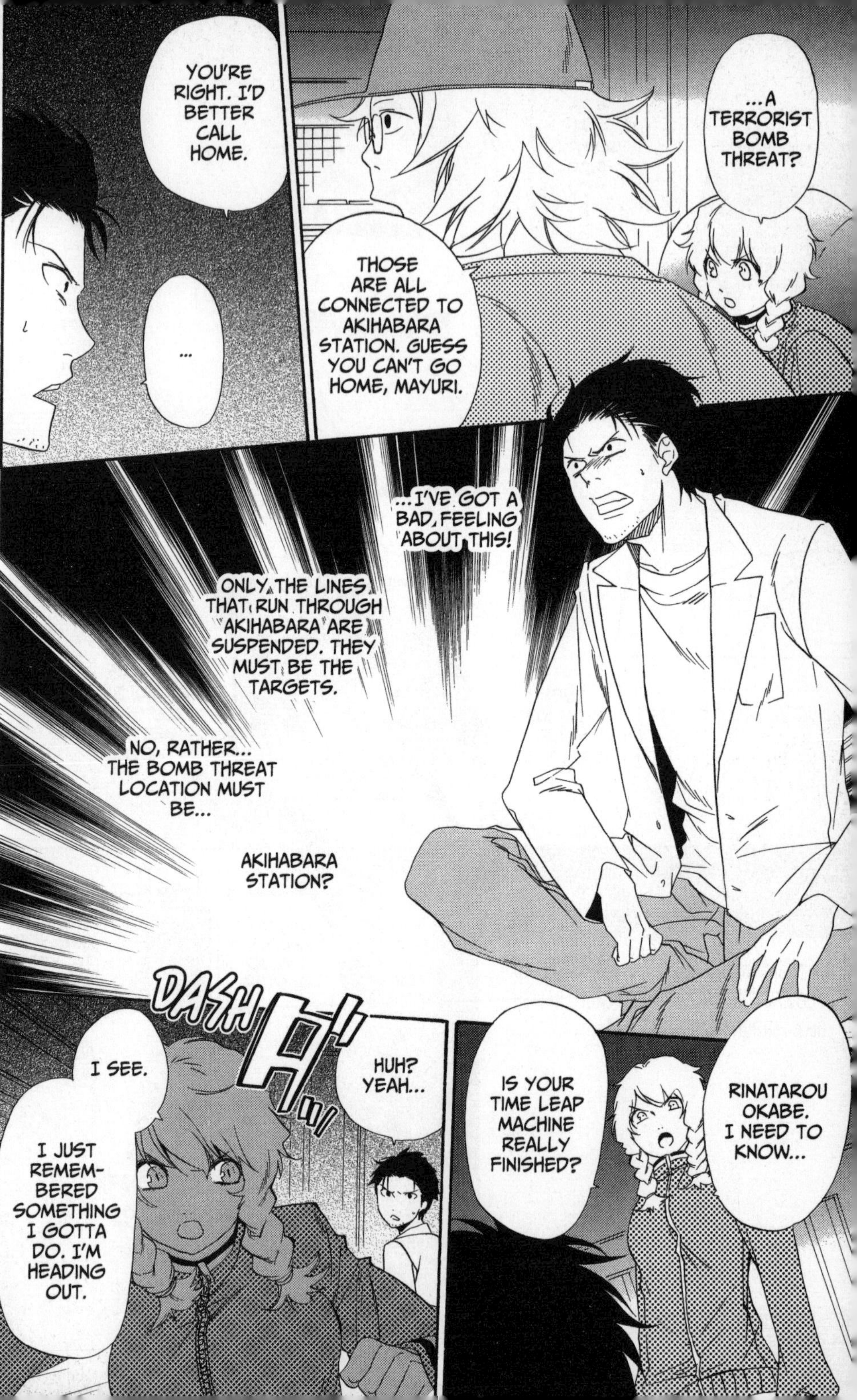
...A TERRORIST BOMB THREAT?
THOSE ARE ALL CONNECTED TO AKIHABARA STATION. GUESS YOU CAN'T GO HOME, MAYURI.
YOU'RE RIGHT. I'D BETTER CALL HOME.
...
...I'VE GOT A BAD FEELING ABOUT THIS!
ONLY THE LINES THAT RUN THROUGH AKIHABARA ARE SUSPENDED. THEY MUST BE THE TARGETS.
NO, RATHER... THE BOMB THREAT LOCATION MUST BE...
AKIHABARA STATION?
RINATAROU OKABE. I NEED TO KNOW...
IS YOUR TIME LEAP MACHINE REALLY FINISHED?
HUH? YEAH...
I SEE.
I JUST REMEMBERED SOMETHING I GOTTA DO. I'M HEADING OUT.
DASH

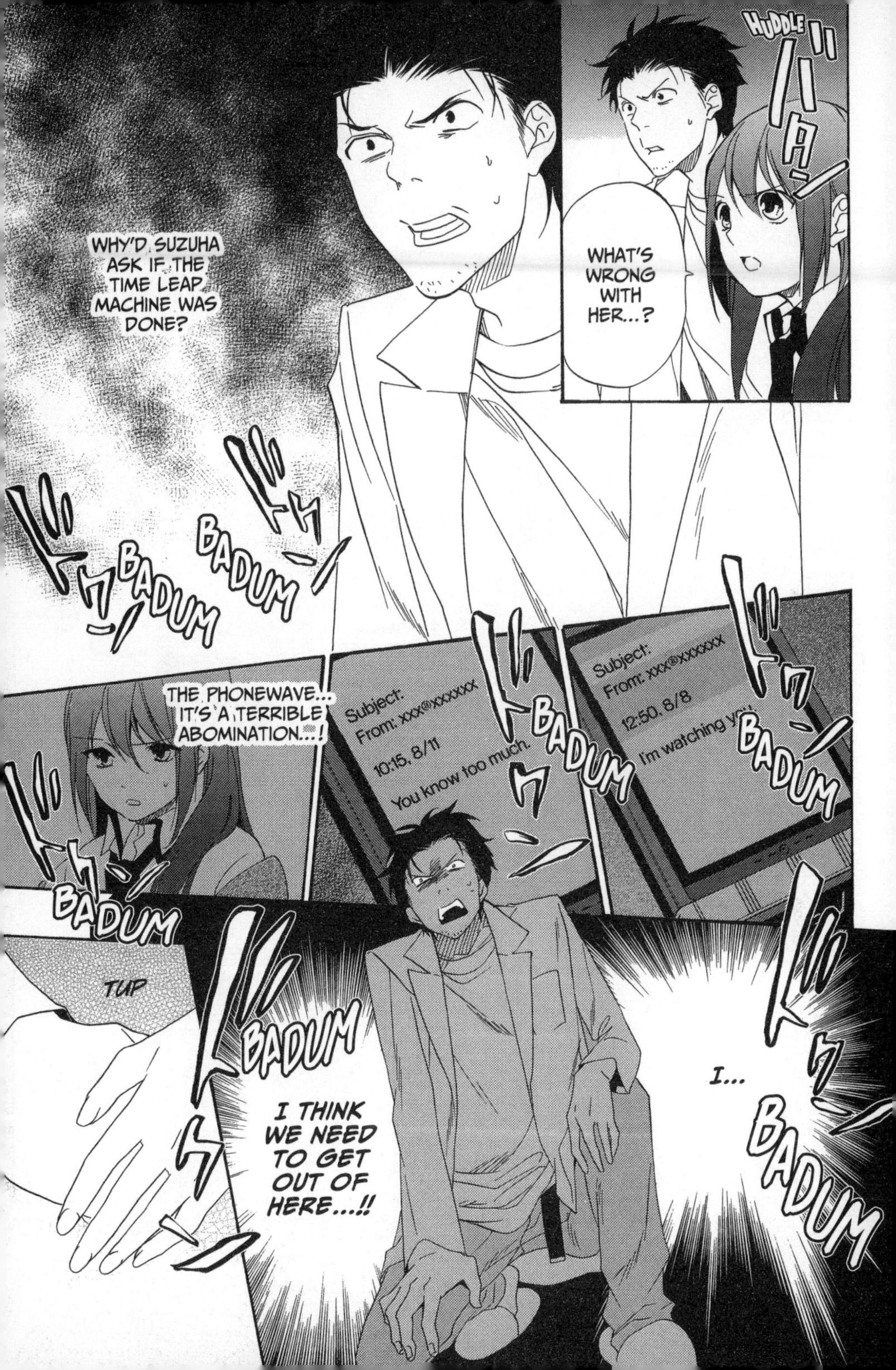
HUDDLE
WHAT'S WRONG WITH HER...?
WHY'D SUZUHA ASK IF THE TIME LEAP MACHINE WAS DONE?
BADUM
BADUM
Subject:
From: xxx@xxxxxx
12:50, 8/8
I'm watching yo
BADUM
Subject:
From: xxx@xxxxxx
10:15, 8/11
You know too much.
BADUM
THE PHONEWAVE... IT'S A TERRIBLE ABOMINATION...!
BADUM
I...
BADUM
I THINK WE NEED TO GET OUT OF HERE...!!
BADUM
TUP

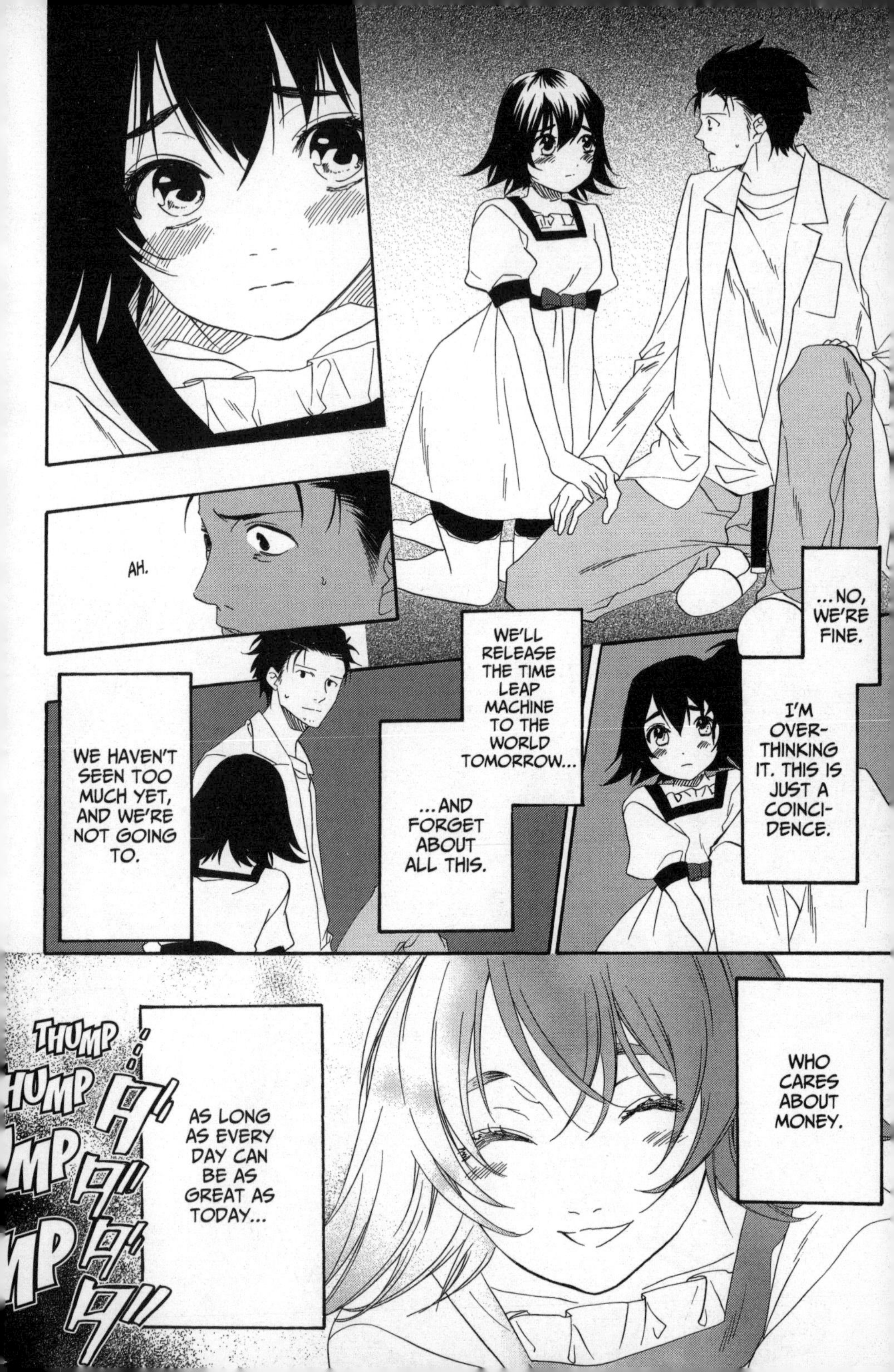
AH.
...NO, WE'RE FINE.
I'M OVER-THINKING IT. THIS IS JUST A COINCI-DENCE.
WE'LL RELEASE THE TIME LEAP MACHINE TO THE WORLD TOMORROW...
...AND FORGET ABOUT ALL THIS.
WE HAVEN'T SEEN TOO MUCH YET, AND WE'RE NOT GOING TO.
WHO CARES ABOUT MONEY.
AS LONG AS EVERY DAY CAN BE AS GREAT AS TODAY...
THUMP
THUMP

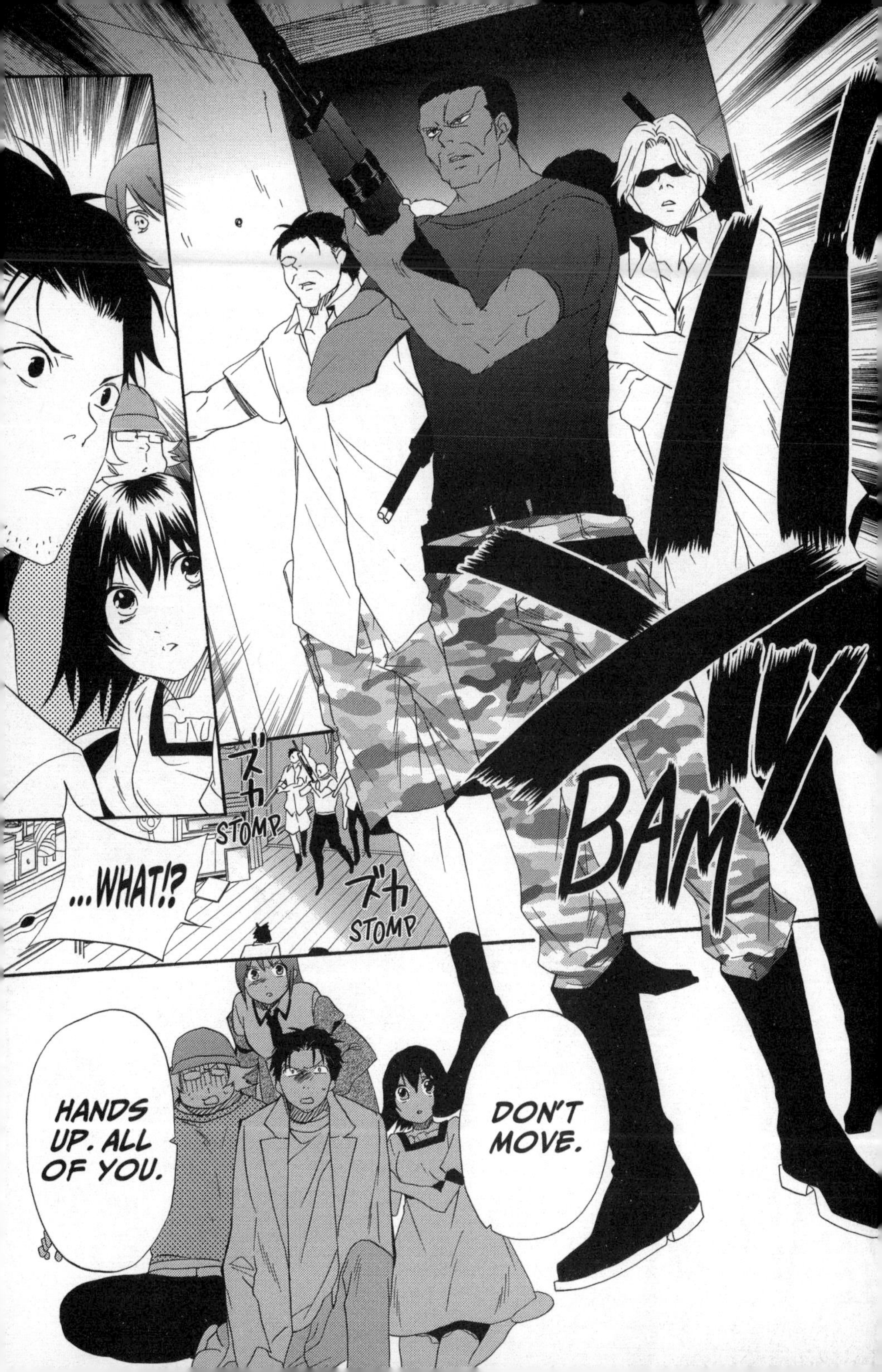
BAM
ズカ
STOMP
ズカ
STOMP
...WHAT!?
DON'T MOVE.
HANDS UP. ALL OF YOU.

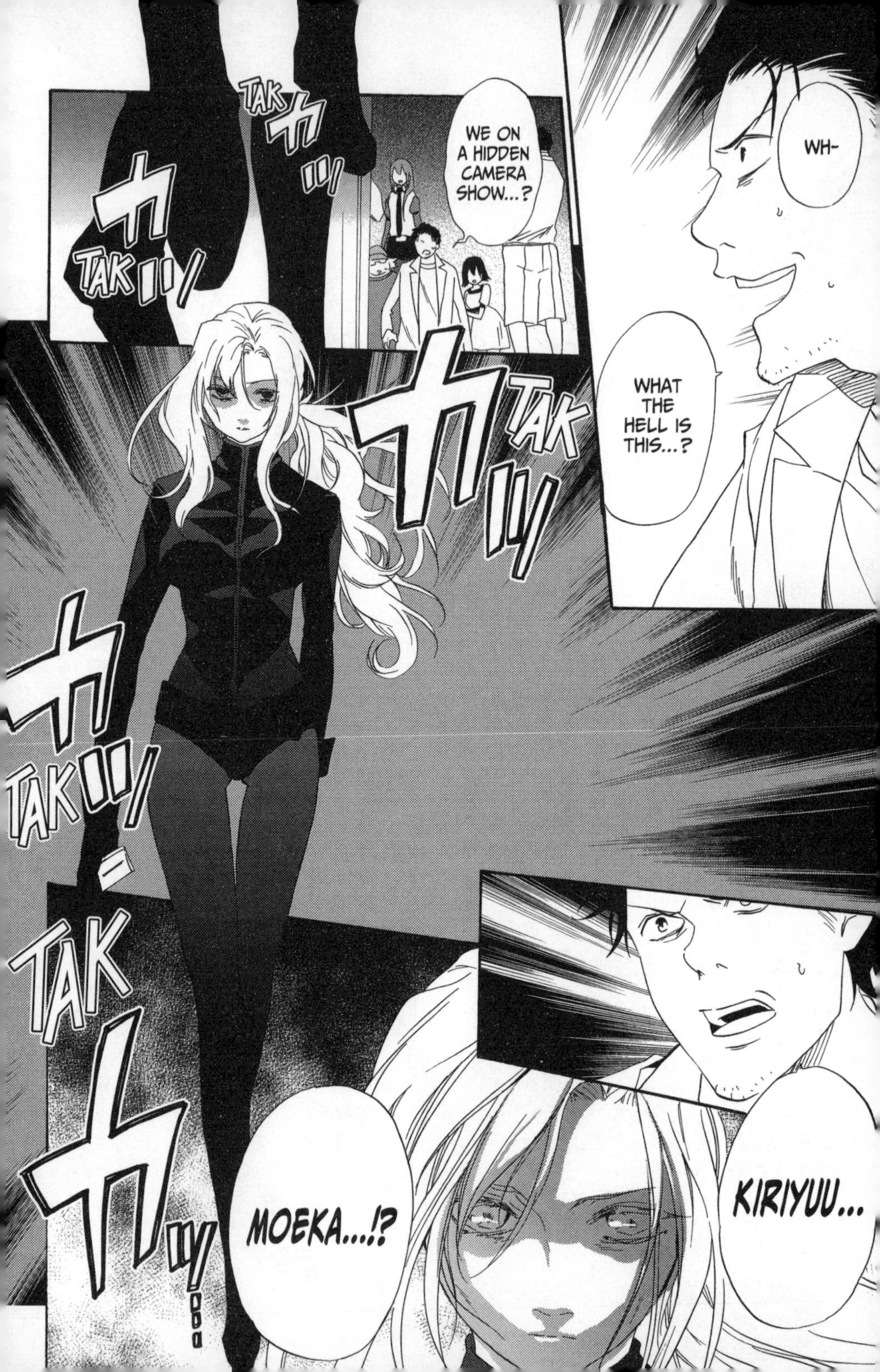
WH-
WHAT THE HELL IS THIS...?
WE ON A HIDDEN CAMERA SHOW...?
TAK
TAK
TAK
TAK
TAK
KIRIYUU...
MOEKA...!?

[BRAUN TUBE WORKSHOP]

The good old parts shop that occupies the first floor of the "Daihiyama Building", below Future Gadget Labs. It specializes in Braun tubes. They're all it carries, in fact. Its proprietor is Tennouji Yuugo. Customers rarely come, and no one could claim that the business is thriving, but Tennouji doesn't seem to be concerned about that. The primary service seems to be the repair of Braun tube-based television sets, which sometimes necessitates home visits. As Tennouji used to run the shop alone, he would close up the business when making home visits, but ever since Suzuha started working there, she's been able to manage the store while Tennouji is out.

The universe has no end, though it does have a beginning. --- Infinite.
Stars too have a beginning, though they are destroyed by their own power. --- Finite.
Those who believe they have wisdom, are often shown by history to be the most foolish.
The fish in the sea don't know what the world is like on the land. Wisdom would destroy them as well.
Man to exceeding the speed of light would be more ridiculous than fish to living on land.
This is God's final warning to any who rebel.

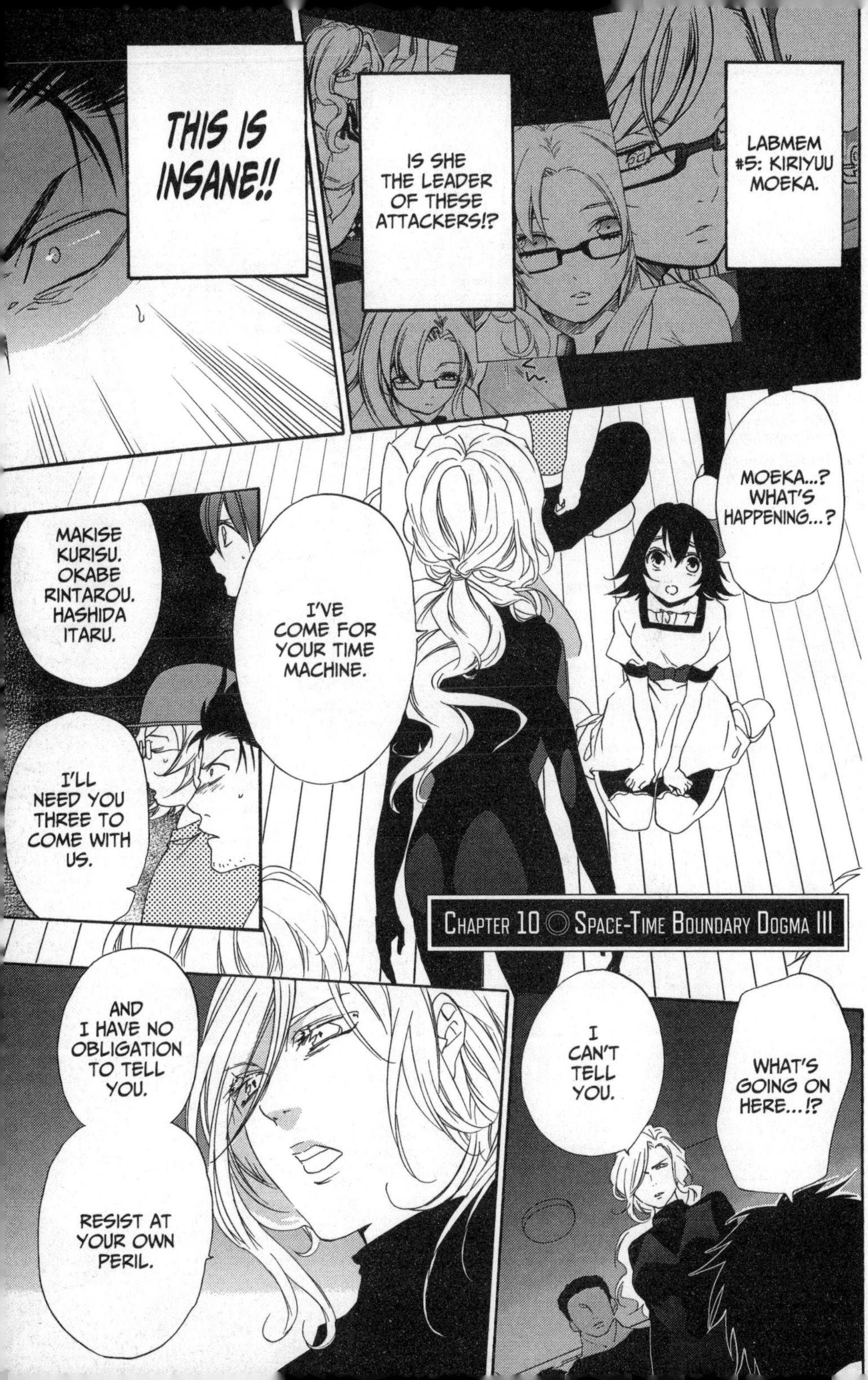
LABMEM #5: KIRIYUU MOEKA.
IS SHE THE LEADER OF THESE ATTACKERS!?
THIS IS INSANE!!
MOEKA...? WHAT'S HAPPENING...?
I'VE COME FOR YOUR TIME MACHINE.
MAKISE KURISU. OKABE RINTAROU. HASHIDA ITARU.
I'LL NEED YOU THREE TO COME WITH US.
CHAPTER 10 ◎ SPACE-TIME BOUNDARY DOGMA III
WHAT'S GOING ON HERE...!?
I CAN'T TELL YOU.
AND I HAVE NO OBLIGATION TO TELL YOU.
RESIST AT YOUR OWN PERIL.

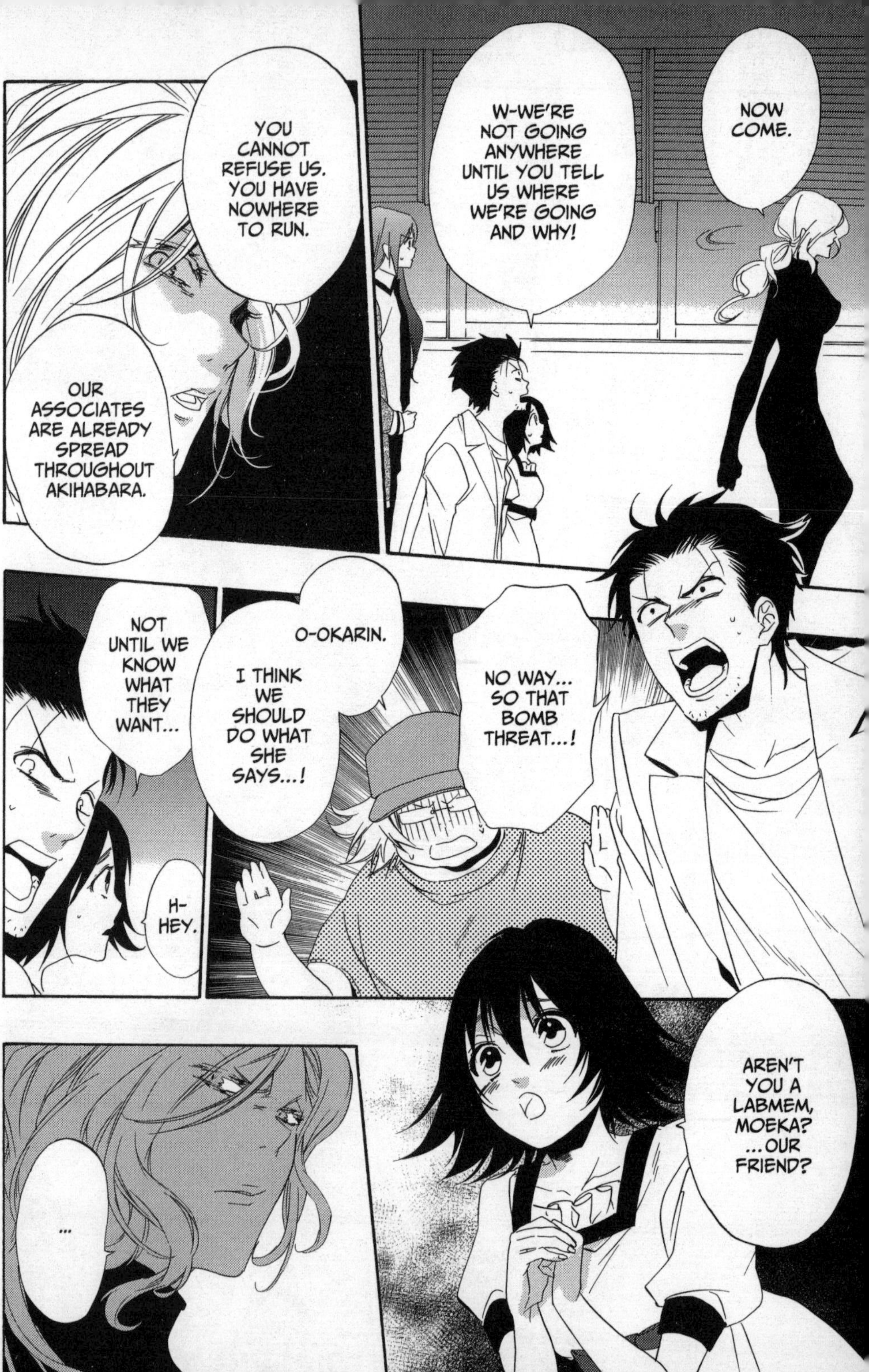
NOW COME.
W-WE'RE NOT GOING ANYWHERE UNTIL YOU TELL US WHERE WE'RE GOING AND WHY!
YOU CANNOT REFUSE US. YOU HAVE NOWHERE TO RUN.
OUR ASSOCIATES ARE ALREADY SPREAD THROUGHOUT AKIHABARA.
NO WAY... SO THAT BOMB THREAT...!
O-OKARIN.
I THINK WE SHOULD DO WHAT SHE SAYS...!
NOT UNTIL WE KNOW WHAT THEY WANT...
H-HEY.
AREN'T YOU A LABMEM, MOEKA? ...OUR FRIEND?
...

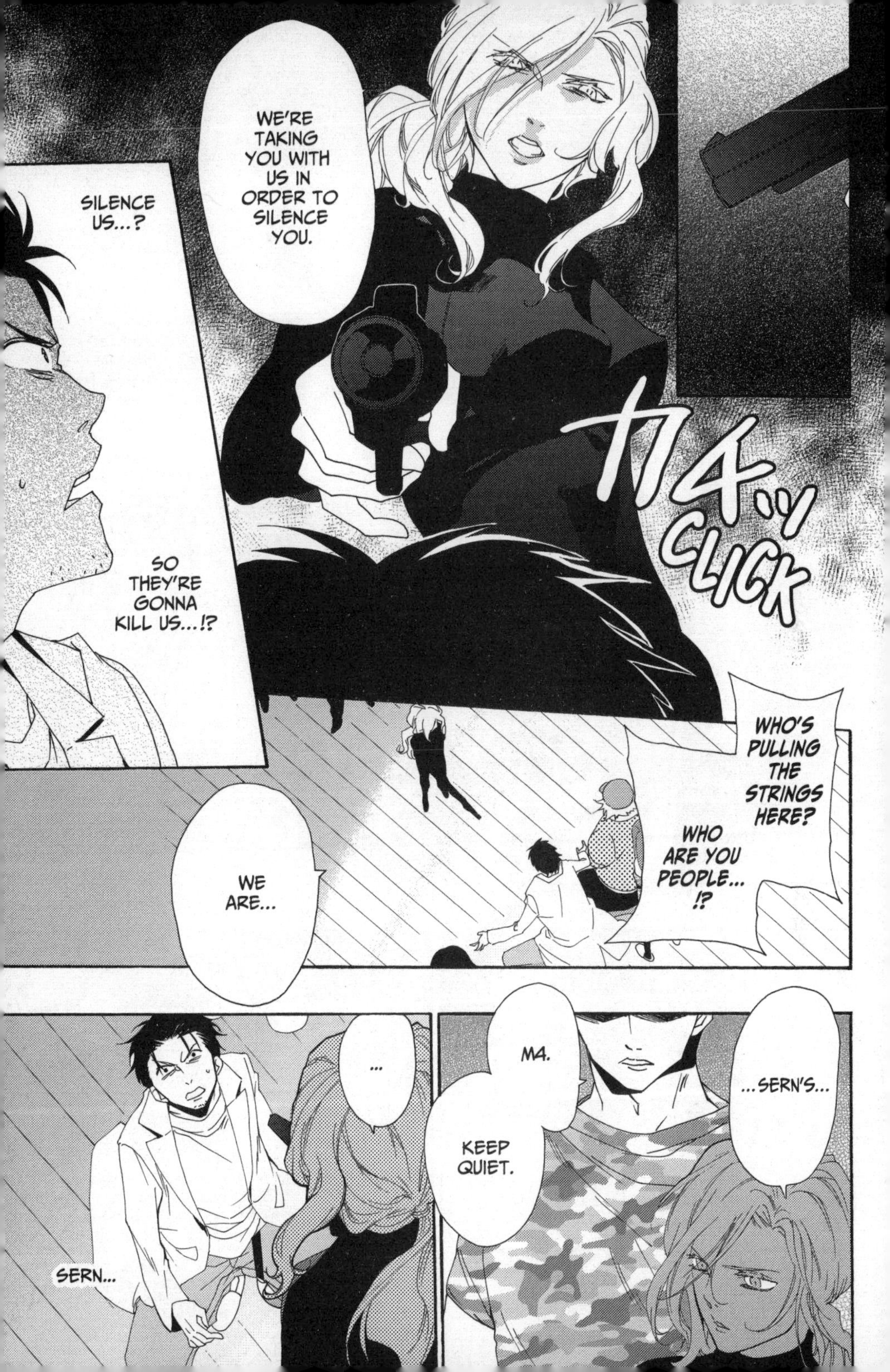
WE'RE TAKING YOU WITH US IN ORDER TO SILENCE YOU.
CLICK
SILENCE US...?
SO THEY'RE GONNA KILL US...!?
WHO'S PULLING THE STRINGS HERE?
WHO ARE YOU PEOPLE...!?
WE ARE...
...SERN'S...
M4.
KEEP QUIET.
...
SERN...

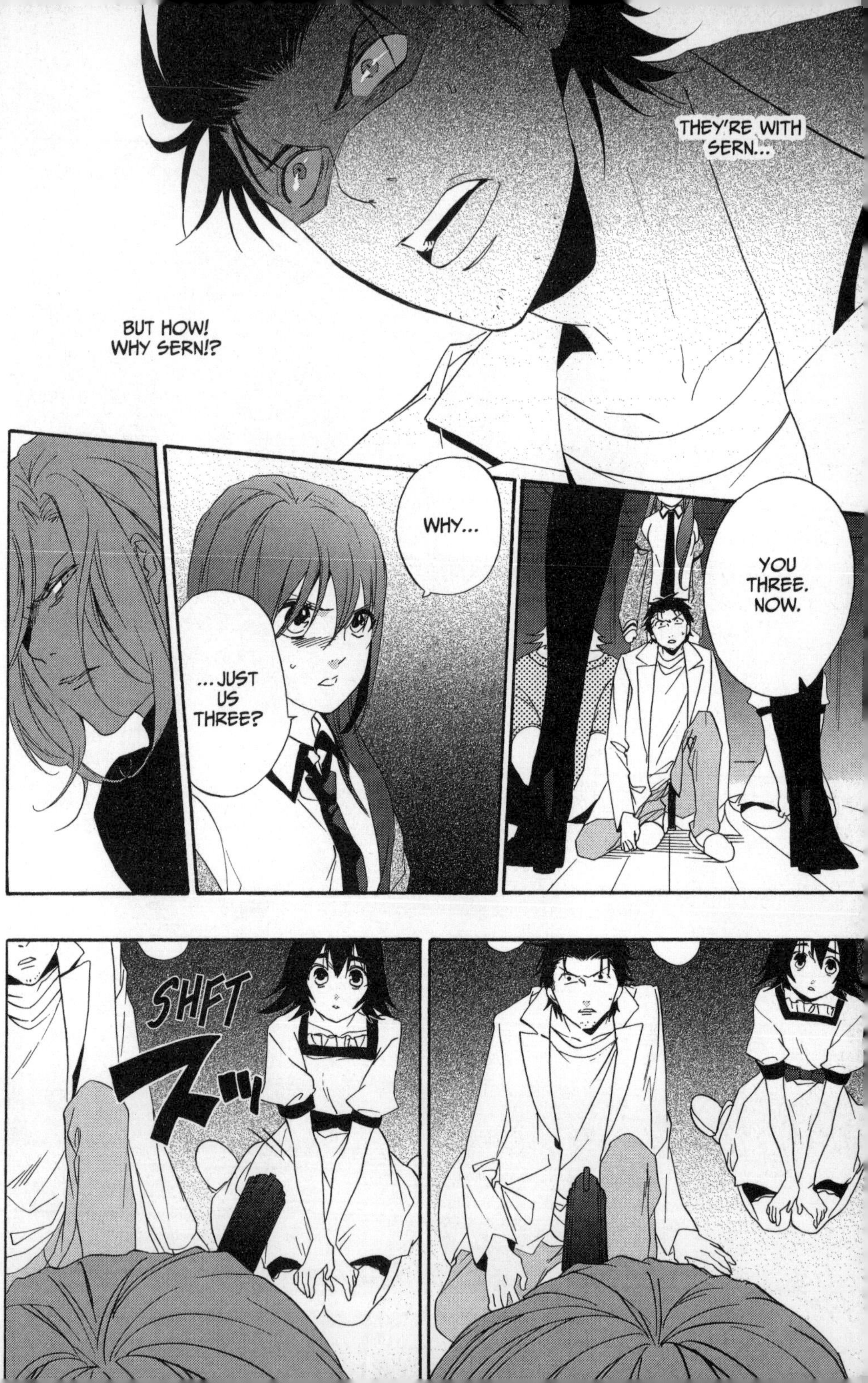
THEY'RE WITH SERN...
BUT HOW! WHY SERN!?
YOU THREE. NOW.
WHY...
...JUST US THREE?
SHFT
ズッ

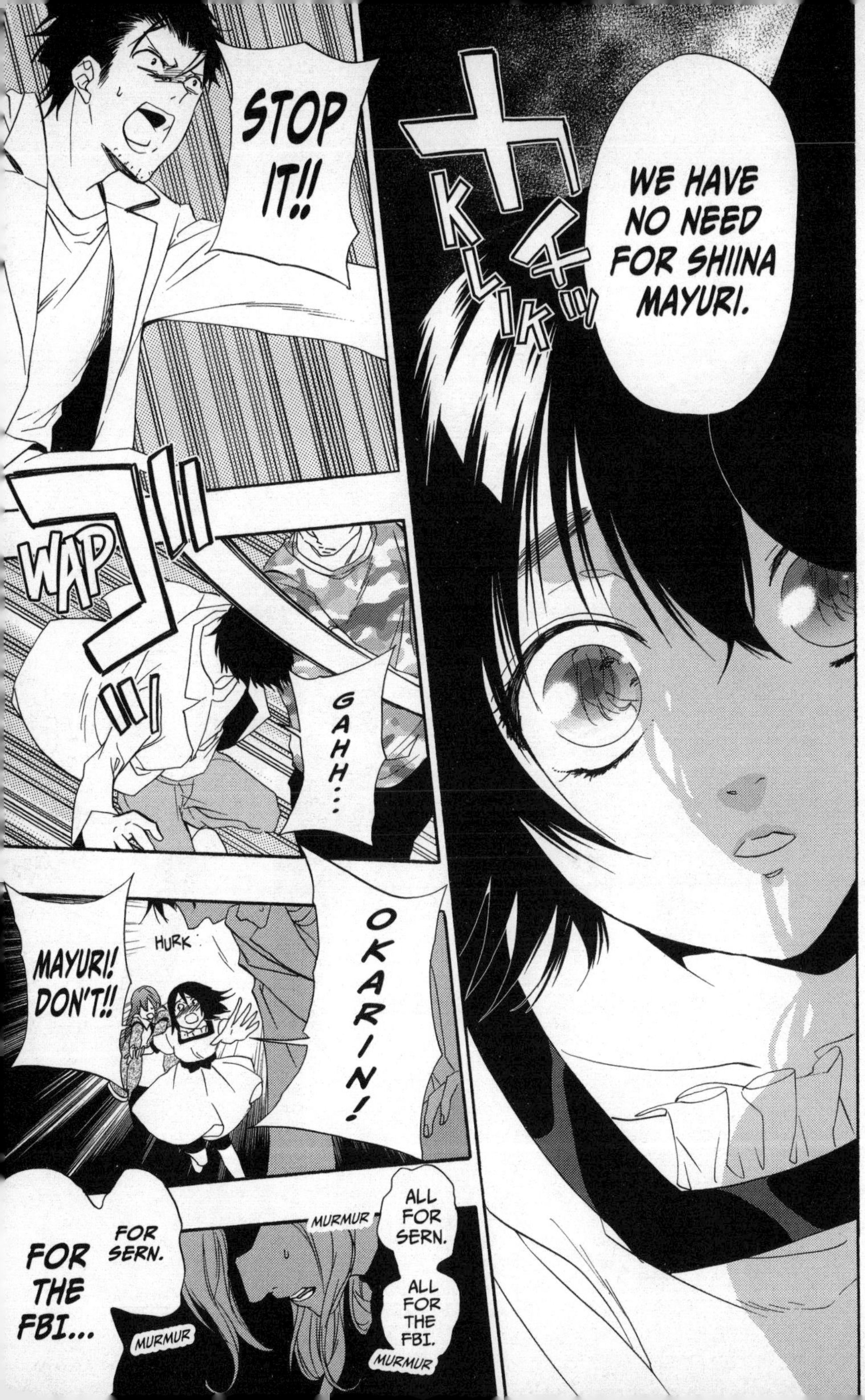
WE HAVE NO NEED FOR SHIINA MAYURI.
KLIK
STOP IT!!
WAP
GAHH...
OKARIN!
HURK
MAYURI! DON'T!!
ALL FOR SERN.
MURMUR
ALL FOR THE FBI.
MURMUR
FOR SERN.
FOR THE FBI...
MURMUR

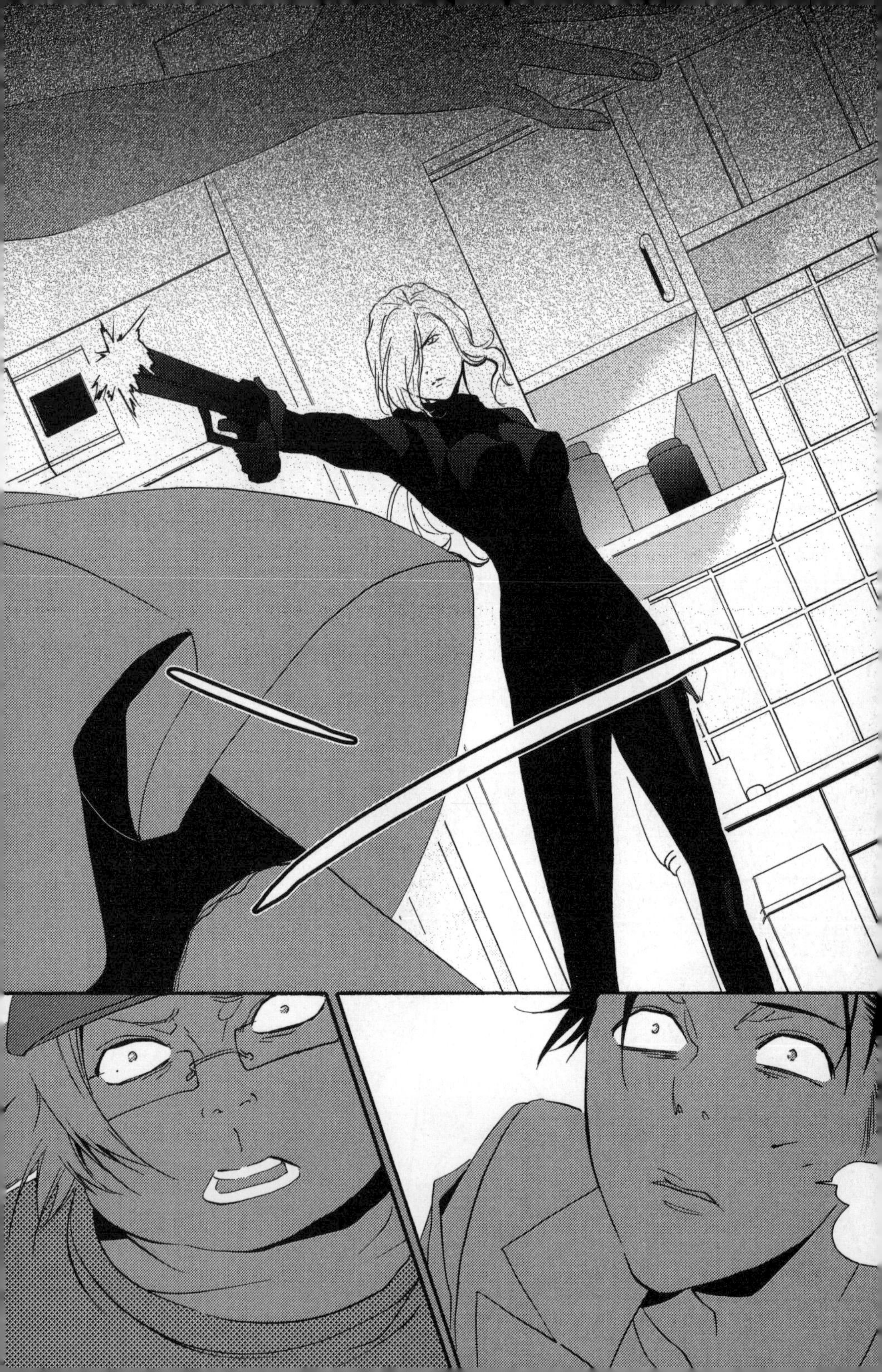

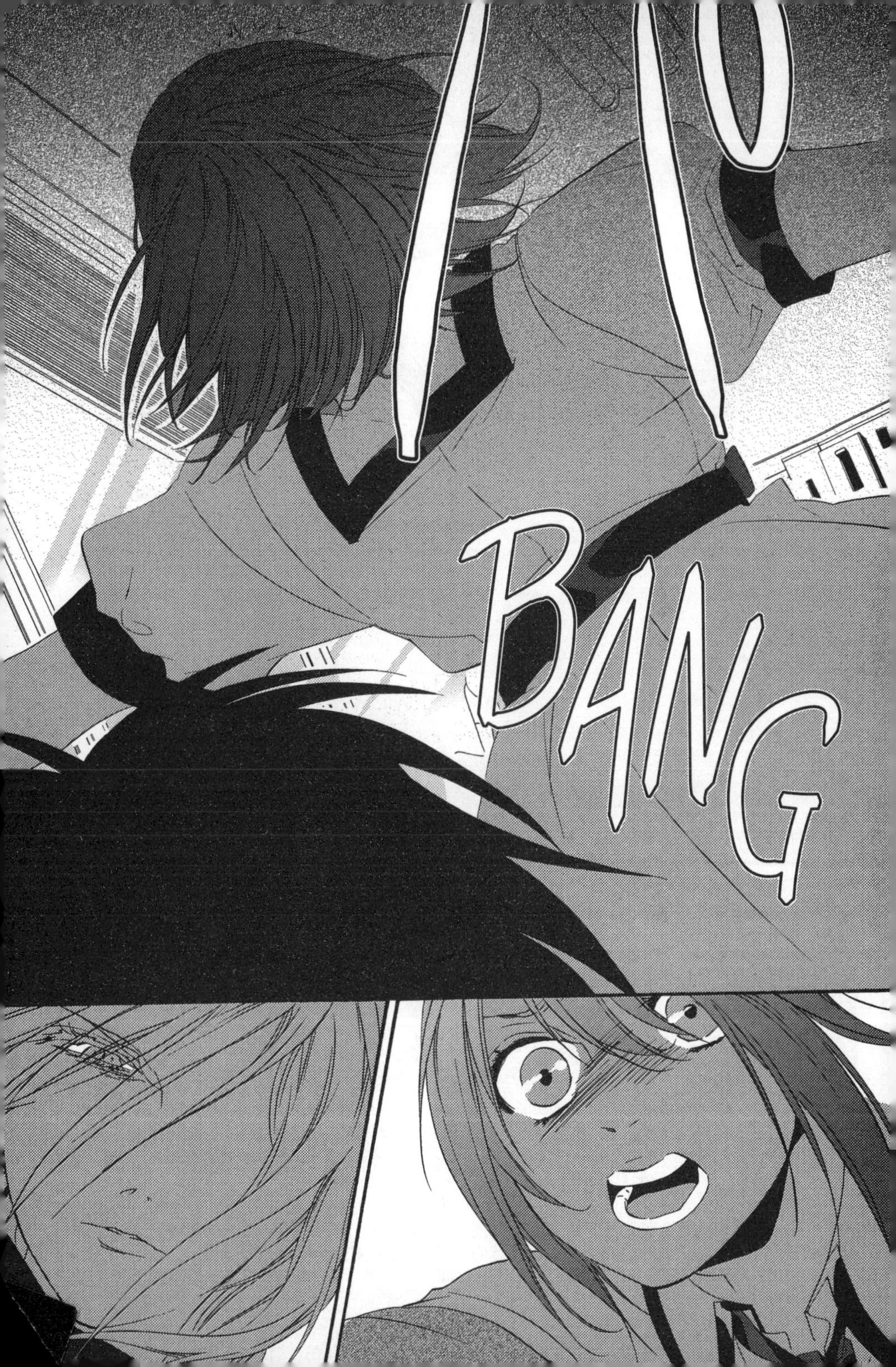
BANG

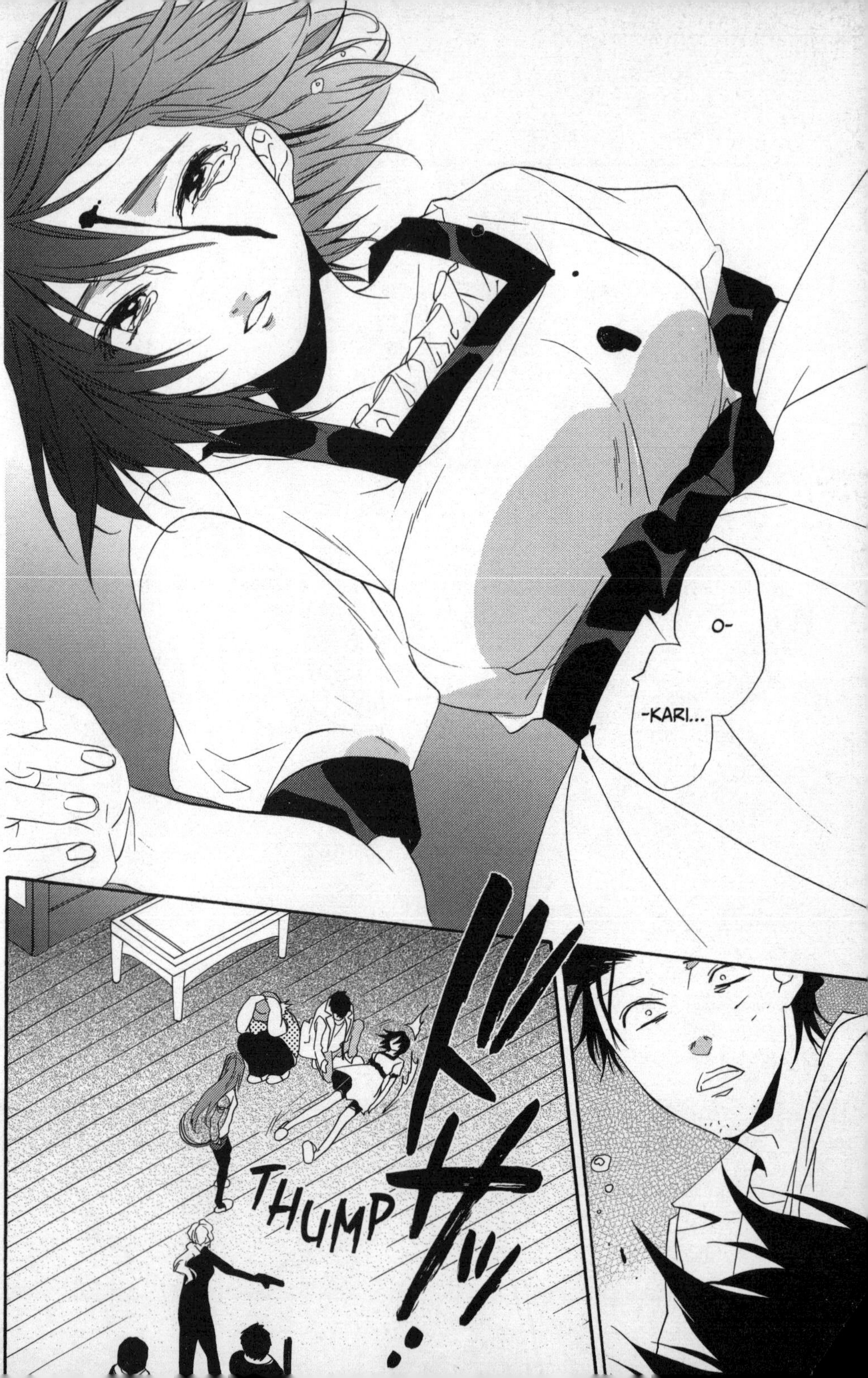

O- -KARI...
THUMP

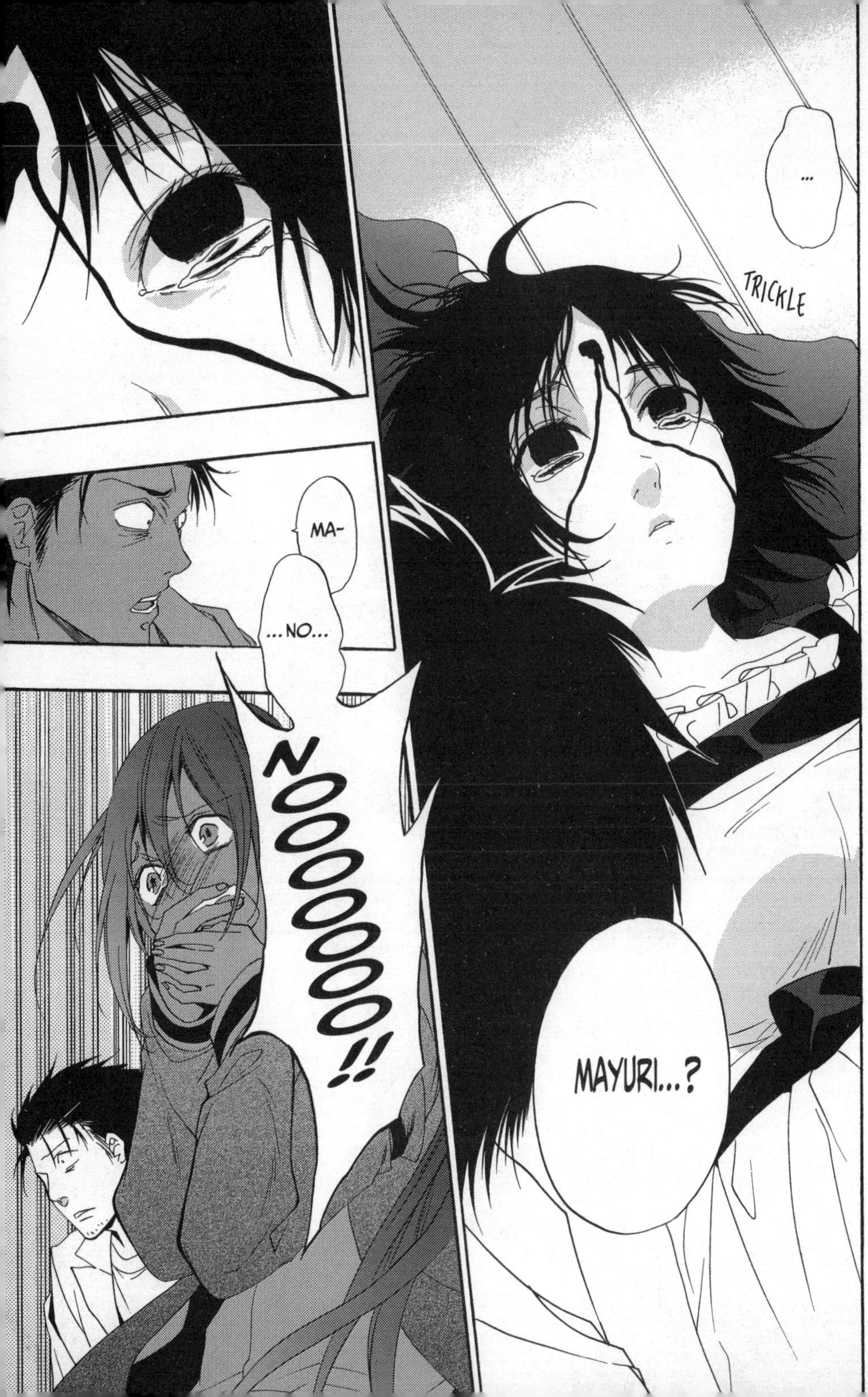
...
TRICKLE
MAYURI...?
MA-
...NO...
NOOOOOOOO!!

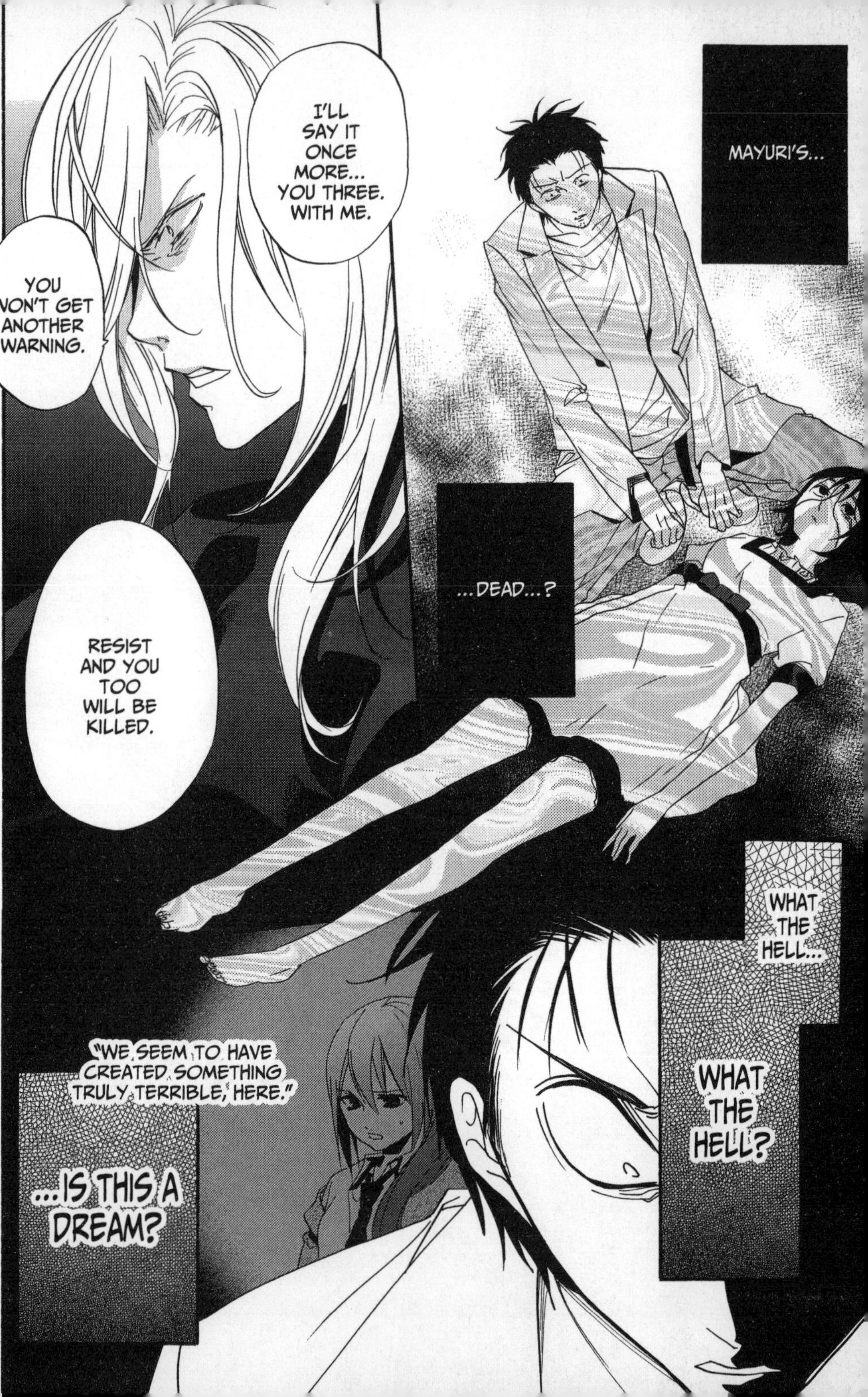
MAYURI'S...
...DEAD...?
I'LL SAY IT ONCE MORE... YOU THREE. WITH ME.
YOU WON'T GET ANOTHER WARNING.
RESIST AND YOU TOO WILL BE KILLED.
WHAT THE HELL...
WHAT THE HELL?
"WE SEEM TO HAVE CREATED SOMETHING TRULY TERRIBLE, HERE."
...IS THIS A DREAM?

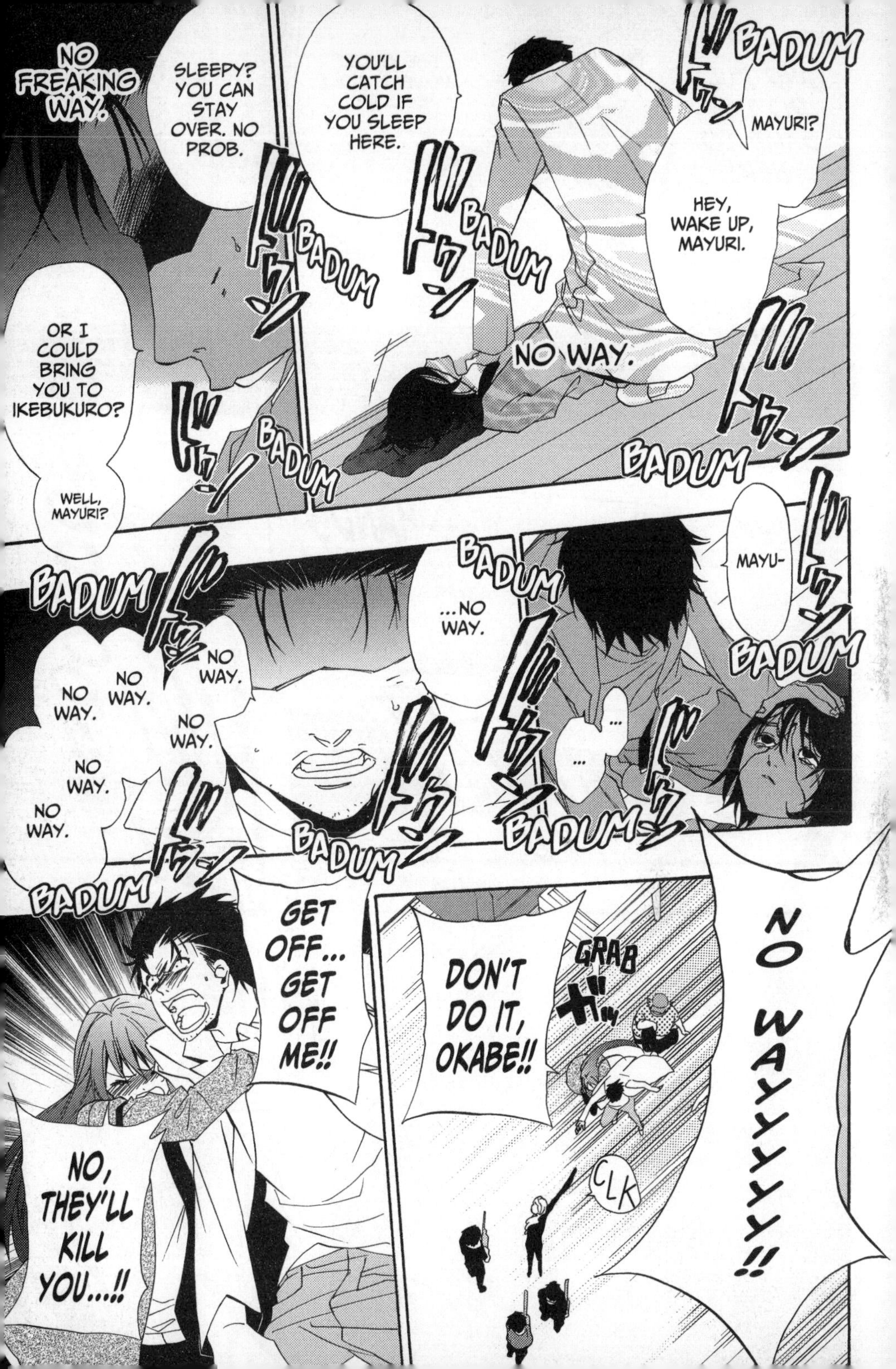
BADUM
MAYURI?
HEY, WAKE UP, MAYURI.
YOU'LL CATCH COLD IF YOU SLEEP HERE.
BADUM
BADUM
NO WAY.
BADUM
SLEEPY? YOU CAN STAY OVER. NO PROB.
NO FREAKING WAY.
BADUM
OR I COULD BRING YOU TO IKEBUKURO?
BADUM
WELL, MAYURI?
MAYU-
BADUM
BADUM
...
...
BADUM
...NO WAY.
BADUM
BADUM
NO WAY.
NO WAY.
NO WAY.
NO WAY.
NO WAY.
NO WAY.
BADUM
BADUM
NO WAYYYYYYY!!
GRAB
DON'T DO IT, OKABE!!
CLK
GET OFF... GET OFF ME!!
NO, THEY'LL KILL YOU...!!

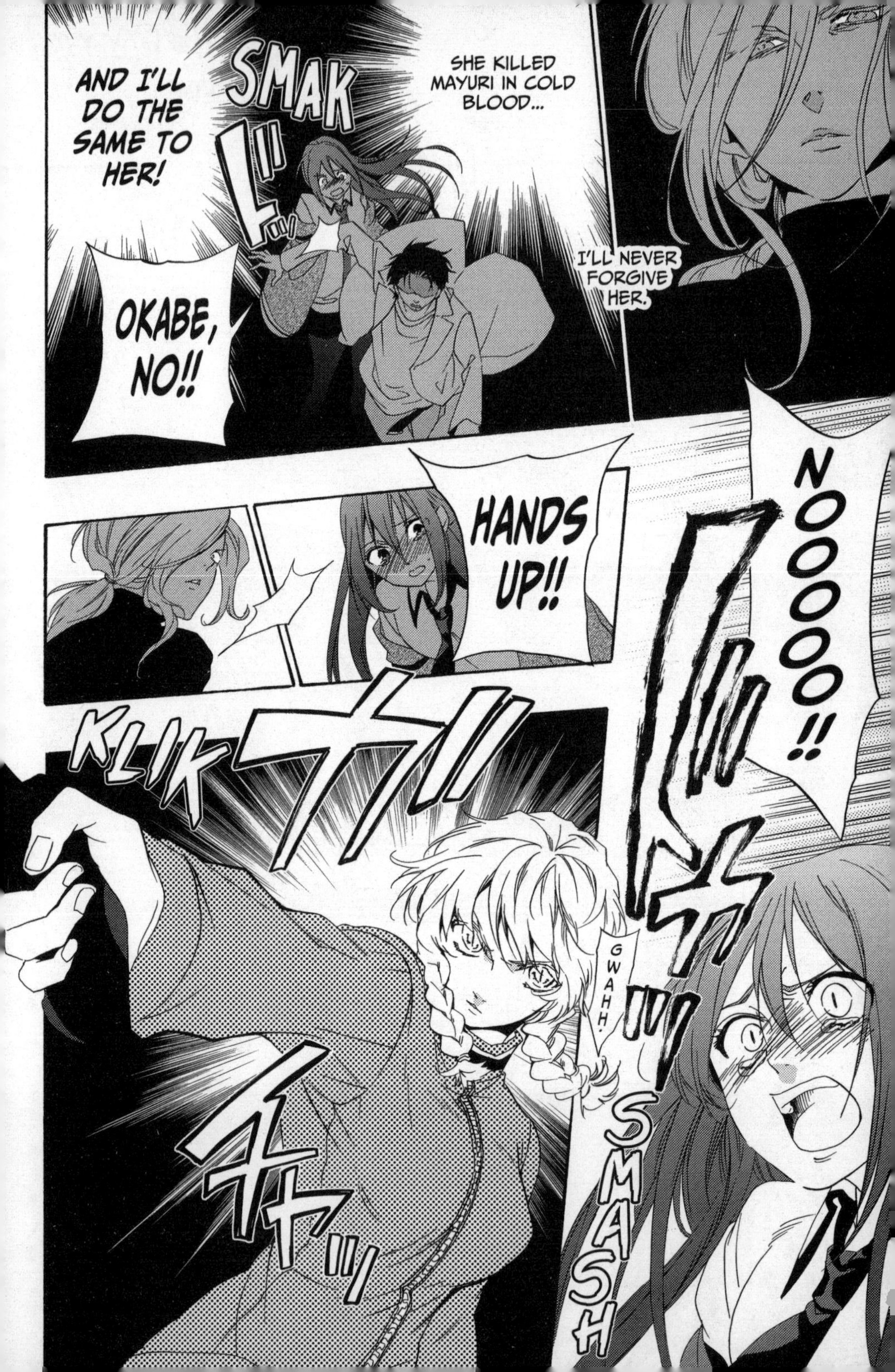
I'LL NEVER FORGIVE HER.
SHE KILLED MAYURI IN COLD BLOOD...
SMAK
AND I'LL DO THE SAME TO HER!
OKABE, NO!!
NOOOOOO!!
HANDS UP!!
SMASH
GWAHH.
KLIK

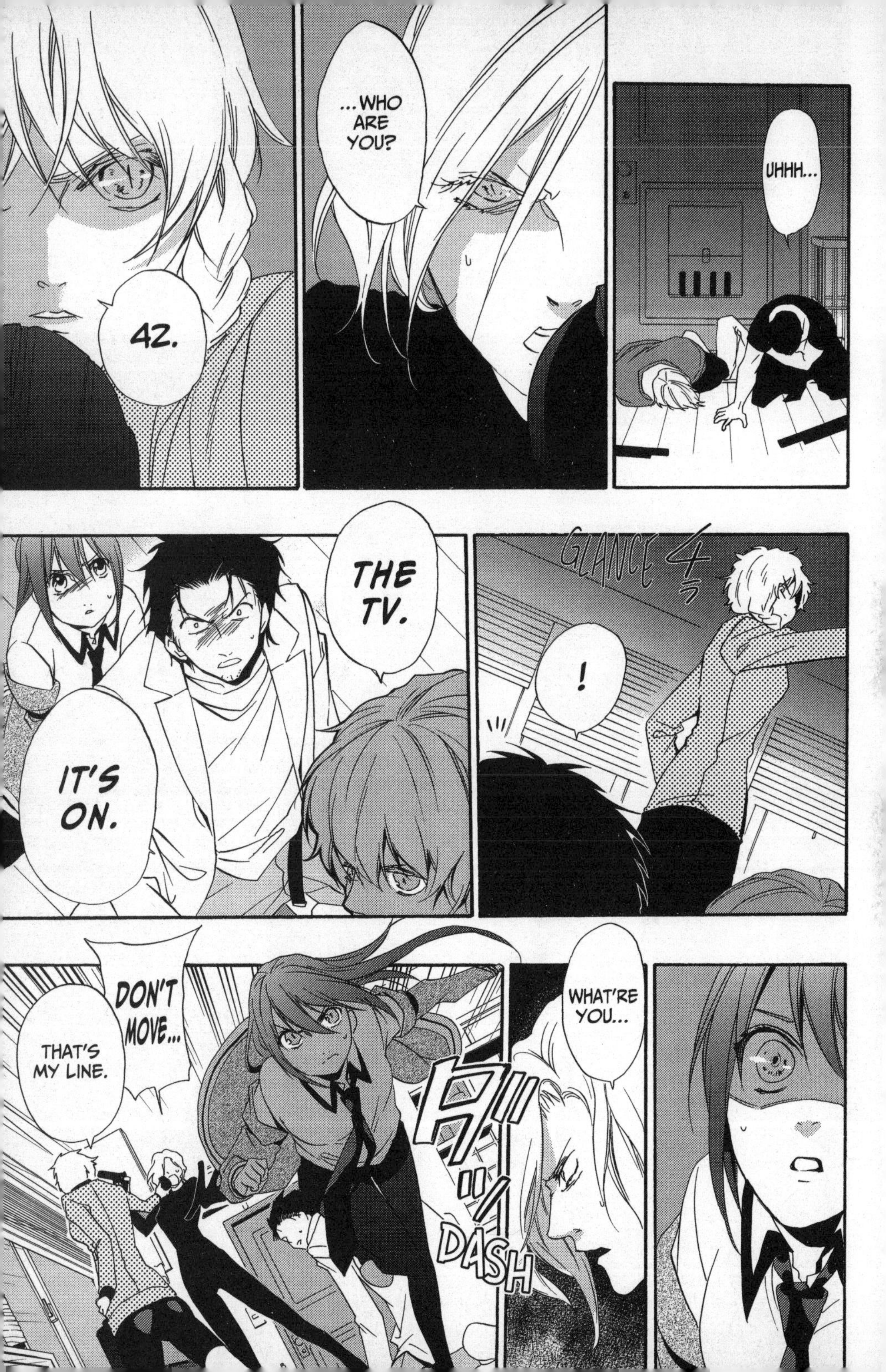
UHHH...
...WHO ARE YOU?
42.
GLANCE
!
THE TV.
IT'S ON.
WHAT'RE YOU...
DASH
DON'T MOVE...
THAT'S MY LINE.

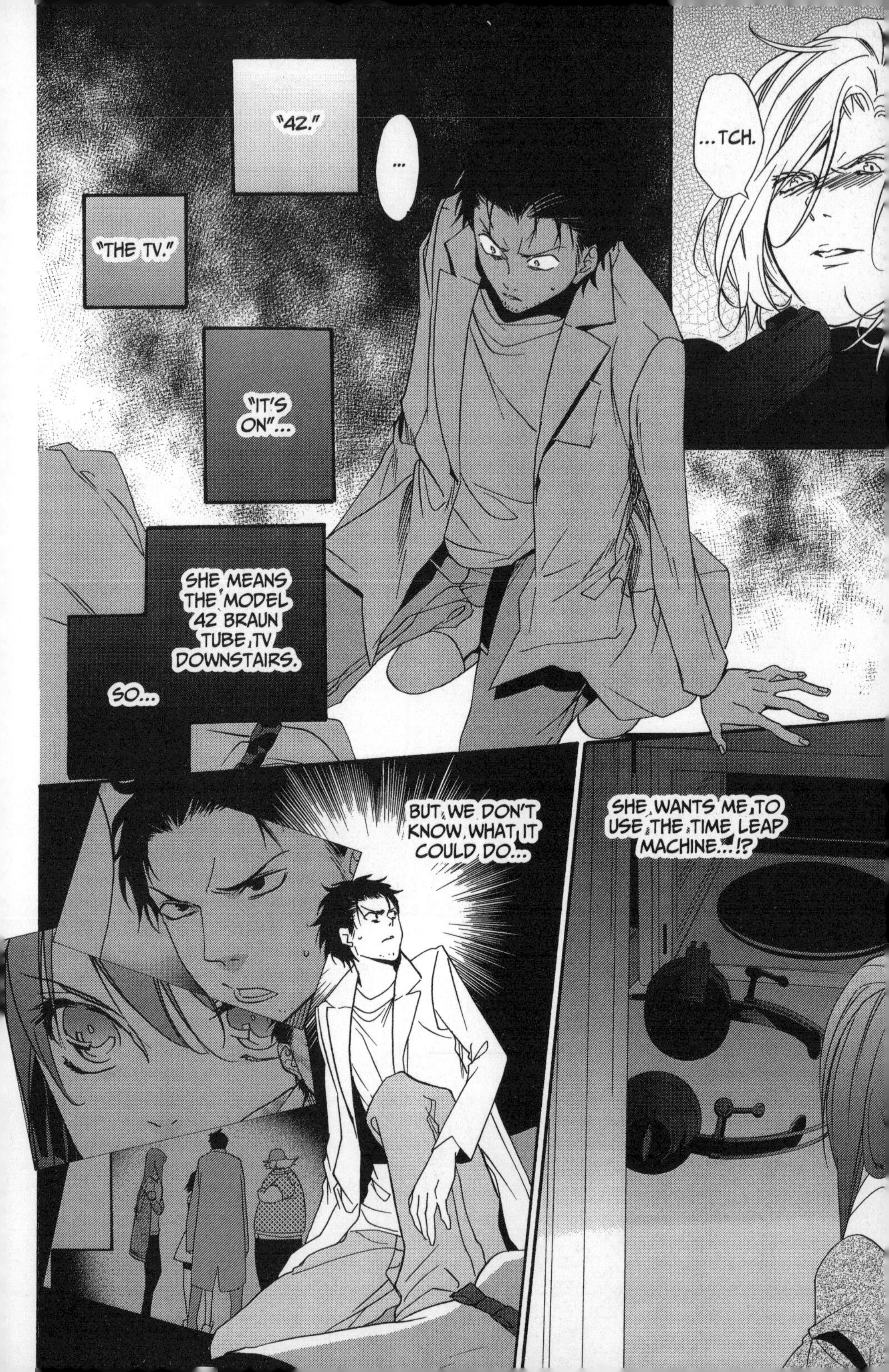
...TCH.
...
"42."
"THE TV."
"IT'S ON"...
SHE MEANS THE MODEL 42 BRAUN TUBE TV DOWNSTAIRS.
SO...
SHE WANTS ME TO USE THE TIME LEAP MACHINE...!?
BUT WE DON'T KNOW WHAT IT COULD DO...

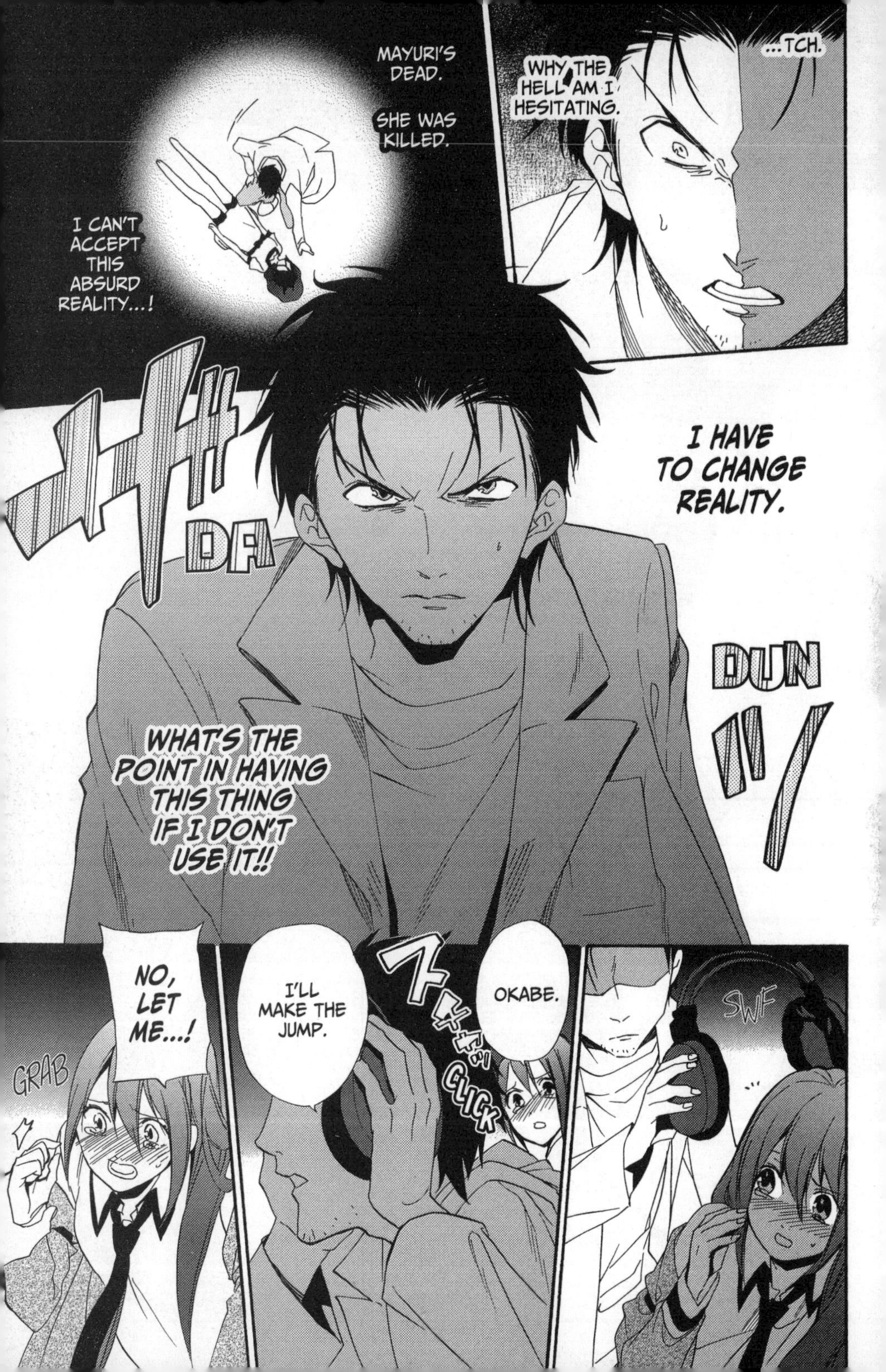
...TCH.
WHY THE HELL AM I HESITATING.
MAYURI'S DEAD.
SHE WAS KILLED.
I CAN'T ACCEPT THIS ABSURD REALITY...!
I HAVE TO CHANGE REALITY.
DUN
WHAT'S THE POINT IN HAVING THIS THING IF I DON'T USE IT!!
DA
SWF
...
OKABE.
CLICK
I'LL MAKE THE JUMP.
NO, LET ME...!
GRAB

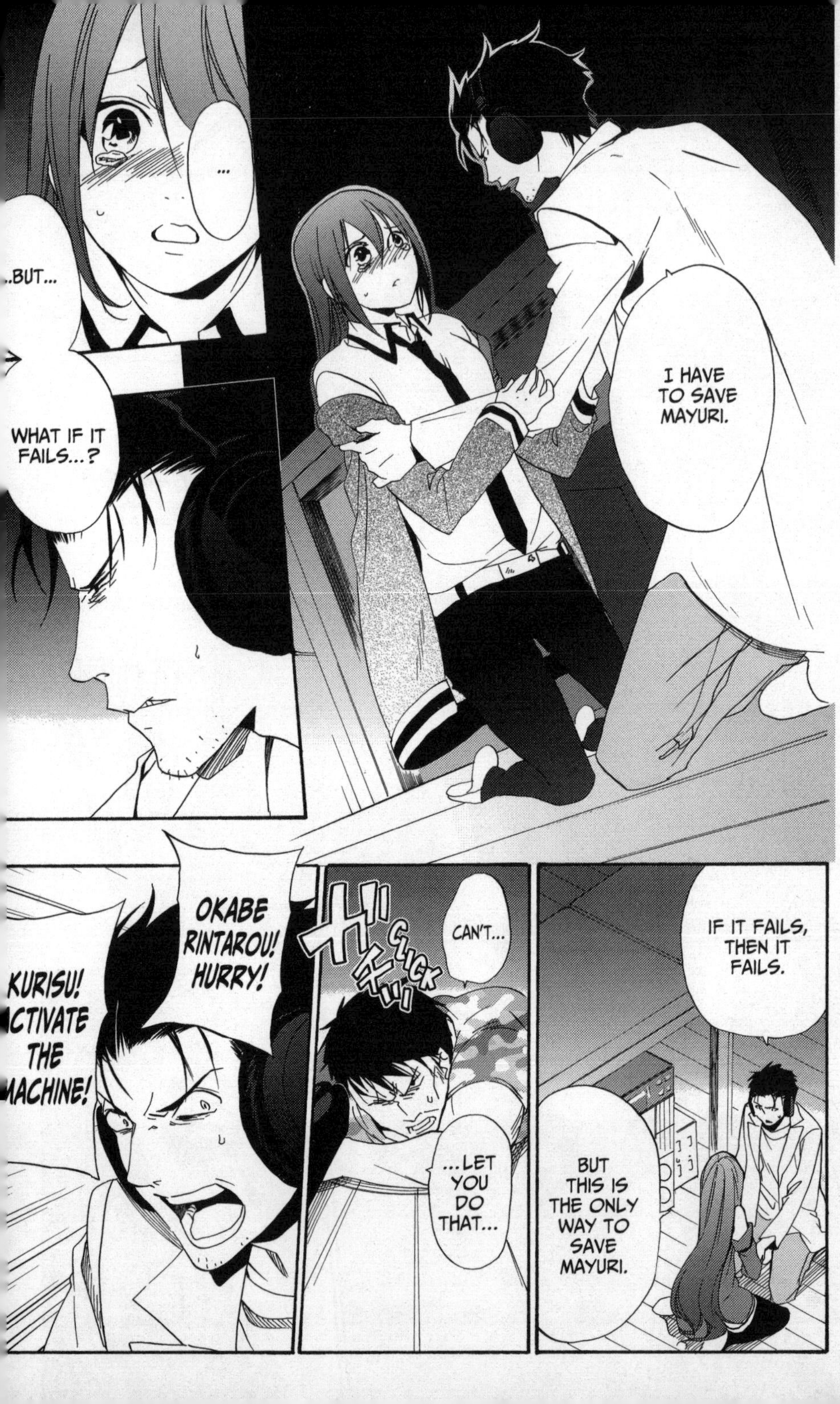
I HAVE TO SAVE MAYURI.
...
..BUT...
WHAT IF IT FAILS...?
IF IT FAILS, THEN IT FAILS.
BUT THIS IS THE ONLY WAY TO SAVE MAYURI.
CAN'T...
CLICK
...LET YOU DO THAT...
OKABE RINTAROU! HURRY!
KURISU! CTIVATE THE ACHINE!

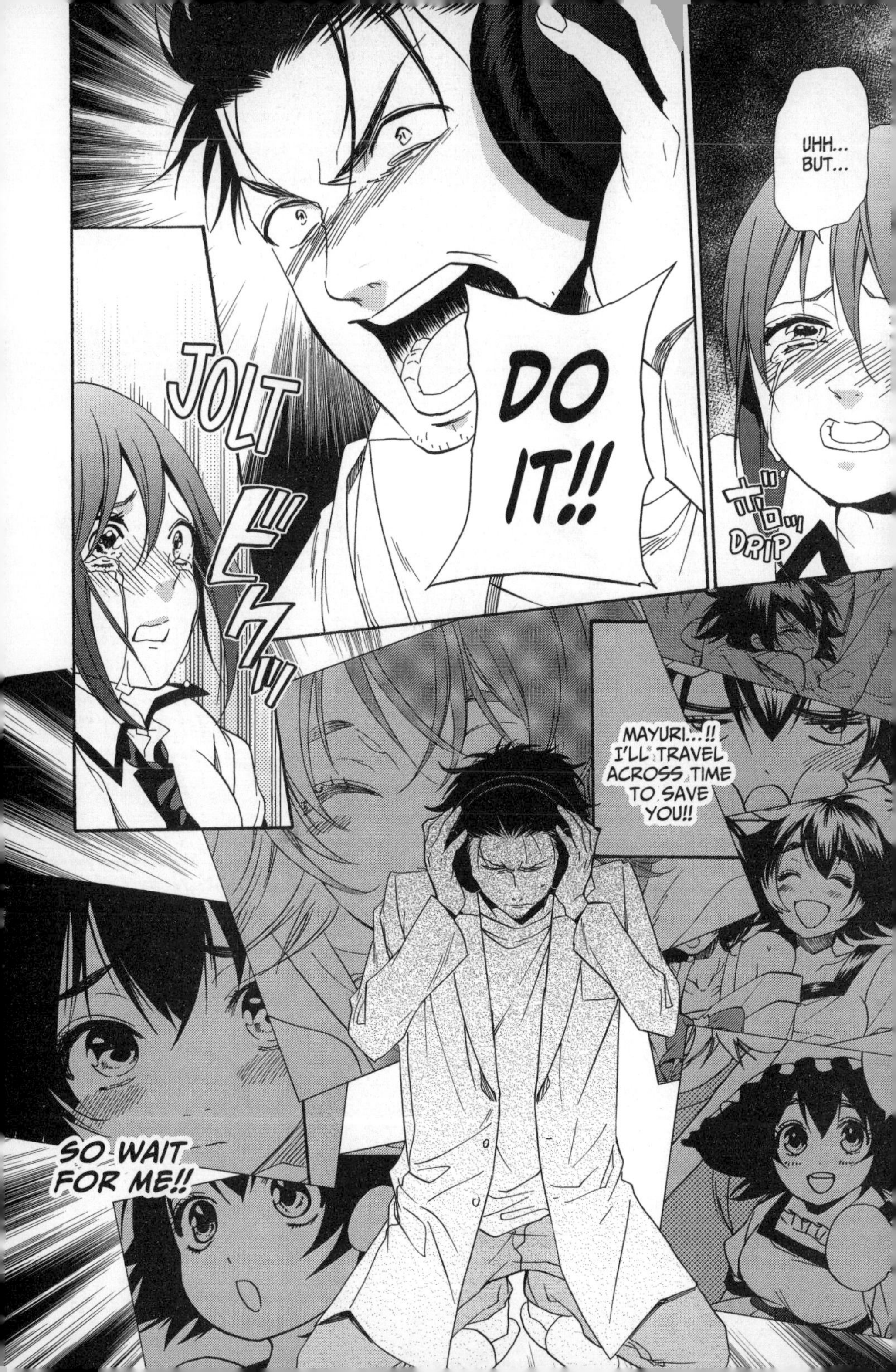
UHH... BUT...
DRIP
DO IT!!
JOLT
ビクッ
MAYURI...!! I'LL TRAVEL ACROSS TIME TO SAVE YOU!!
SO WAIT FOR ME!!

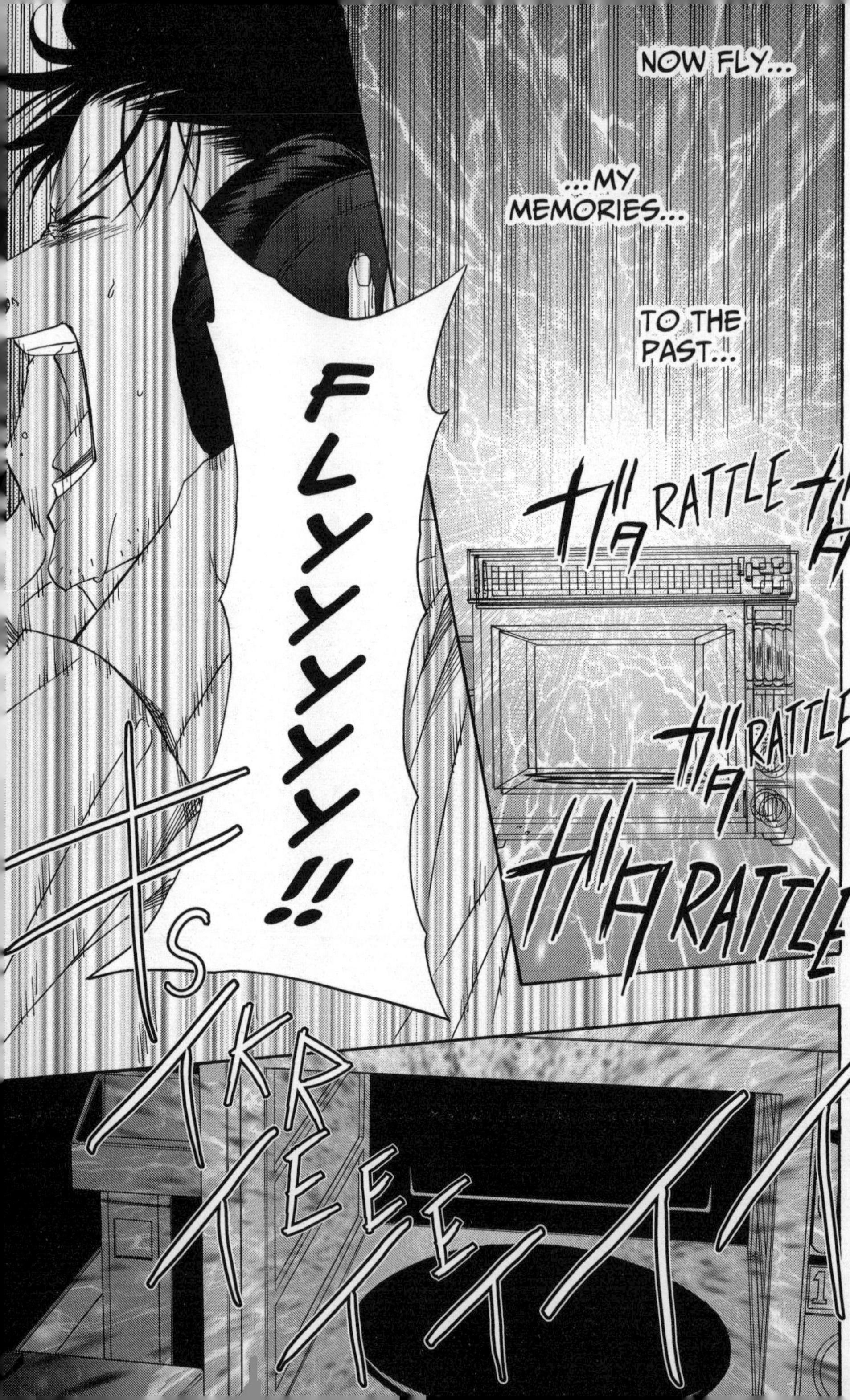
NOW FLY...
...MY MEMORIES...
TO THE PAST...
FLYYYYYY!!
RATTLE
RATTLE
RATTLE
SKREEE

[IBN-5100]

A desktop computer put on the market in June of 1975 by IBN; full
name "IBN-5100 Portable Computer". John Titor said the following
about the computer: "It has the ability to read the older IBM
programming languages in addition to APL and BASIC." This was not
public knowledge until John Titor revealed it; it was even a secret to
the hardware developers themselves. Immediately after Titor said as
much on a message board in February 2001, IBN went into a panic
and publicly released a statement that confirmed what Titor had said.
Thus, the public learned of the IBN-5100's hidden features that hadn't
even been mentioned in the manual.

The universe has no end, though it does have a beginning. --- Infinite.
Stars too have a beginning, though they are destroyed by their own power. --- Finite.
Those who believe they have wisdom, are often shown by history to be the most foolish.
The fish in the sea don't know what the world is like on the land. Wisdom would destroy them as well.
Man to exceeding the speed of light would be more ridiculous than fish to living on land.
This is God's final warning to any who rebel.

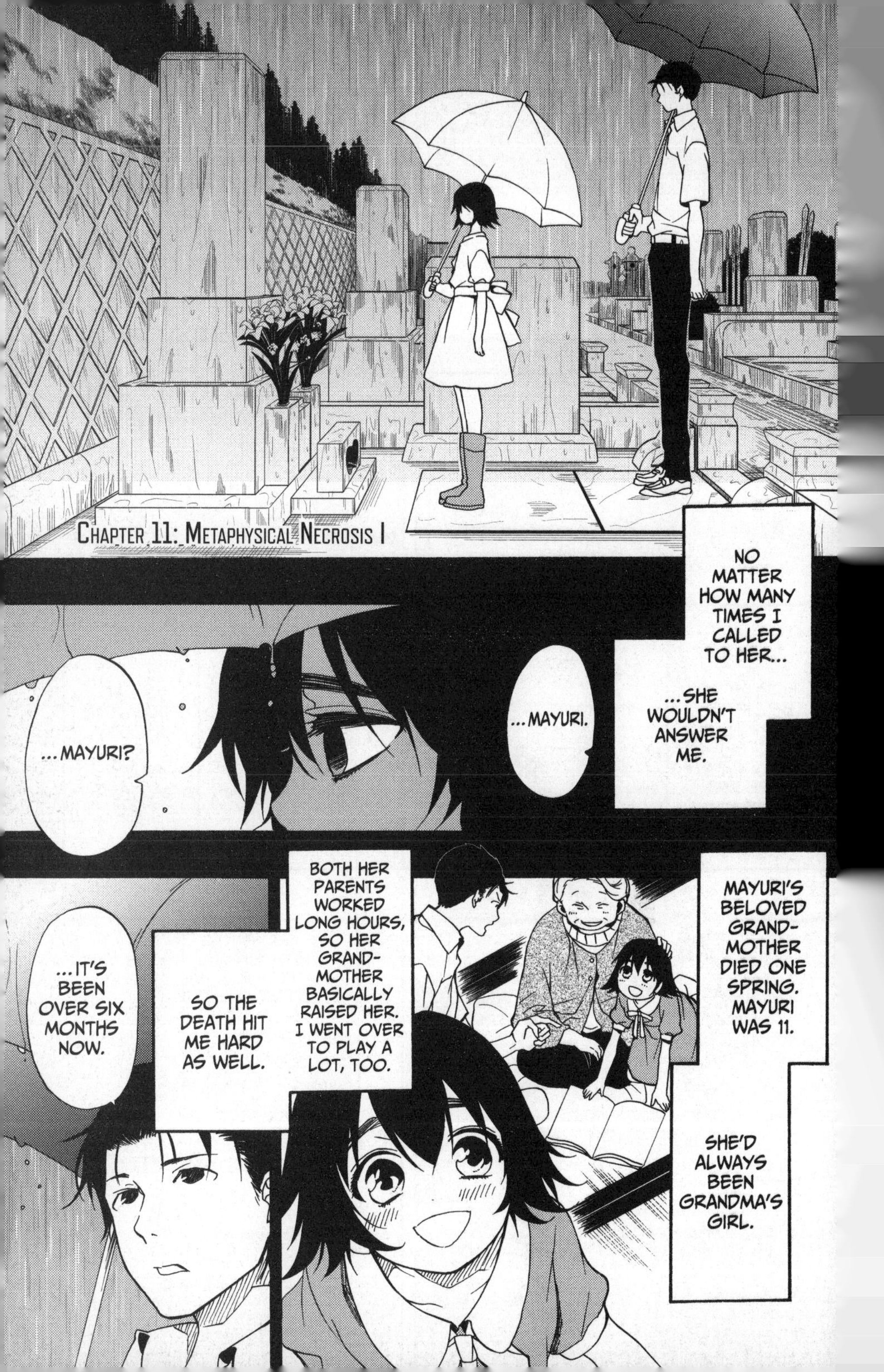
Chapter 11: Metaphysical Necrosis I
NO MATTER HOW MANY TIMES I CALLED TO HER...
...SHE WOULDN'T ANSWER ME.
...MAYURI.
...MAYURI?
MAYURI'S BELOVED GRAND-MOTHER DIED ONE SPRING. MAYURI WAS 11.
SHE'D ALWAYS BEEN GRANDMA'S GIRL.
BOTH HER PARENTS WORKED LONG HOURS, SO HER GRAND-MOTHER BASICALLY RAISED HER. I WENT OVER TO PLAY A LOT, TOO.
SO THE DEATH HIT ME HARD AS WELL.
...IT'S BEEN OVER SIX MONTHS NOW.

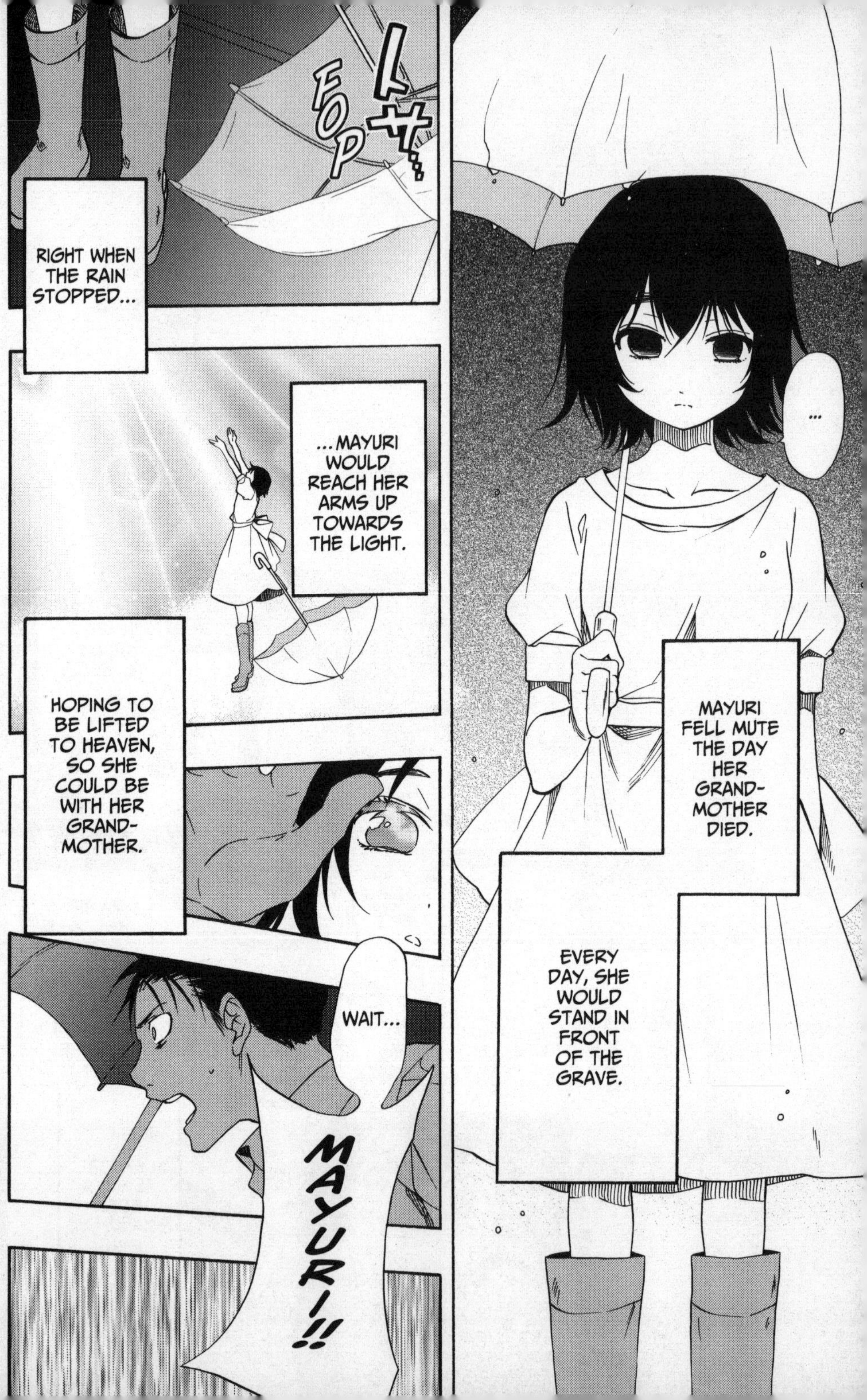
...
MAYURI FELL MUTE THE DAY HER GRAND-MOTHER DIED.
EVERY DAY, SHE WOULD STAND IN FRONT OF THE GRAVE.
FOP
RIGHT WHEN THE RAIN STOPPED...
...MAYURI WOULD REACH HER ARMS UP TOWARDS THE LIGHT.
HOPING TO BE LIFTED TO HEAVEN, SO SHE COULD BE WITH HER GRAND-MOTHER.
WAIT...
MAYURI!!

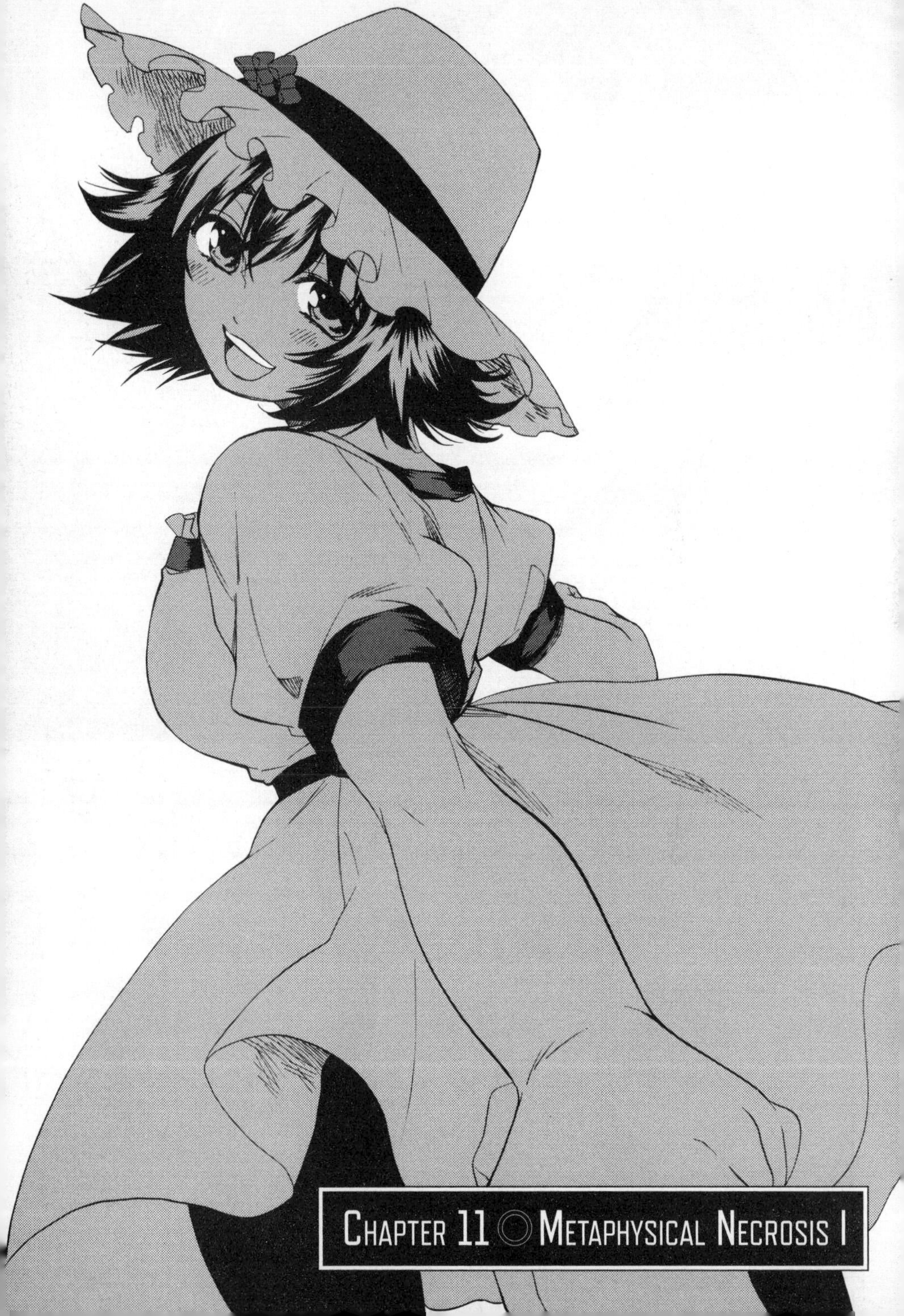

Chapter 11 ◎ Metaphysical Necrosis I

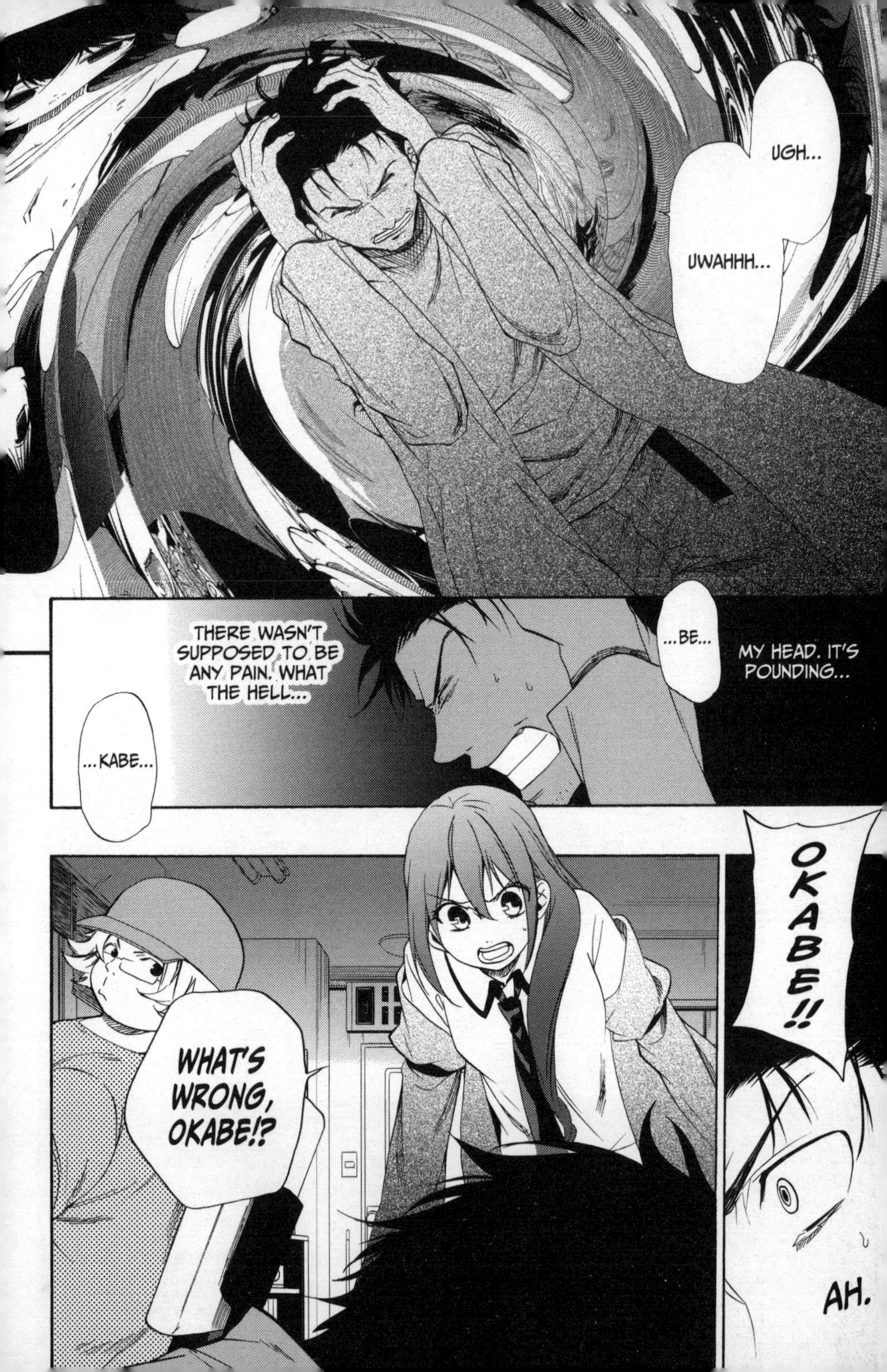
UGH...
UWAHHH...
MY HEAD. IT'S POUNDING...
...BE...
THERE WASN'T SUPPOSED TO BE ANY PAIN. WHAT THE HELL...
...KABE...
OKABE!!
AH.
WHAT'S WRONG, OKABE!?

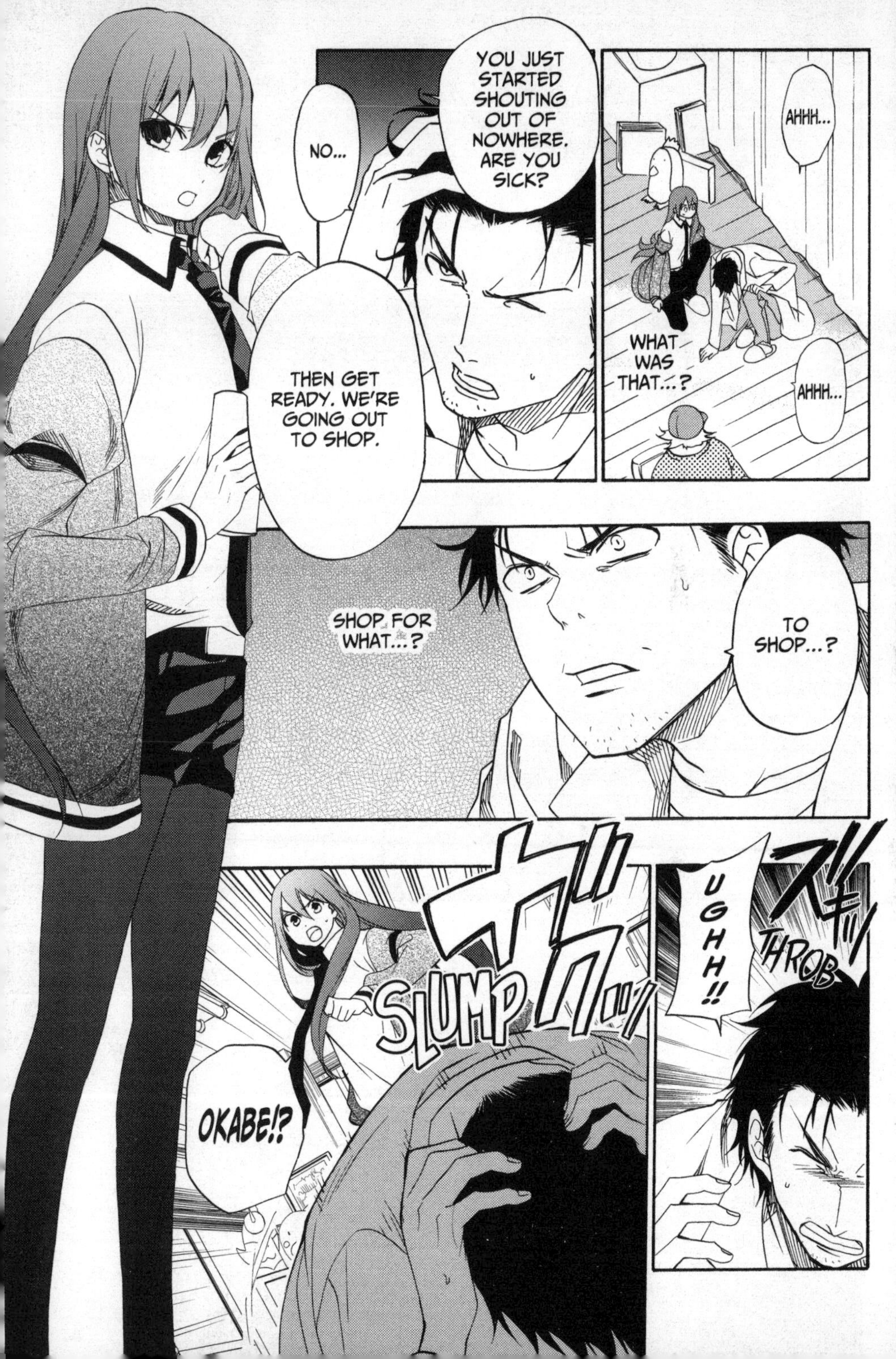
AHHH...
AHHH...
WHAT WAS THAT...?
YOU JUST STARTED SHOUTING OUT OF NOWHERE. ARE YOU SICK?
NO...
THEN GET READY. WE'RE GOING OUT TO SHOP.
TO SHOP...?
SHOP FOR WHAT...?
UGHH!!
THROB
SLUMP
OKABE!?

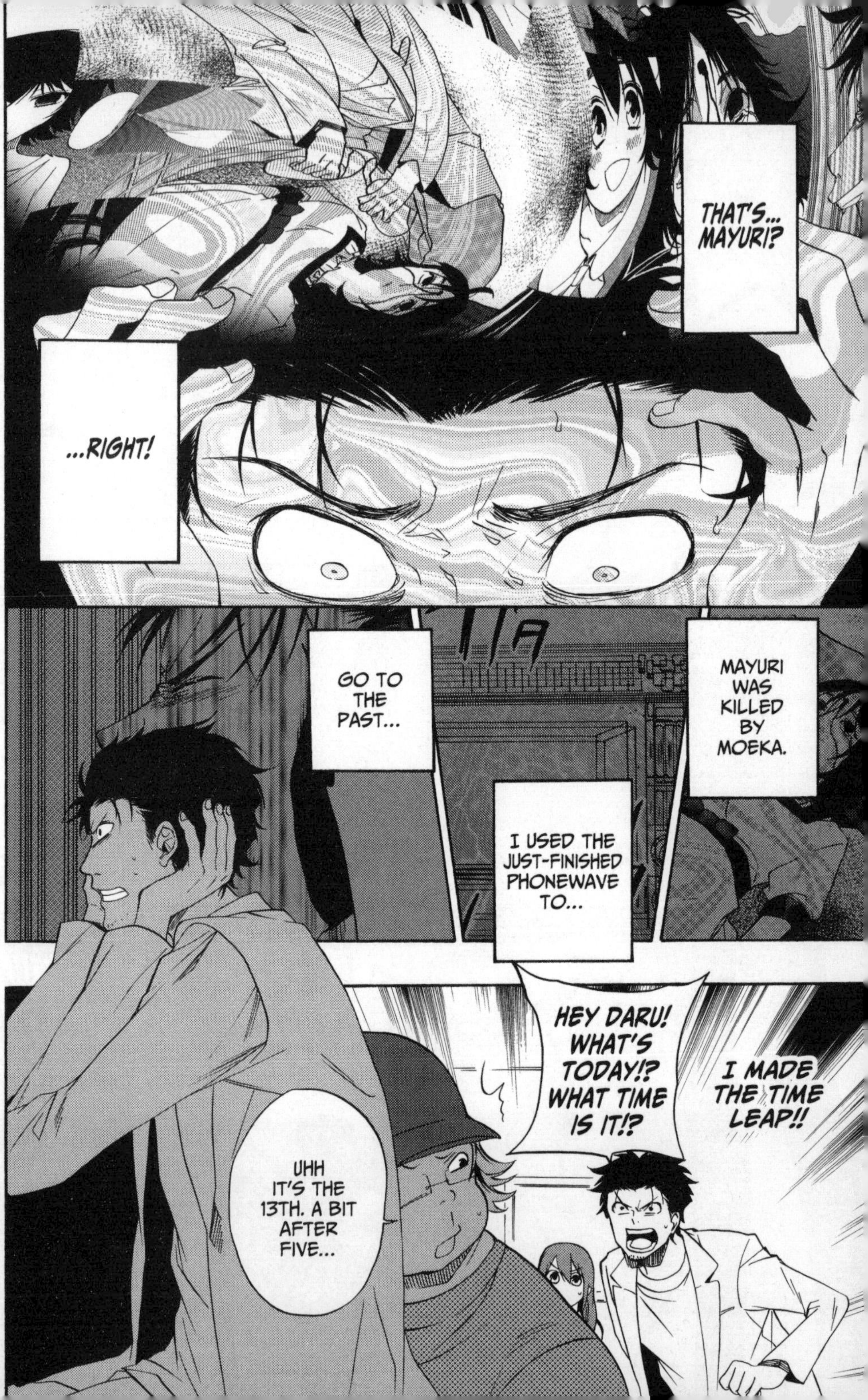
THAT'S... MAYURI?
...RIGHT!
MAYURI WAS KILLED BY MOEKA.
I USED THE JUST-FINISHED PHONEWAVE TO...
GO TO THE PAST...
I MADE THE TIME LEAP!!
HEY DARU! WHAT'S TODAY!? WHAT TIME IS IT!?
UHH IT'S THE 13TH. A BIT AFTER FIVE...

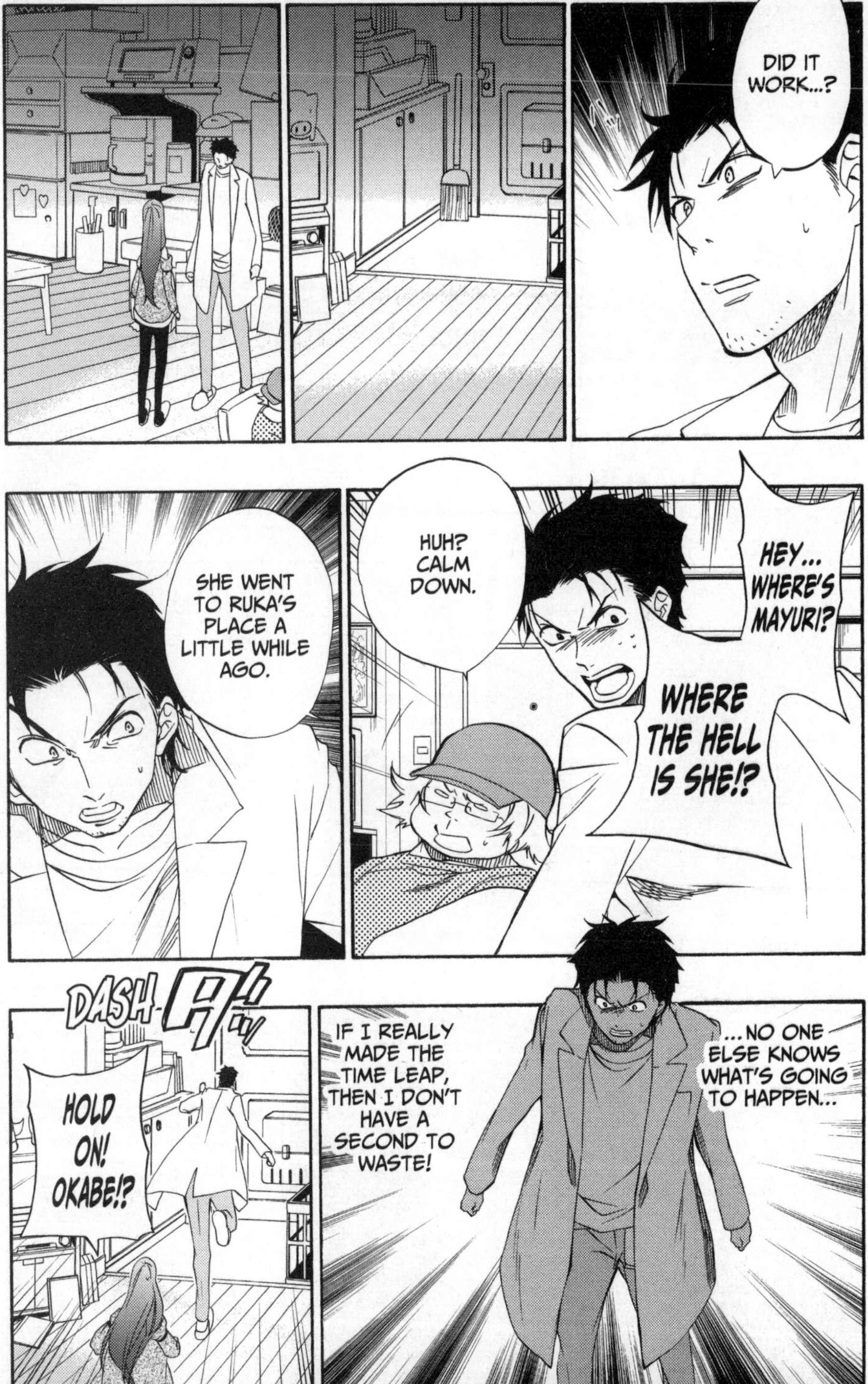
DID IT WORK...?
HEY... WHERE'S MAYURI?
WHERE THE HELL IS SHE!?
HUH? CALM DOWN.
SHE WENT TO RUKA'S PLACE A LITTLE WHILE AGO.
...NO ONE ELSE KNOWS WHAT'S GOING TO HAPPEN...
IF I REALLY MADE THE TIME LEAP, THEN I DON'T HAVE A SECOND TO WASTE!
DASH
HOLD ON! OKABE!?

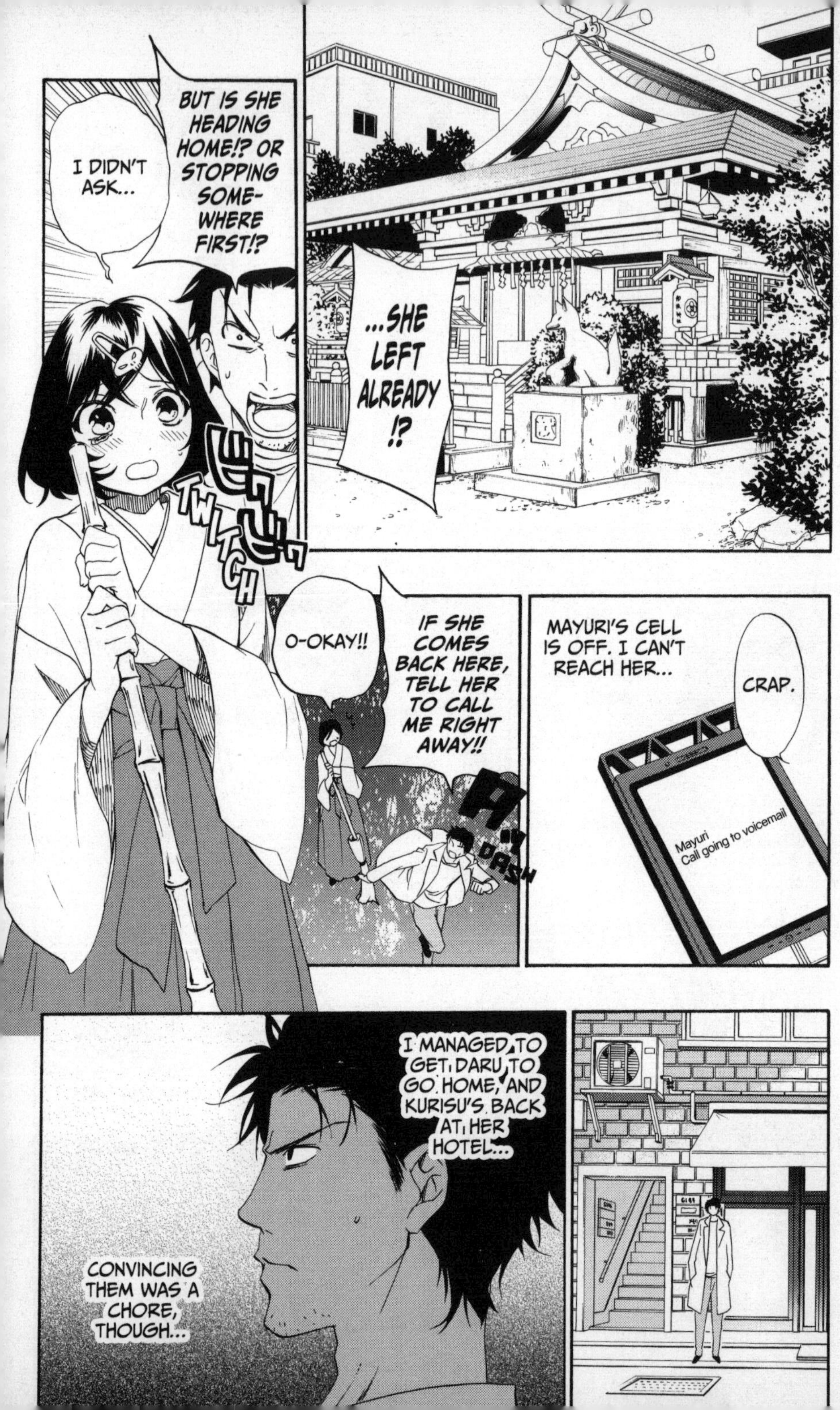
...SHE LEFT ALREADY!?
BUT IS SHE HEADING HOME!? OR STOPPING SOMEWHERE FIRST!?
I DIDN'T ASK...
TWITCH
IF SHE COMES BACK HERE, TELL HER TO CALL ME RIGHT AWAY!!
O-OKAY!!
DASH
MAYURI'S CELL IS OFF. I CAN'T REACH HER...
CRAP.
Mayuri
Call going to voicemail
I MANAGED TO GET DARU TO GO HOME, AND KURISU'S BACK AT HER HOTEL...
CONVINCING THEM WAS A CHORE, THOUGH...

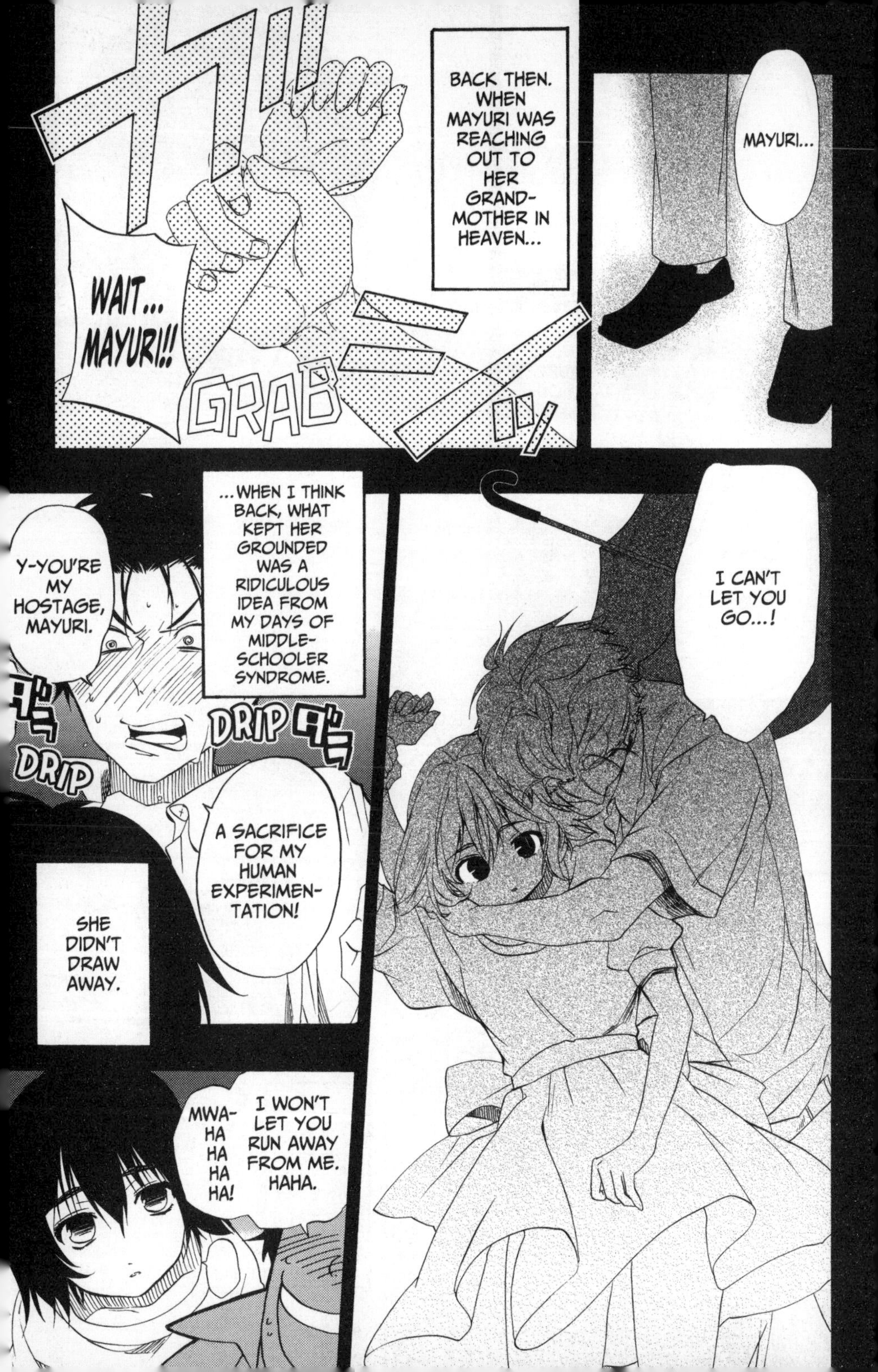
MAYURI...
BACK THEN. WHEN MAYURI WAS REACHING OUT TO HER GRANDMOTHER IN HEAVEN...
WAIT... MAYURI!!
GRAB
I CAN'T LET YOU GO...!
...WHEN I THINK BACK, WHAT KEPT HER GROUNDED WAS A RIDICULOUS IDEA FROM MY DAYS OF MIDDLE-SCHOOLER SYNDROME.
Y-YOU'RE MY HOSTAGE, MAYURI.
DRIP
DRIP
A SACRIFICE FOR MY HUMAN EXPERIMENTATION!
SHE DIDN'T DRAW AWAY.
I WON'T LET YOU RUN AWAY FROM ME. HAHA.
MWA-HA HA HA HA!

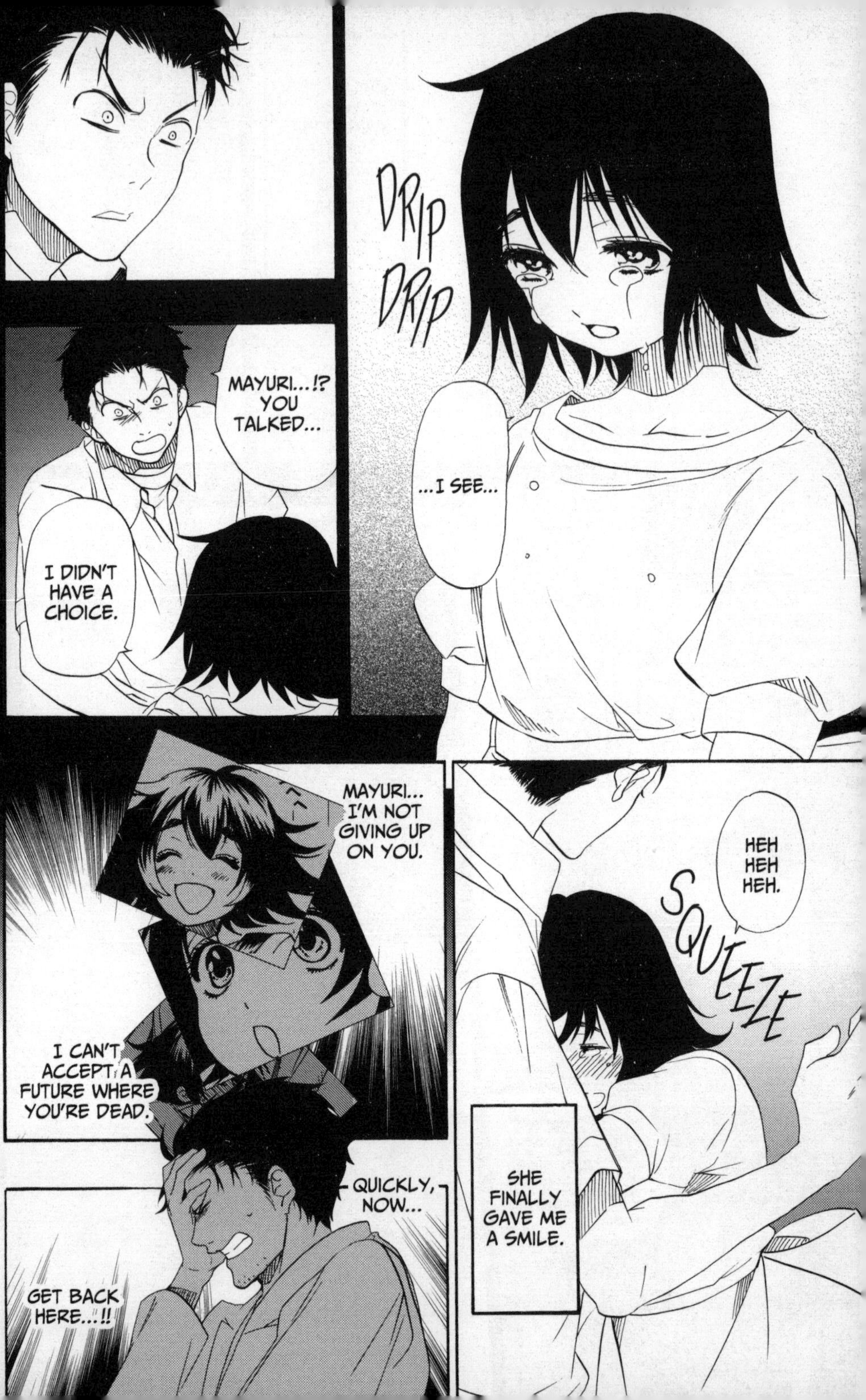
DRIP
DRIP
...I SEE...
MAYURI...!? YOU TALKED...
I DIDN'T HAVE A CHOICE.
HEH HEH HEH.
SQUEEZE
SHE FINALLY GAVE ME A SMILE.
MAYURI... I'M NOT GIVING UP ON YOU.
I CAN'T ACCEPT A FUTURE WHERE YOU'RE DEAD.
QUICKLY, NOW...
GET BACK HERE...!!

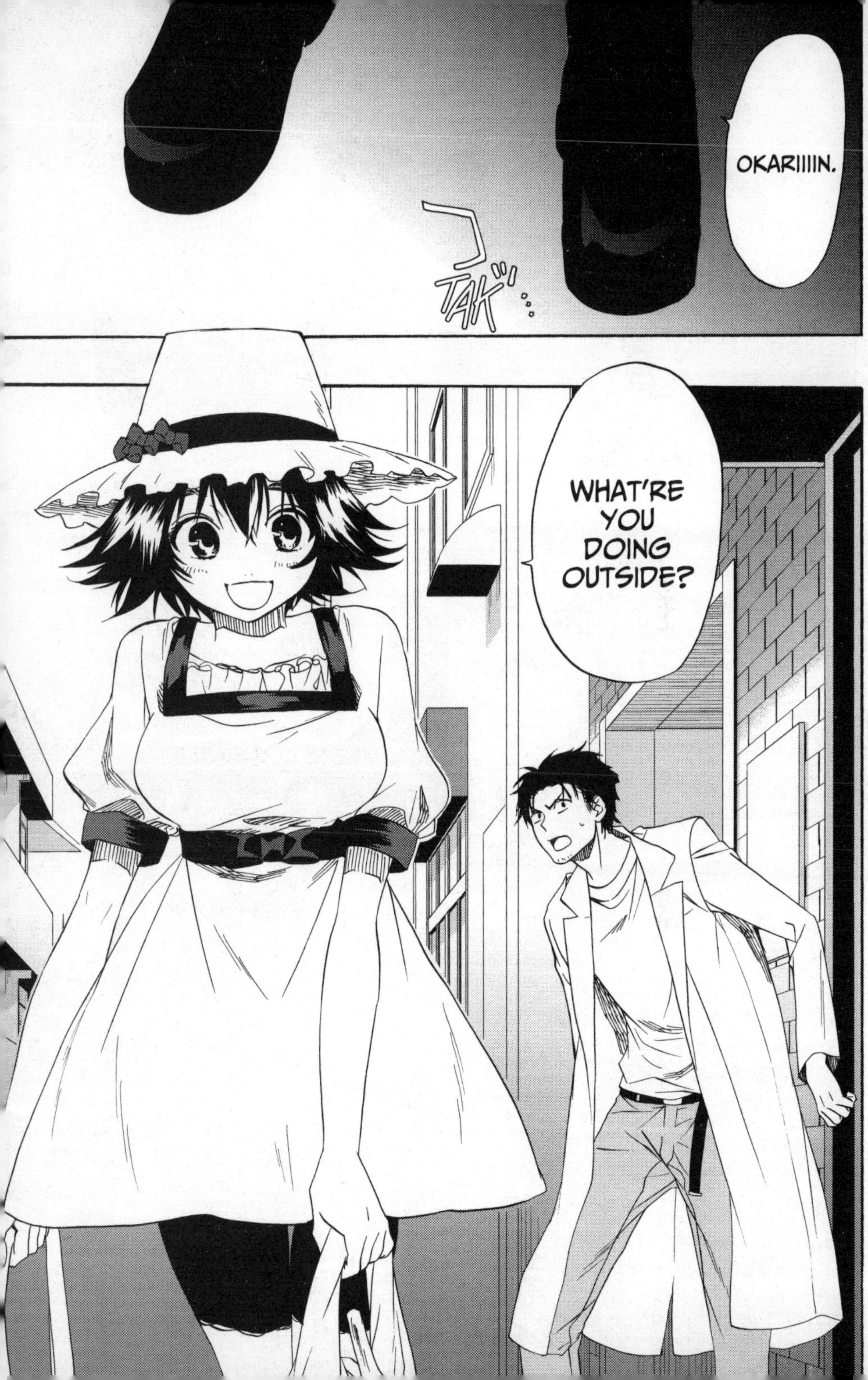
OKARIIIIN.
TAK...
WHAT'RE YOU DOING OUTSIDE?

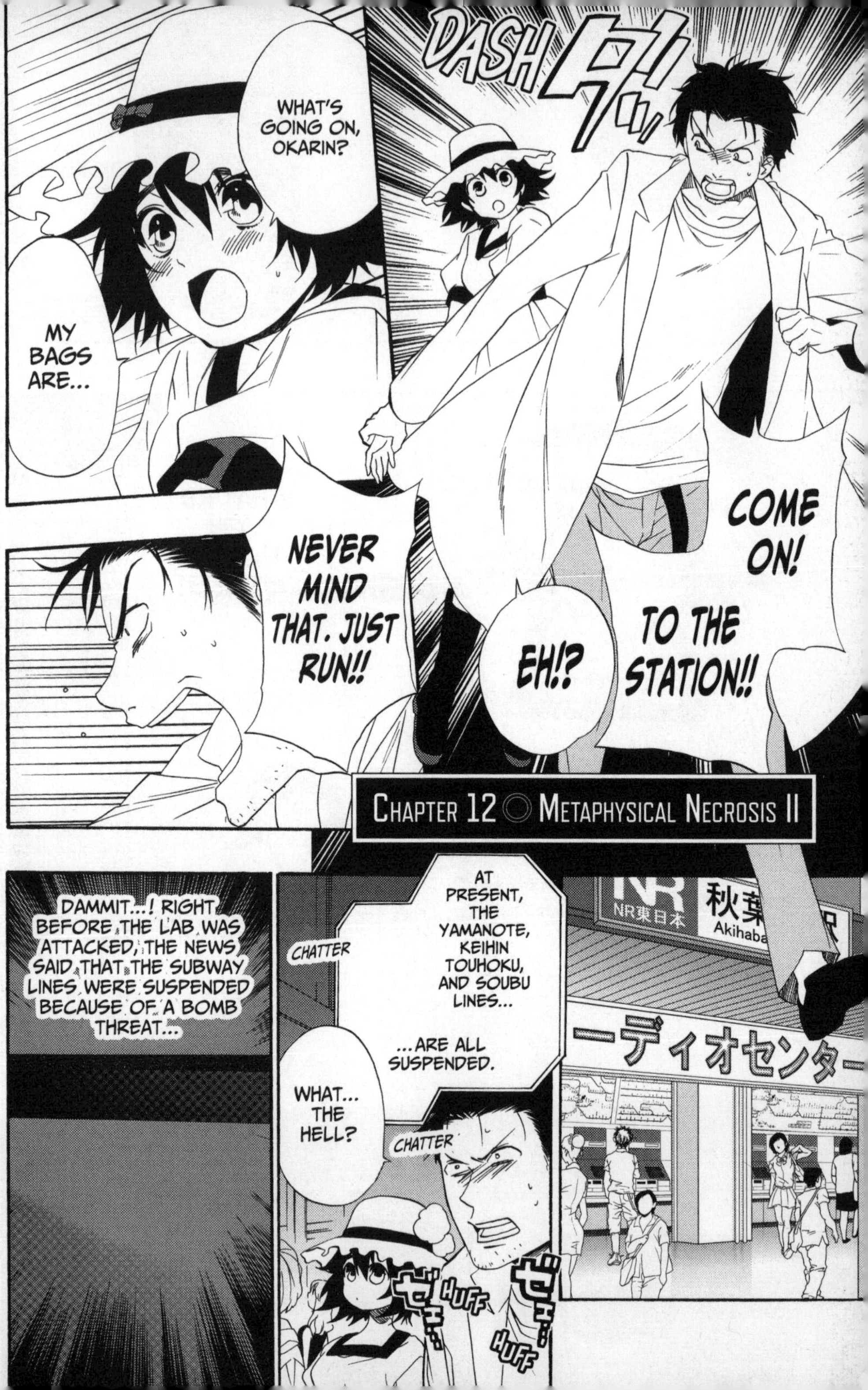
DASH
COME ON!
TO THE STATION!!
EH!?
WHAT'S GOING ON, OKARIN?
MY BAGS ARE...
NEVER MIND THAT. JUST RUN!!
Chapter 12 ◎ Metaphysical Necrosis II
NR
NR東日本
Akihaba
ーディオセンター
AT PRESENT, THE YAMANOTE, KEIHIN TOUHOKU, AND SOUBU LINES...
CHATTER
...ARE ALL SUSPENDED.
WHAT... THE HELL?
CHATTER
HUFF
HUFF
DAMMIT...! RIGHT BEFORE THE LAB WAS ATTACKED, THE NEWS SAID THAT THE SUBWAY LINES WERE SUSPENDED BECAUSE OF A BOMB THREAT...

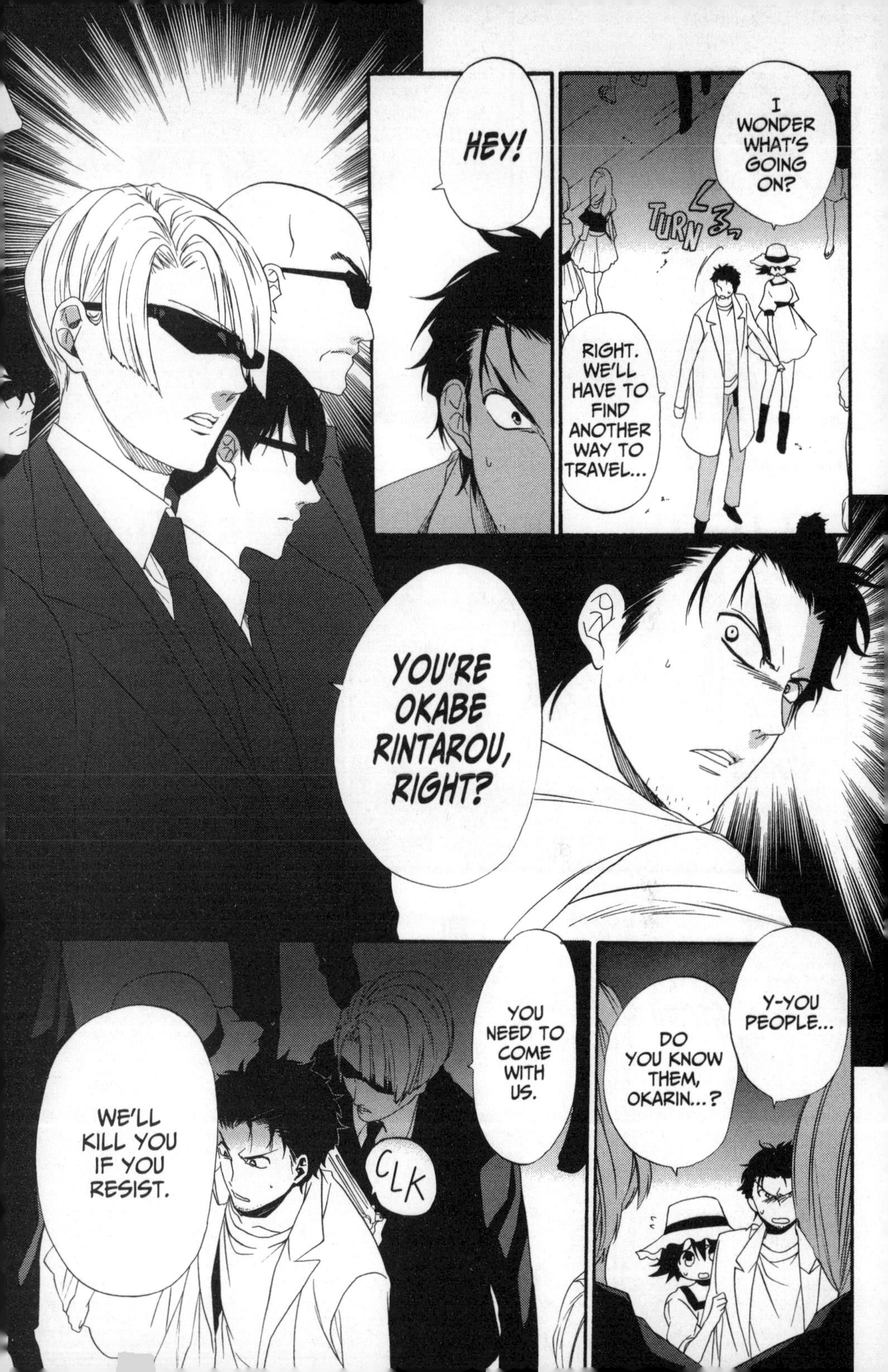
I WONDER WHAT'S GOING ON?
TURN
RIGHT. WE'LL HAVE TO FIND ANOTHER WAY TO TRAVEL...
HEY!
YOU'RE OKABE RINTAROU, RIGHT?
Y-YOU PEOPLE...
DO YOU KNOW THEM, OKARIN...?
YOU NEED TO COME WITH US.
CLK
WE'LL KILL YOU IF YOU RESIST.

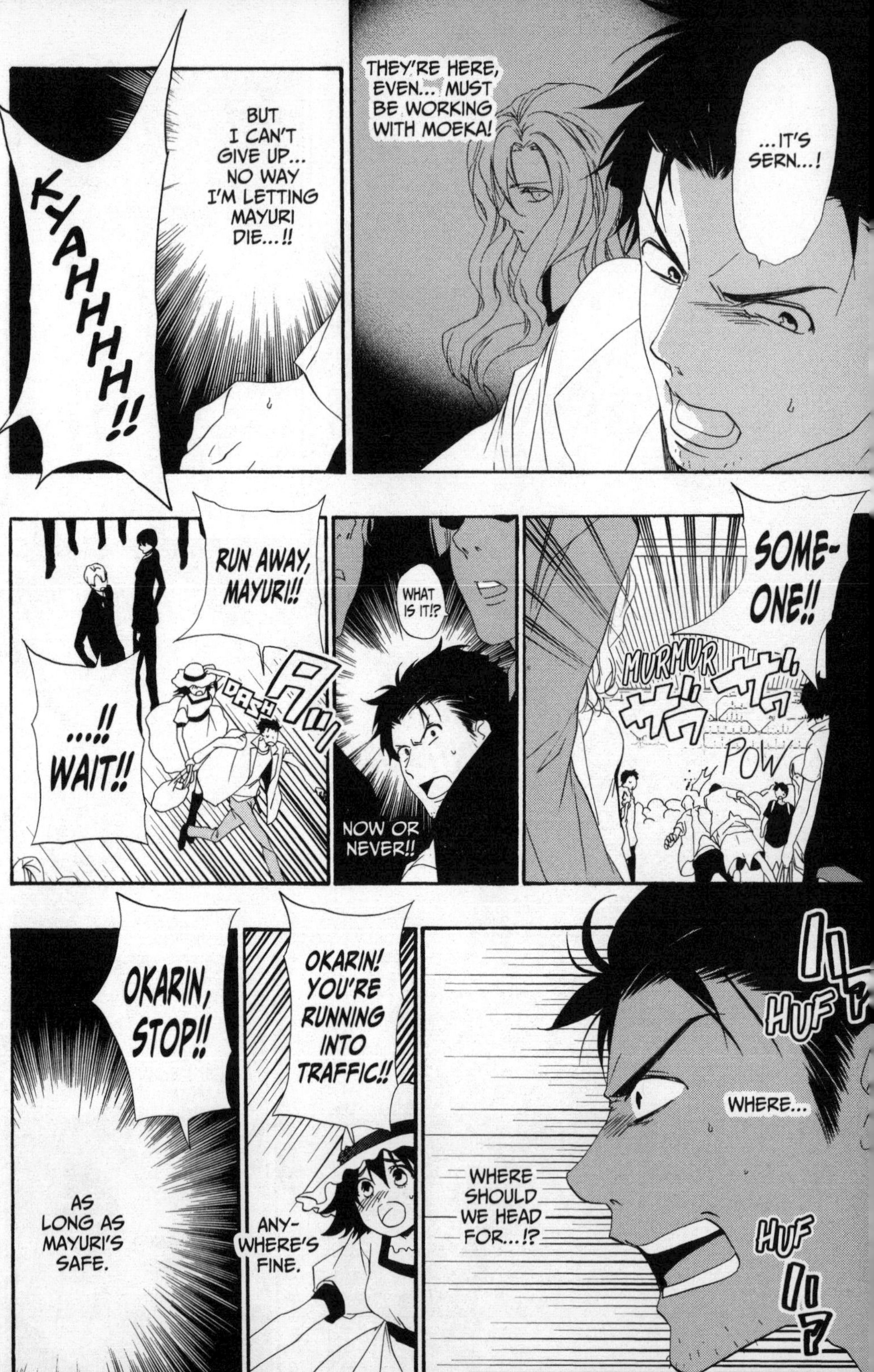
...IT'S SERN...!
THEY'RE HERE, EVEN... MUST BE WORKING WITH MOEKA!
BUT I CAN'T GIVE UP... NO WAY I'M LETTING MAYURI DIE...!!
KYAHHHH!!
SOME-ONE!!
MURMUR
POW
WHAT IS IT!?
NOW OR NEVER!!
RUN AWAY, MAYURI!!
DASH
...!! WAIT!!
HUF
WHERE...
WHERE SHOULD WE HEAD FOR...!?
HUF
OKARIN! YOU'RE RUNNING INTO TRAFFIC!!
ANY-WHERE'S FINE.
OKARIN, STOP!!
AS LONG AS MAYURI'S SAFE.

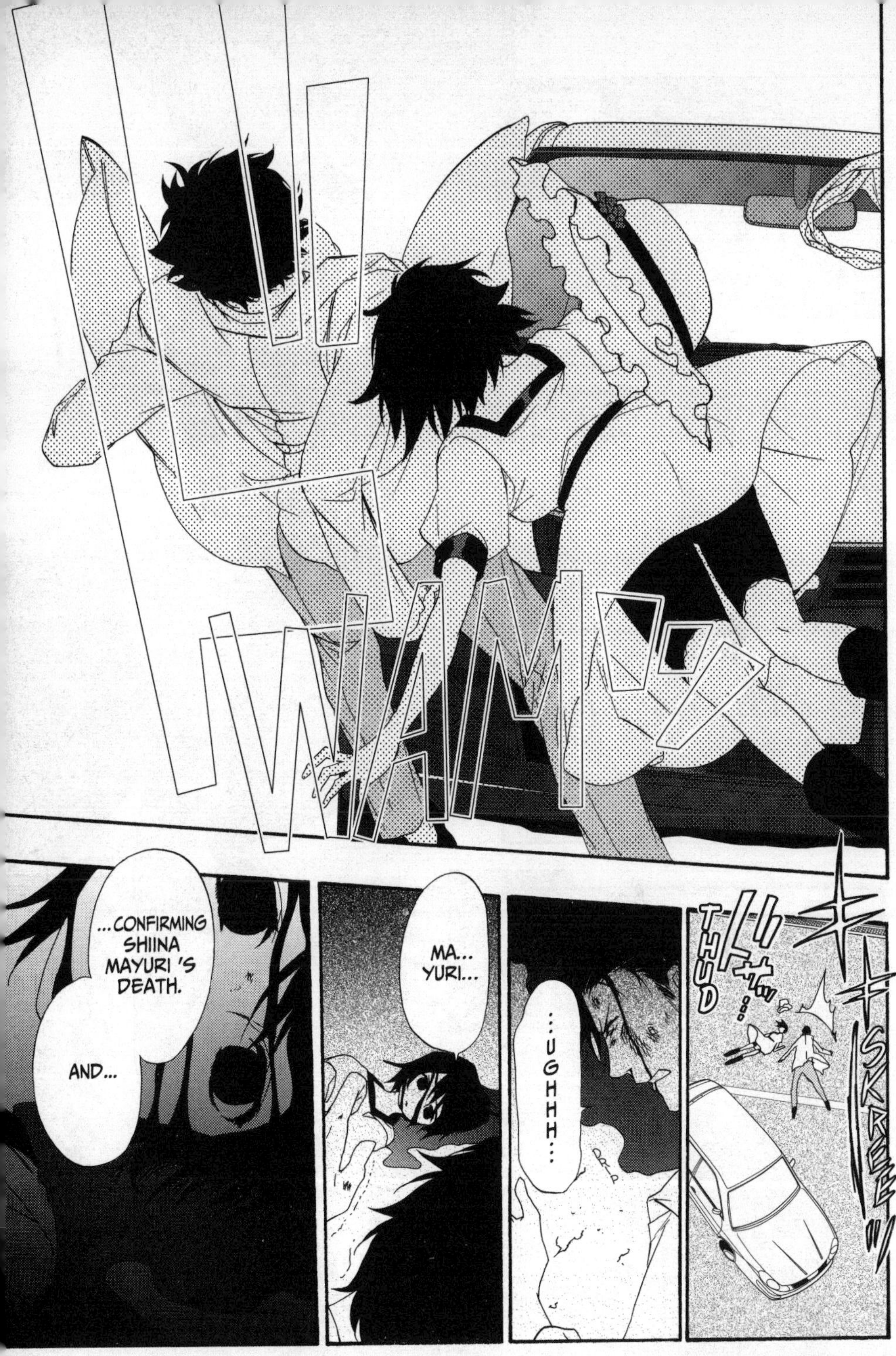
WHAM
SKREE
THUD
...UGHHH...
MA... YURI...
...CONFIRMING SHIINA MAYURI 'S DEATH.
AND...

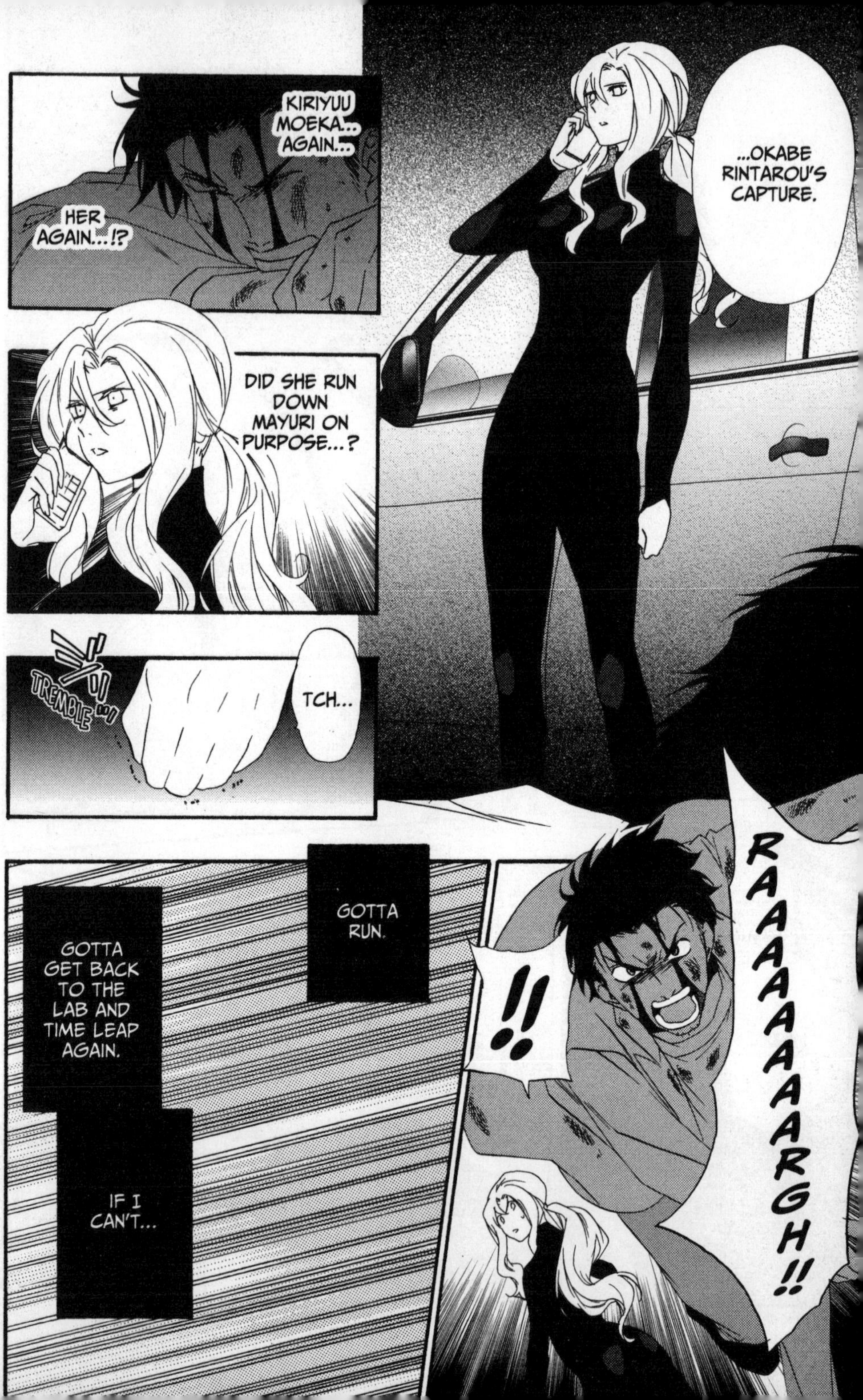
...OKABE RINTAROU'S CAPTURE.
KIRIYUU MOEKA... AGAIN...
HER AGAIN...!?
DID SHE RUN DOWN MAYURI ON PURPOSE...?
TREMBLE
TCH...
RAAAAAAAARGH!!
!!
GOTTA RUN.
GOTTA GET BACK TO THE LAB AND TIME LEAP AGAIN.
IF I CAN'T...

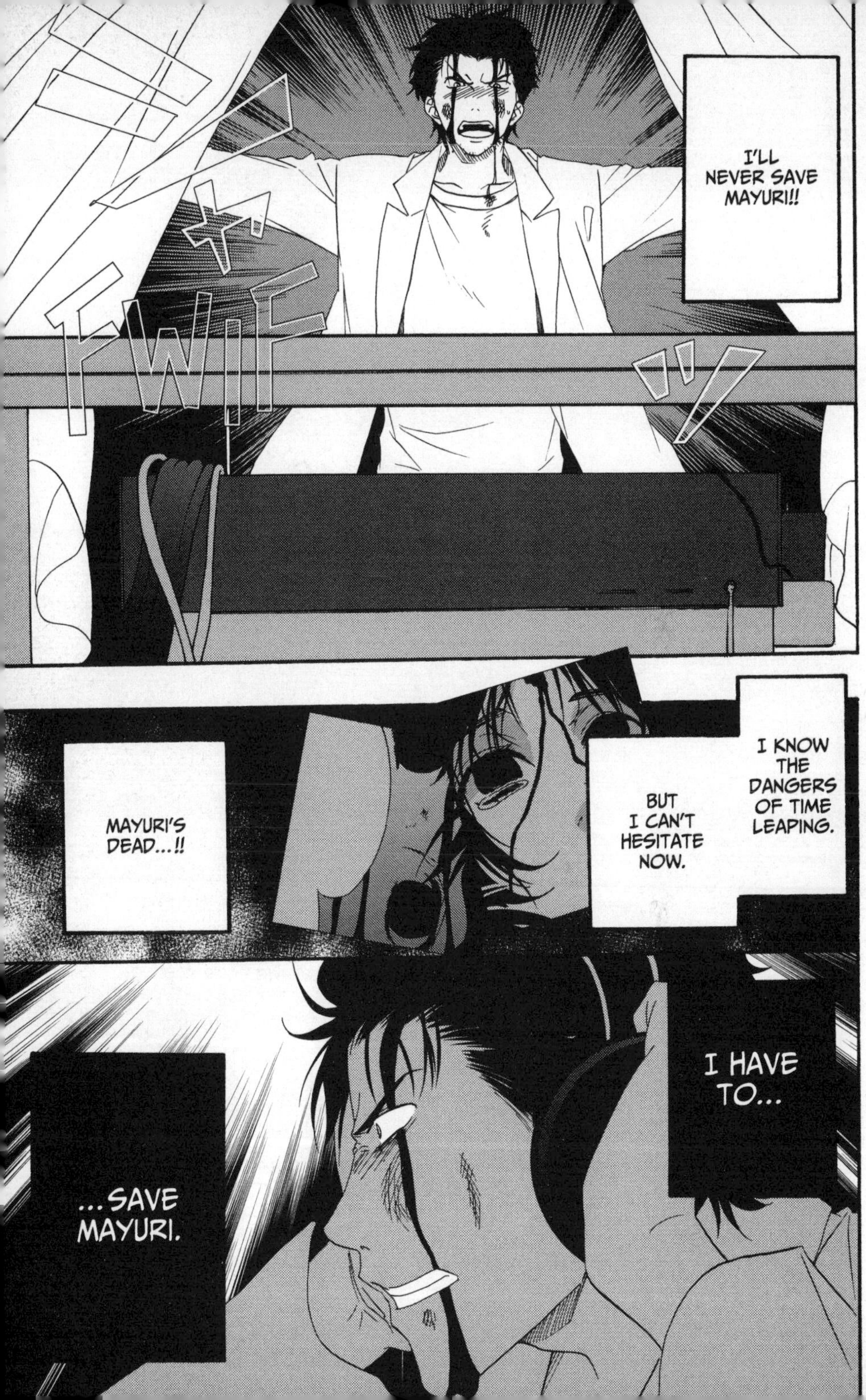
I'LL NEVER SAVE MAYURI!!
FWIP
I KNOW THE DANGERS OF TIME LEAPING.
BUT I CAN'T HESITATE NOW.
MAYURI'S DEAD...!!
I HAVE TO...
...SAVE MAYURI.

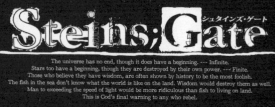

The universe has no end, though it does have a beginning. --- Infinite.
Stars too have a beginning, though they are destroyed by their own power. --- Finite.
Those who believe they have wisdom, are often shown by history to be the most foolish.
The fish in the sea don't know what the world is like on the land. Wisdom would destroy them as well.
Man to exceeding the speed of light would be more ridiculous than fish to living on land.
This is God's final warning to any who rebel.

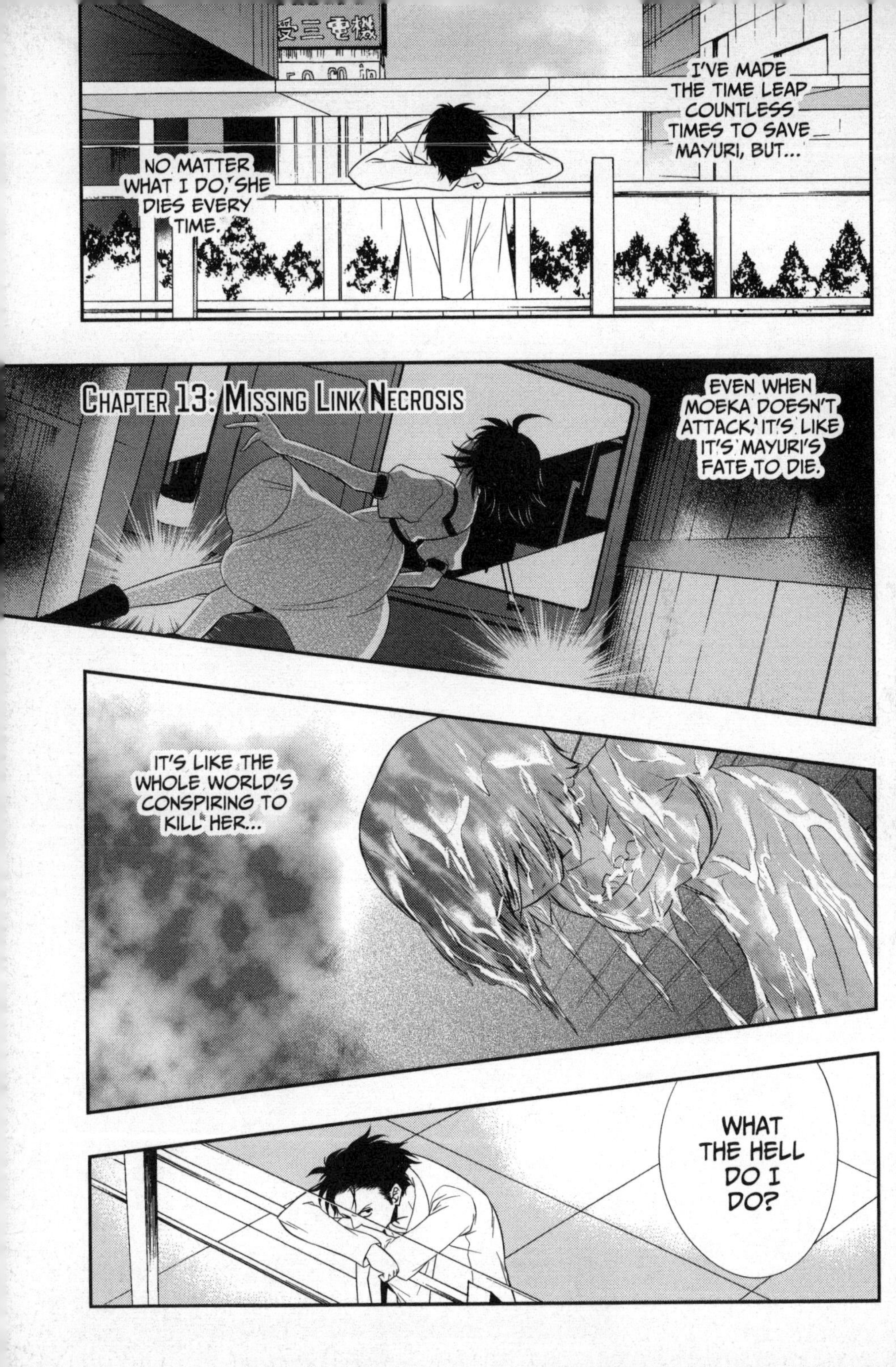

I'VE MADE THE TIME LEAP COUNTLESS TIMES TO SAVE MAYURI, BUT...
NO MATTER WHAT I DO, SHE DIES EVERY TIME.
EVEN WHEN MOEKA DOESN'T ATTACK, IT'S LIKE IT'S MAYURI'S FATE TO DIE.
CHAPTER 13: MISSING LINK NECROSIS
IT'S LIKE THE WHOLE WORLD'S CONSPIRING TO KILL HER...
WHAT THE HELL DO I DO?

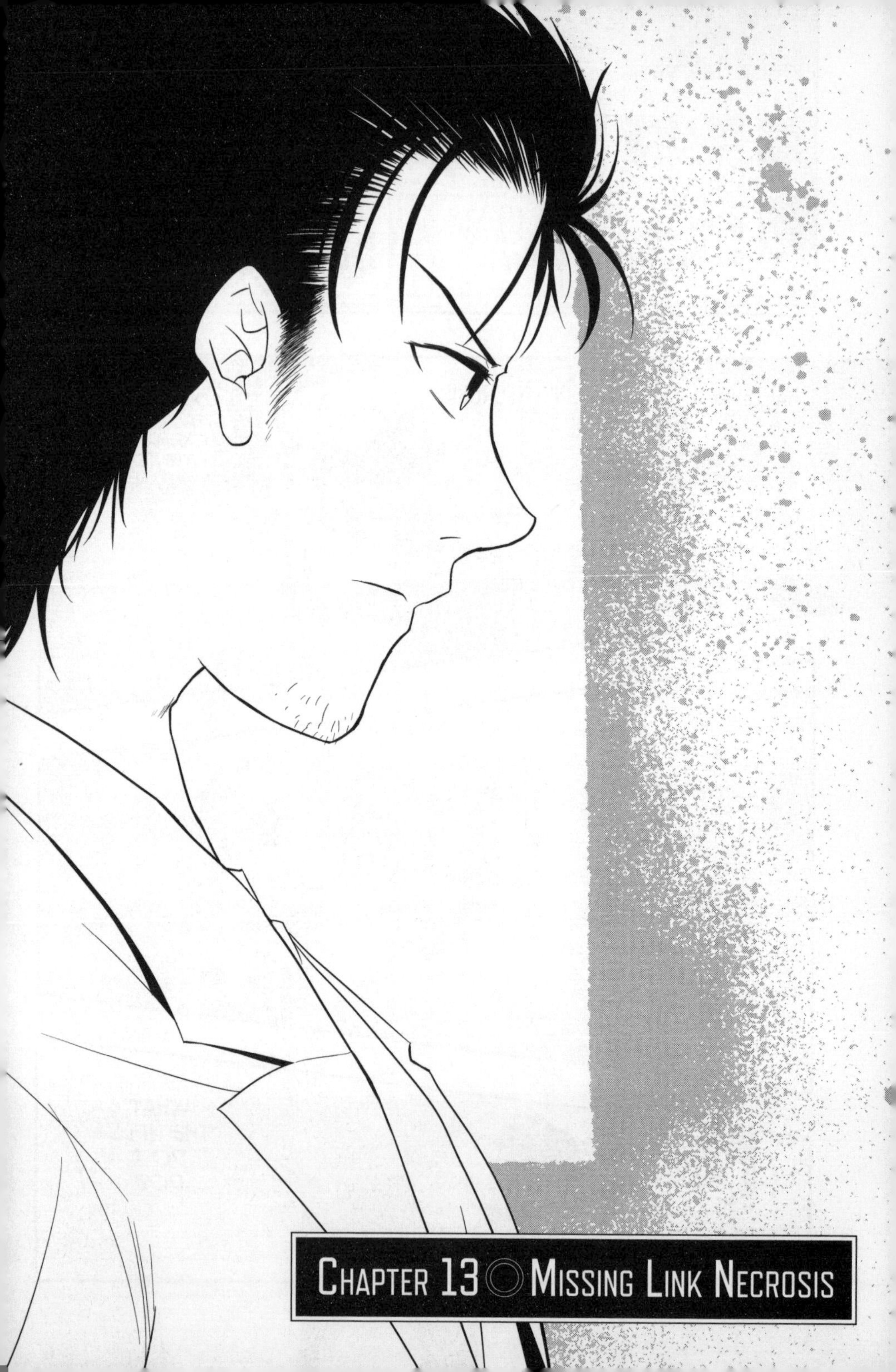

Chapter 13 ◎ Missing Link Necrosis

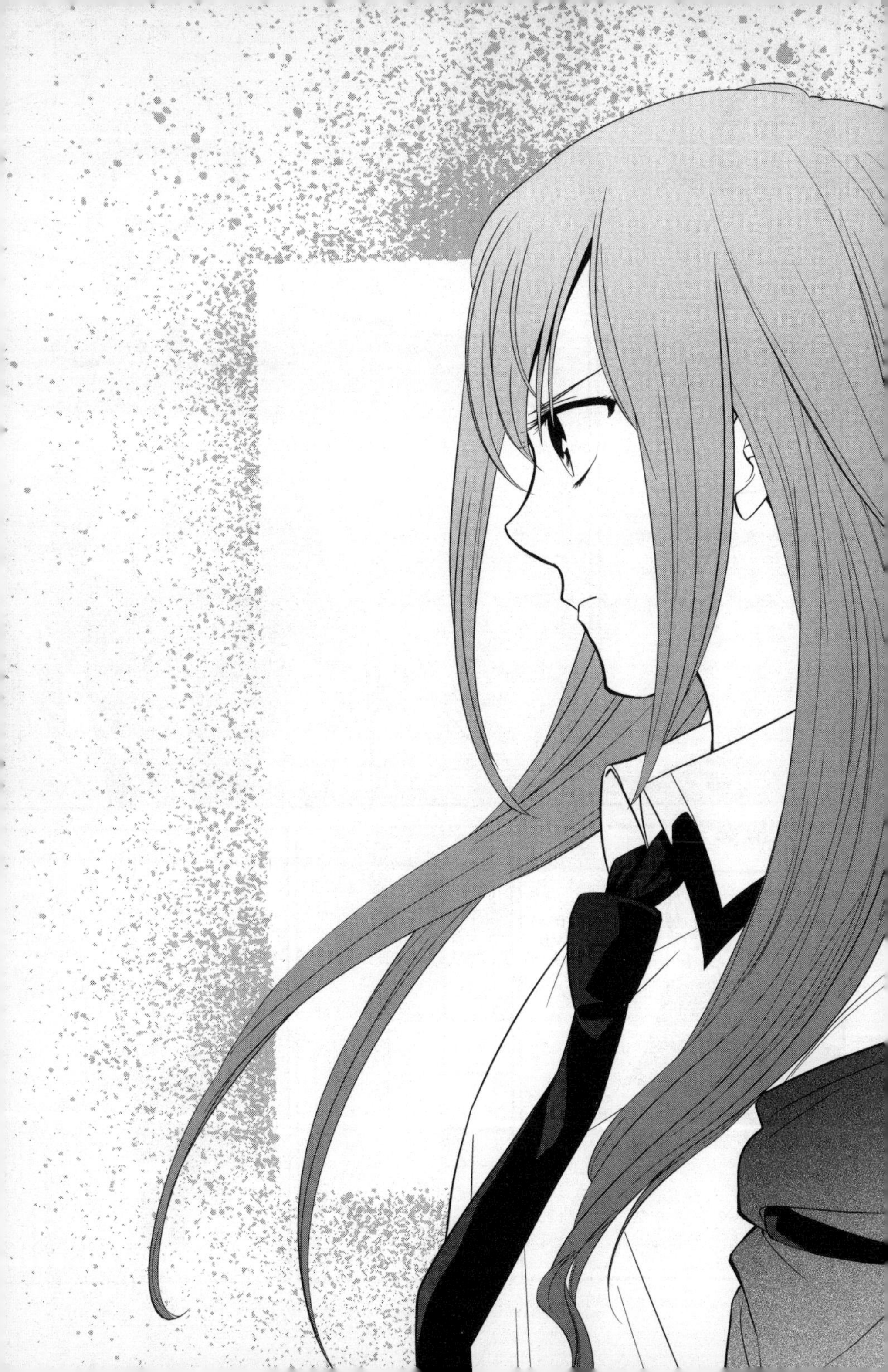

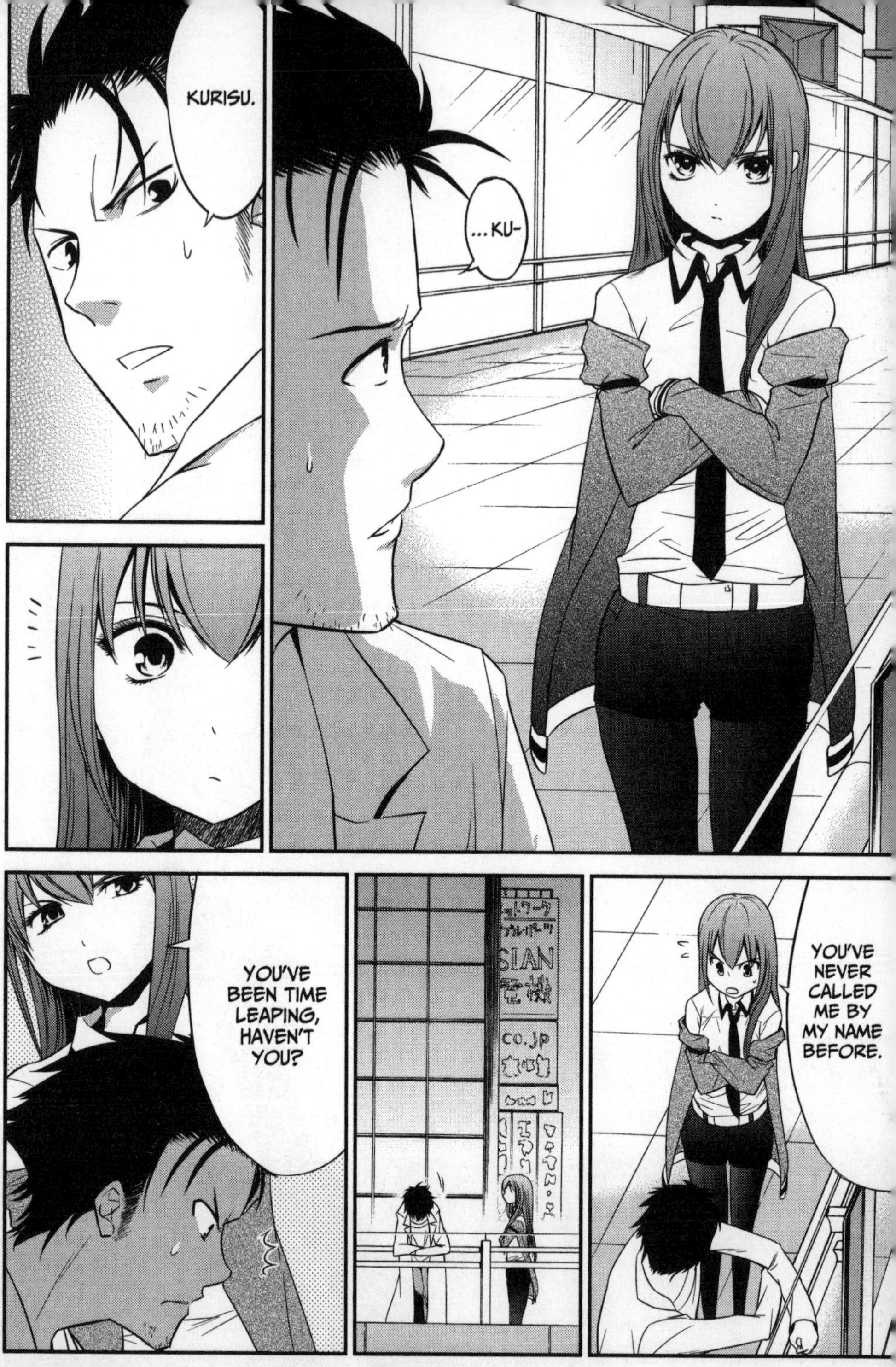
...KU-
KURISU.
YOU'VE NEVER CALLED ME BY MY NAME BEFORE.
YOU'VE BEEN TIME LEAPING, HAVEN'T YOU?

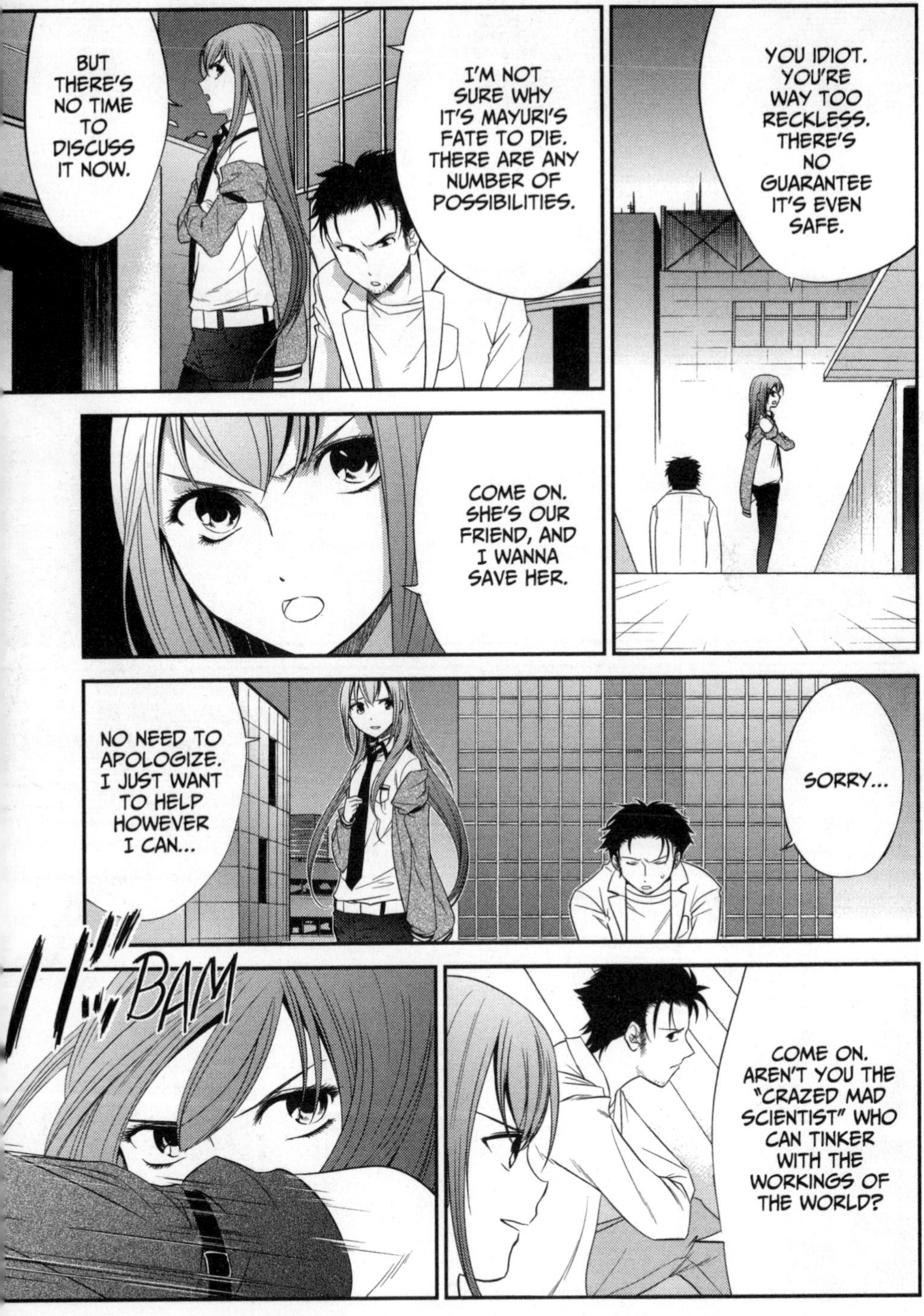
YOU IDIOT. YOU'RE WAY TOO RECKLESS. THERE'S NO GUARANTEE IT'S EVEN SAFE.
I'M NOT SURE WHY IT'S MAYURI'S FATE TO DIE. THERE ARE ANY NUMBER OF POSSIBILITIES.
BUT THERE'S NO TIME TO DISCUSS IT NOW.
COME ON. SHE'S OUR FRIEND, AND I WANNA SAVE HER.
SORRY...
NO NEED TO APOLOGIZE. I JUST WANT TO HELP HOWEVER I CAN...
COME ON. AREN'T YOU THE "CRAZED MAD SCIENTIST" WHO CAN TINKER WITH THE WORKINGS OF THE WORLD?
BAM

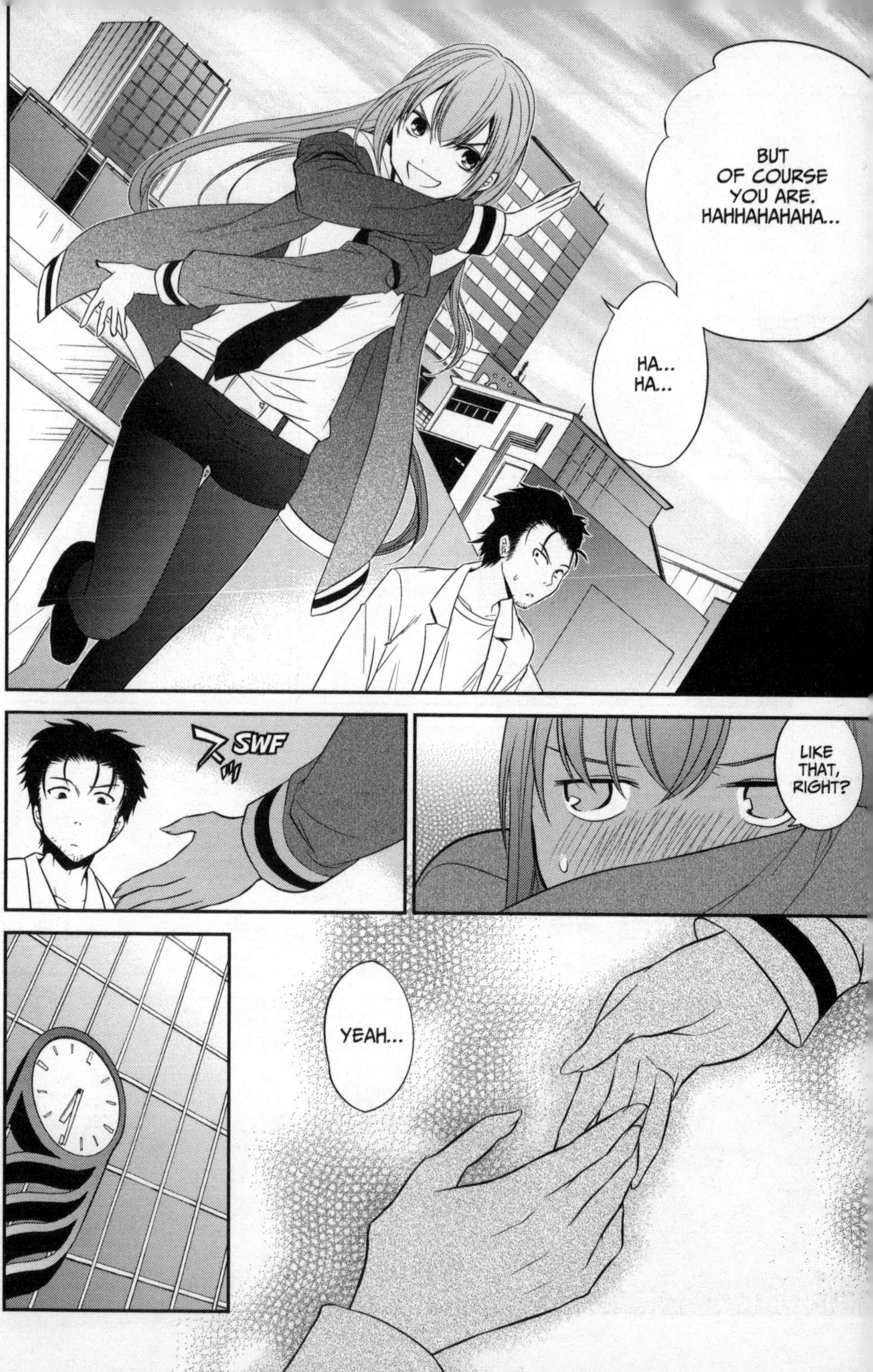
BUT OF COURSE YOU ARE. HAHHAHAHAHA...
HA... HA...
LIKE THAT, RIGHT?
SWF
YEAH...

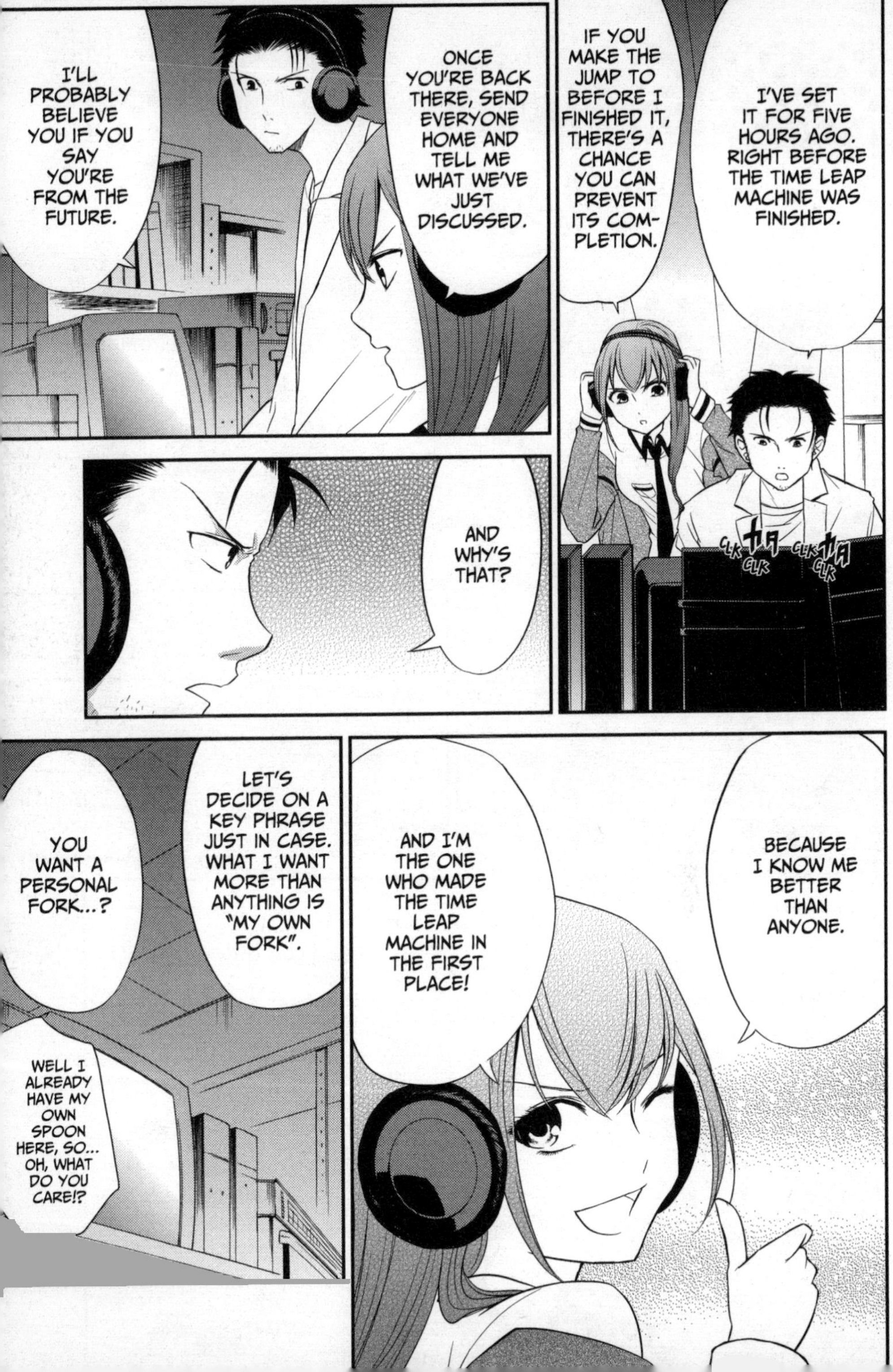
I'VE SET IT FOR FIVE HOURS AGO. RIGHT BEFORE THE TIME LEAP MACHINE WAS FINISHED.
IF YOU MAKE THE JUMP TO BEFORE I FINISHED IT, THERE'S A CHANCE YOU CAN PREVENT ITS COMPLETION.
カタ CLK CLK
カタ CLK CLK
ONCE YOU'RE BACK THERE, SEND EVERYONE HOME AND TELL ME WHAT WE'VE JUST DISCUSSED.
I'LL PROBABLY BELIEVE YOU IF YOU SAY YOU'RE FROM THE FUTURE.
AND WHY'S THAT?
BECAUSE I KNOW ME BETTER THAN ANYONE.
AND I'M THE ONE WHO MADE THE TIME LEAP MACHINE IN THE FIRST PLACE!
LET'S DECIDE ON A KEY PHRASE JUST IN CASE. WHAT I WANT MORE THAN ANYTHING IS "MY OWN FORK".
YOU WANT A PERSONAL FORK...?
WELL I ALREADY HAVE MY OWN SPOON HERE, SO... OH, WHAT DO YOU CARE!?

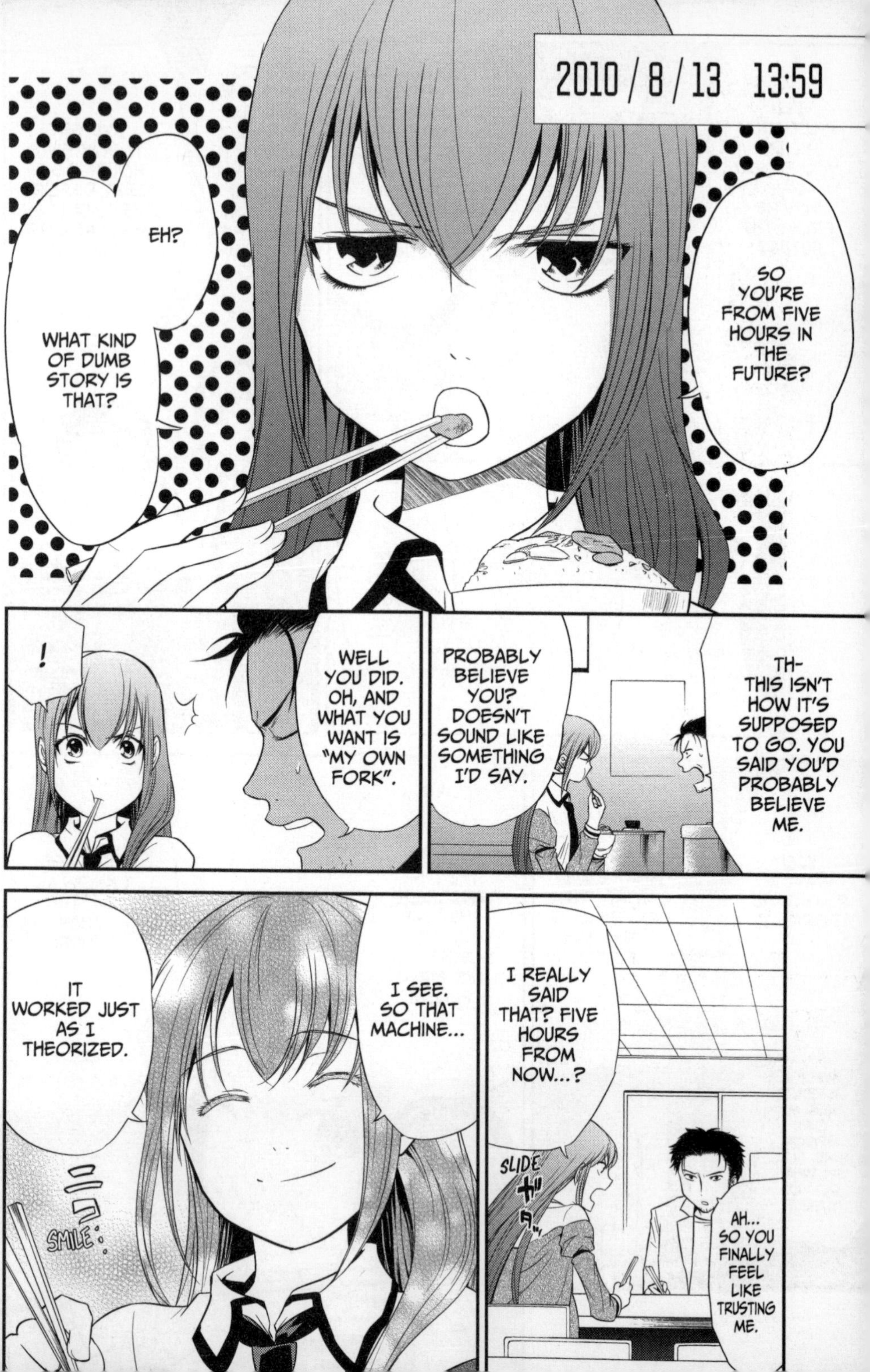
2010 / 8 / 13 13:59
SO YOU'RE FROM FIVE HOURS IN THE FUTURE?
EH? WHAT KIND OF DUMB STORY IS THAT?
TH- THIS ISN'T HOW IT'S SUPPOSED TO GO. YOU SAID YOU'D PROBABLY BELIEVE ME.
PROBABLY BELIEVE YOU? DOESN'T SOUND LIKE SOMETHING I'D SAY.
WELL YOU DID. OH, AND WHAT YOU WANT IS "MY OWN FORK".
!
I REALLY SAID THAT? FIVE HOURS FROM NOW...?
SLIDE
AH... SO YOU FINALLY FEEL LIKE TRUSTING ME.
I SEE. SO THAT MACHINE...
IT WORKED JUST AS I THEORIZED.
SMILE

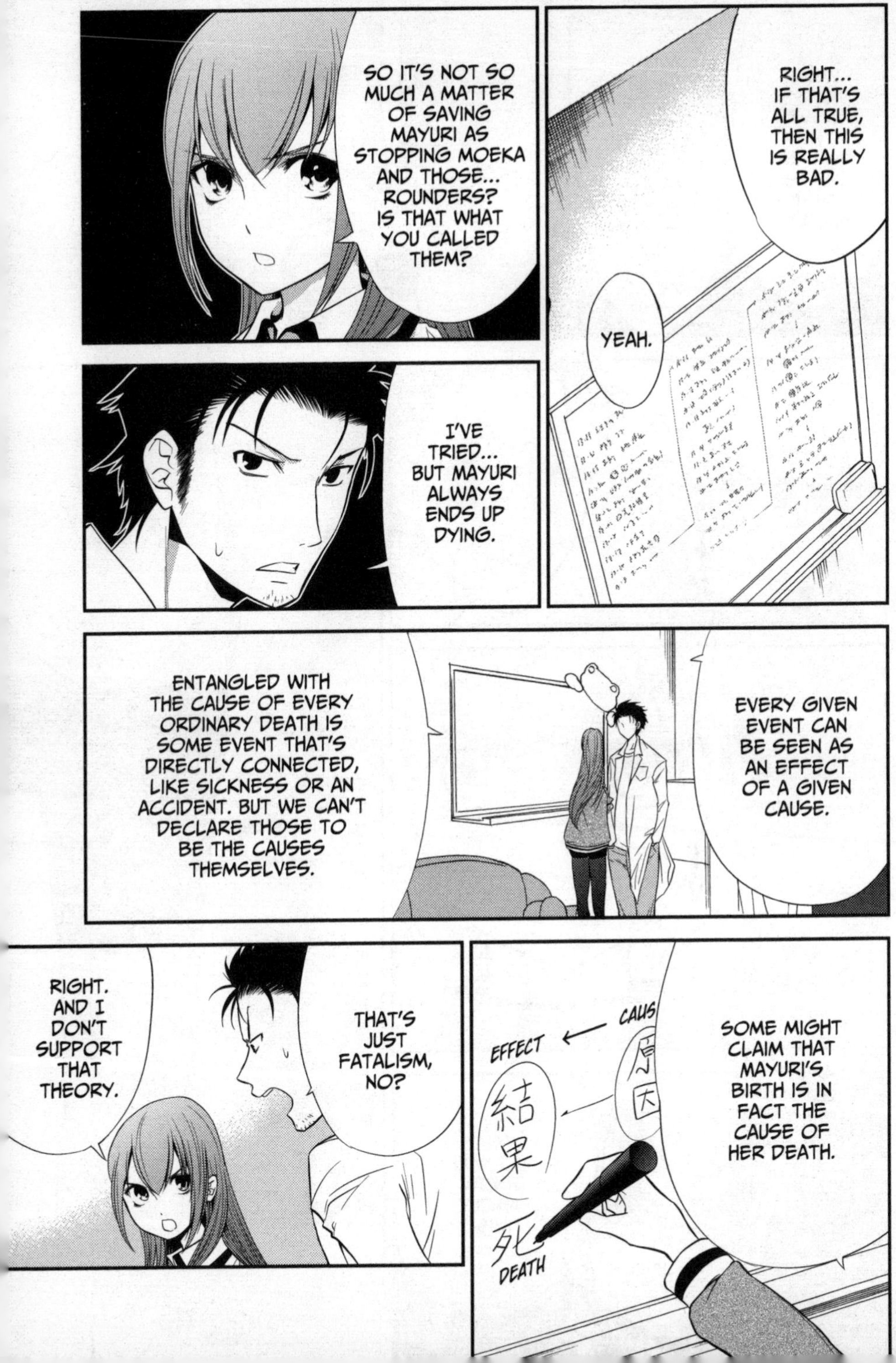
RIGHT... IF THAT'S ALL TRUE, THEN THIS IS REALLY BAD.
YEAH.
SO IT'S NOT SO MUCH A MATTER OF SAVING MAYURI AS STOPPING MOEKA AND THOSE... ROUNDERS? IS THAT WHAT YOU CALLED THEM?
I'VE TRIED... BUT MAYURI ALWAYS ENDS UP DYING.
EVERY GIVEN EVENT CAN BE SEEN AS AN EFFECT OF A GIVEN CAUSE.
ENTANGLED WITH THE CAUSE OF EVERY ORDINARY DEATH IS SOME EVENT THAT'S DIRECTLY CONNECTED, LIKE SICKNESS OR AN ACCIDENT. BUT WE CAN'T DECLARE THOSE TO BE THE CAUSES THEMSELVES.
SOME MIGHT CLAIM THAT MAYURI'S BIRTH IS IN FACT THE CAUSE OF HER DEATH.
CAUS
原因
EFFECT
結果
死
DEATH
THAT'S JUST FATALISM, NO?
RIGHT. AND I DON'T SUPPORT THAT THEORY.

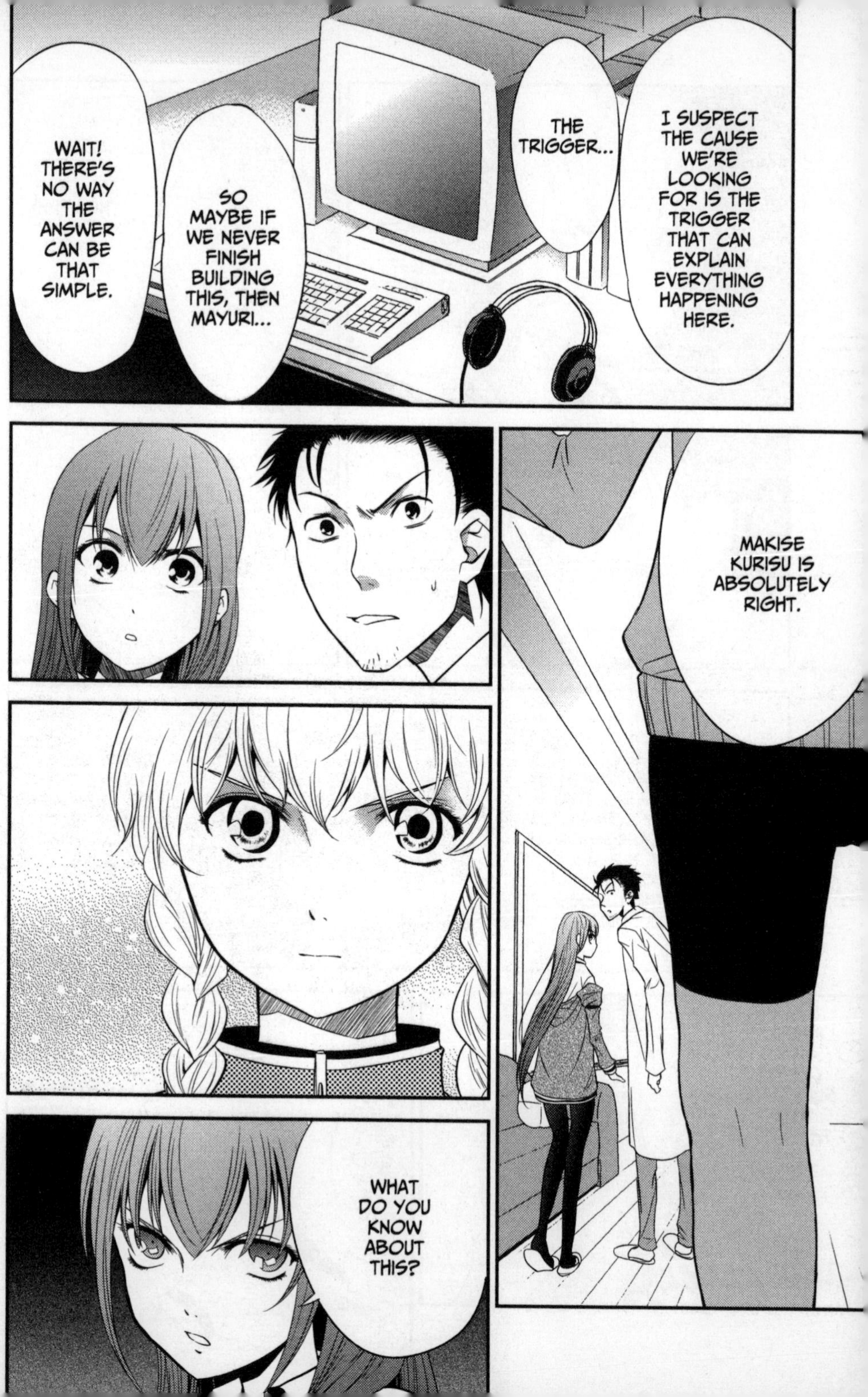
I SUSPECT THE CAUSE WE'RE LOOKING FOR IS THE TRIGGER THAT CAN EXPLAIN EVERYTHING HAPPENING HERE.
THE TRIGGER...
SO MAYBE IF WE NEVER FINISH BUILDING THIS, THEN MAYURI...
WAIT! THERE'S NO WAY THE ANSWER CAN BE THAT SIMPLE.
MAKISE KURISU IS ABSOLUTELY RIGHT.
WHAT DO YOU KNOW ABOUT THIS?

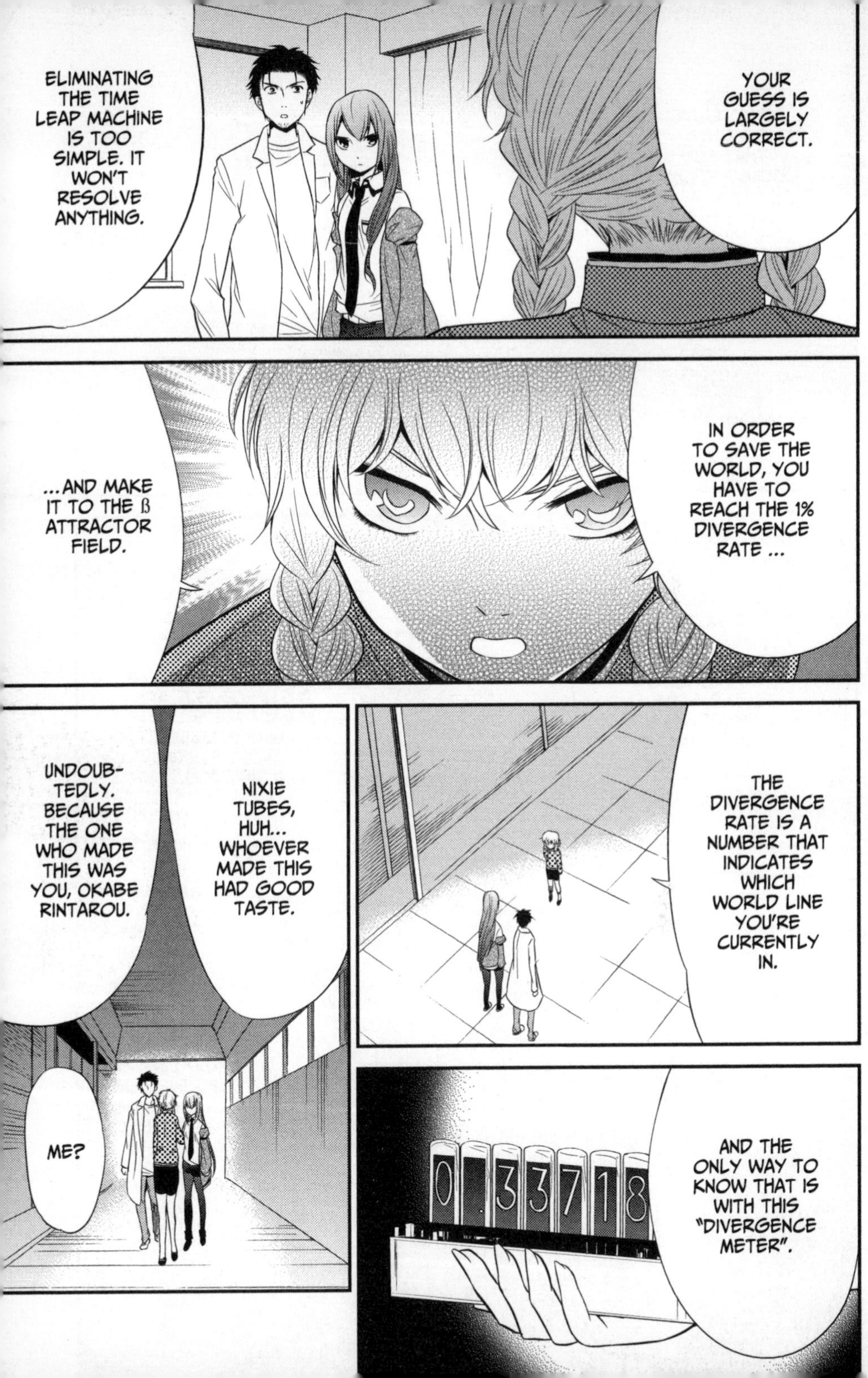

YOUR GUESS IS LARGELY CORRECT.
ELIMINATING THE TIME LEAP MACHINE IS TOO SIMPLE. IT WON'T RESOLVE ANYTHING.
IN ORDER TO SAVE THE WORLD, YOU HAVE TO REACH THE 1% DIVERGENCE RATE ...
...AND MAKE IT TO THE ß ATTRACTOR FIELD.
THE DIVERGENCE RATE IS A NUMBER THAT INDICATES WHICH WORLD LINE YOU'RE CURRENTLY IN.
AND THE ONLY WAY TO KNOW THAT IS WITH THIS "DIVERGENCE METER".
NIXIE TUBES, HUH... WHOEVER MADE THIS HAD GOOD TASTE.
UNDOUB-TEDLY. BECAUSE THE ONE WHO MADE THIS WAS YOU, OKABE RINTAROU.
ME?

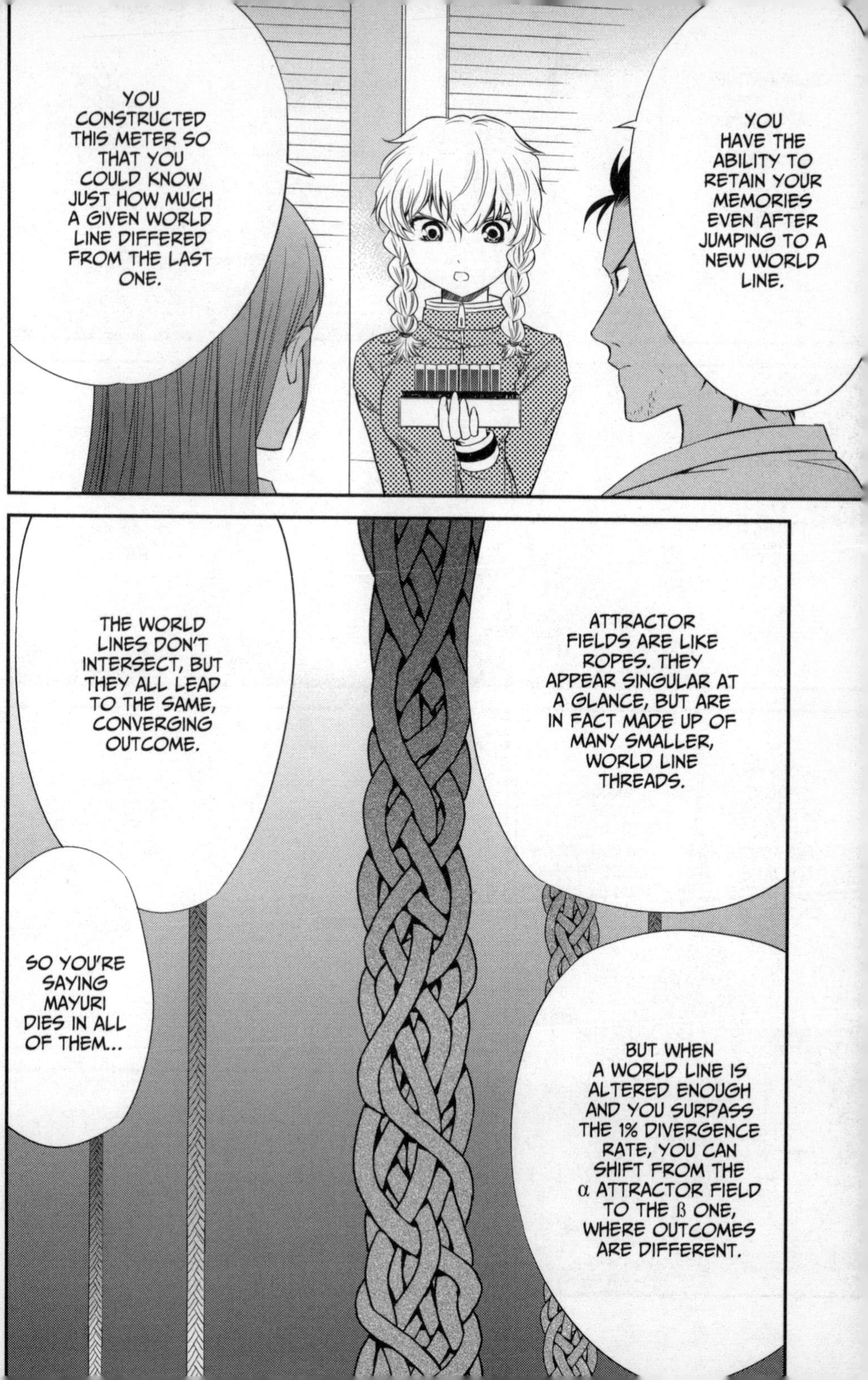
YOU HAVE THE ABILITY TO RETAIN YOUR MEMORIES EVEN AFTER JUMPING TO A NEW WORLD LINE.
YOU CONSTRUCTED THIS METER SO THAT YOU COULD KNOW JUST HOW MUCH A GIVEN WORLD LINE DIFFERED FROM THE LAST ONE.
ATTRACTOR FIELDS ARE LIKE ROPES. THEY APPEAR SINGULAR AT A GLANCE, BUT ARE IN FACT MADE UP OF MANY SMALLER, WORLD LINE THREADS.
THE WORLD LINES DON'T INTERSECT, BUT THEY ALL LEAD TO THE SAME, CONVERGING OUTCOME.
BUT WHEN A WORLD LINE IS ALTERED ENOUGH AND YOU SURPASS THE 1% DIVERGENCE RATE, YOU CAN SHIFT FROM THE α ATTRACTOR FIELD TO THE ß ONE, WHERE OUTCOMES ARE DIFFERENT.
SO YOU'RE SAYING MAYURI DIES IN ALL OF THEM...

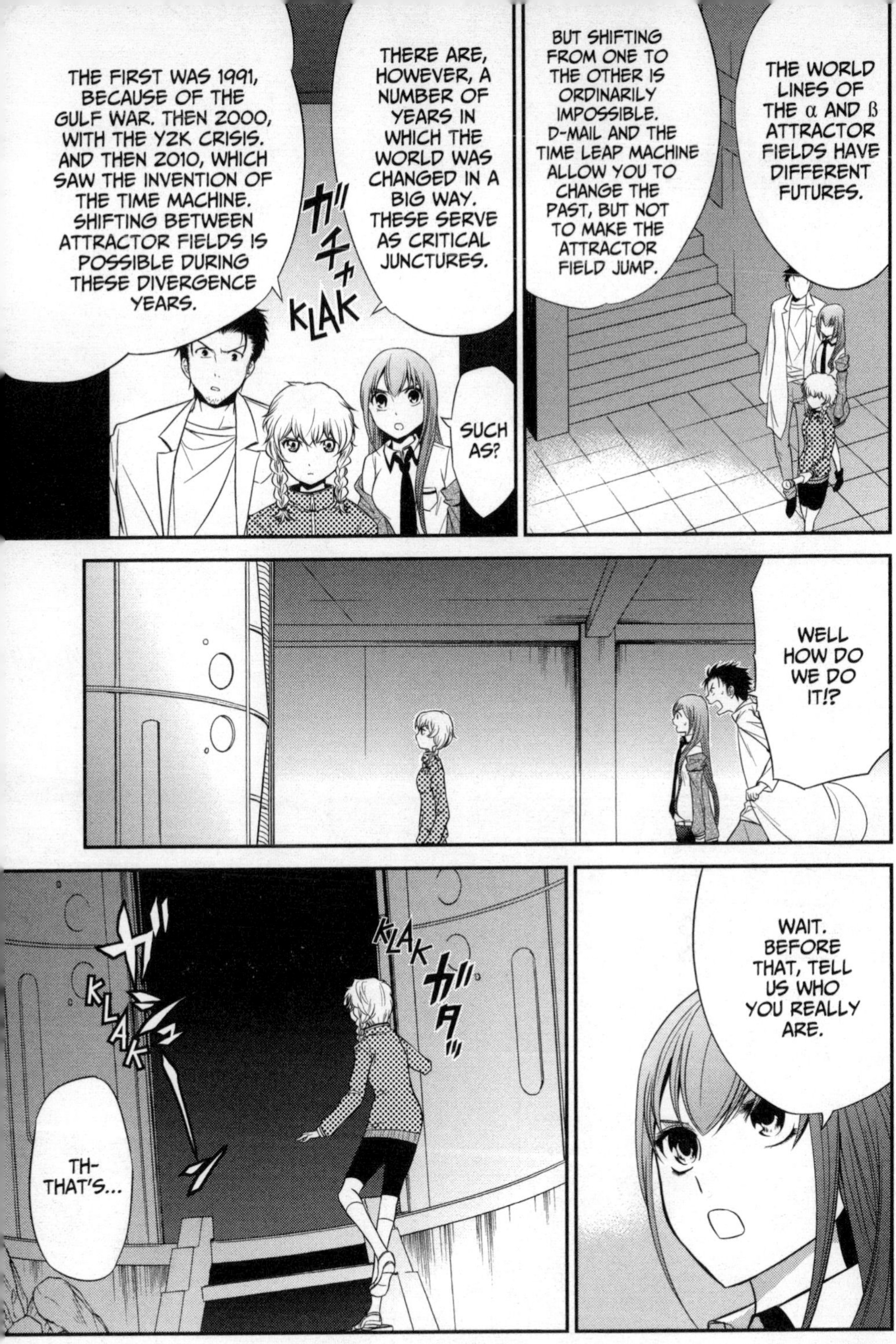
THE WORLD LINES OF THE α AND β ATTRACTOR FIELDS HAVE DIFFERENT FUTURES.
BUT SHIFTING FROM ONE TO THE OTHER IS ORDINARILY IMPOSSIBLE. D-MAIL AND THE TIME LEAP MACHINE ALLOW YOU TO CHANGE THE PAST, BUT NOT TO MAKE THE ATTRACTOR FIELD JUMP.
THERE ARE, HOWEVER, A NUMBER OF YEARS IN WHICH THE WORLD WAS CHANGED IN A BIG WAY. THESE SERVE AS CRITICAL JUNCTURES.
KLAK
SUCH AS?
THE FIRST WAS 1991, BECAUSE OF THE GULF WAR. THEN 2000, WITH THE Y2K CRISIS. AND THEN 2010, WHICH SAW THE INVENTION OF THE TIME MACHINE. SHIFTING BETWEEN ATTRACTOR FIELDS IS POSSIBLE DURING THESE DIVERGENCE YEARS.
WELL HOW DO WE DO IT!?
WAIT. BEFORE THAT, TELL US WHO YOU REALLY ARE.
KLAK
KLAK
TH- THAT'S...

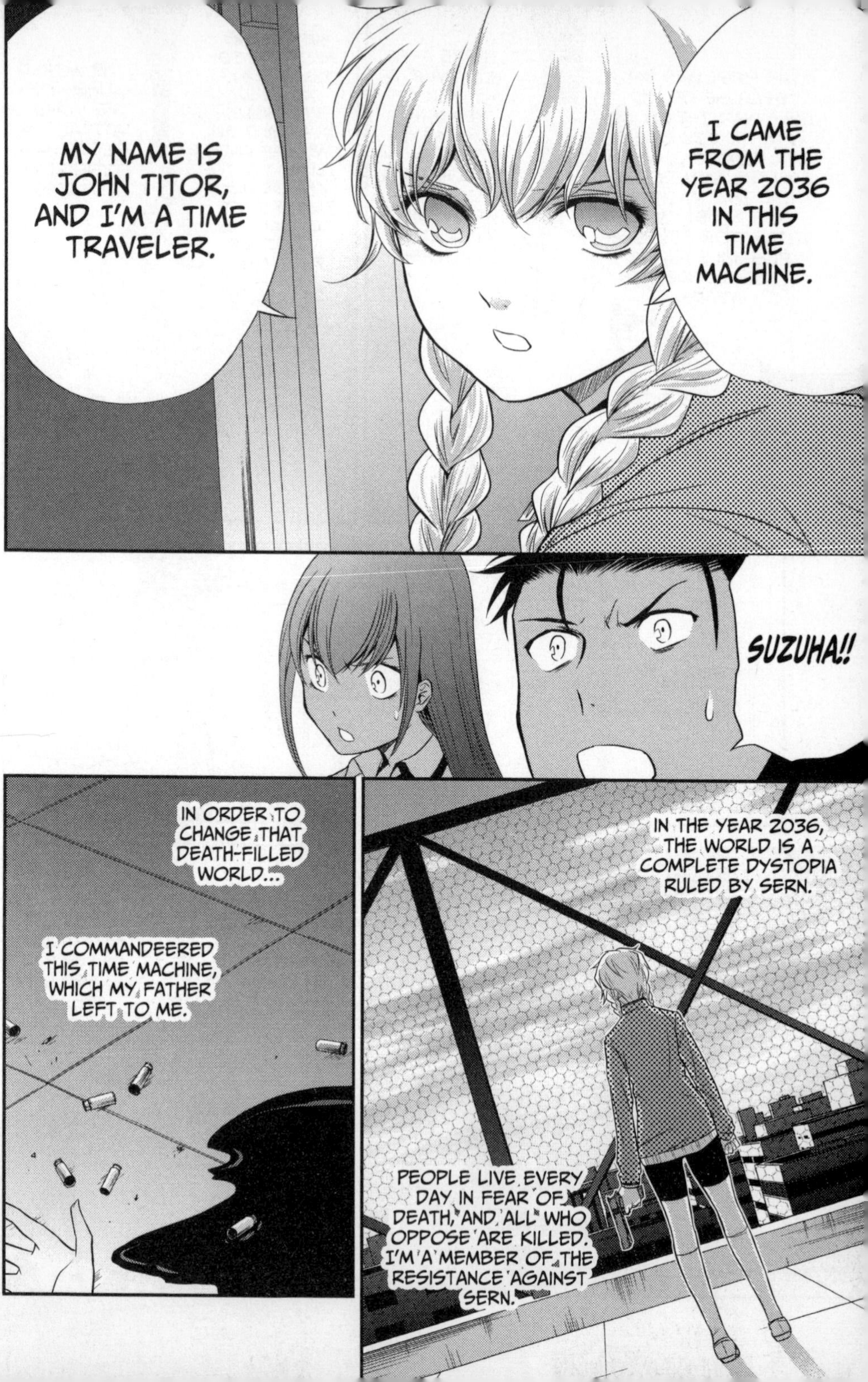
I CAME FROM THE YEAR 2036 IN THIS TIME MACHINE.
MY NAME IS JOHN TITOR, AND I'M A TIME TRAVELER.
SUZUHA!!
IN THE YEAR 2036, THE WORLD IS A COMPLETE DYSTOPIA RULED BY SERN.
PEOPLE LIVE EVERY DAY IN FEAR OF DEATH, AND ALL WHO OPPOSE ARE KILLED. I'M A MEMBER OF THE RESISTANCE AGAINST SERN.
IN ORDER TO CHANGE THAT DEATH-FILLED WORLD...
I COMMANDEERED THIS TIME MACHINE, WHICH MY FATHER LEFT TO ME.

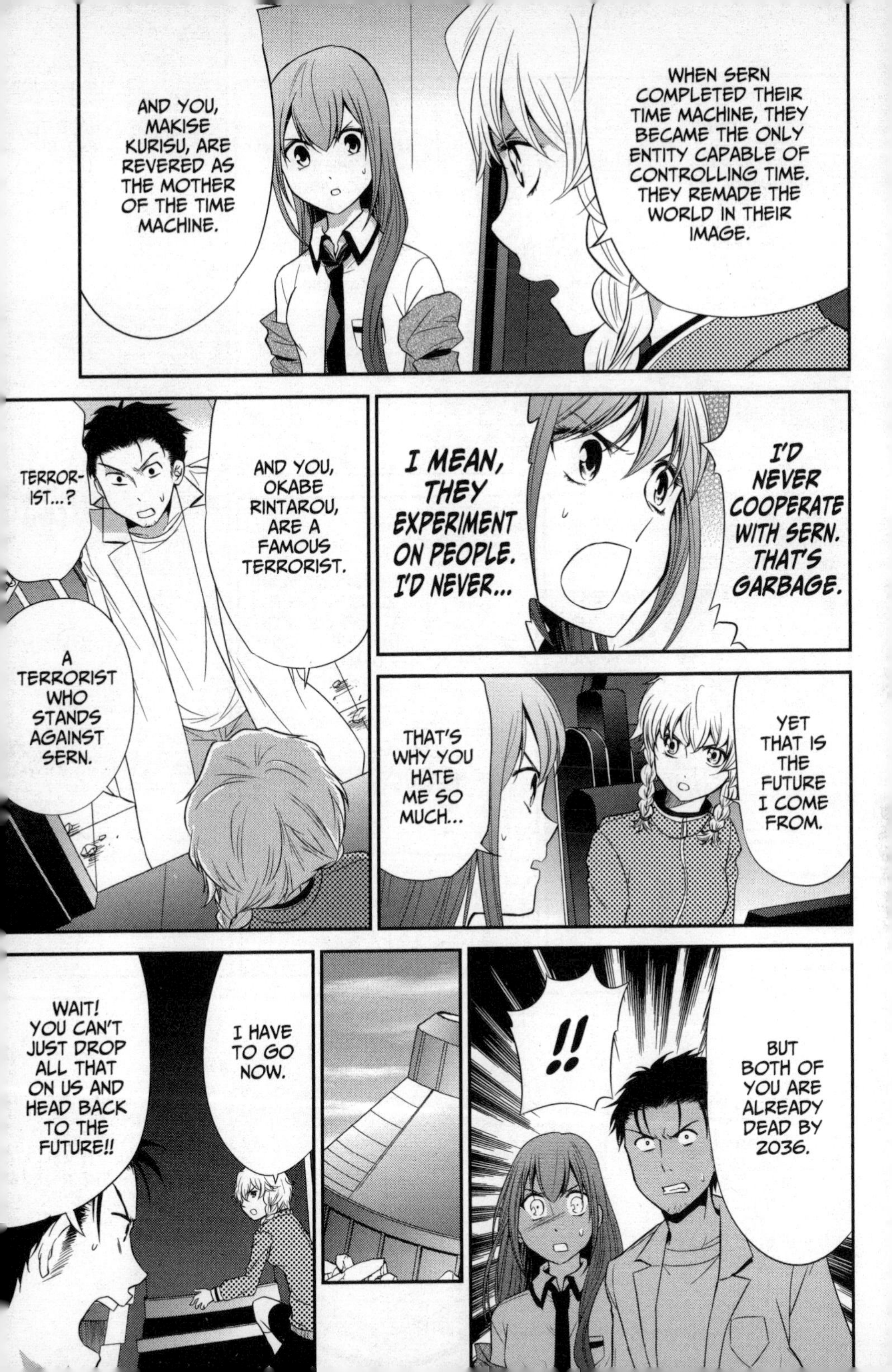
WHEN SERN COMPLETED THEIR TIME MACHINE, THEY BECAME THE ONLY ENTITY CAPABLE OF CONTROLLING TIME. THEY REMADE THE WORLD IN THEIR IMAGE.
AND YOU, MAKISE KURISU, ARE REVERED AS THE MOTHER OF THE TIME MACHINE.
I'D NEVER COOPERATE WITH SERN. THAT'S GARBAGE.
I MEAN, THEY EXPERIMENT ON PEOPLE. I'D NEVER...
YET THAT IS THE FUTURE I COME FROM.
THAT'S WHY YOU HATE ME SO MUCH...
AND YOU, OKABE RINTAROU, ARE A FAMOUS TERRORIST.
TERROR-IST...?
A TERRORIST WHO STANDS AGAINST SERN.
BUT BOTH OF YOU ARE ALREADY DEAD BY 2036.
!!
I HAVE TO GO NOW.
WAIT! YOU CAN'T JUST DROP ALL THAT ON US AND HEAD BACK TO THE FUTURE!!

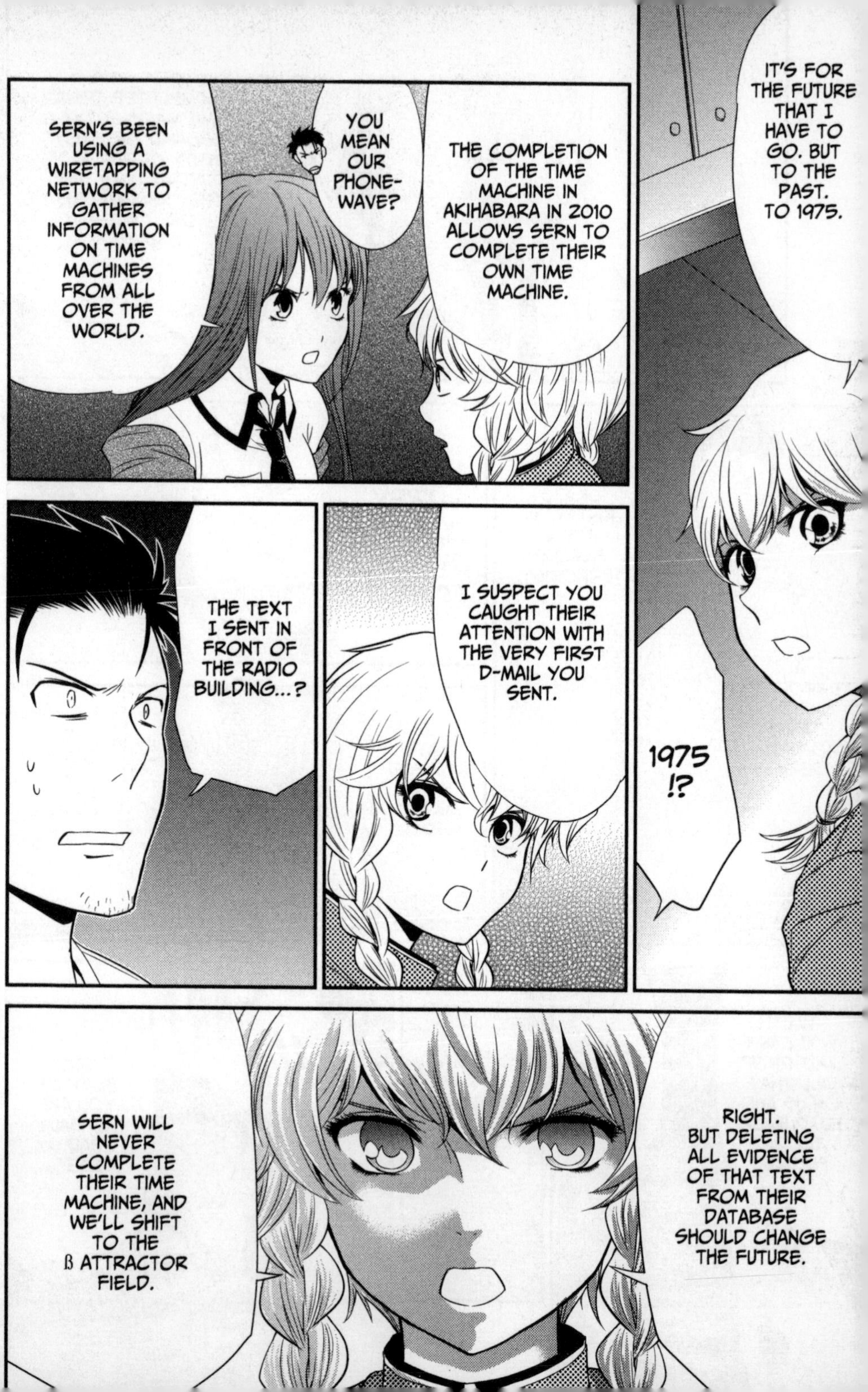
IT'S FOR THE FUTURE THAT I HAVE TO GO. BUT TO THE PAST. TO 1975.
1975!?
THE COMPLETION OF THE TIME MACHINE IN AKIHABARA IN 2010 ALLOWS SERN TO COMPLETE THEIR OWN TIME MACHINE.
YOU MEAN OUR PHONE-WAVE?
SERN'S BEEN USING A WIRETAPPING NETWORK TO GATHER INFORMATION ON TIME MACHINES FROM ALL OVER THE WORLD.
I SUSPECT YOU CAUGHT THEIR ATTENTION WITH THE VERY FIRST D-MAIL YOU SENT.
THE TEXT I SENT IN FRONT OF THE RADIO BUILDING...?
RIGHT. BUT DELETING ALL EVIDENCE OF THAT TEXT FROM THEIR DATABASE SHOULD CHANGE THE FUTURE.
SERN WILL NEVER COMPLETE THEIR TIME MACHINE, AND WE'LL SHIFT TO THE ß ATTRACTOR FIELD.

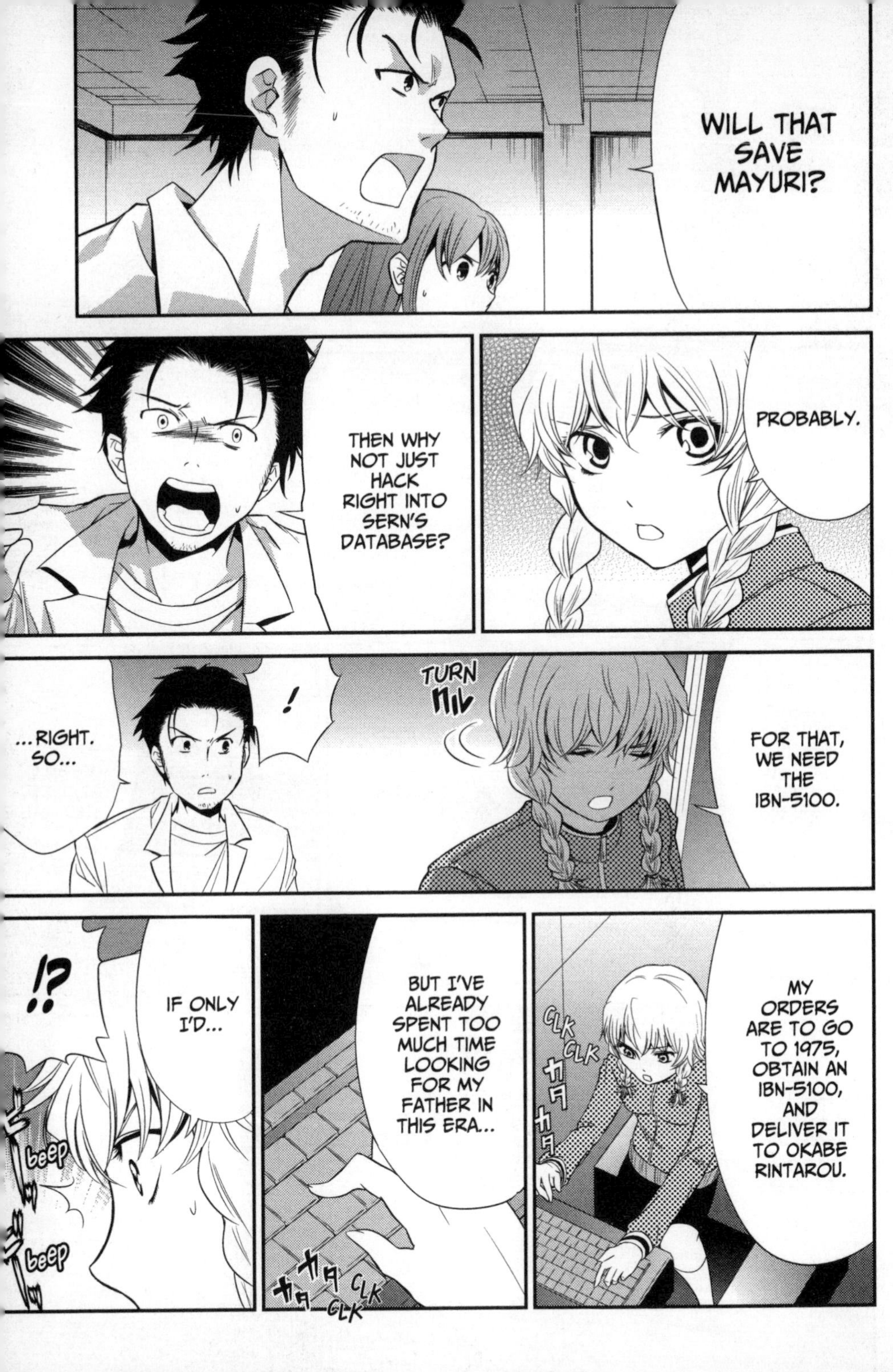
WILL THAT SAVE MAYURI?
PROBABLY.
THEN WHY NOT JUST HACK RIGHT INTO SERN'S DATABASE?
FOR THAT, WE NEED THE IBN-5100.
TURN
!
...RIGHT. SO...
MY ORDERS ARE TO GO TO 1975, OBTAIN AN IBN-5100, AND DELIVER IT TO OKABE RINTAROU.
CLK CLK
BUT I'VE ALREADY SPENT TOO MUCH TIME LOOKING FOR MY FATHER IN THIS ERA...
CLK CLK
!?
IF ONLY I'D...
beep
beep

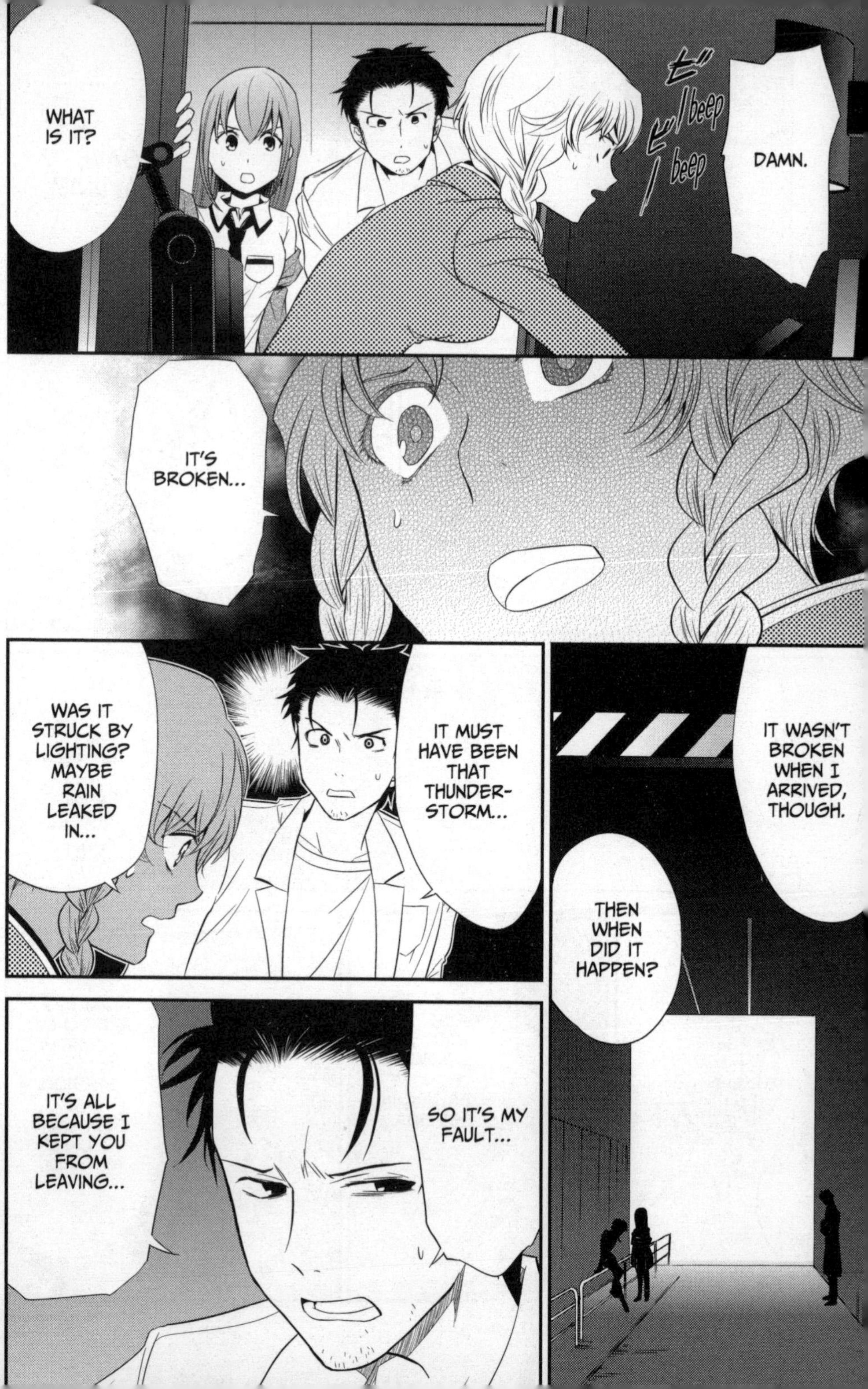
DAMN.
ビ/beep
ビ/beep
WHAT IS IT?
IT'S BROKEN...
IT WASN'T BROKEN WHEN I ARRIVED, THOUGH.
THEN WHEN DID IT HAPPEN?
IT MUST HAVE BEEN THAT THUNDER-STORM...
WAS IT STRUCK BY LIGHTING? MAYBE RAIN LEAKED IN...
SO IT'S MY FAULT...
IT'S ALL BECAUSE I KEPT YOU FROM LEAVING...

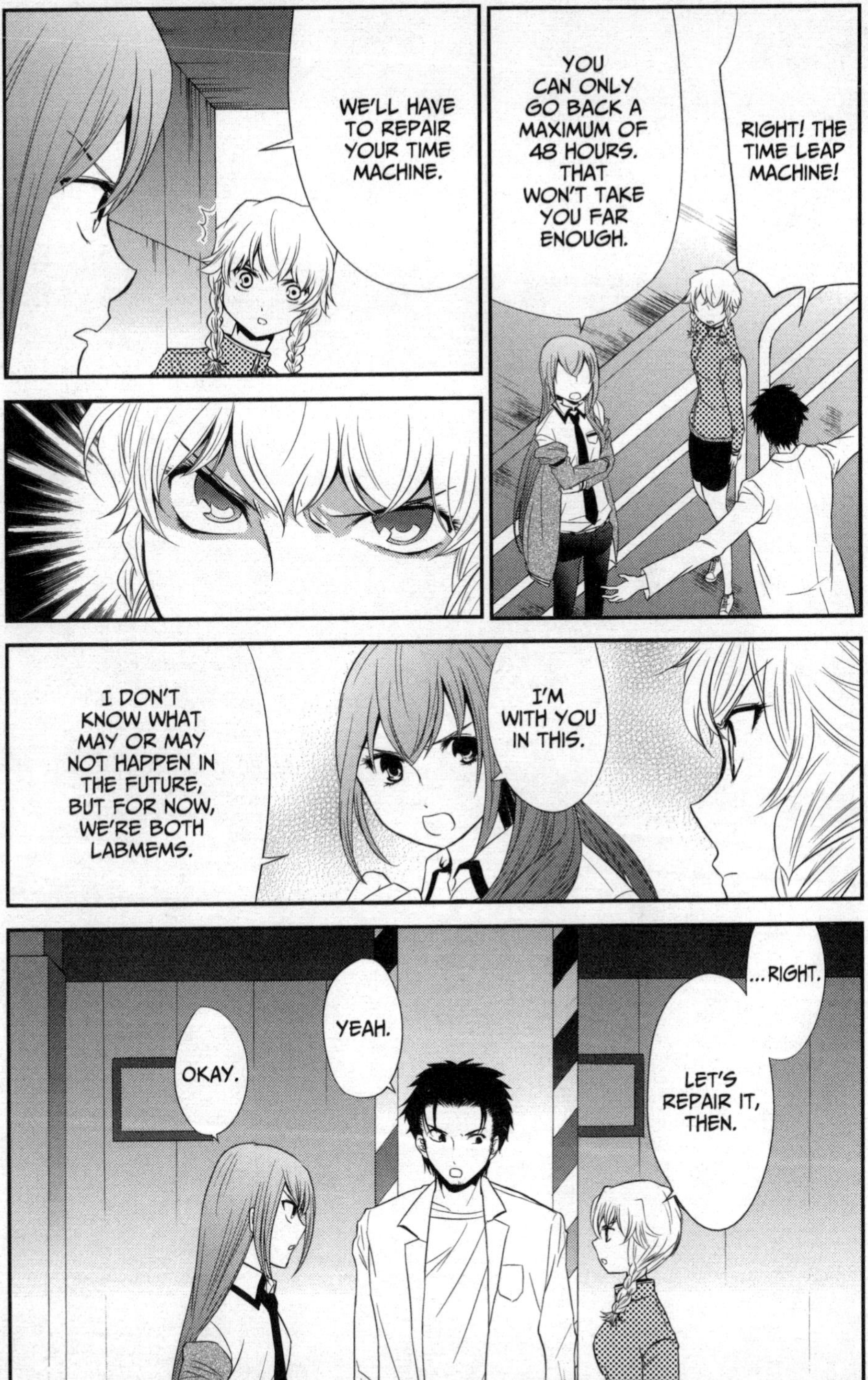
RIGHT! THE TIME LEAP MACHINE!
YOU CAN ONLY GO BACK A MAXIMUM OF 48 HOURS. THAT WON'T TAKE YOU FAR ENOUGH.
WE'LL HAVE TO REPAIR YOUR TIME MACHINE.
I'M WITH YOU IN THIS.
I DON'T KNOW WHAT MAY OR MAY NOT HAPPEN IN THE FUTURE, BUT FOR NOW, WE'RE BOTH LABMEMS.
...RIGHT.
LET'S REPAIR IT, THEN.
YEAH.
OKAY.

The universe has no end, though it does have a beginning. --- Infinite.
Stars too have a beginning, though they are destroyed by their own power. --- Finite.
Those who believe they have wisdom, are often shown by history to be the most foolish.
The fish in the sea don't know what the world is like on the land. Wisdom would destroy them as well.
Man to exceeding the speed of light would be more ridiculous than fish to living on land.
This is God's final warning to any who rebel.

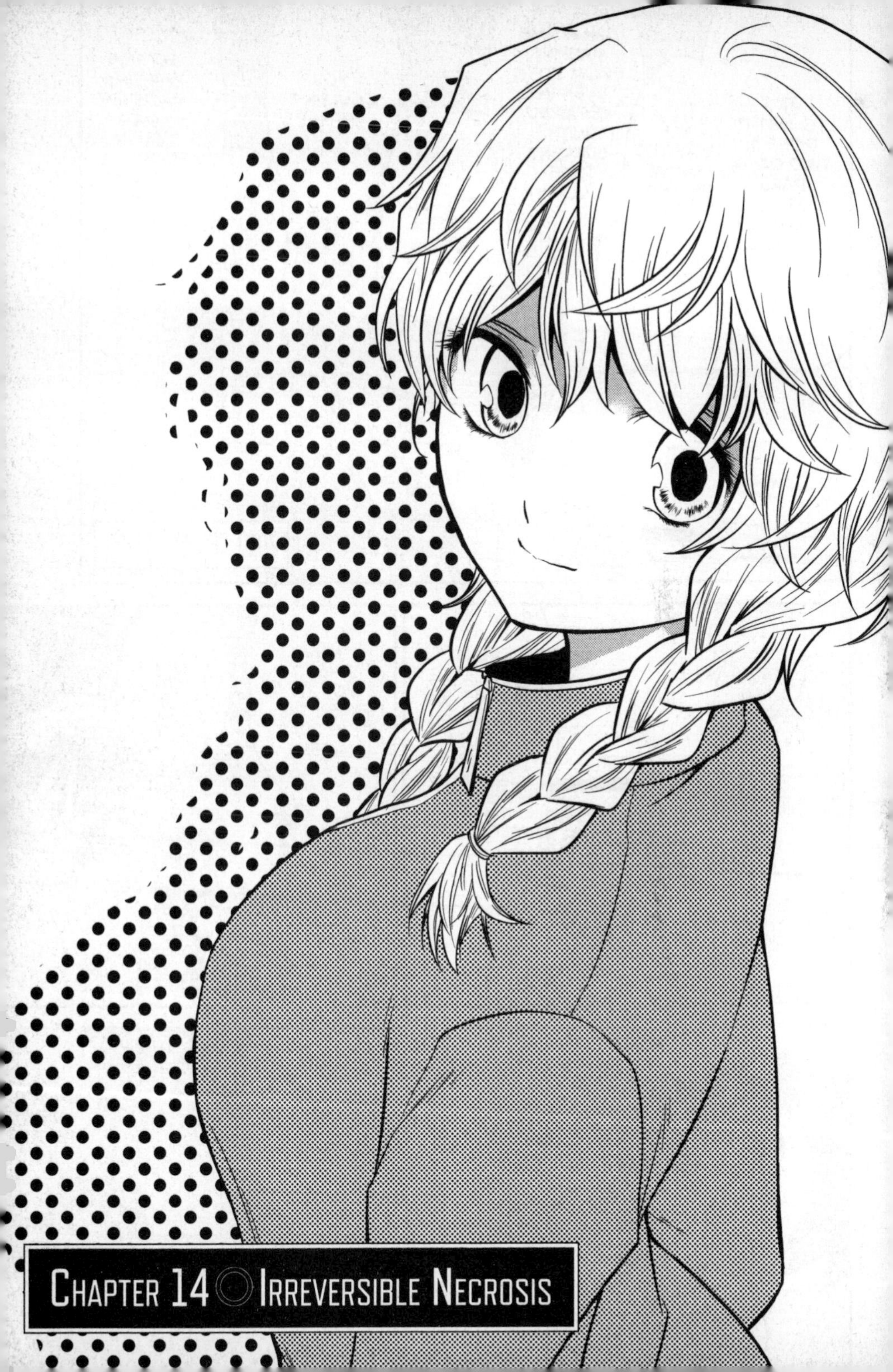

Chapter 14 ◎ Irreversible Necrosis

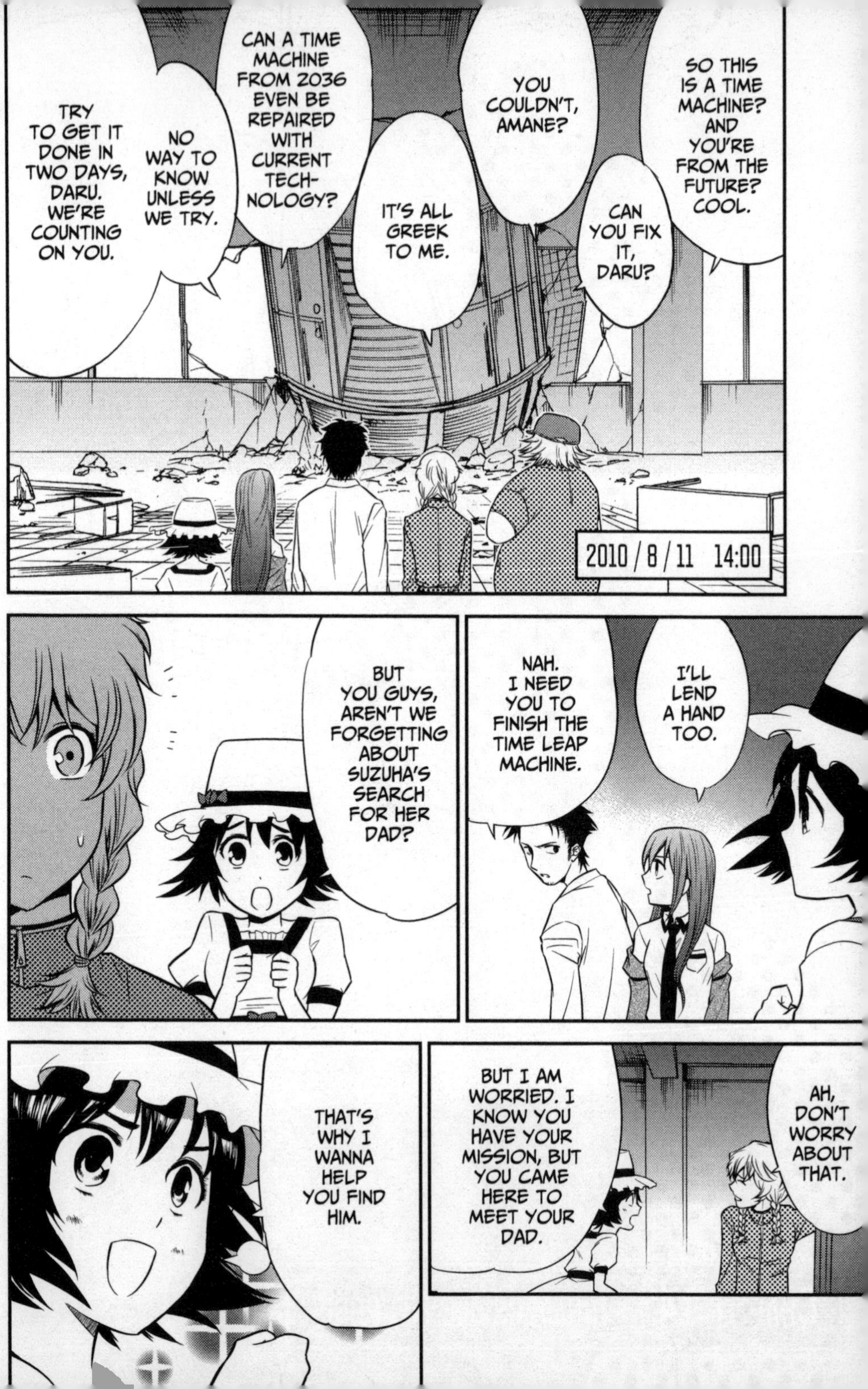
SO THIS IS A TIME MACHINE? AND YOU'RE FROM THE FUTURE? COOL.
CAN YOU FIX IT, DARU?
YOU COULDN'T, AMANE?
IT'S ALL GREEK TO ME.
CAN A TIME MACHINE FROM 2036 EVEN BE REPAIRED WITH CURRENT TECH-NOLOGY?
NO WAY TO KNOW UNLESS WE TRY.
TRY TO GET IT DONE IN TWO DAYS, DARU. WE'RE COUNTING ON YOU.
2010/8/11 14:00
I'LL LEND A HAND TOO.
NAH. I NEED YOU TO FINISH THE TIME LEAP MACHINE.
BUT YOU GUYS, AREN'T WE FORGETTING ABOUT SUZUHA'S SEARCH FOR HER DAD?
AH, DON'T WORRY ABOUT THAT.
BUT I AM WORRIED. I KNOW YOU HAVE YOUR MISSION, BUT YOU CAME HERE TO MEET YOUR DAD.
THAT'S WHY I WANNA HELP YOU FIND HIM.

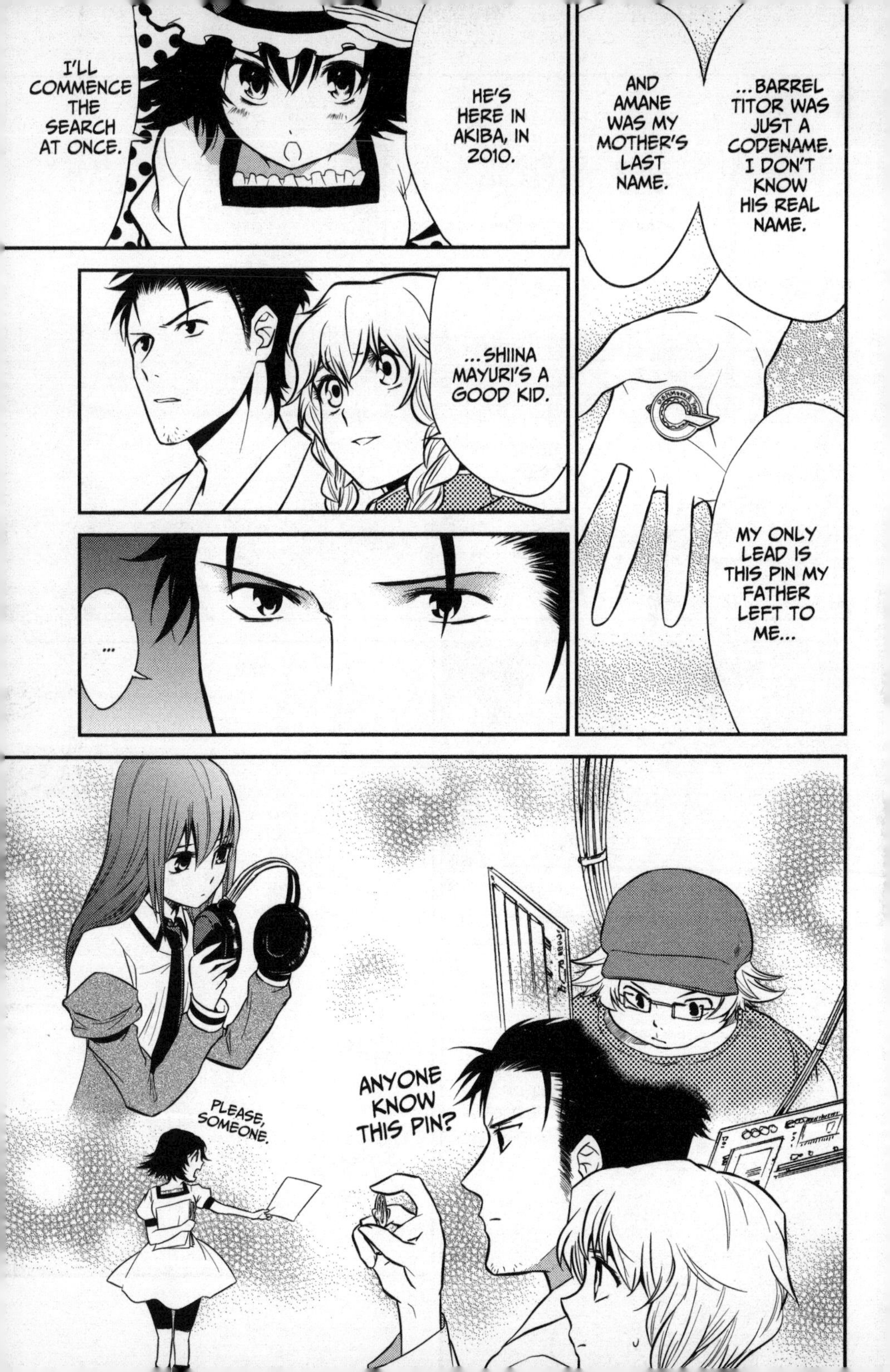
...BARREL TITOR WAS JUST A CODENAME. I DON'T KNOW HIS REAL NAME.
AND AMANE WAS MY MOTHER'S LAST NAME.
MY ONLY LEAD IS THIS PIN MY FATHER LEFT TO ME...
HE'S HERE IN AKIBA, IN 2010.
I'LL COMMENCE THE SEARCH AT ONCE.
...SHIINA MAYURI'S A GOOD KID.
...
ANYONE KNOW THIS PIN?
PLEASE, SOMEONE.

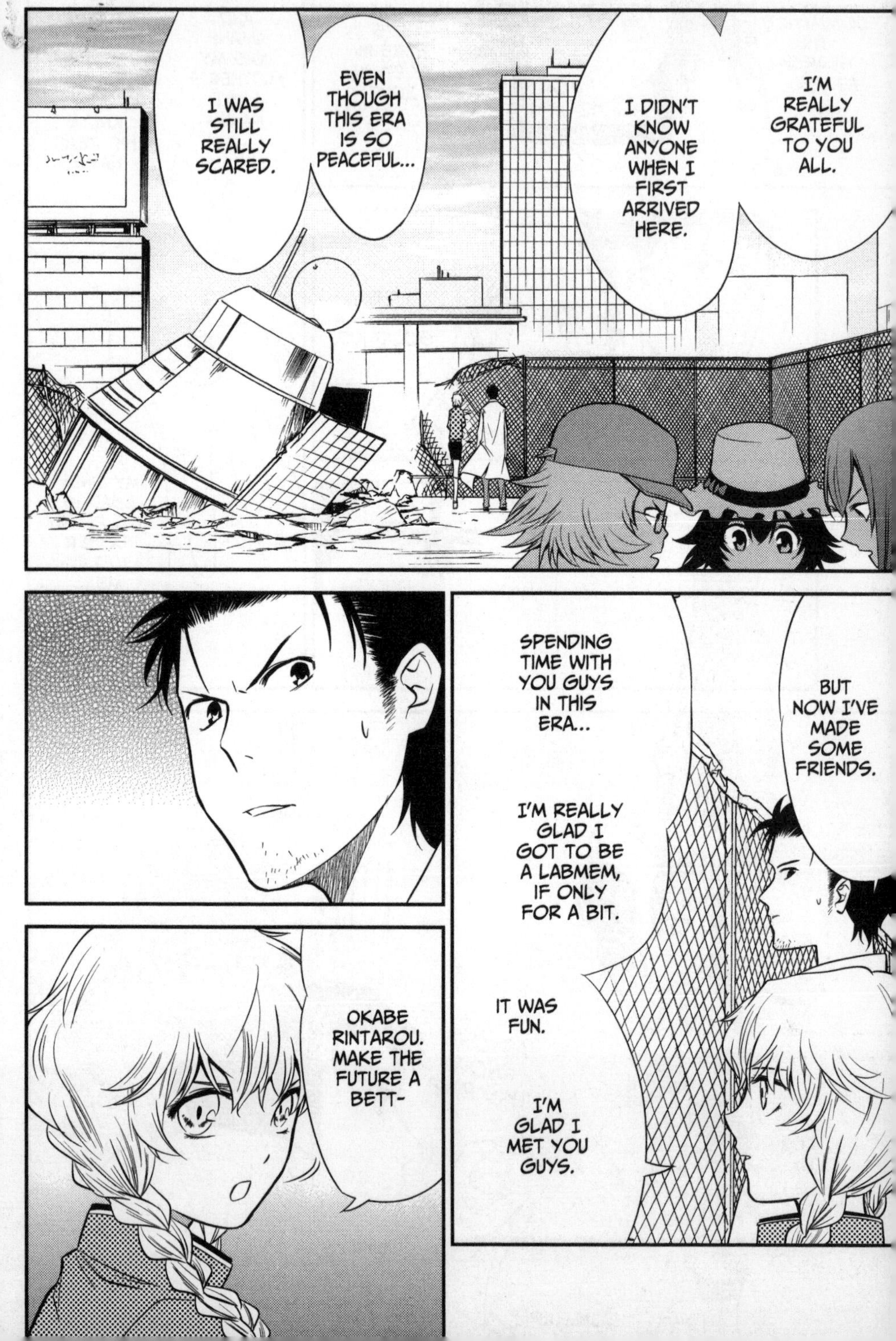

I'M REALLY GRATEFUL TO YOU ALL.
I DIDN'T KNOW ANYONE WHEN I FIRST ARRIVED HERE.
EVEN THOUGH THIS ERA IS SO PEACEFUL...
I WAS STILL REALLY SCARED.
BUT NOW I'VE MADE SOME FRIENDS.
SPENDING TIME WITH YOU GUYS IN THIS ERA...
I'M REALLY GLAD I GOT TO BE A LABMEM, IF ONLY FOR A BIT.
IT WAS FUN.
I'M GLAD I MET YOU GUYS.
OKABE RINTAROU. MAKE THE FUTURE A BETT-

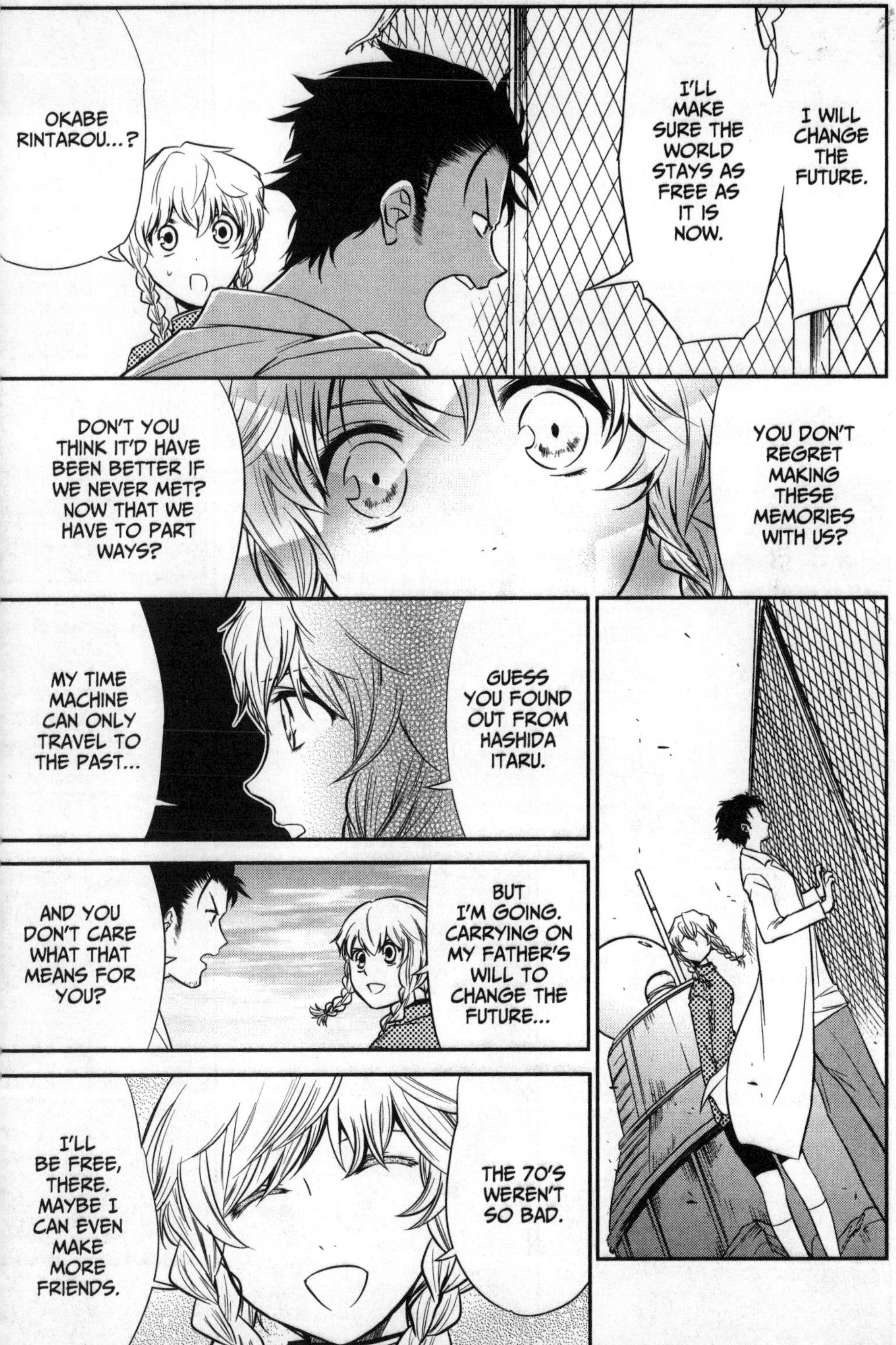
I WILL CHANGE THE FUTURE.
I'LL MAKE SURE THE WORLD STAYS AS FREE AS IT IS NOW.
OKABE RINTAROU...?
YOU DON'T REGRET MAKING THESE MEMORIES WITH US?
DON'T YOU THINK IT'D HAVE BEEN BETTER IF WE NEVER MET? NOW THAT WE HAVE TO PART WAYS?
GUESS YOU FOUND OUT FROM HASHIDA ITARU.
MY TIME MACHINE CAN ONLY TRAVEL TO THE PAST...
BUT I'M GOING. CARRYING ON MY FATHER'S WILL TO CHANGE THE FUTURE...
AND YOU DON'T CARE WHAT THAT MEANS FOR YOU?
THE 70'S WEREN'T SO BAD.
I'LL BE FREE, THERE. MAYBE I CAN EVEN MAKE MORE FRIENDS.

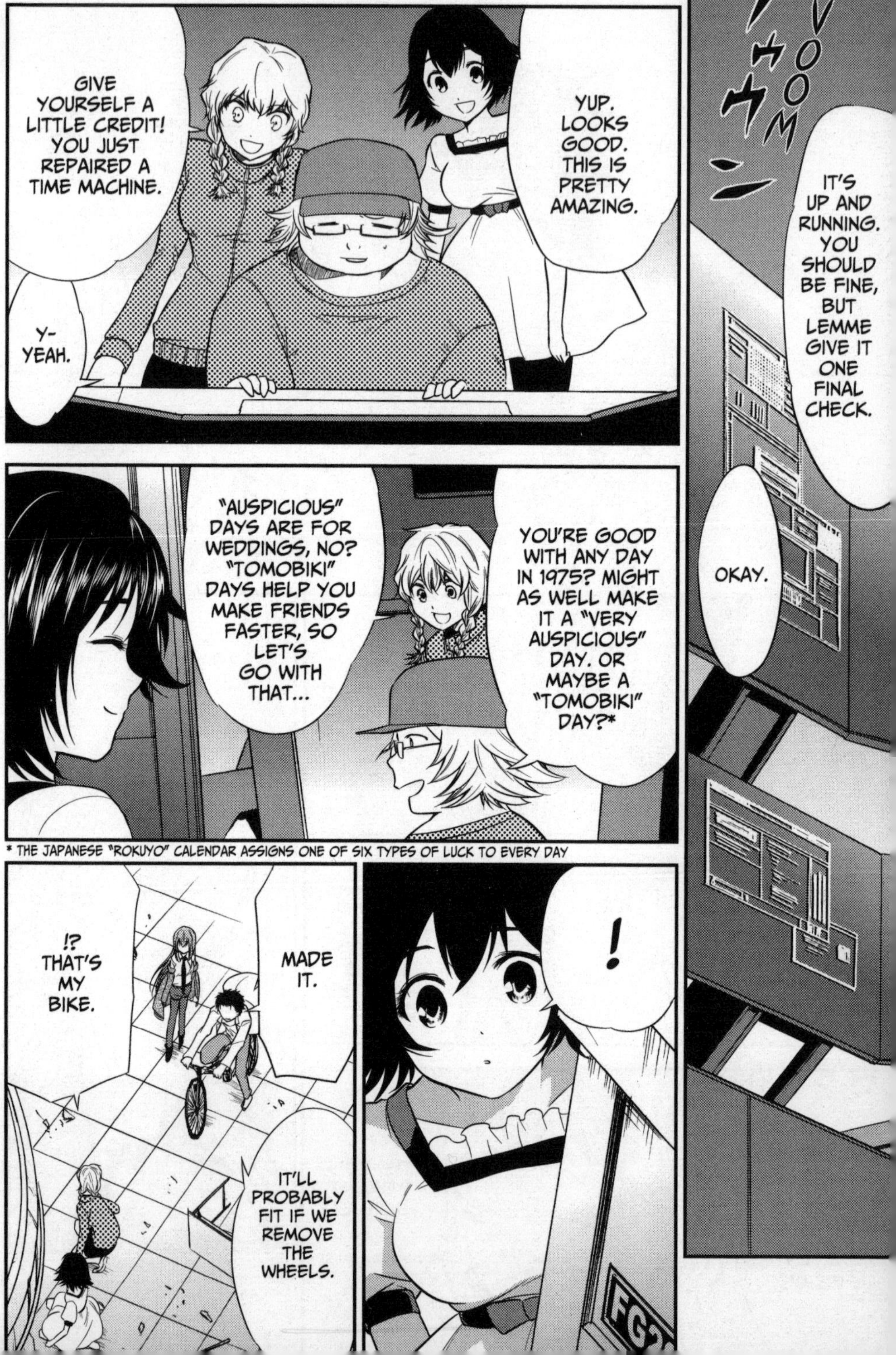
ブゥゥン
VOOM
IT'S UP AND RUNNING. YOU SHOULD BE FINE, BUT LEMME GIVE IT ONE FINAL CHECK.
OKAY.
YUP. LOOKS GOOD. THIS IS PRETTY AMAZING.
GIVE YOURSELF A LITTLE CREDIT! YOU JUST REPAIRED A TIME MACHINE.
Y-YEAH.
YOU'RE GOOD WITH ANY DAY IN 1975? MIGHT AS WELL MAKE IT A "VERY AUSPICIOUS" DAY. OR MAYBE A "TOMOBIKI" DAY?*
"AUSPICIOUS" DAYS ARE FOR WEDDINGS, NO? "TOMOBIKI" DAYS HELP YOU MAKE FRIENDS FASTER, SO LET'S GO WITH THAT...
!
MADE IT.
!? THAT'S MY BIKE.
IT'LL PROBABLY FIT IF WE REMOVE THE WHEELS.
* THE JAPANESE "ROKUYO" CALENDAR ASSIGNS ONE OF SIX TYPES OF LUCK TO EVERY DAY

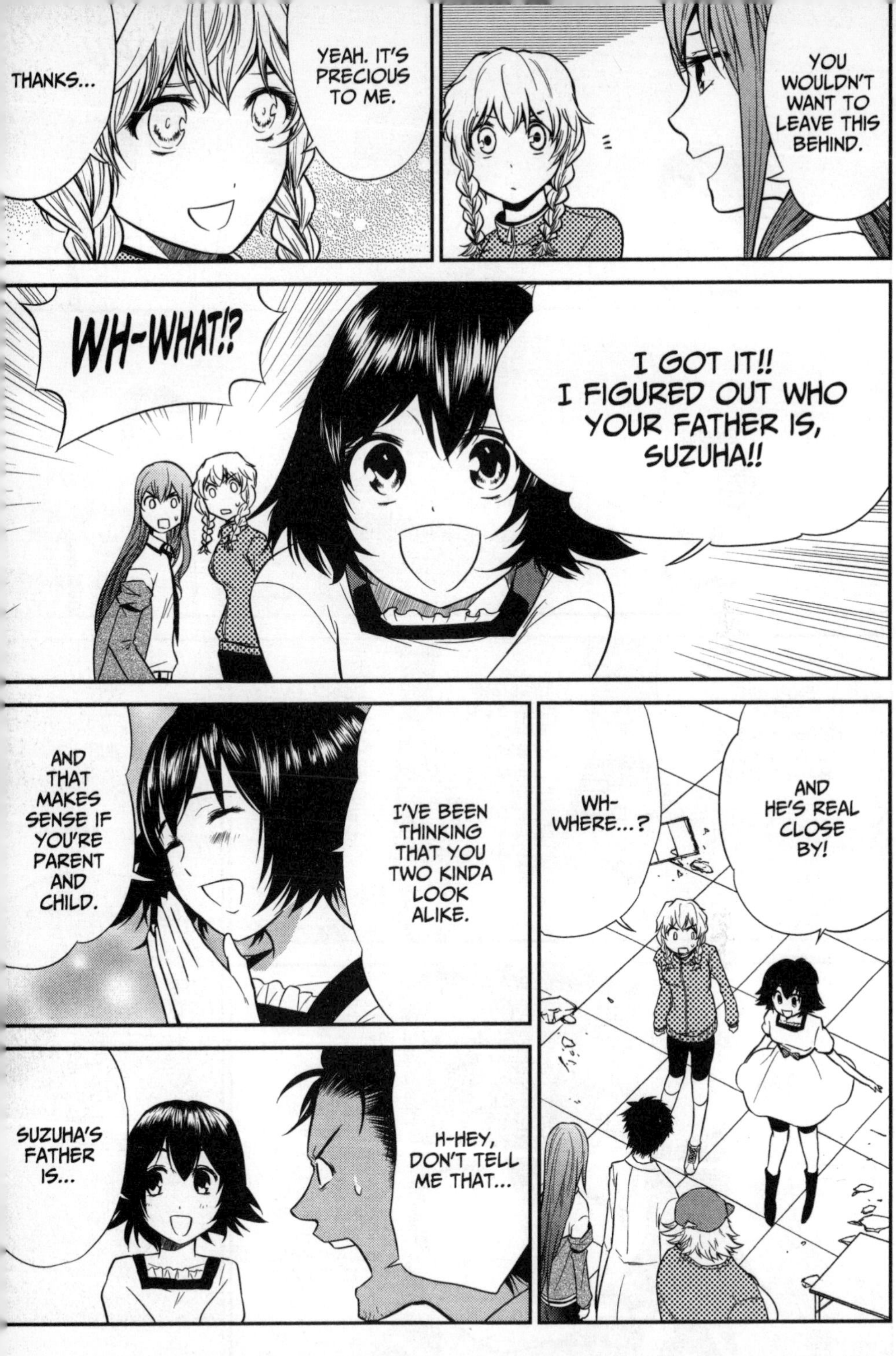
YOU WOULDN'T WANT TO LEAVE THIS BEHIND.
YEAH. IT'S PRECIOUS TO ME.
THANKS...
I GOT IT!! I FIGURED OUT WHO YOUR FATHER IS, SUZUHA!!
WH-WHAT!?
AND HE'S REAL CLOSE BY!
WH- WHERE...?
I'VE BEEN THINKING THAT YOU TWO KINDA LOOK ALIKE.
AND THAT MAKES SENSE IF YOU'RE PARENT AND CHILD.
H-HEY, DON'T TELL ME THAT...
SUZUHA'S FATHER IS...

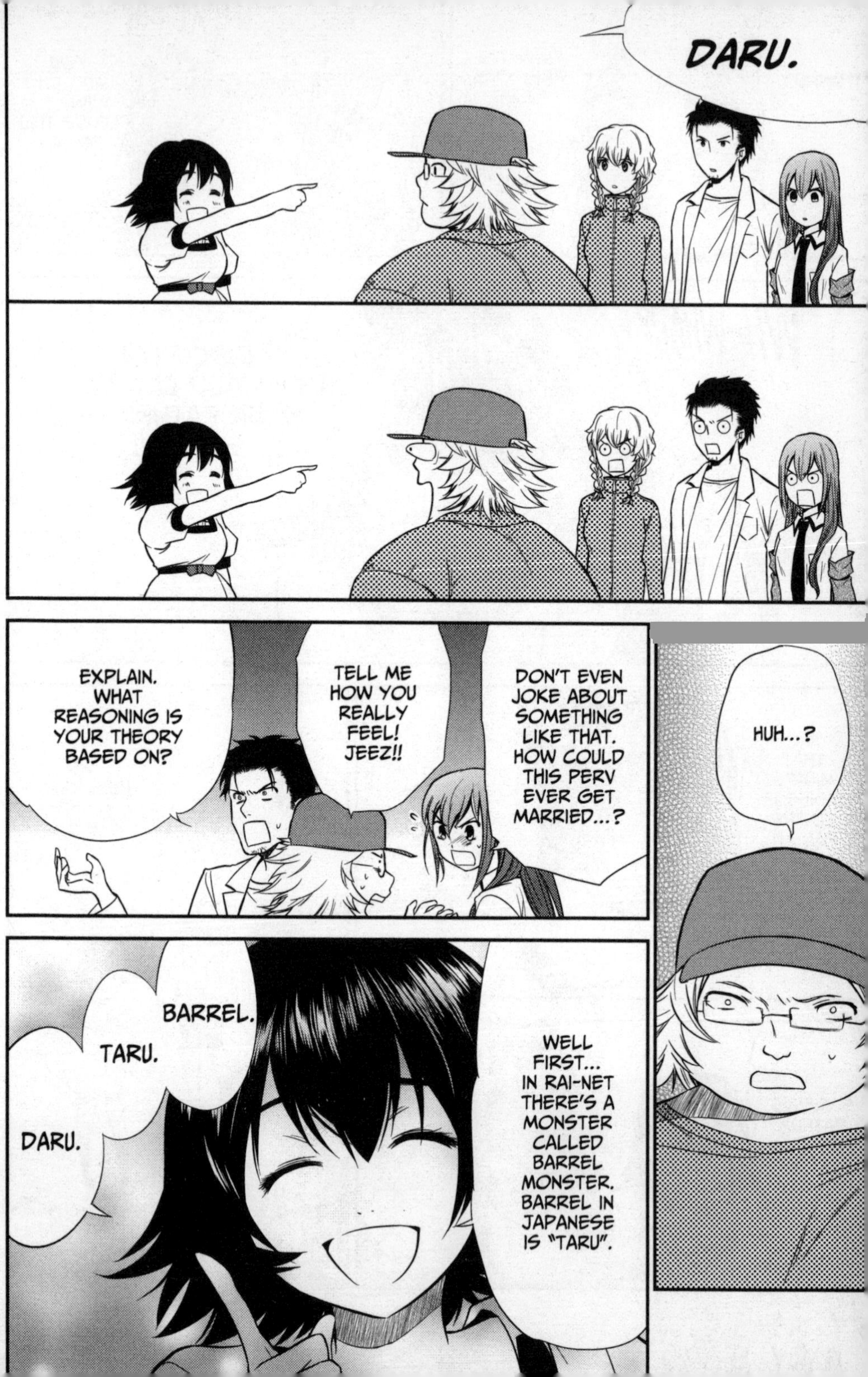
DARU.
HUH...?
DON'T EVEN JOKE ABOUT SOMETHING LIKE THAT. HOW COULD THIS PERV EVER GET MARRIED...?
TELL ME HOW YOU REALLY FEEL! JEEZ!!
EXPLAIN. WHAT REASONING IS YOUR THEORY BASED ON?
WELL FIRST... IN RAI-NET THERE'S A MONSTER CALLED BARREL MONSTER. BARREL IN JAPANESE IS "TARU".
BARREL.
TARU.
DARU.

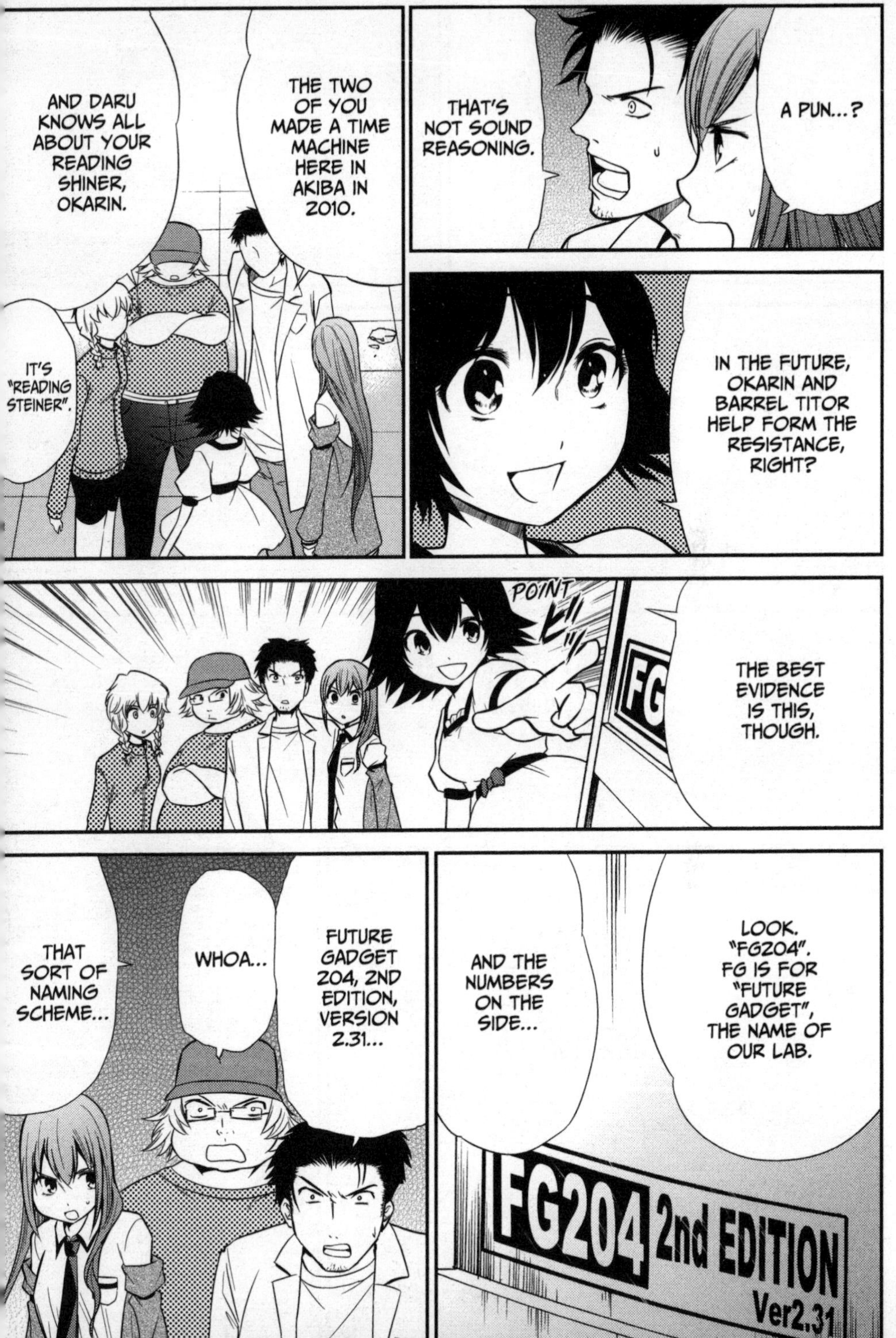
A PUN...?
THAT'S NOT SOUND REASONING.
IN THE FUTURE, OKARIN AND BARREL TITOR HELP FORM THE RESISTANCE, RIGHT?
THE TWO OF YOU MADE A TIME MACHINE HERE IN AKIBA IN 2010.
AND DARU KNOWS ALL ABOUT YOUR READING SHINER, OKARIN.
IT'S "READING STEINER".
THE BEST EVIDENCE IS THIS, THOUGH.
POINT
FG
LOOK. "FG204". FG IS FOR "FUTURE GADGET", THE NAME OF OUR LAB.
AND THE NUMBERS ON THE SIDE...
FG204 2nd EDITION Ver2.31
FUTURE GADGET 204, 2ND EDITION, VERSION 2.31...
WHOA...
THAT SORT OF NAMING SCHEME...

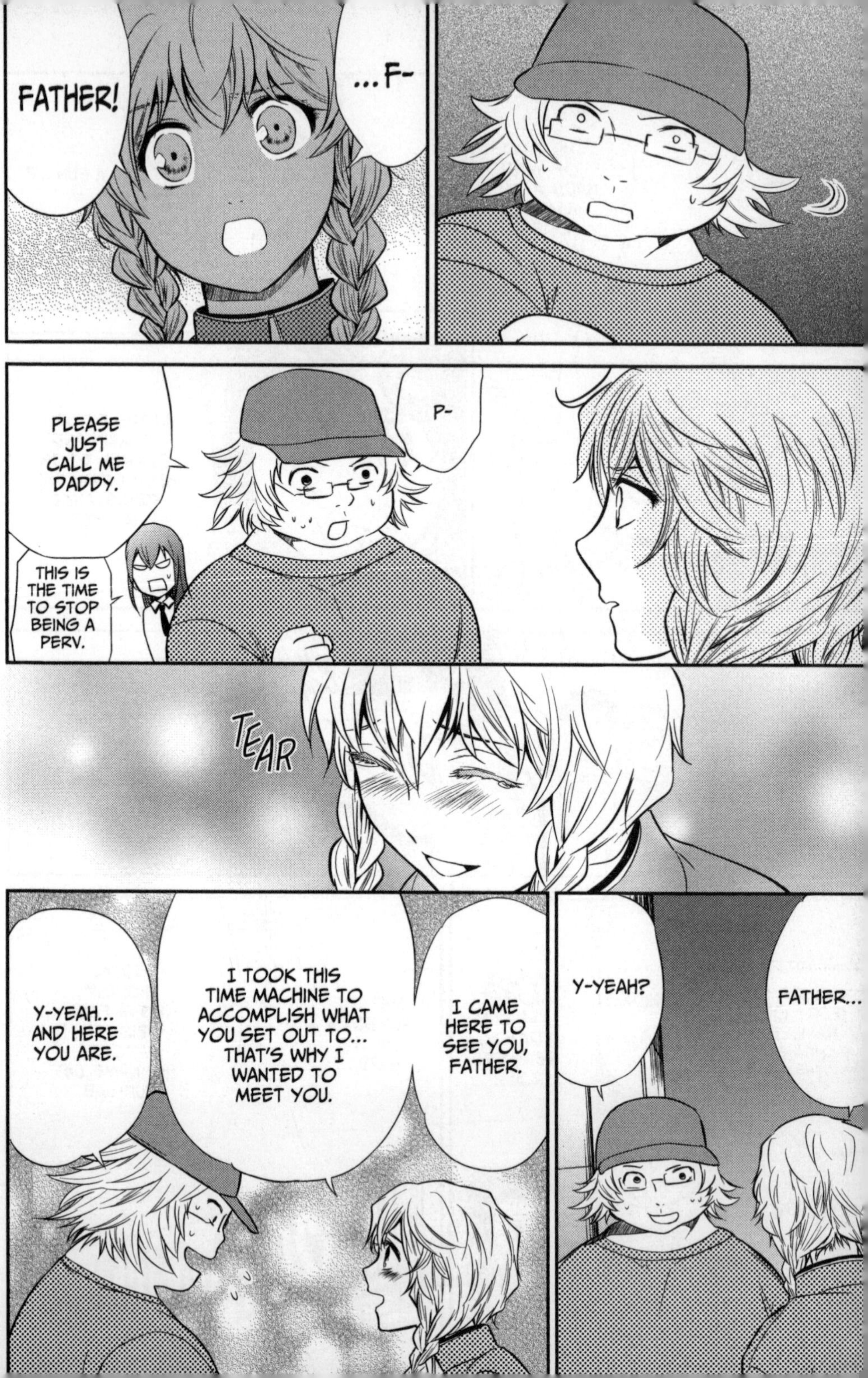
...F-
FATHER!
P-
PLEASE JUST CALL ME DADDY.
THIS IS THE TIME TO STOP BEING A PERV.
TEAR
FATHER...
Y-YEAH?
I CAME HERE TO SEE YOU, FATHER.
I TOOK THIS TIME MACHINE TO ACCOMPLISH WHAT YOU SET OUT TO... THAT'S WHY I WANTED TO MEET YOU.
Y-YEAH... AND HERE YOU ARE.

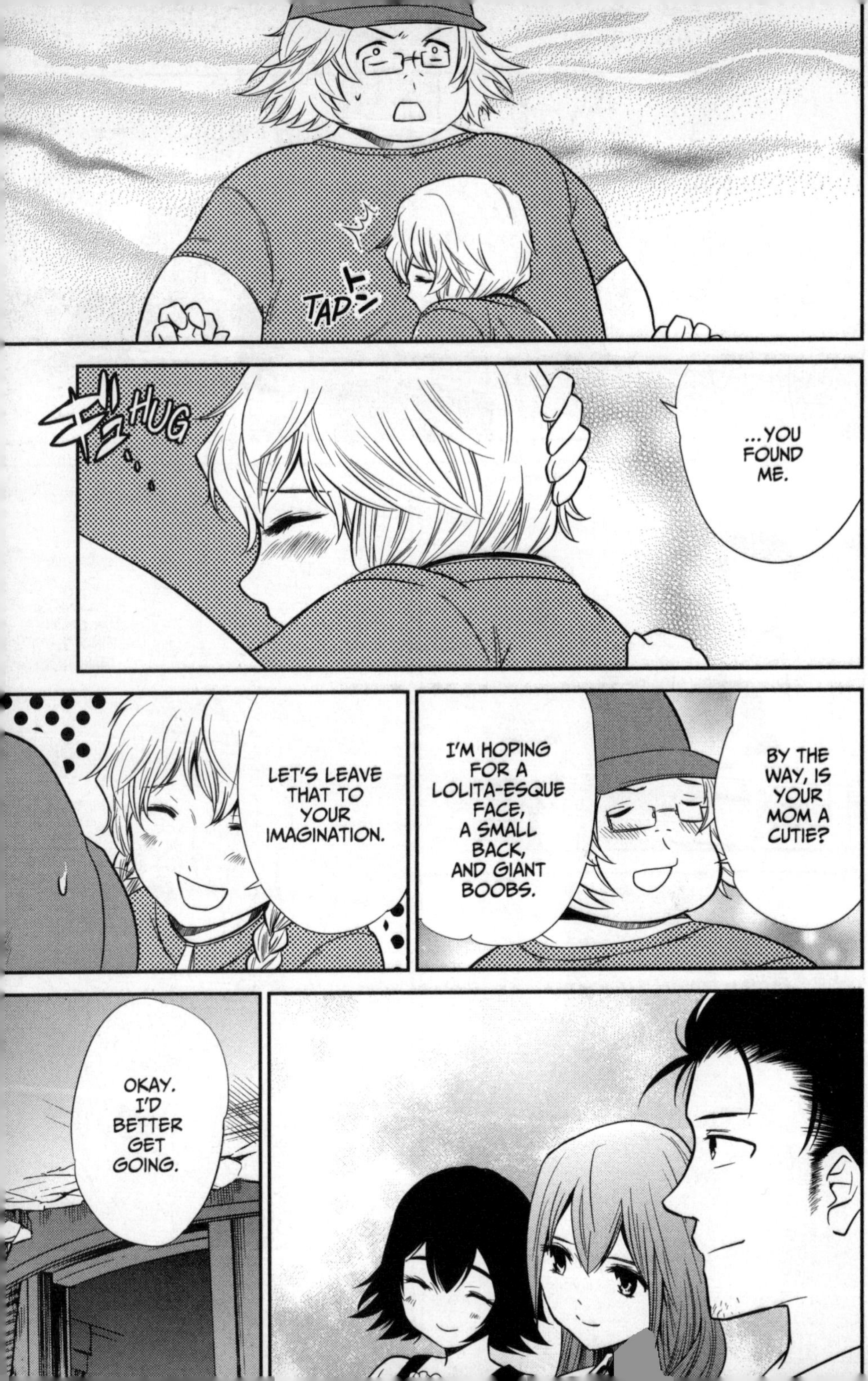
TAP
...YOU FOUND ME.
HUG
BY THE WAY, IS YOUR MOM A CUTIE?
I'M HOPING FOR A LOLITA-ESQUE FACE, A SMALL BACK, AND GIANT BOOBS.
LET'S LEAVE THAT TO YOUR IMAGINATION.
OKAY. I'D BETTER GET GOING.

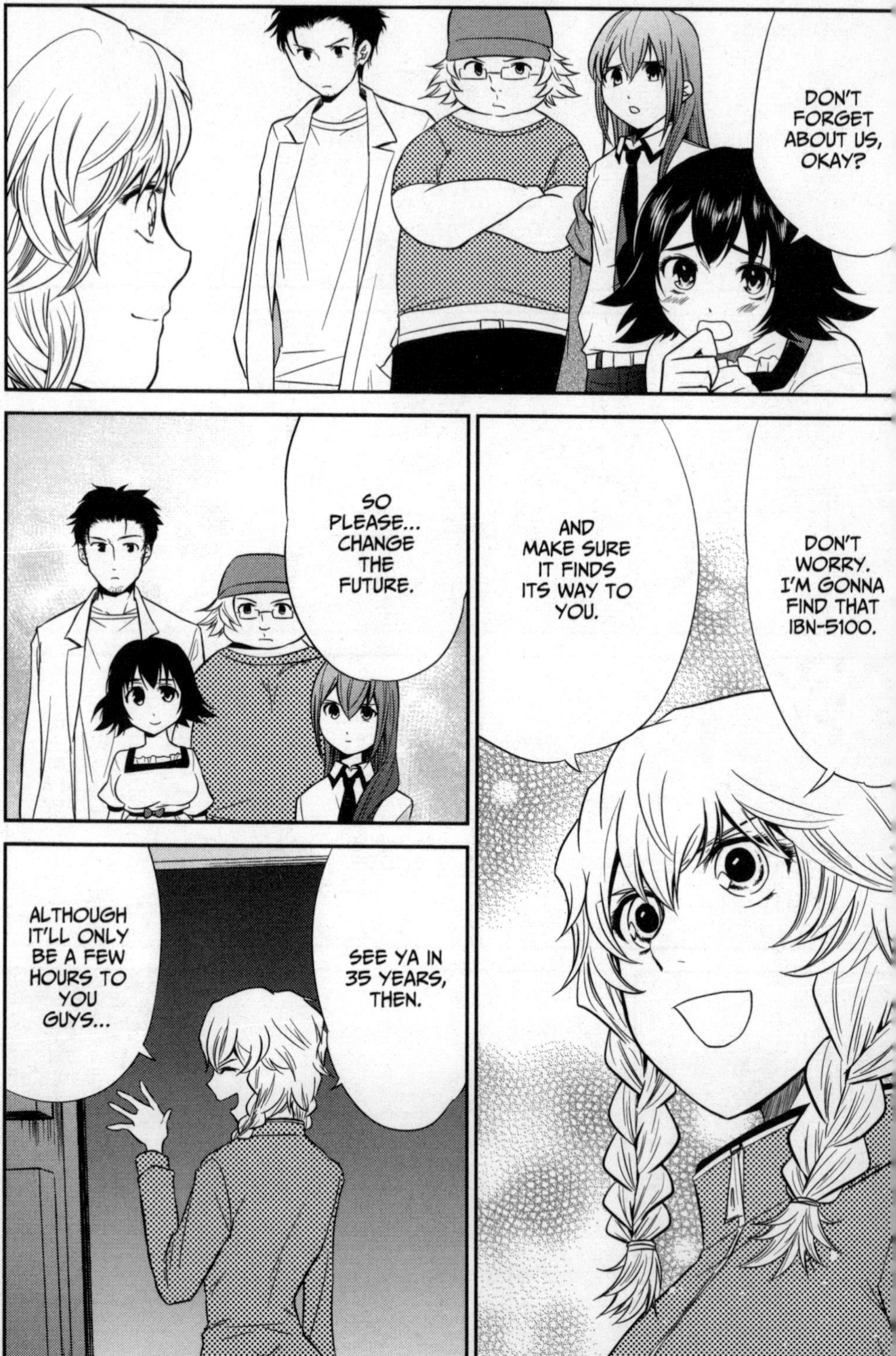
DON'T FORGET ABOUT US, OKAY?
DON'T WORRY. I'M GONNA FIND THAT IBN-5100.
AND MAKE SURE IT FINDS ITS WAY TO YOU.
SO PLEASE... CHANGE THE FUTURE.
SEE YA IN 35 YEARS, THEN.
ALTHOUGH IT'LL ONLY BE A FEW HOURS TO YOU GUYS...

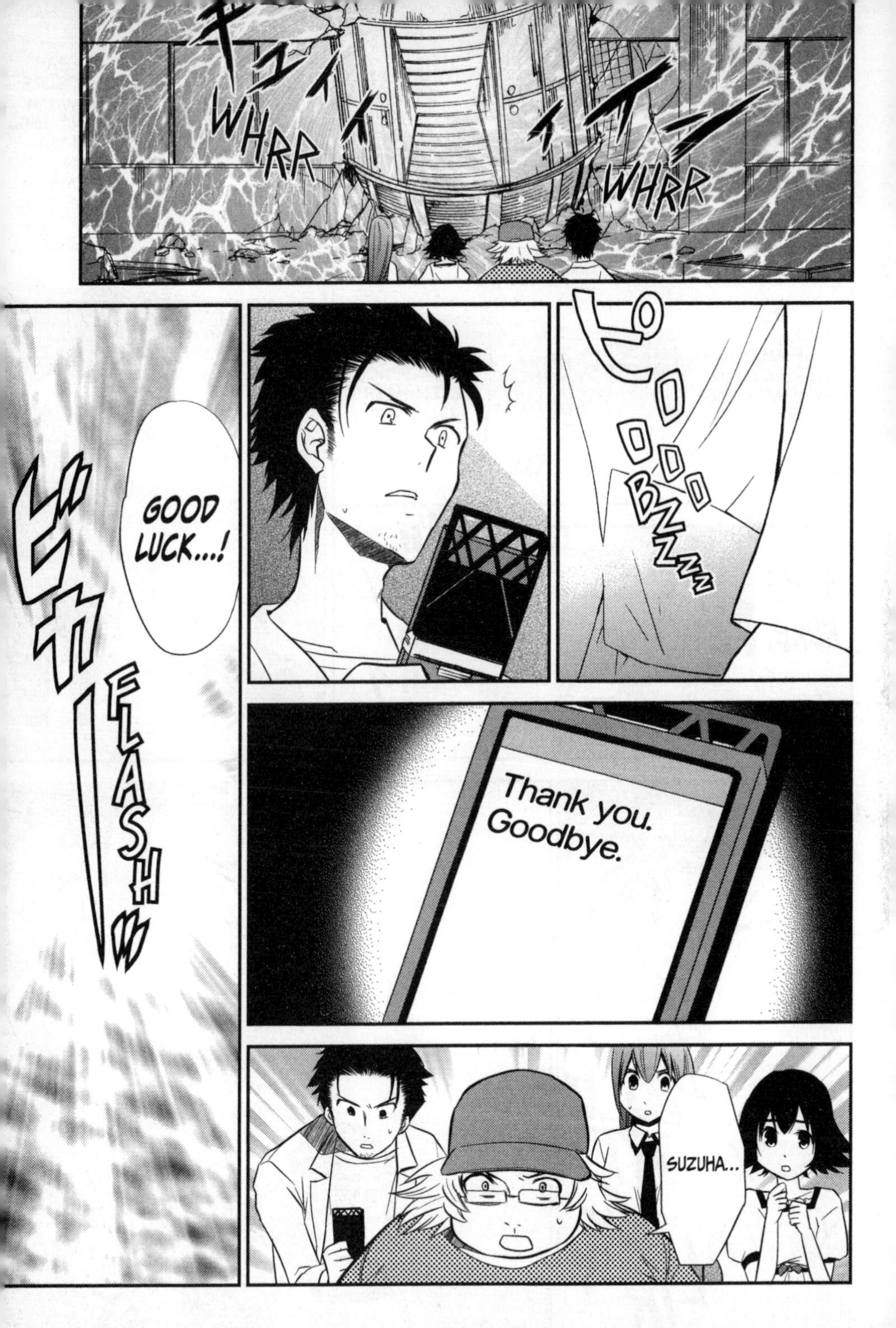
WHRR
WHRR
BZZZZ
GOOD LUCK...!
FLASH!!
Thank you.
Goodbye.
SUZUHA...

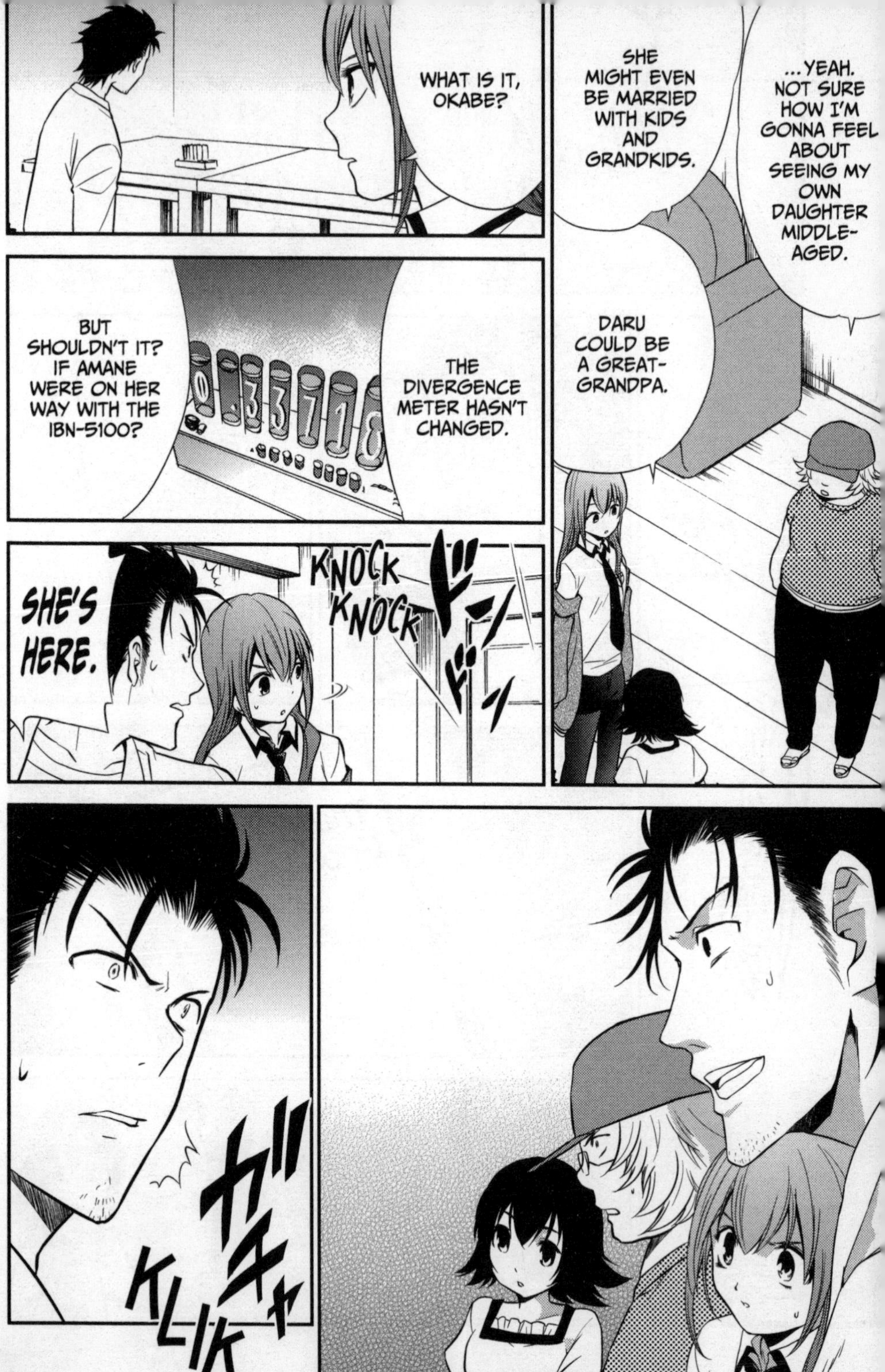
...YEAH. NOT SURE HOW I'M GONNA FEEL ABOUT SEEING MY OWN DAUGHTER MIDDLE-AGED.
SHE MIGHT EVEN BE MARRIED WITH KIDS AND GRANDKIDS.
DARU COULD BE A GREAT-GRANDPA.
WHAT IS IT, OKABE?
THE DIVERGENCE METER HASN'T CHANGED.
BUT SHOULDN'T IT? IF AMANE WERE ON HER WAY WITH THE IBN-5100?
ドンドン
KNOCK KNOCK
SHE'S HERE.
ガチャ
KLIK

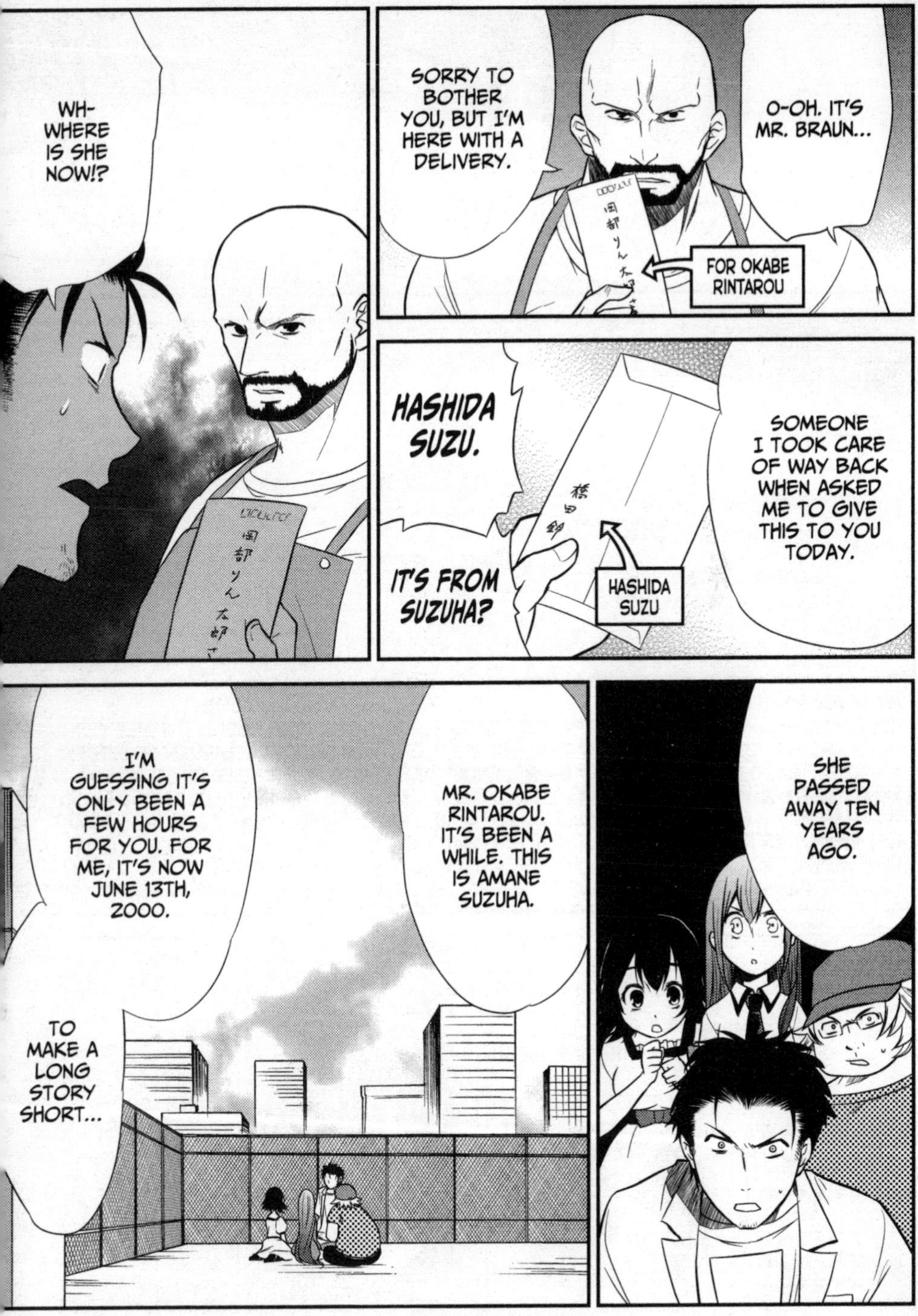
O-OH. IT'S MR. BRAUN...
SORRY TO BOTHER YOU, BUT I'M HERE WITH A DELIVERY.
FOR OKABE RINTAROU
SOMEONE I TOOK CARE OF WAY BACK WHEN ASKED ME TO GIVE THIS TO YOU TODAY.
HASHIDA SUZU
HASHIDA SUZU.
IT'S FROM SUZUHA?
WH-WHERE IS SHE NOW!?
SHE PASSED AWAY TEN YEARS AGO.
MR. OKABE RINTAROU. IT'S BEEN A WHILE. THIS IS AMANE SUZUHA.
I'M GUESSING IT'S ONLY BEEN A FEW HOURS FOR YOU. FOR ME, IT'S NOW JUNE 13TH, 2000.
TO MAKE A LONG STORY SHORT...

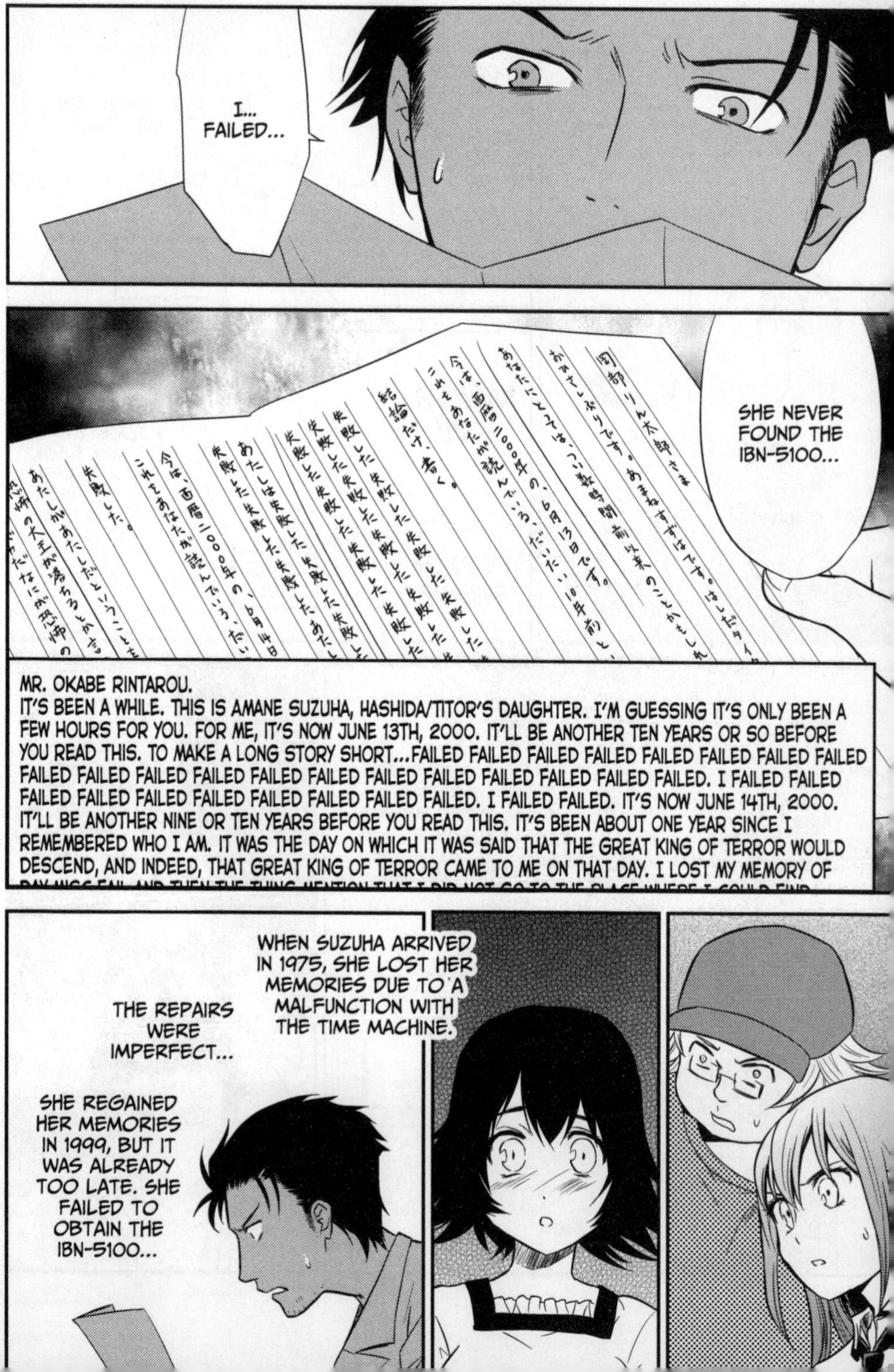
I... FAILED...
SHE NEVER FOUND THE IBN-5100...
MR. OKABE RINTAROU.
IT'S BEEN A WHILE. THIS IS AMANE SUZUHA, HASHIDA/TITOR'S DAUGHTER. I'M GUESSING IT'S ONLY BEEN A FEW HOURS FOR YOU. FOR ME, IT'S NOW JUNE 13TH, 2000. IT'LL BE ANOTHER TEN YEARS OR SO BEFORE YOU READ THIS. TO MAKE A LONG STORY SHORT...FAILED FAILED FAILED FAILED FAILED FAILED FAILED FAILED FAILED FAILED FAILED FAILED FAILED FAILED FAILED FAILED FAILED FAILED FAILED FAILED. I FAILED FAILED FAILED FAILED FAILED FAILED FAILED FAILED FAILED FAILED. I FAILED FAILED. IT'S NOW JUNE 14TH, 2000. IT'LL BE ANOTHER NINE OR TEN YEARS BEFORE YOU READ THIS. IT'S BEEN ABOUT ONE YEAR SINCE I REMEMBERED WHO I AM. IT WAS THE DAY ON WHICH IT WAS SAID THAT THE GREAT KING OF TERROR WOULD DESCEND, AND INDEED, THAT GREAT KING OF TERROR CAME TO ME ON THAT DAY. I LOST MY MEMORY OF
WHEN SUZUHA ARRIVED IN 1975, SHE LOST HER MEMORIES DUE TO A MALFUNCTION WITH THE TIME MACHINE.
THE REPAIRS WERE IMPERFECT...
SHE REGAINED HER MEMORIES IN 1999, BUT IT WAS ALREADY TOO LATE. SHE FAILED TO OBTAIN THE IBN-5100...

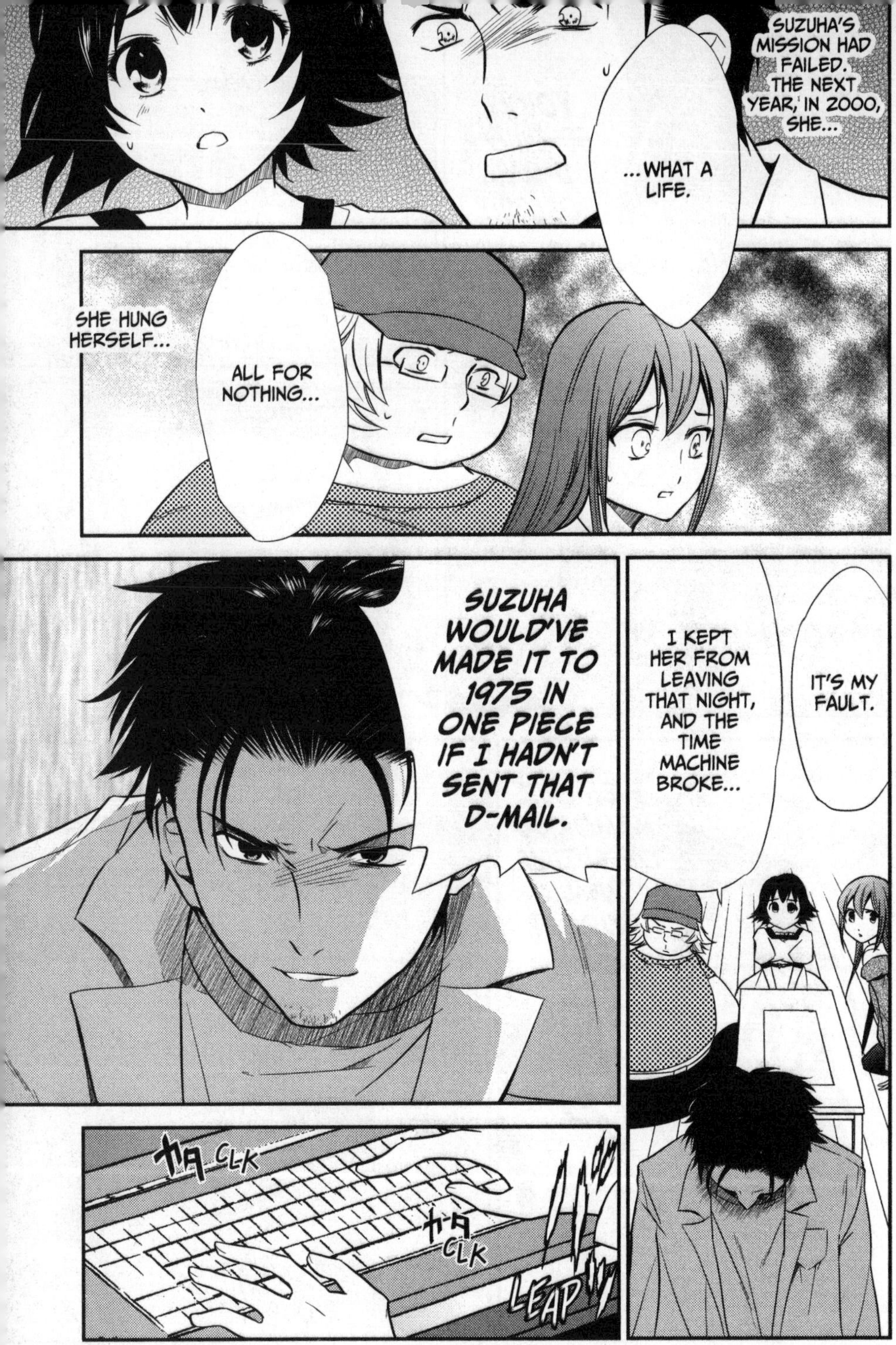
SUZUHA'S MISSION HAD FAILED. THE NEXT YEAR, IN 2000, SHE...
...WHAT A LIFE.
SHE HUNG HERSELF...
ALL FOR NOTHING...
IT'S MY FAULT.
I KEPT HER FROM LEAVING THAT NIGHT, AND THE TIME MACHINE BROKE...
SUZUHA WOULD'VE MADE IT TO 1975 IN ONE PIECE IF I HADN'T SENT THAT D-MAIL.
カタ CLK
カタ CLK
LEAP

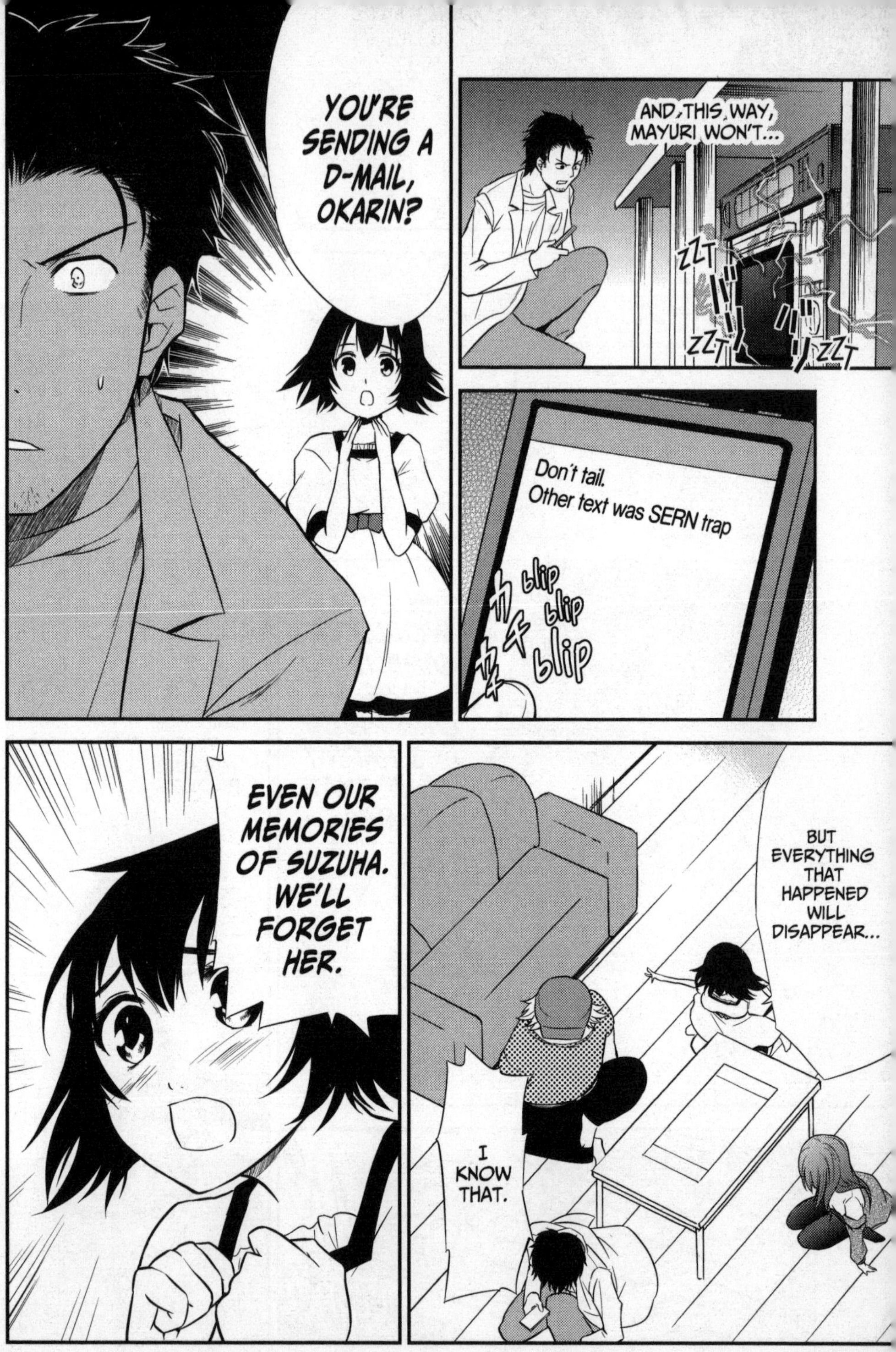
AND THIS WAY, MAYURI WON'T...
ZZT
ZZT
ZZT
Don't tail.
Other text was SERN trap
blip
blip
blip
YOU'RE SENDING A D-MAIL, OKARIN?
BUT EVERYTHING THAT HAPPENED WILL DISAPPEAR...
I KNOW THAT.
EVEN OUR MEMORIES OF SUZUHA. WE'LL FORGET HER.

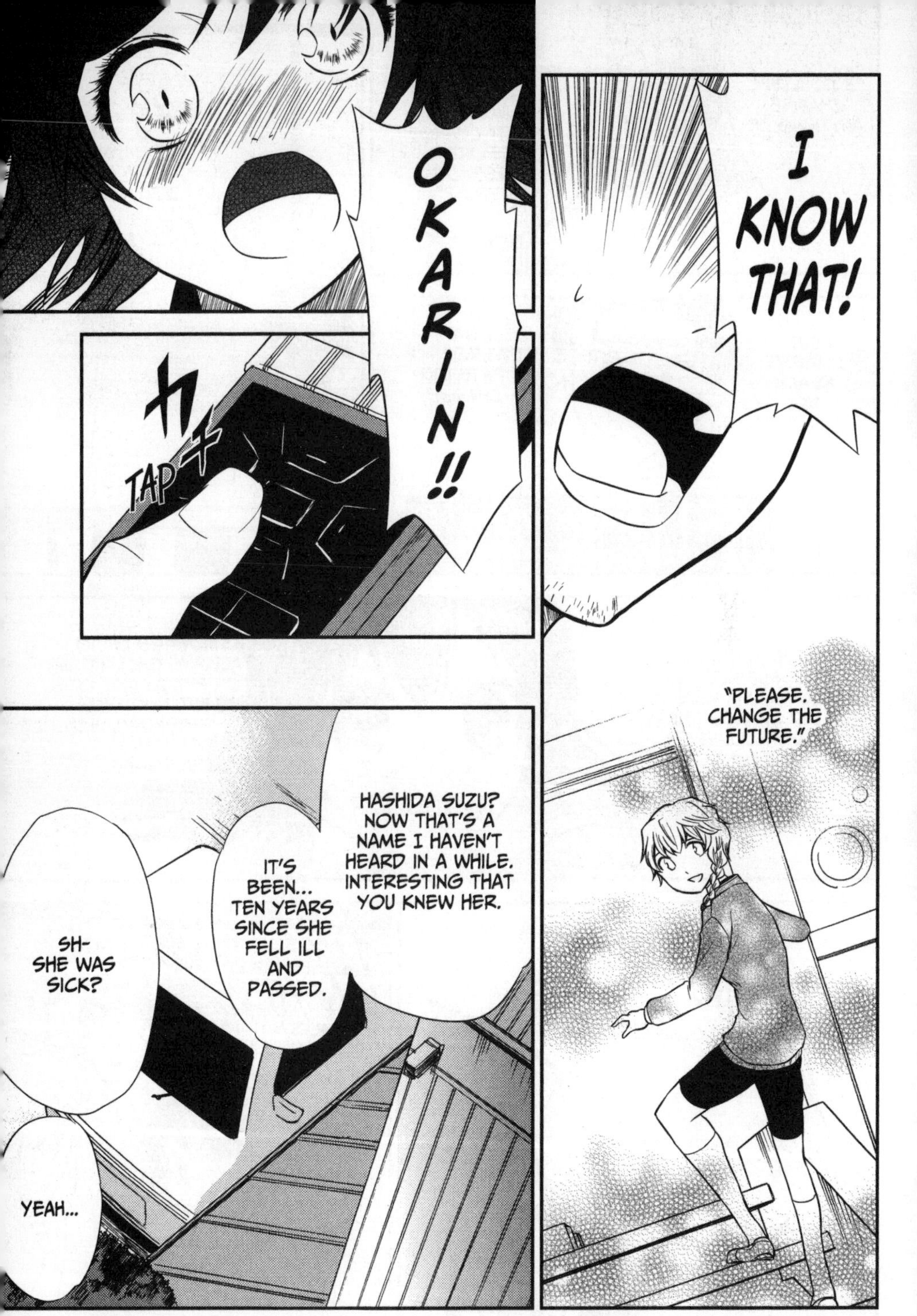
I KNOW THAT!
OKARIN!!
カチ
TAP
"PLEASE. CHANGE THE FUTURE."
HASHIDA SUZU? NOW THAT'S A NAME I HAVEN'T HEARD IN A WHILE. INTERESTING THAT YOU KNEW HER.
IT'S BEEN... TEN YEARS SINCE SHE FELL ILL AND PASSED.
SH- SHE WAS SICK?
YEAH...

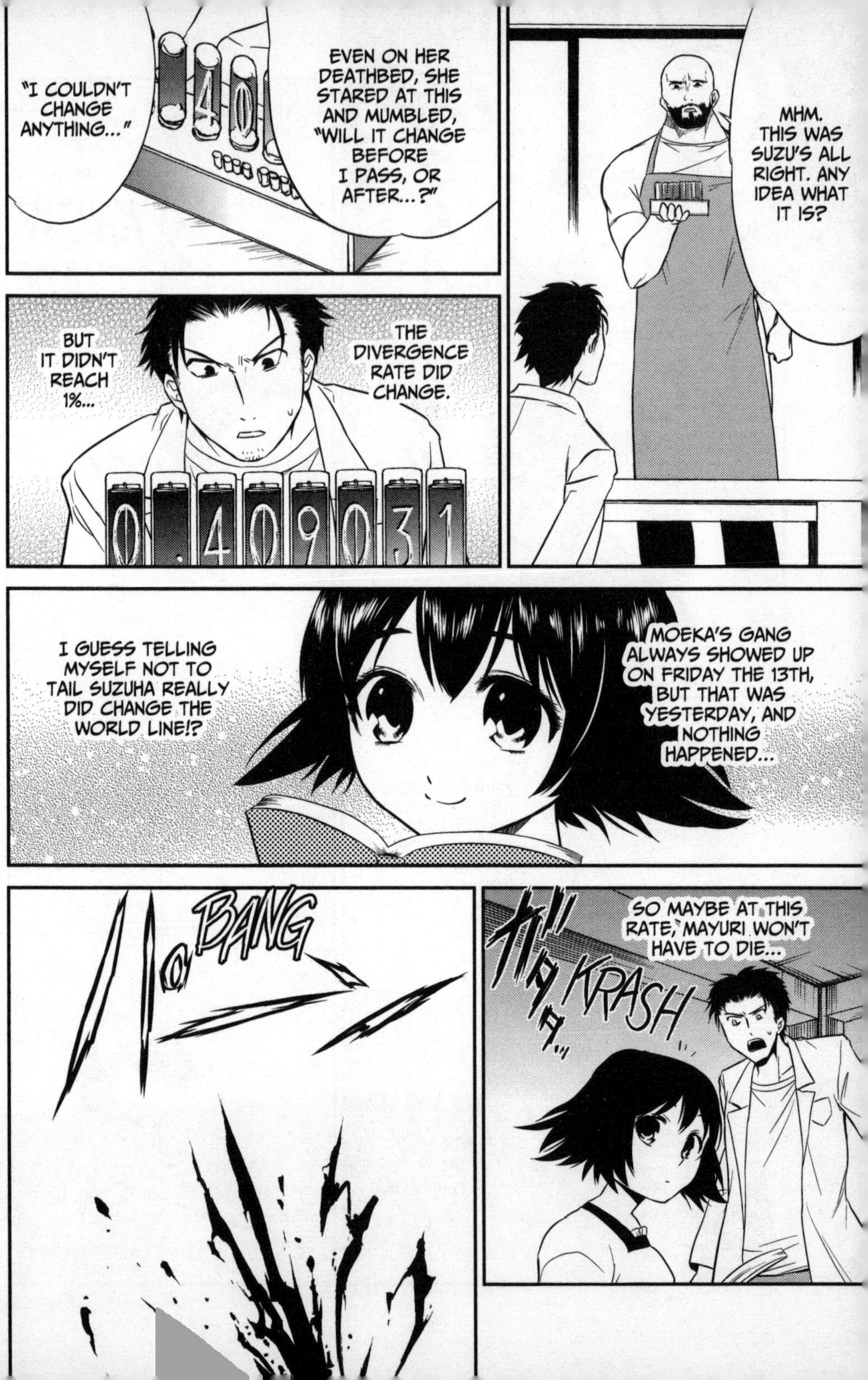
MHM. THIS WAS SUZU'S ALL RIGHT. ANY IDEA WHAT IT IS?
EVEN ON HER DEATHBED, SHE STARED AT THIS AND MUMBLED, "WILL IT CHANGE BEFORE I PASS, OR AFTER...?"
"I COULDN'T CHANGE ANYTHING..."
THE DIVERGENCE RATE DID CHANGE.
BUT IT DIDN'T REACH 1%...
0.409031
MOEKA'S GANG ALWAYS SHOWED UP ON FRIDAY THE 13TH, BUT THAT WAS YESTERDAY, AND NOTHING HAPPENED...
I GUESS TELLING MYSELF NOT TO TAIL SUZUHA REALLY DID CHANGE THE WORLD LINE!?
SO MAYBE AT THIS RATE, MAYURI WON'T HAVE TO DIE...
KRASH
BANG

[TIME MACHINE]

The revolutionary device completed in 2034. Its appearance is that of an ordinary satellite, but it has a cockpit and controls that allow a pilot to travel through time. The craft was used by John Titor, who also elaborated on its design. The mechanisms behind its functions and development differ between attractor fields α and β.

[D-MAIL]

"Texts sent to the past" via the Phonewave (real name T.B.A.). Every second on the microwave's timer translates to one hour farther back in the past. The maximum message length is three messages of six full-width or 12 half-width characters, each. Characters beyond that limit will be lost.

[READING STEINER]

Okabe's ability to detect when the world line has changed. He becomes very dizzy whenever a D-Mail is sent. When the world line changes, most people lose their memories and have them replaced with reconstructed ones, but Okabe retains his old memories. The downside is that he doesn't receive reconstructed memories of the new world line.

The universe has no end, though it does have a beginning. --- Infinite.
Stars too have a beginning, though they are destroyed by their own power. --- Finite.
Those who believe they have wisdom, are often shown by history to be the most foolish.
The fish in the sea don't know what the world is like on the land. Wisdom would destroy them as well.
Man to exceeding the speed of light would be more ridiculous than fish to living on land.
This is God's final warning to any who rebel.

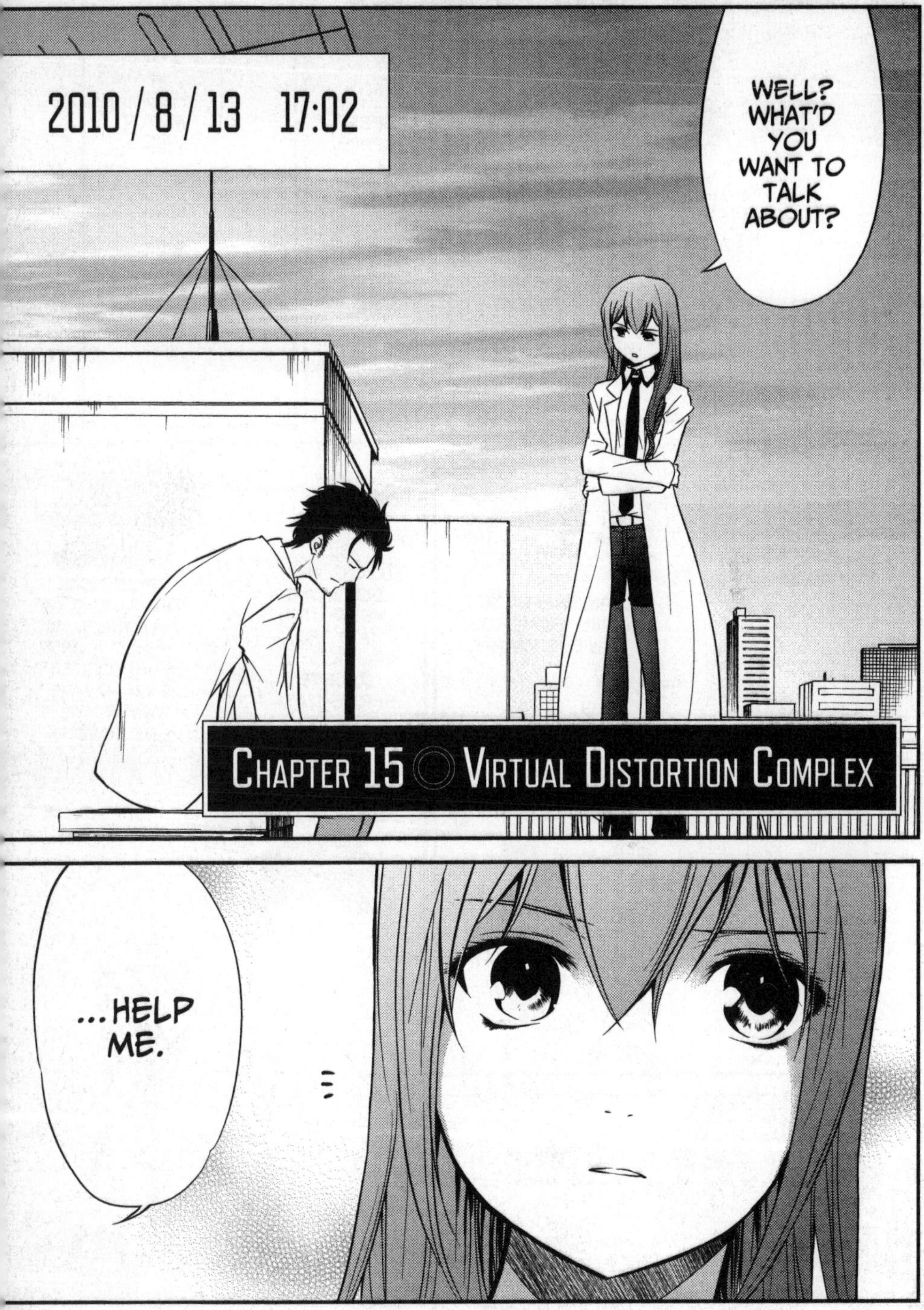
WELL? WHAT'D YOU WANT TO TALK ABOUT?
2010 / 8 / 13 17:02
CHAPTER 15 ◎ VIRTUAL DISTORTION COMPLEX
...HELP ME.

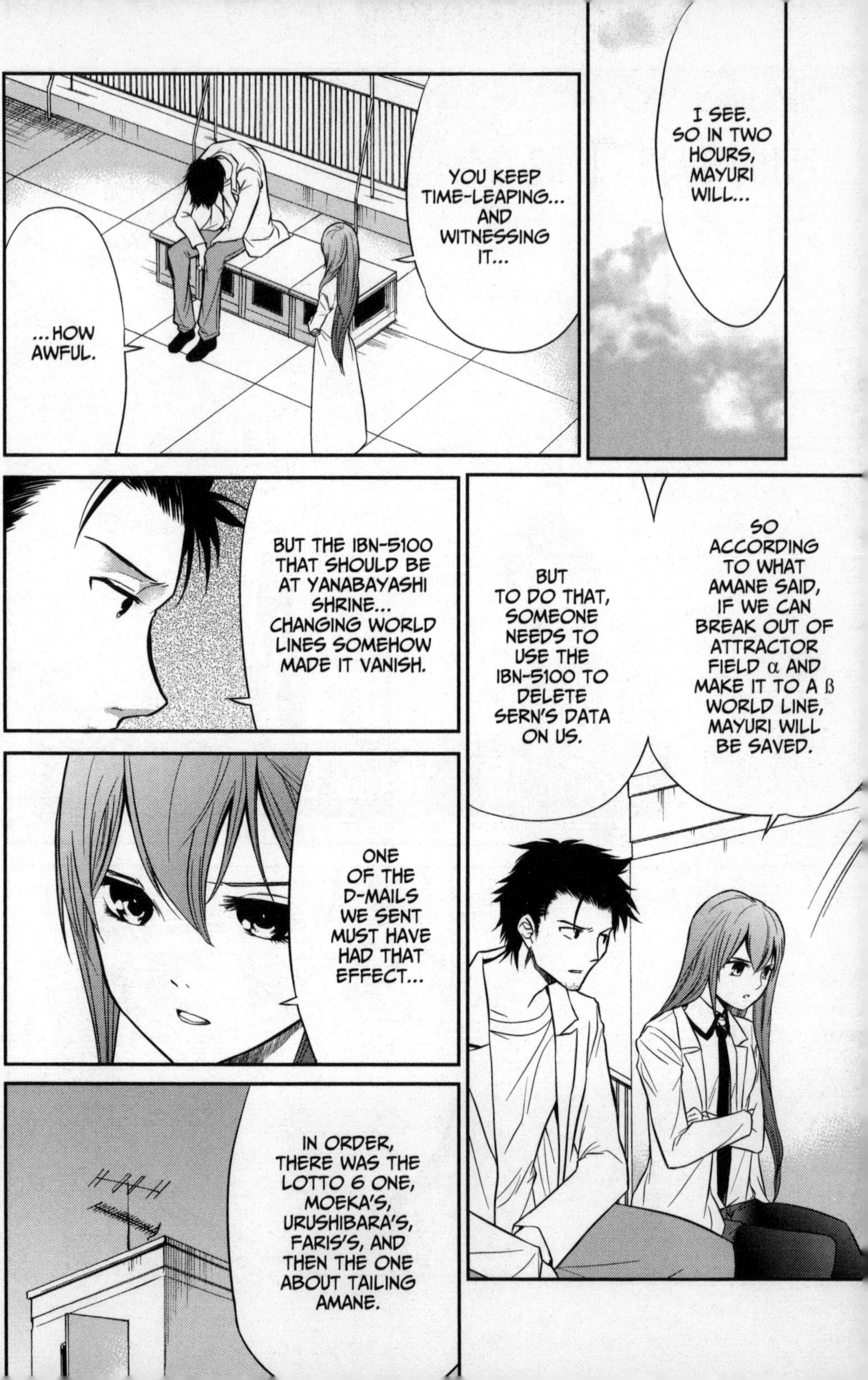
I SEE. SO IN TWO HOURS, MAYURI WILL...
YOU KEEP TIME-LEAPING... AND WITNESSING IT...
...HOW AWFUL.
SO ACCORDING TO WHAT AMANE SAID, IF WE CAN BREAK OUT OF ATTRACTOR FIELD α AND MAKE IT TO A β WORLD LINE, MAYURI WILL BE SAVED.
BUT TO DO THAT, SOMEONE NEEDS TO USE THE IBN-5100 TO DELETE SERN'S DATA ON US.
BUT THE IBN-5100 THAT SHOULD BE AT YANABAYASHI SHRINE... CHANGING WORLD LINES SOMEHOW MADE IT VANISH.
ONE OF THE D-MAILS WE SENT MUST HAVE HAD THAT EFFECT...
IN ORDER, THERE WAS THE LOTTO 6 ONE, MOEKA'S, URUSHIBARA'S, FARIS'S, AND THEN THE ONE ABOUT TAILING AMANE.

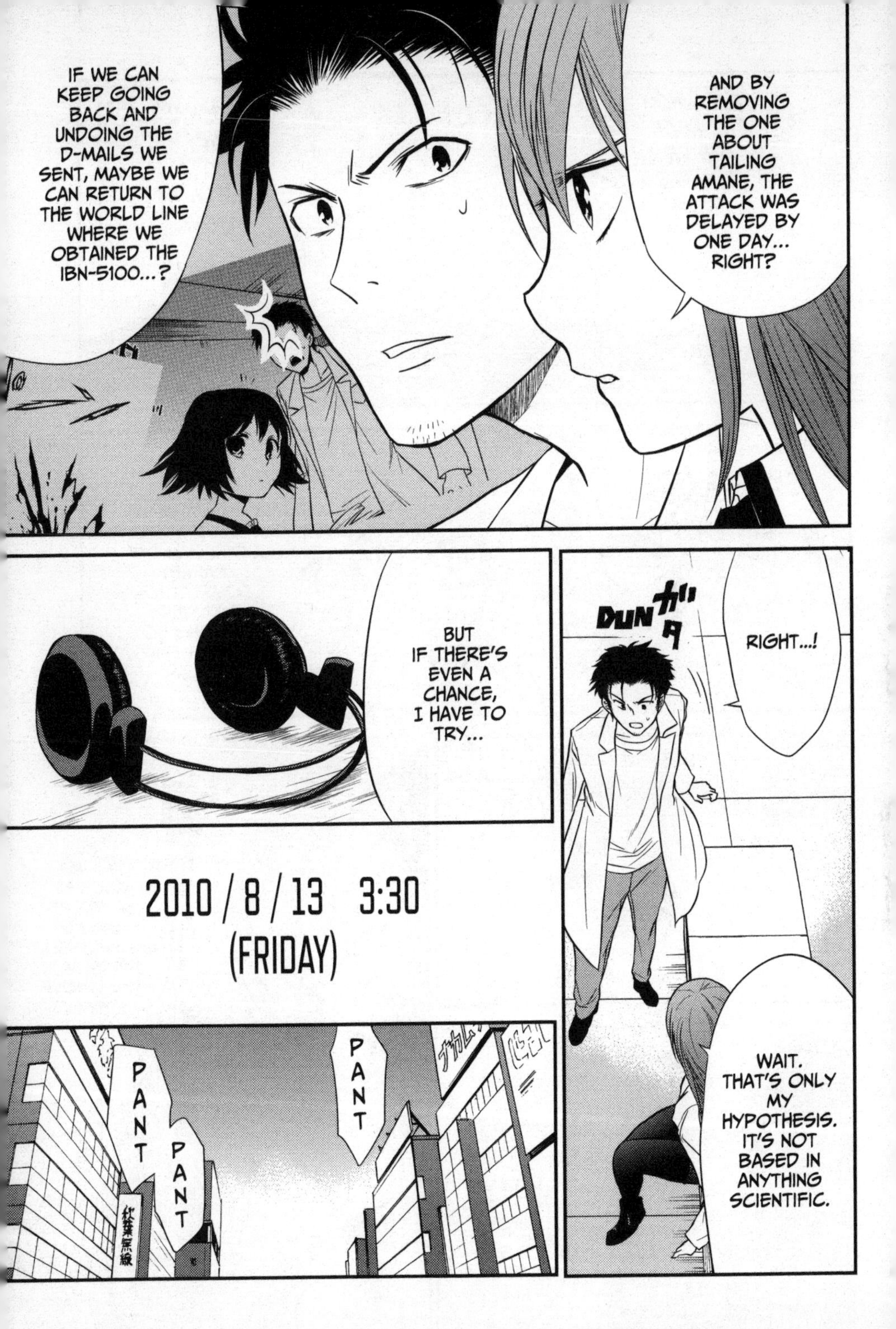
AND BY REMOVING THE ONE ABOUT TAILING AMANE, THE ATTACK WAS DELAYED BY ONE DAY... RIGHT?
IF WE CAN KEEP GOING BACK AND UNDOING THE D-MAILS WE SENT, MAYBE WE CAN RETURN TO THE WORLD LINE WHERE WE OBTAINED THE IBN-5100...?
RIGHT...!
DUN ガタ
WAIT. THAT'S ONLY MY HYPOTHESIS. IT'S NOT BASED IN ANYTHING SCIENTIFIC.
BUT IF THERE'S EVEN A CHANCE, I HAVE TO TRY...
2010 / 8 / 13 3:30 (FRIDAY)
PANT
PANT
PANT

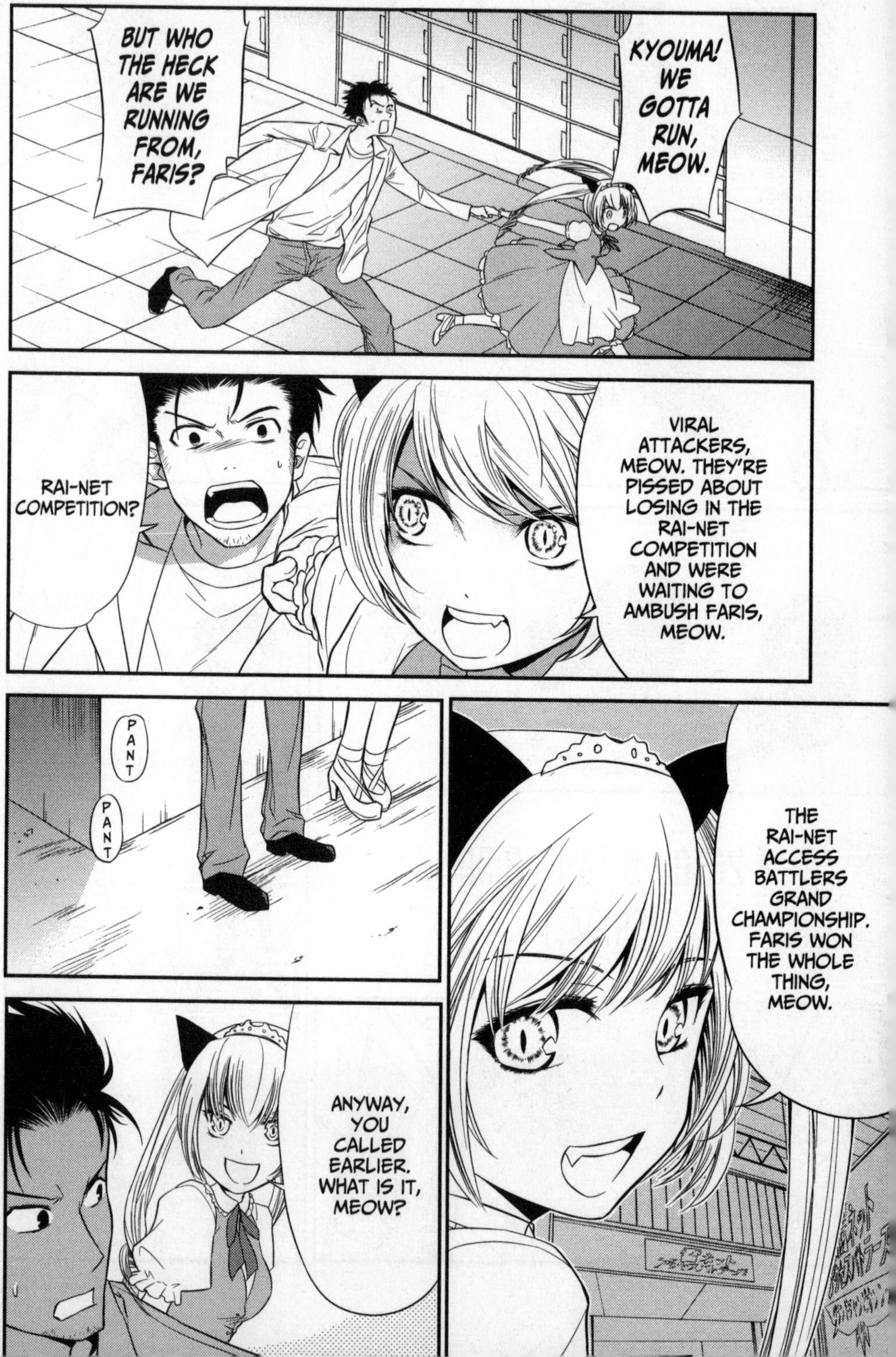
KYOUMA! WE GOTTA RUN, MEOW.
BUT WHO THE HECK ARE WE RUNNING FROM, FARIS?
VIRAL ATTACKERS, MEOW. THEY'RE PISSED ABOUT LOSING IN THE RAI-NET COMPETITION AND WERE WAITING TO AMBUSH FARIS, MEOW.
RAI-NET COMPETITION?
THE RAI-NET ACCESS BATTLERS GRAND CHAMPIONSHIP. FARIS WON THE WHOLE THING, MEOW.
PANT
PANT
ANYWAY, YOU CALLED EARLIER. WHAT IS IT, MEOW?

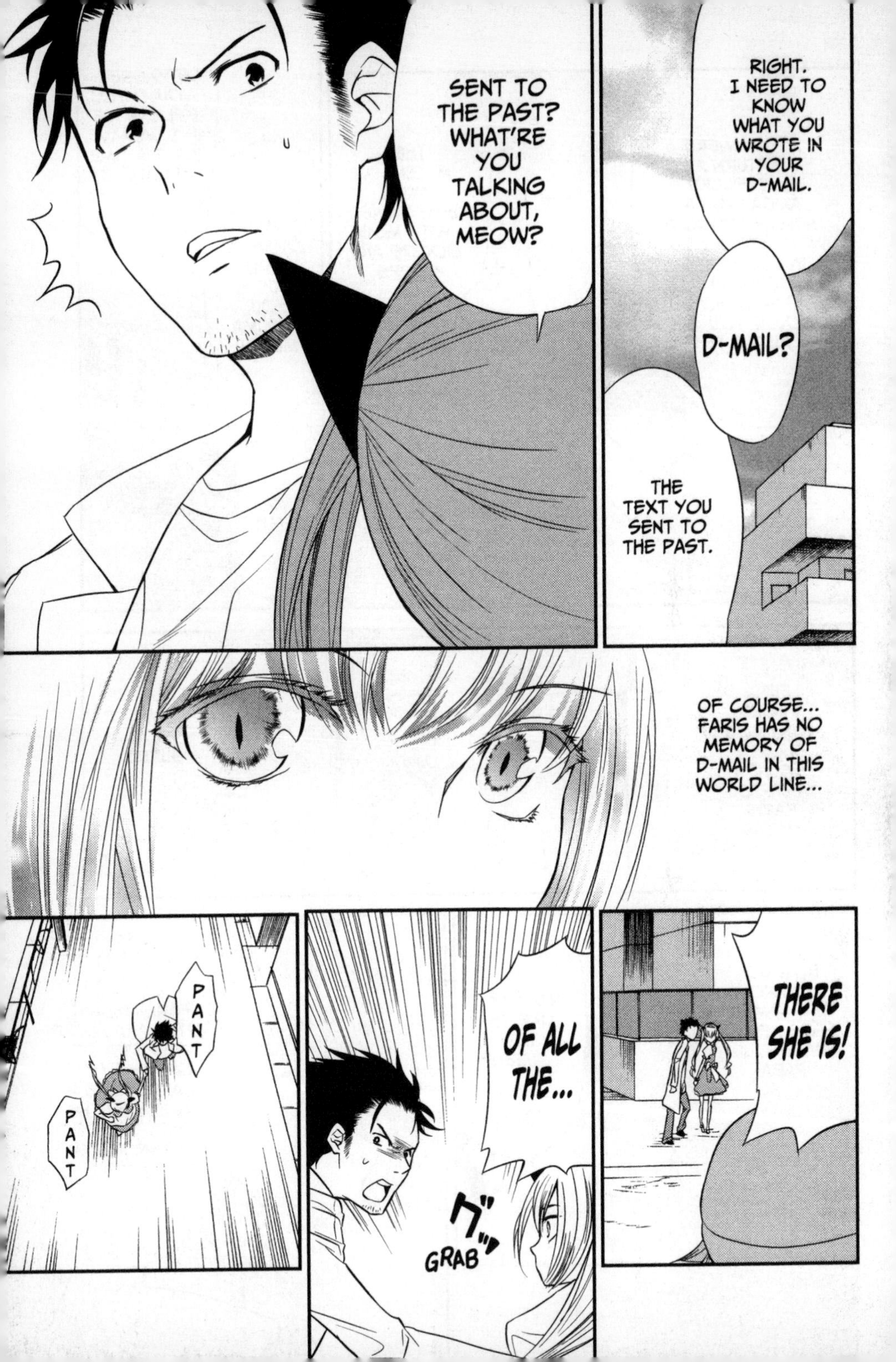
RIGHT. I NEED TO KNOW WHAT YOU WROTE IN YOUR D-MAIL.
D-MAIL?
THE TEXT YOU SENT TO THE PAST.
SENT TO THE PAST? WHAT'RE YOU TALKING ABOUT, MEOW?
OF COURSE... FARIS HAS NO MEMORY OF D-MAIL IN THIS WORLD LINE...
THERE SHE IS!
OF ALL THE...
グッ
GRAB
PANT
PANT

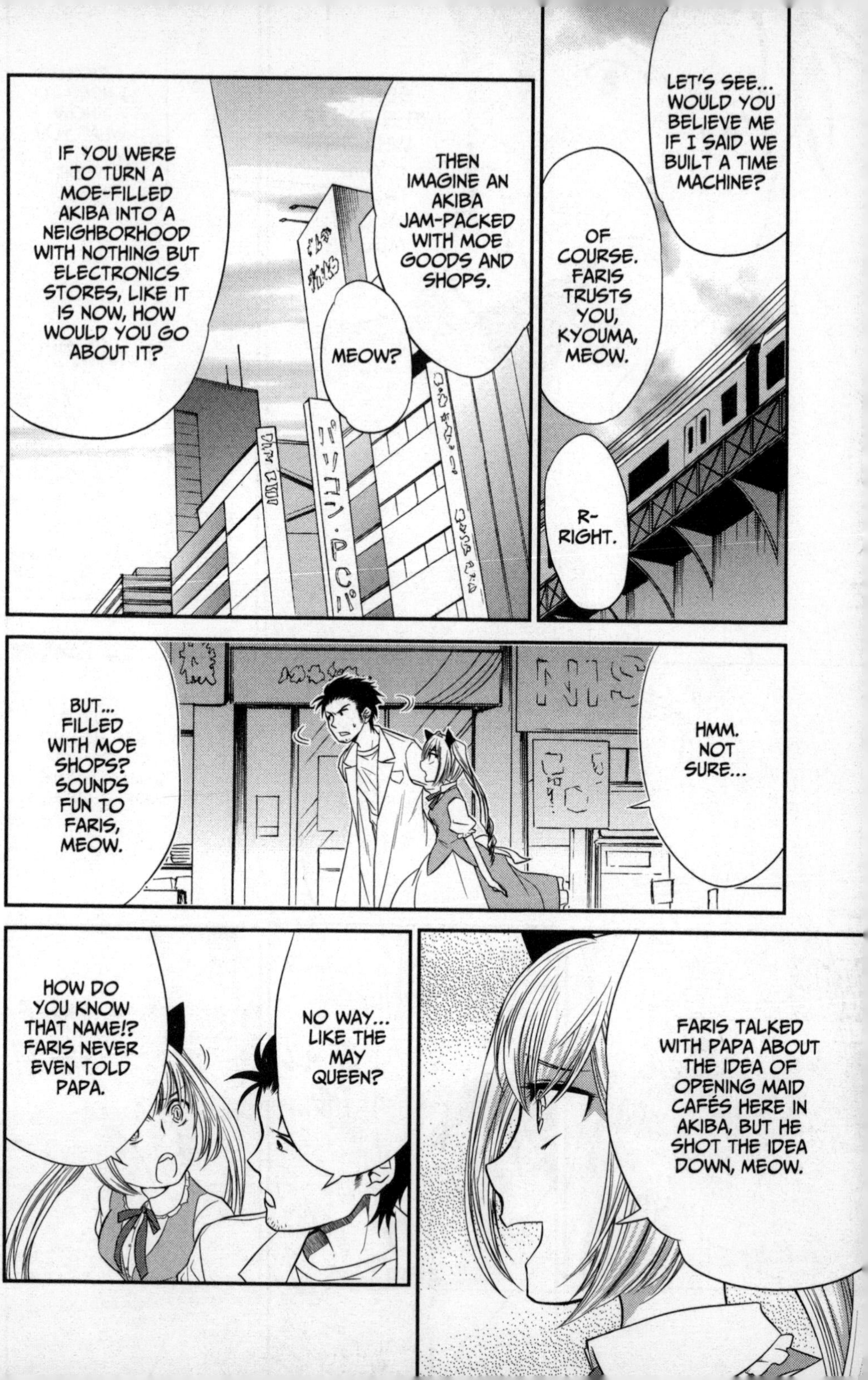
LET'S SEE... WOULD YOU BELIEVE ME IF I SAID WE BUILT A TIME MACHINE?
OF COURSE. FARIS TRUSTS YOU, KYOUMA, MEOW.
R-RIGHT.
THEN IMAGINE AN AKIBA JAM-PACKED WITH MOE GOODS AND SHOPS.
MEOW?
IF YOU WERE TO TURN A MOE-FILLED AKIBA INTO A NEIGHBORHOOD WITH NOTHING BUT ELECTRONICS STORES, LIKE IT IS NOW, HOW WOULD YOU GO ABOUT IT?
HMM. NOT SURE...
BUT... FILLED WITH MOE SHOPS? SOUNDS FUN TO FARIS, MEOW.
FARIS TALKED WITH PAPA ABOUT THE IDEA OF OPENING MAID CAFÉS HERE IN AKIBA, BUT HE SHOT THE IDEA DOWN, MEOW.
NO WAY... LIKE THE MAY QUEEN?
HOW DO YOU KNOW THAT NAME!? FARIS NEVER EVEN TOLD PAPA.

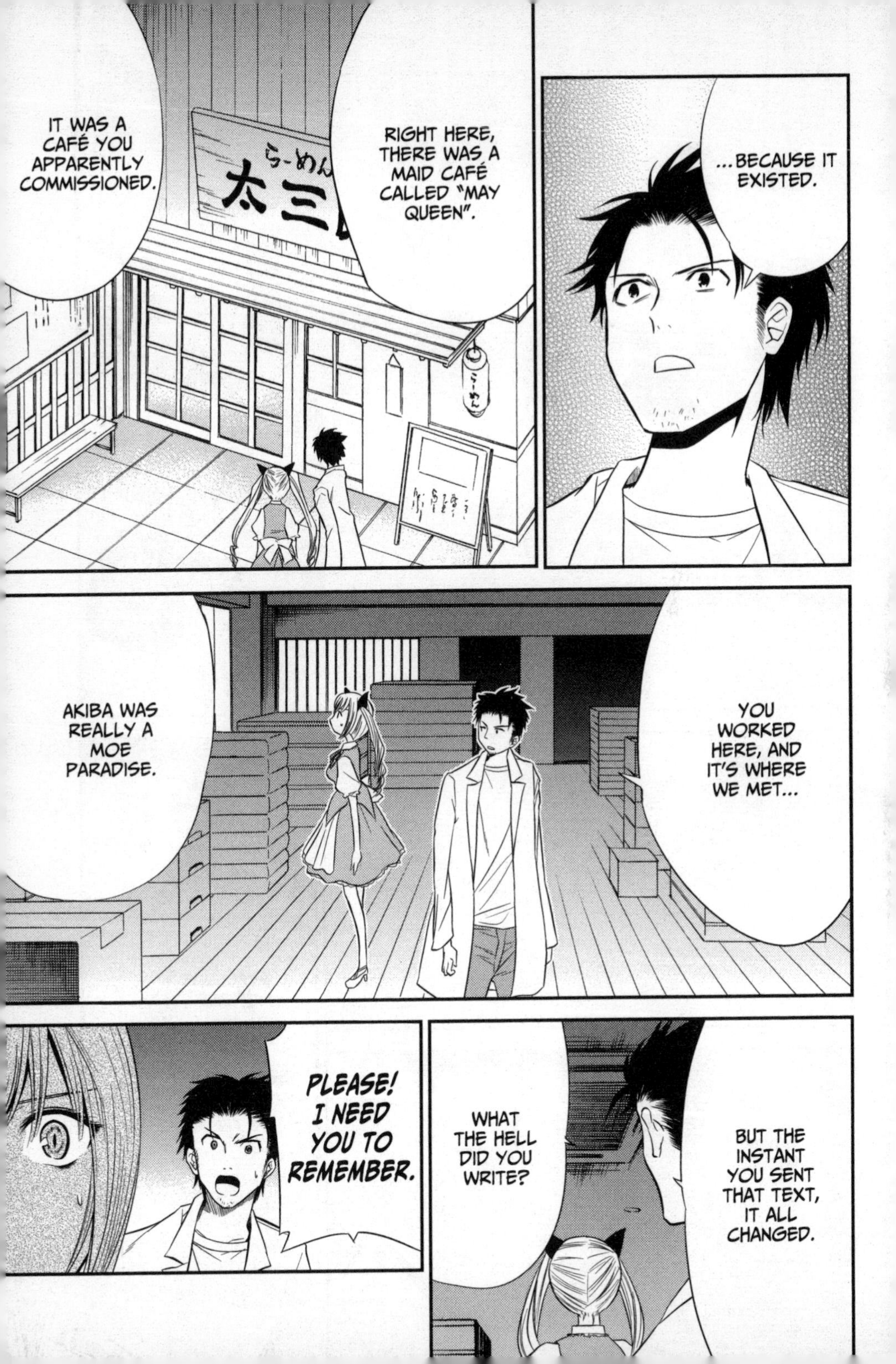
...BECAUSE IT EXISTED.
RIGHT HERE, THERE WAS A MAID CAFÉ CALLED "MAY QUEEN".
IT WAS A CAFÉ YOU APPARENTLY COMMISSIONED.
YOU WORKED HERE, AND IT'S WHERE WE MET...
AKIBA WAS REALLY A MOE PARADISE.
BUT THE INSTANT YOU SENT THAT TEXT, IT ALL CHANGED.
WHAT THE HELL DID YOU WRITE?
PLEASE! I NEED YOU TO REMEMBER.

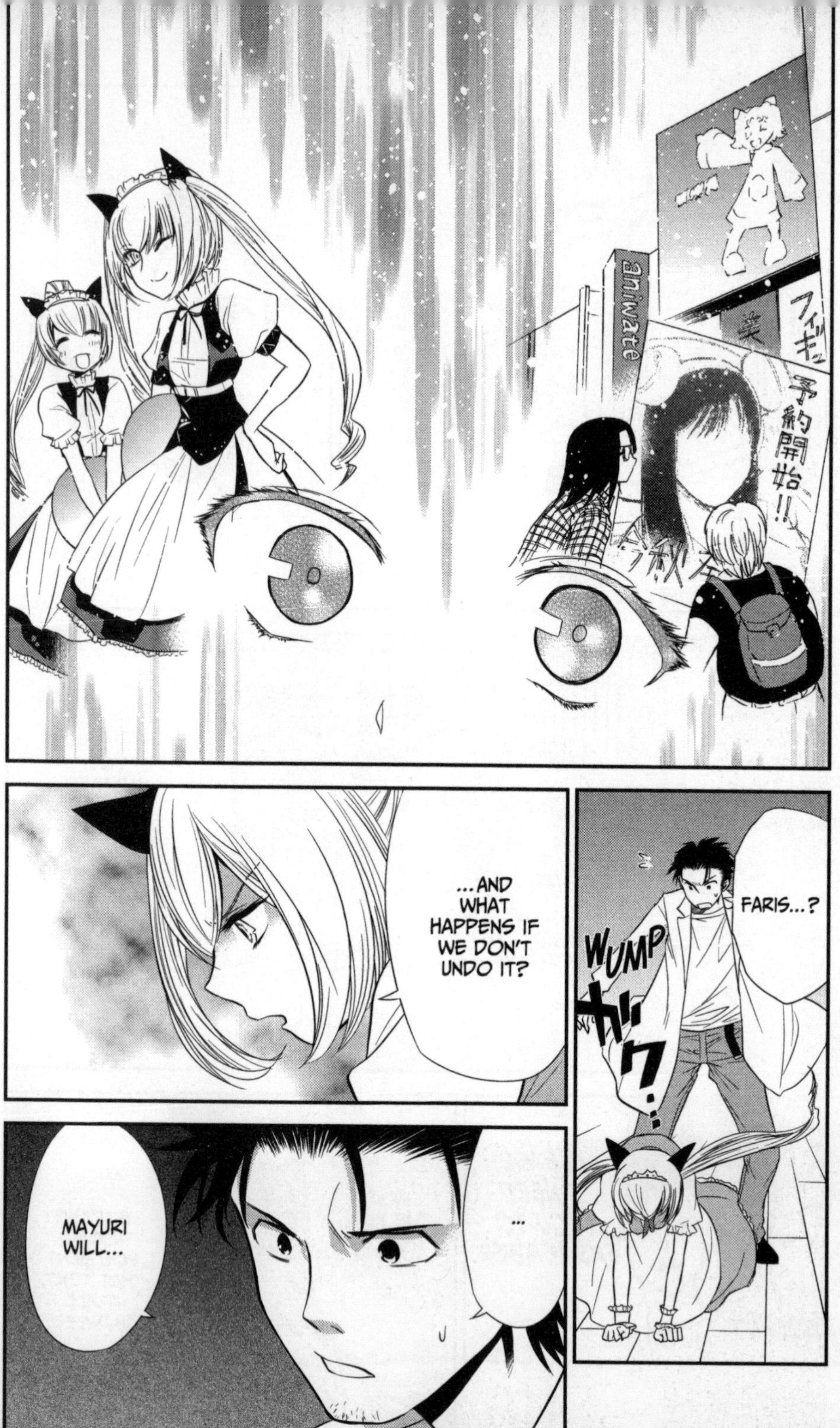

予約開始!!
FARIS...?
WUMP
...AND WHAT HAPPENS IF WE DON'T UNDO IT?
...
MAYURI WILL...

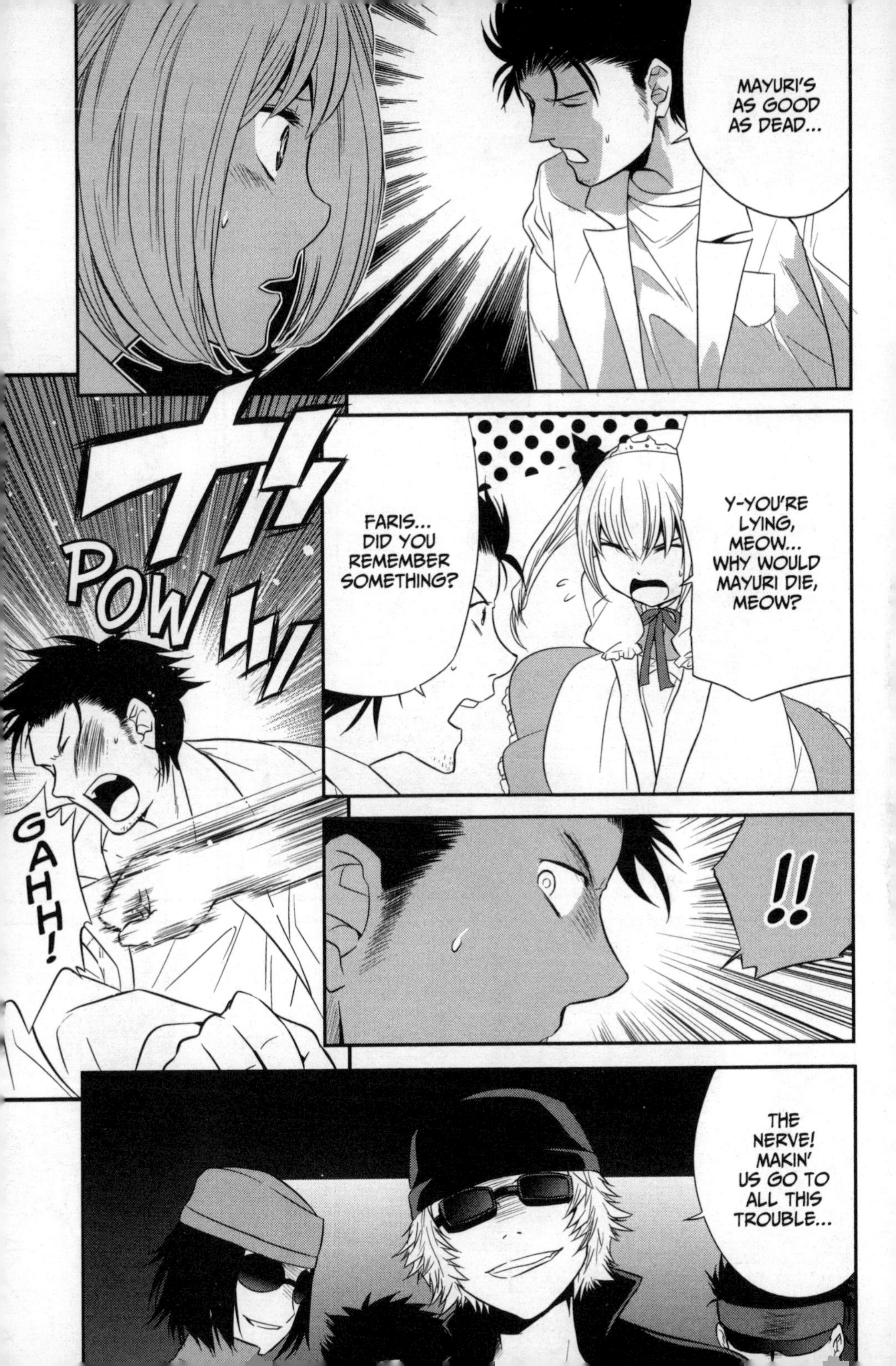
MAYURI'S AS GOOD AS DEAD...
Y-YOU'RE LYING, MEOW... WHY WOULD MAYURI DIE, MEOW?
FARIS... DID YOU REMEMBER SOMETHING?
!!
POW
GAHH!
THE NERVE! MAKIN' US GO TO ALL THIS TROUBLE...

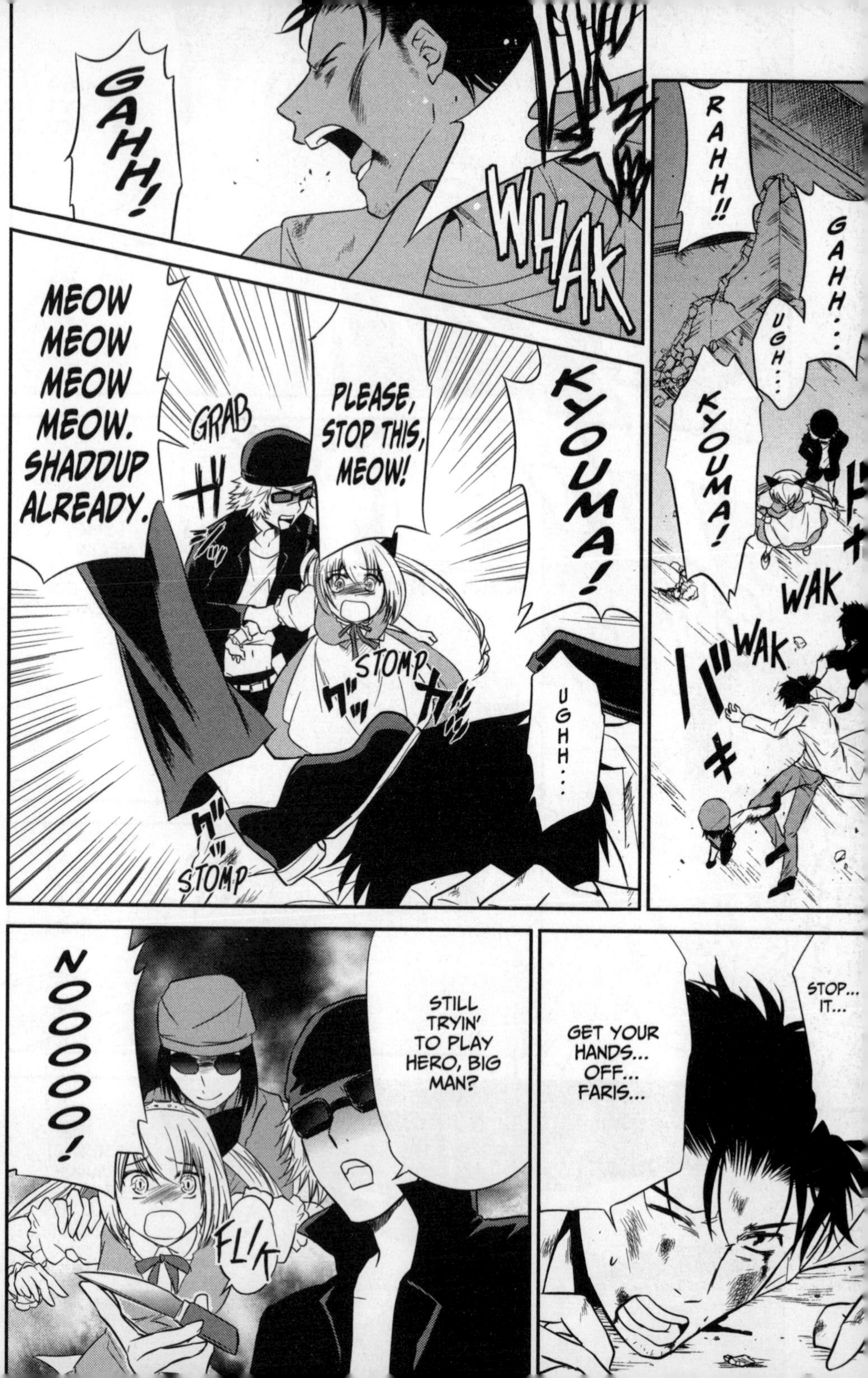

RAHH!!
GAHH...
UGH...
KYOUMA!
WAK
WAK
GAHH!
WHAK
KYOUMA!
PLEASE, STOP THIS, MEOW!
MEOW MEOW MEOW MEOW. SHADDUP ALREADY.
GRAB
STOMP
UGHH...
STOMP
STOP... IT...
GET YOUR HANDS... OFF... FARIS...
STILL TRYIN' TO PLAY HERO, BIG MAN?
NOOOOOO!
FLIK

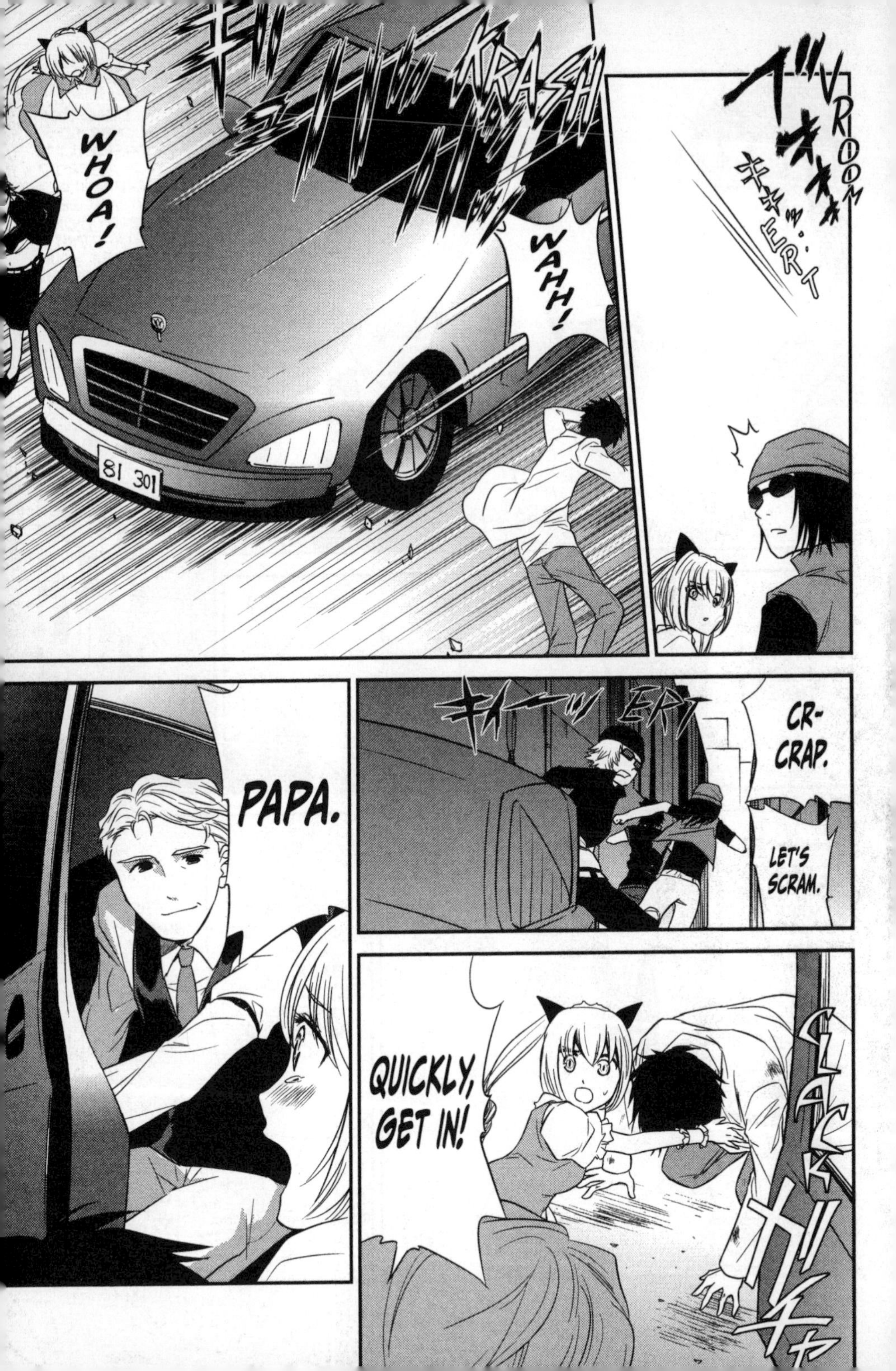
VROOM
ERT
KRASH
WAHH!
WHOA!
CR-CRAP.
LET'S SCRAM.
ERT
CLACK
QUICKLY, GET IN!
PAPA.

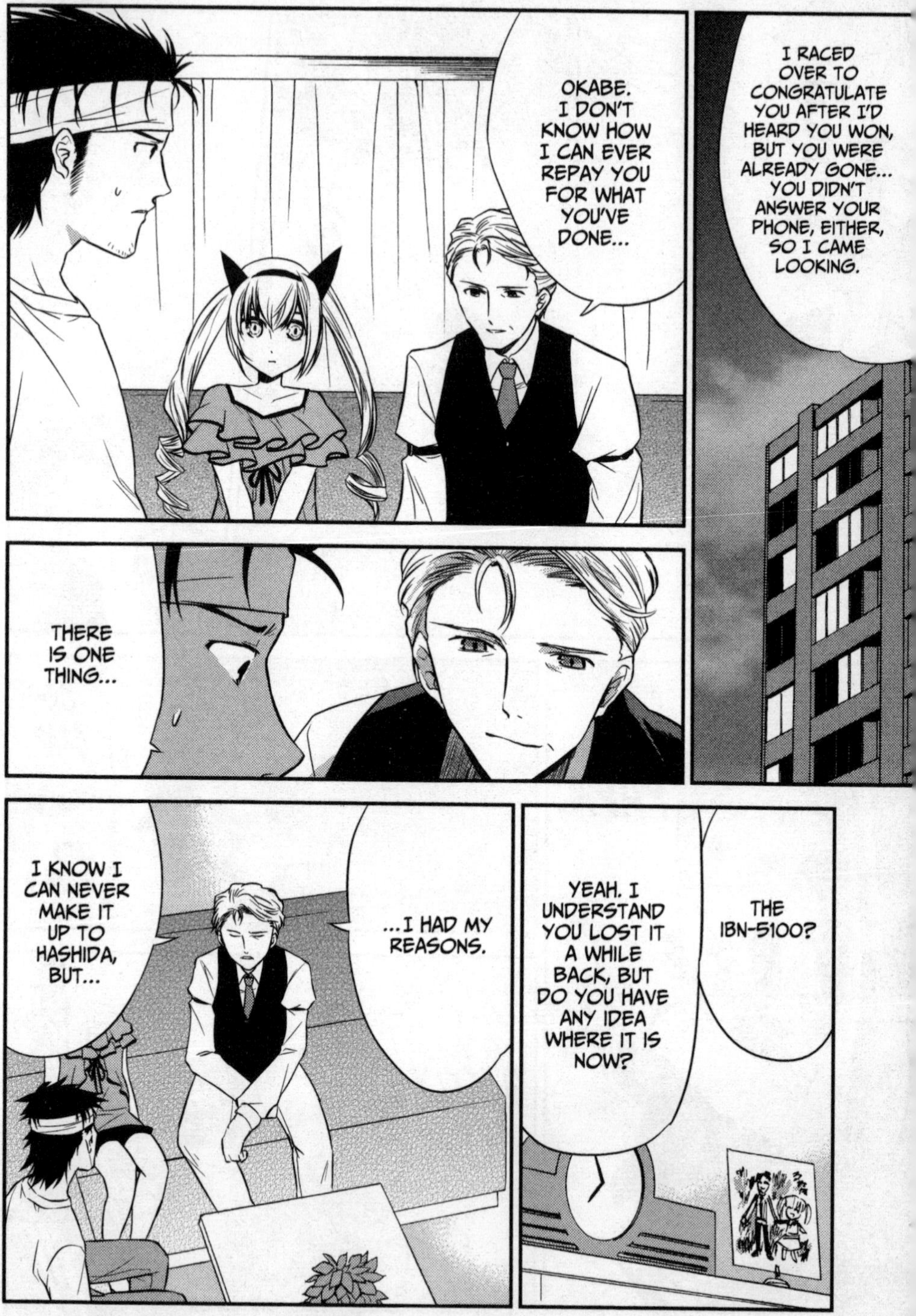
I RACED OVER TO CONGRATULATE YOU AFTER I'D HEARD YOU WON, BUT YOU WERE ALREADY GONE... YOU DIDN'T ANSWER YOUR PHONE, EITHER, SO I CAME LOOKING.
OKABE. I DON'T KNOW HOW I CAN EVER REPAY YOU FOR WHAT YOU'VE DONE...
THERE IS ONE THING...
THE IBN-5100?
YEAH. I UNDERSTAND YOU LOST IT A WHILE BACK, BUT DO YOU HAVE ANY IDEA WHERE IT IS NOW?
...I HAD MY REASONS.
I KNOW I CAN NEVER MAKE IT UP TO HASHIDA, BUT...

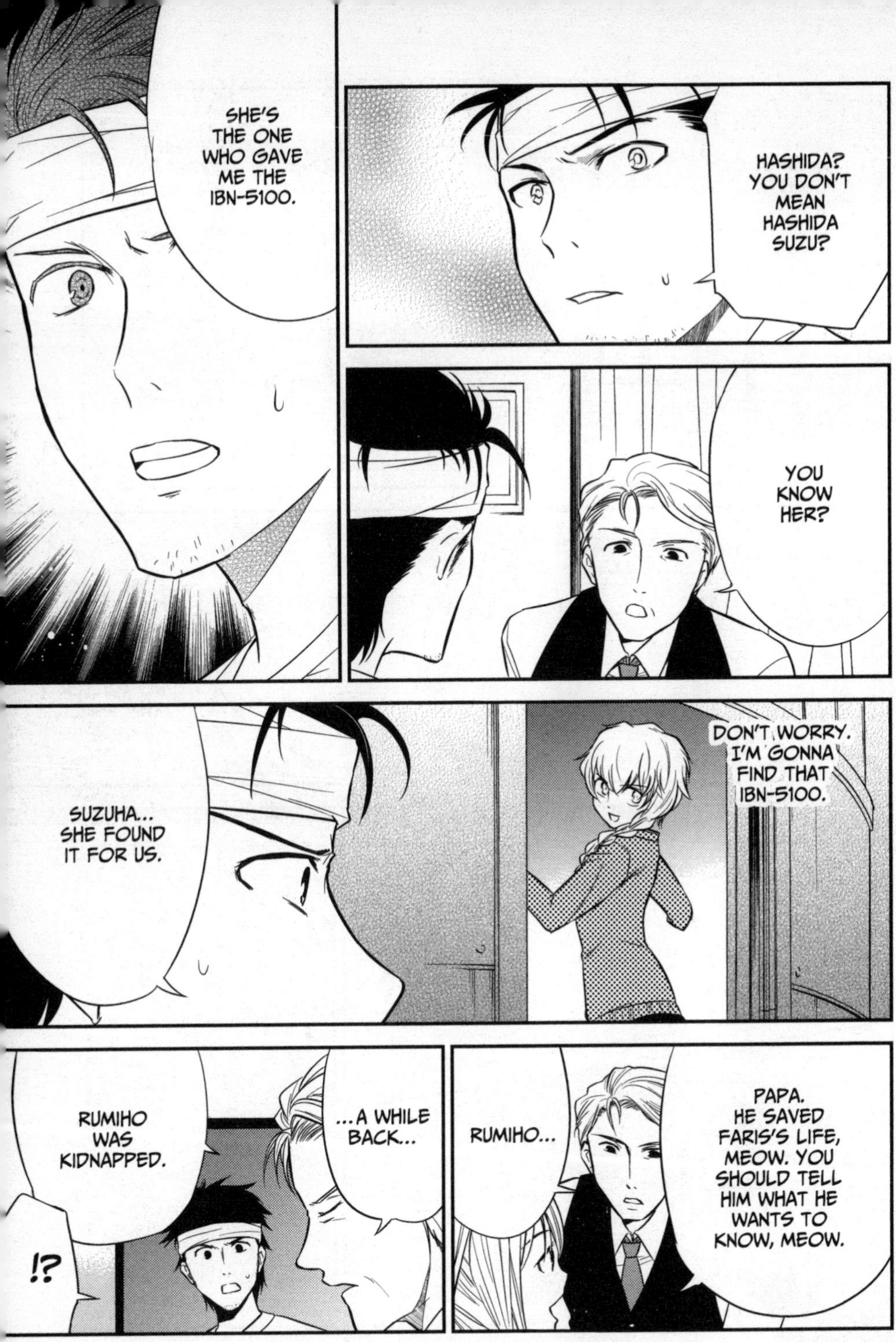
HASHIDA? YOU DON'T MEAN HASHIDA SUZU?
YOU KNOW HER?
SHE'S THE ONE WHO GAVE ME THE IBN-5100.
DON'T WORRY. I'M GONNA FIND THAT IBN-5100.
SUZUHA... SHE FOUND IT FOR US.
PAPA. HE SAVED FARIS'S LIFE, MEOW. YOU SHOULD TELL HIM WHAT HE WANTS TO KNOW, MEOW.
RUMIHO...
...A WHILE BACK...
RUMIHO WAS KIDNAPPED.
!?

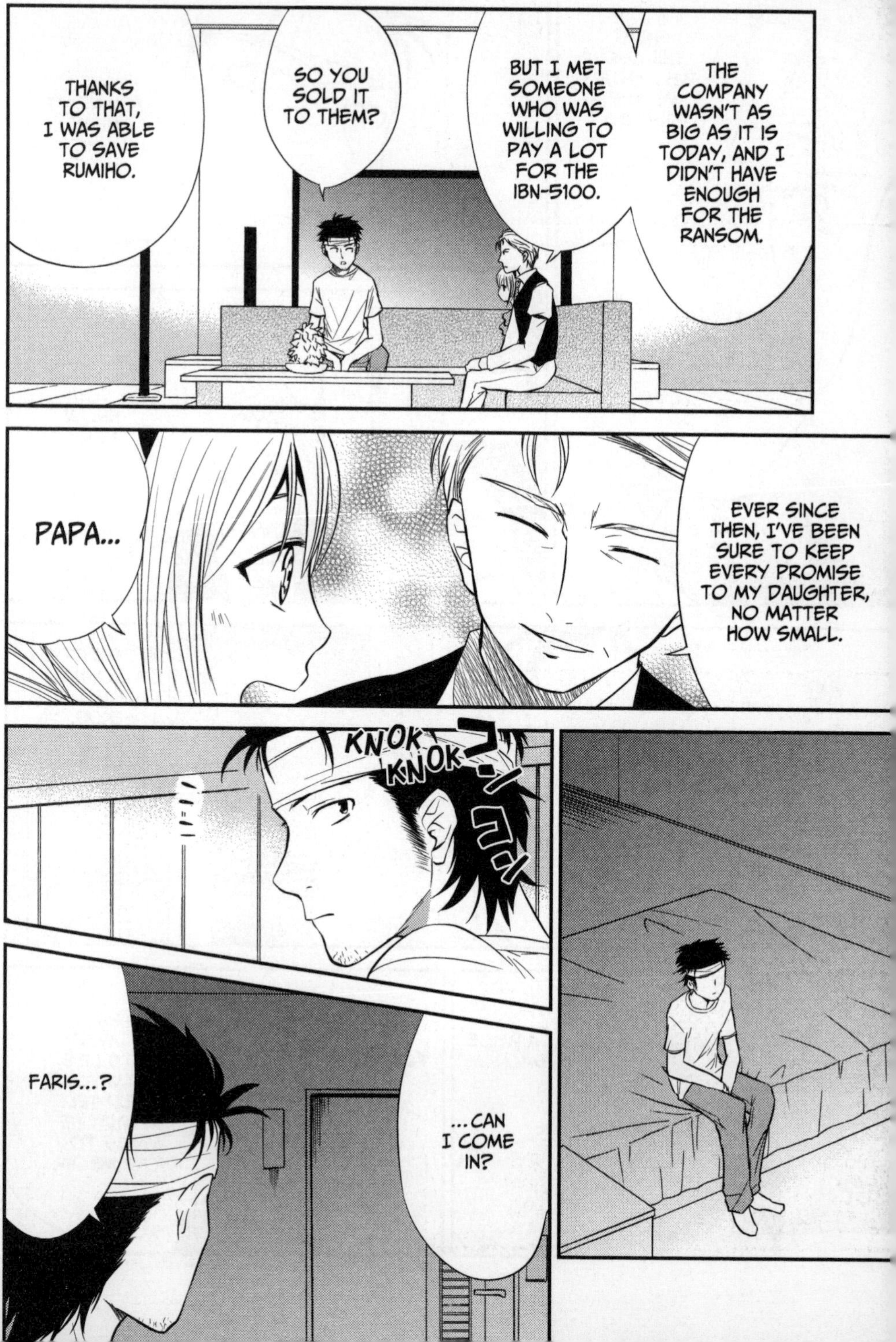
THE COMPANY WASN'T AS BIG AS IT IS TODAY, AND I DIDN'T HAVE ENOUGH FOR THE RANSOM.
BUT I MET SOMEONE WHO WAS WILLING TO PAY A LOT FOR THE IBN-5100.
SO YOU SOLD IT TO THEM?
THANKS TO THAT, I WAS ABLE TO SAVE RUMIHO.
EVER SINCE THEN, I'VE BEEN SURE TO KEEP EVERY PROMISE TO MY DAUGHTER, NO MATTER HOW SMALL.
PAPA...
KNOK KNOK
...CAN I COME IN?
FARIS...?

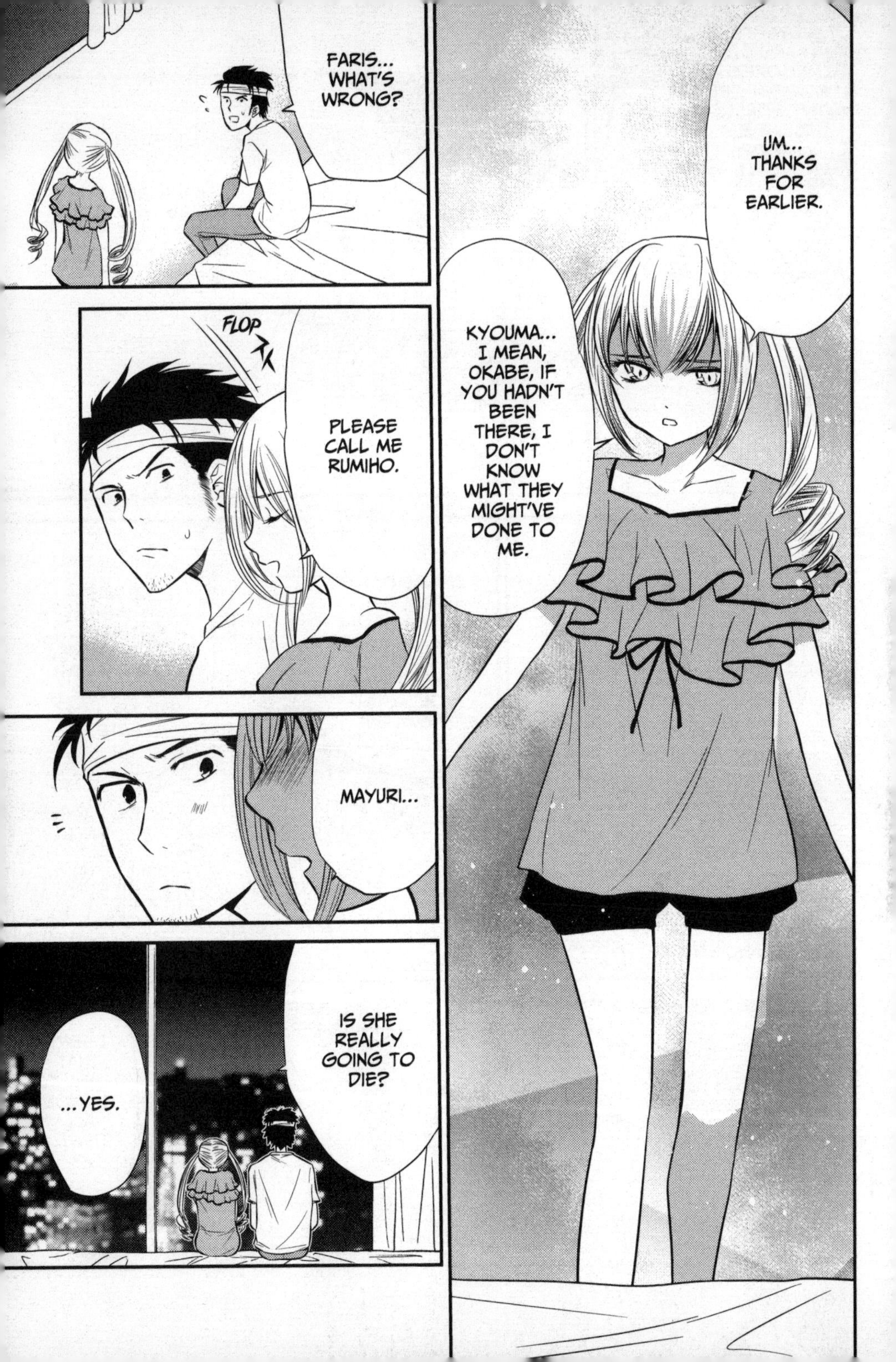
UM... THANKS FOR EARLIER.
KYOUMA... I MEAN, OKABE, IF YOU HADN'T BEEN THERE, I DON'T KNOW WHAT THEY MIGHT'VE DONE TO ME.
FARIS... WHAT'S WRONG?
FLOP
PLEASE CALL ME RUMIHO.
MAYURI...
IS SHE REALLY GOING TO DIE?
...YES.

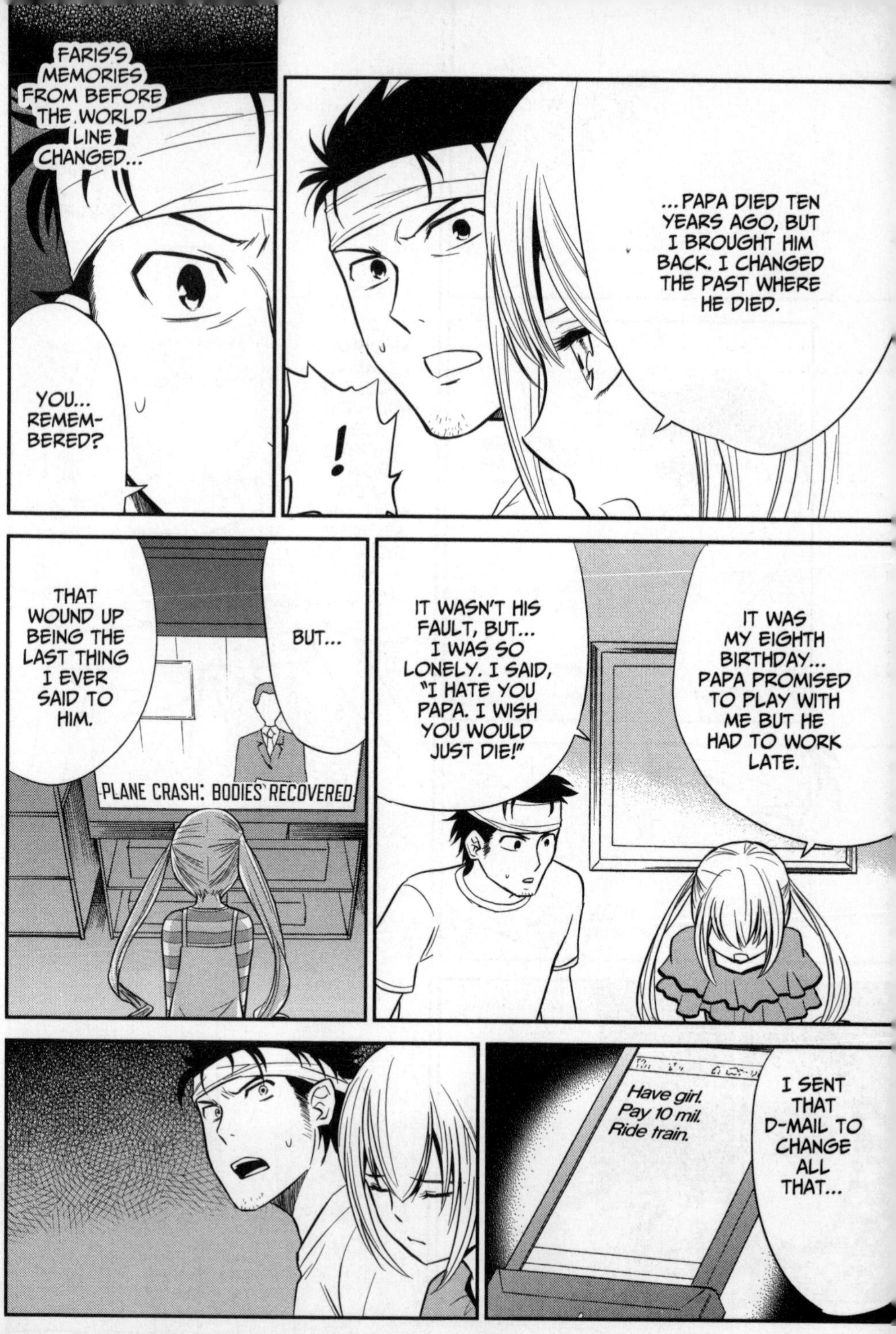
...PAPA DIED TEN YEARS AGO, BUT I BROUGHT HIM BACK. I CHANGED THE PAST WHERE HE DIED.
!
FARIS'S MEMORIES FROM BEFORE THE WORLD LINE CHANGED...
YOU... REMEM-BERED?
IT WAS MY EIGHTH BIRTHDAY... PAPA PROMISED TO PLAY WITH ME BUT HE HAD TO WORK LATE.
IT WASN'T HIS FAULT, BUT... I WAS SO LONELY. I SAID, "I HATE YOU PAPA. I WISH YOU WOULD JUST DIE!"
BUT...
THAT WOUND UP BEING THE LAST THING I EVER SAID TO HIM.
PLANE CRASH: BODIES RECOVERED
I SENT THAT D-MAIL TO CHANGE ALL THAT...
Have girl.
Pay 10 mil.
Ride train.

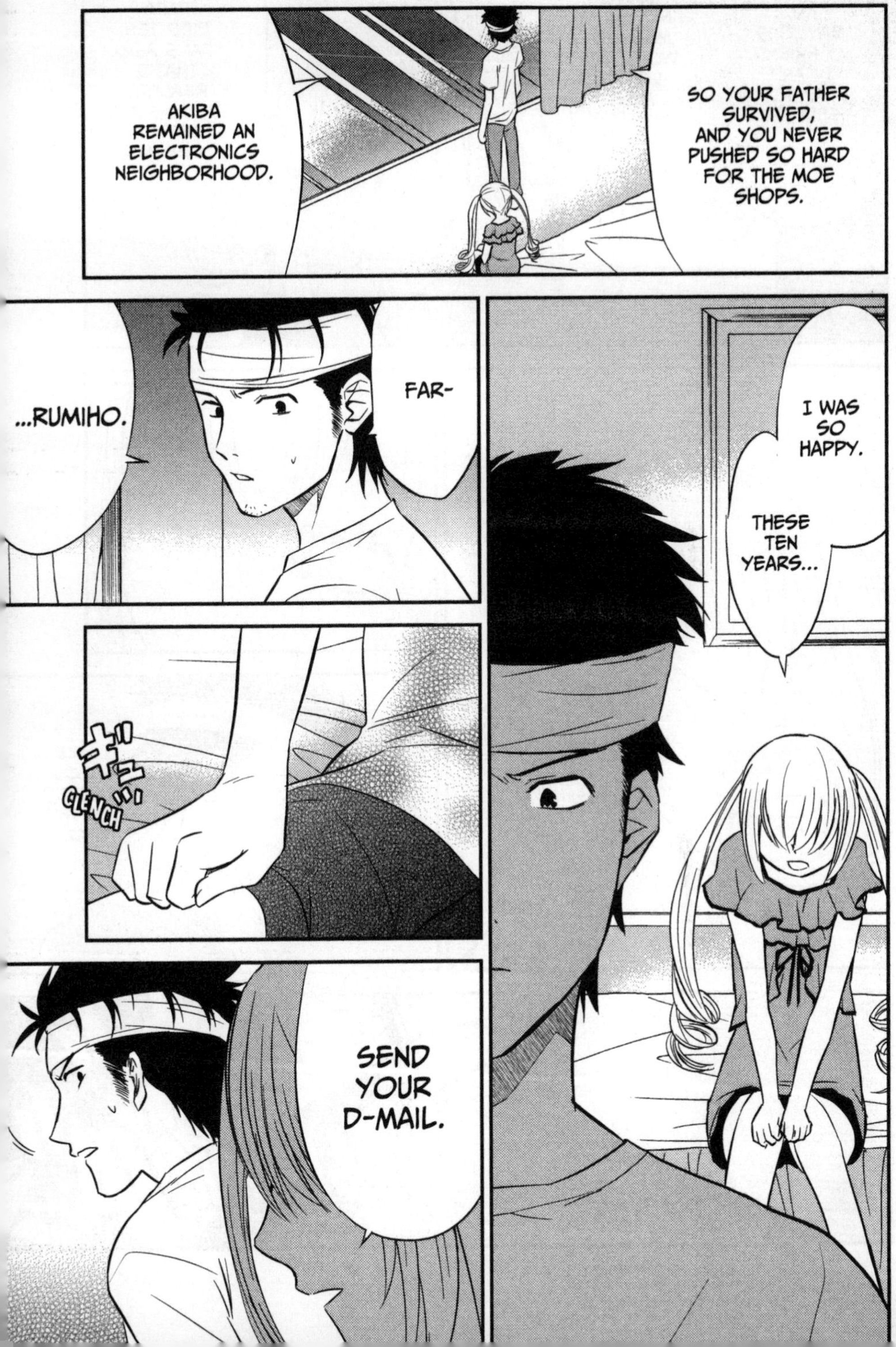
SO YOUR FATHER SURVIVED, AND YOU NEVER PUSHED SO HARD FOR THE MOE SHOPS.
AKIBA REMAINED AN ELECTRONICS NEIGHBORHOOD.
I WAS SO HAPPY.
THESE TEN YEARS...
FAR-
...RUMIHO.
ギュ
CLENCH
SEND YOUR D-MAIL.

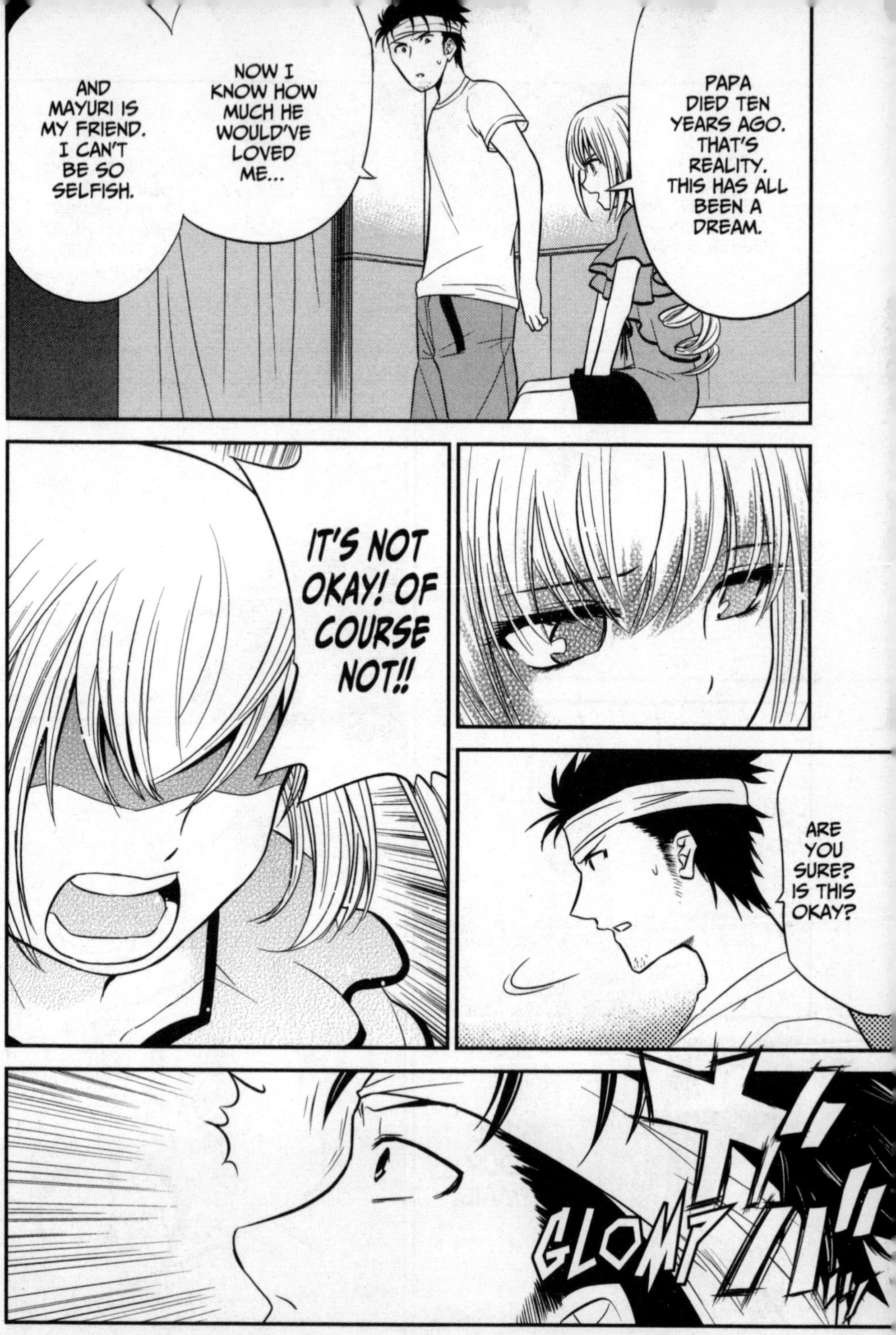
PAPA DIED TEN YEARS AGO. THAT'S REALITY. THIS HAS ALL BEEN A DREAM.
NOW I KNOW HOW MUCH HE WOULD'VE LOVED ME...
AND MAYURI IS MY FRIEND. I CAN'T BE SO SELFISH.
ARE YOU SURE? IS THIS OKAY?
IT'S NOT OKAY! OF COURSE NOT!!
GLOMP

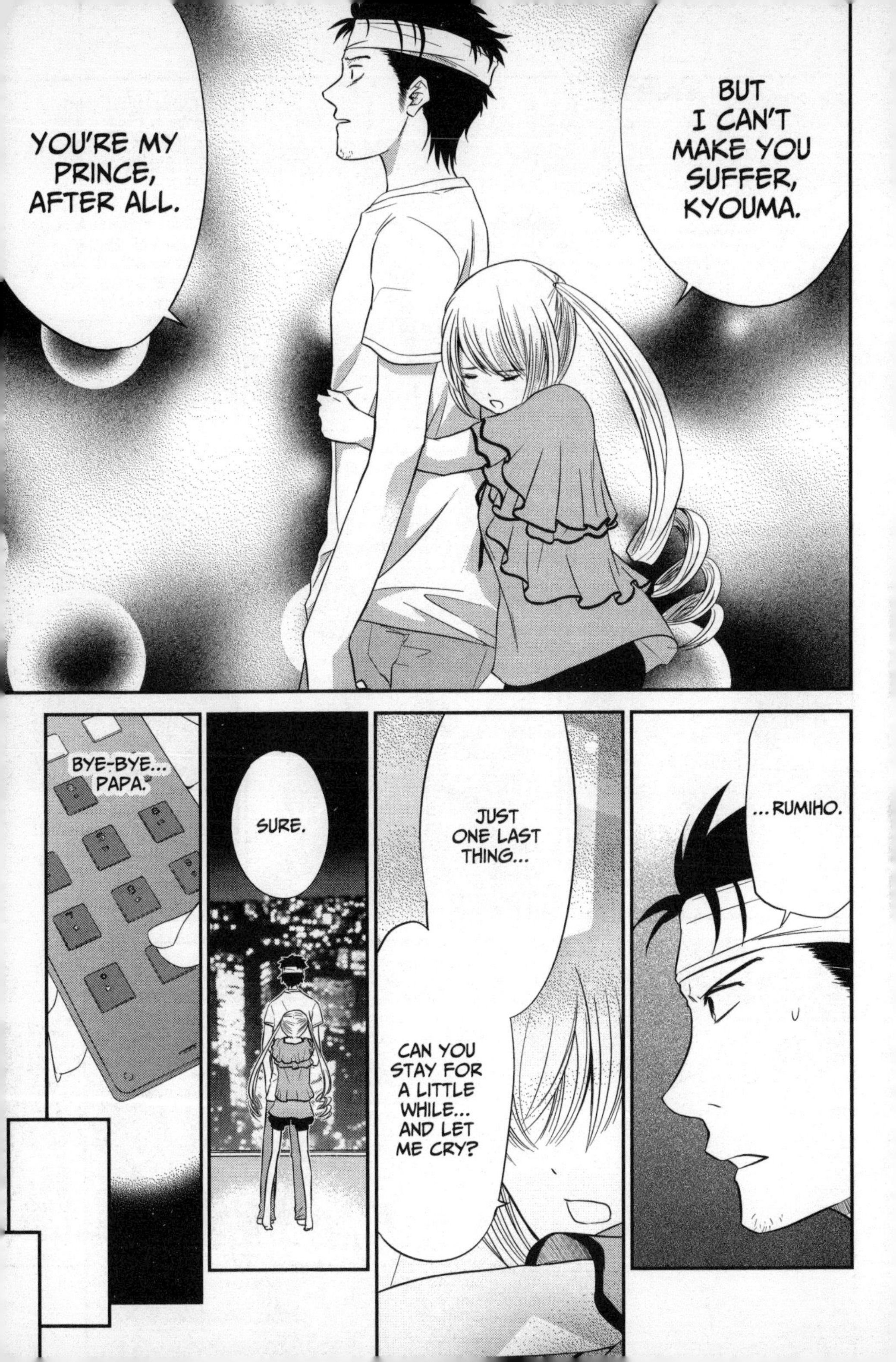
BUT I CAN'T MAKE YOU SUFFER, KYOUMA.
YOU'RE MY PRINCE, AFTER ALL.
...RUMIHO.
JUST ONE LAST THING...
CAN YOU STAY FOR A LITTLE WHILE... AND LET ME CRY?
SURE.
BYE-BYE... PAPA.

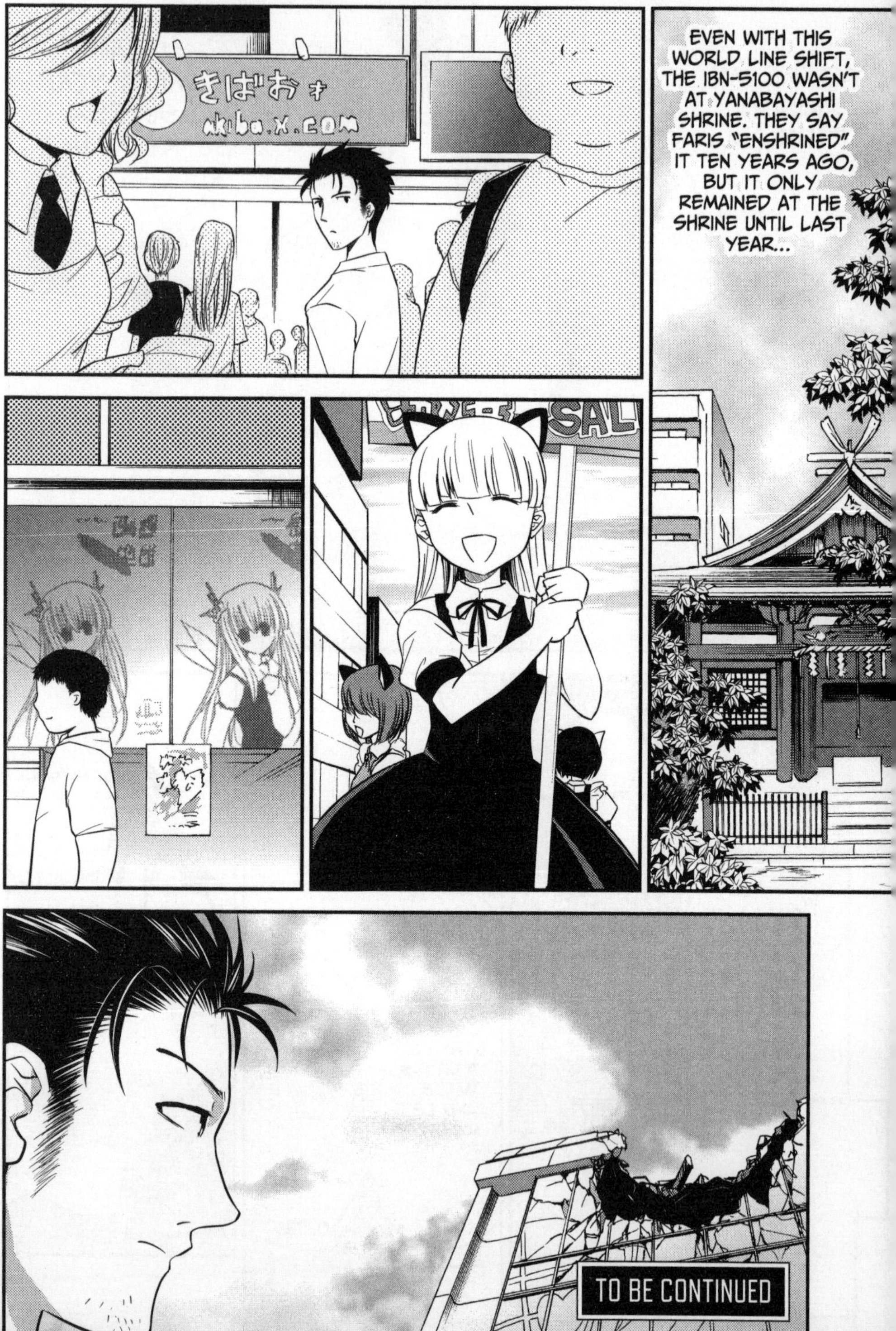
EVEN WITH THIS WORLD LINE SHIFT, THE IBN-5100 WASN'T AT YANABAYASHI SHRINE. THEY SAY FARIS "ENSHRINED" IT TEN YEARS AGO, BUT IT ONLY REMAINED AT THE SHRINE UNTIL LAST YEAR...
akiba.x.com
TO BE CONTINUED

Steins;Gate

The universe has no end, though it does have a beginning. --- Infinite.
Stars too have a beginning, though they are destroyed by their own power. --- Finite.
Those who believe they have wisdom, are often shown by history to be the most foolish.
The fish in the sea don't know what the world is like on the land. Wisdom would destroy them as well.
Man to exceeding the speed of light would be more ridiculous than fish to living on land.
This is God's final warning to any who rebel.

MANGA BY: Yomi Sarachi
ORIGINAL CREATOR: 5pb. Inc. x Nitroplus

ENGLISH EDITION
Translation: CALEB D. COOK
Lettering: MARSHALL DILLON

UDON STAFF
Chief of Operations: ERIK KO
Director of Publishing: MATT MOYLAN
Senior Editor: ASH PAULSEN
VP of Sales - JOHN SHABLESKI
Senior Producer - LONG VO
Marketing Manager: JENNY MYUNG
Production Manager: JANICE LEUNG
Japanese Liaisons: STEVEN CUMMINGS

STEINS;GATE Volume 2
© Yomi Sarachi, Sakae Saitoh 2013
© 2009-2015 MAGES./5pb./Nitroplus.
Edited by MEDIA FACTORY.
First published in Japan in 2013 by KADOKAWA CORPORATION
English translation rights reserved by UDON Entertainment Inc.
Under the license from KADOKAWA CORPORATION.
Through TOHAN CORPORATION, Ltd., Tokyo.

Published by UDON Entertainment Corp.
118 Tower Hill Road, C1, PO Box 20008
Richmond Hill, Ontario, L4K 0K0 CANADA

www.UDONentertainment.com

First Printing: November 2015
ISBN-13: 978-1-927925-55-3
ISBN-10: 1-927925-55-X

Printed in the United States

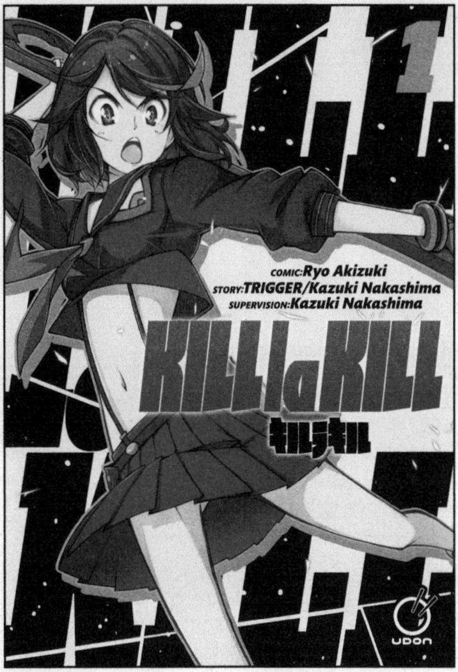
1
COMIC: Ryo Akizuki
STORY: TRIGGER/Kazuki Nakashima
SUPERVISION: Kazuki Nakashima
KILL la KILL
キルラキル
UDON

KILL LA KILL Volume 1

ISBN: 978-1-927925-49-2

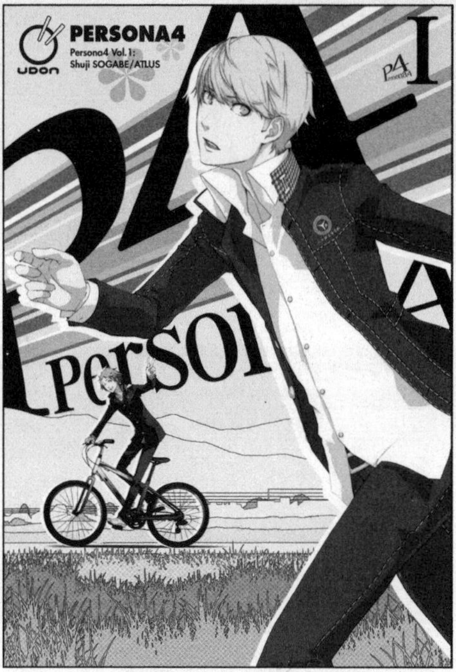
UDON
PERSONA4
Persona4 Vol. 1:
Shuji SOGABE/ATLUS
I

PERSONA 4 Volume 1

ISBN: 978-1-927925-57-7

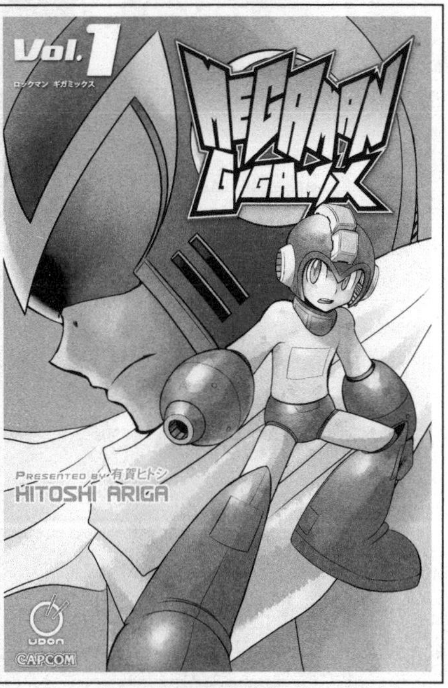
Vol. 1
ロックマン ギガミックス
MEGAMAN GIGAMIX
PRESENTED BY 有賀ヒトシ
HITOSHI ARIGA
UDON
CAPCOM

MEGA MAN GIGAMIX Volume 1

ISBN: 978-1-926778-23-5

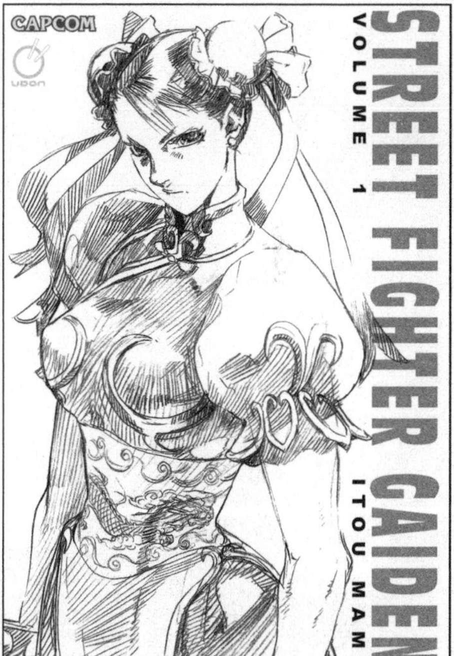
CAPCOM
UDON
STREET FIGHTER GAIDEN
VOLUME 1
ITOU MAMI

STREET FIGHTER GAIDEN Volume 1

ISBN: 978-1-926778-11-2

! WHOOPS !

This is the back of the book!

You're looking at the last page of the book, not the first one.

STEINS;GATE is a comic series originally published in Japan. Japanese comics (known as "manga") are traditionally read from right to left, the reverse of most English comics.

In this English edition, the Japanese format has been left intact. Check the example below to see how to read the word balloons in the proper order.

Now head to the front of the book and enjoy STEINS;GATE!